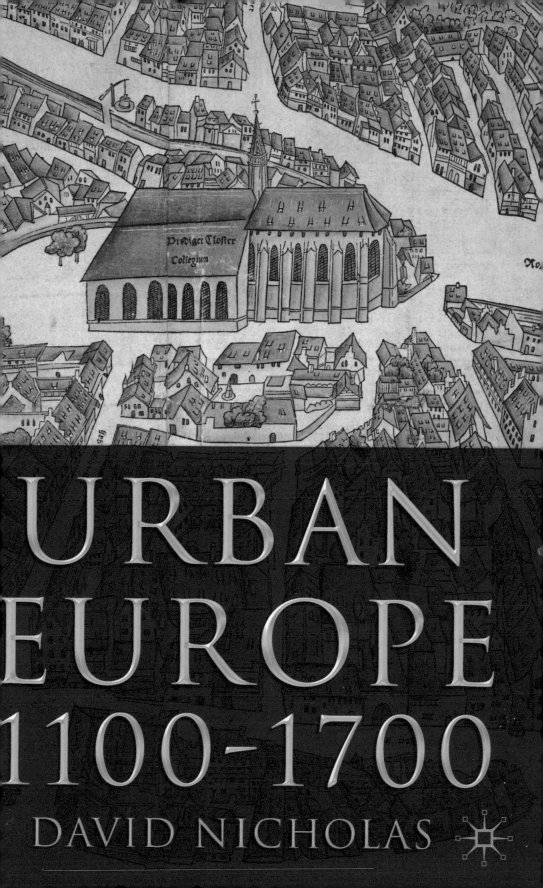

URBAN EUROPE 1100-1700

DAVID NICHOLAS

Urban Europe, 1100–1700

Reflecting the vigour of both urban and medieval history, this timely textbook by a leading scholar is a broadly interdisciplinary work that breaks new ground by emphasising the links between the late medieval and early modern cities.

Urban Europe 1100–1700:

- examines the common social, governmental, economic and intellectual roles played by most pre-modern cities
- views the cities as originating in local market relations, then expanding with the growing complexity of their functions into regional centres of culture, government and exchange
- adopts an organic, evolutionary and environmental approach, particularly in its application of geographical systems to early urbanisation
- makes extensive use of maps and original source material to illustrate aspects of the urban experience.

David Nicholas' study will not only appeal to students and scholars of history, geography and urban studies; sociologists and political economists will value its demonstration of the continuing relevance of the thought of Max Weber, while urban planners will find its analysis of the rationality of pre-modern cities highly useful.

Other books by David Nicholas

The Transformation of Europe, 1300–1600 (1999)

The Growth of the Medieval City: From Late Antiquity to the Early Fourteenth Century (1997)

The Later Medieval City, 1300–1500 (1997)

Medieval Flanders (1992)

The Metamorphosis of a Medieval City: Ghent in the Age of the Arteveldes, 1302–1390 (1987)

The Van Arteveldes of Ghent: The Varieties of Vendetta and the Hero in History (1988)

The Domestic Life of a Medieval City: Women, Children, and the Family in Fourteenth-Century Ghent (1985)

Town and Countryside: Social, Economic, and Political Tensions in Fourteenth-Century Flanders (1971)

With Walter Prevenier (eds.) *Gentse Stads- en Baljuwsrekeningen (1365–1376)* (Accounts of the City and Bailiffs of Ghent, 1365–1376) (1999)

Urban Europe, 1100–1700

David Nicholas

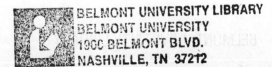

First published 2003 by
PALGRAVE MACMILLAN
Houndmills, Basingstoke, Hampshire RG21 6XS
and 175 Fifth Avenue, New York, N.Y. 10010
Companies and representatives throughout the world

PALGRAVE MACMILLAN is the global academic imprint of the
Palgrave Macmillan division of St. Martin's Press, LLC and of
Palgrave Macmillan Ltd. Macmillan is a registered trademark
in the United States, United Kingdom and other countries.
Palgrave is a registered trademark in the European Union
and other countries.

ISBN 0–333–94982–X hardback
ISBN 0–333–94983–8 paperback

This book is printed on paper suitable for recycling and made
from fully managed and sustained forest sources.

A catalogue record for this book is available from the British Library.

Library of Congress Cataloging-in-Publication Data
Nicholas, David, 1939–
    Urban Europe, 1100–1700 / David Nicholas.
      p. cm
    Includes bibliographical reference and index.
    ISBN 0-333-94982-X (cloth) – ISBN 0-333-94983-8 (pbk.)
      1. Cities and towns, Medieval – Europe. 2. City and town life – Europe. 3.
    Europe-Economic conditions – To 1492. 4. Europe – Economic conditions – 16th
century. 5. Europe – Social life and customs. I. Title.

CB351.N55 2003
940'.091732–dc21   2003051934

10   9   8   7   6   5   4   3   2   1
12   11   10   09   08   07   06   05   04   03

Typeset in Great Britain by
Aarontype Limited, Easton, Bristol

Printed and bound in Great Britain by
Creative Print and Design (Wales), Ebbw Vale

Contents

List of Figures

Preface

The history of European urbanisation is too often treated as a juxtaposition of typologies. Some have claimed that the 'medieval' city was 'closed' to the outside, while simultaneously presenting evidence that shows that the city was then, as it remains, the most mobile form of human association. Fernand Braudel, for example, caricatures medieval urbanisation as the

> closed city, a self-sufficient unit, an exclusive, Lilliputian empire. Entering its gates was like crossing one of the serious frontiers of the world today. You were free to thumb your nose at your neighbour from the other side of the barrier. He could not touch you.

Yet Braudel blithely, although correctly, associates the towns with the rise of capitalism, without realising that he has just undermined his own formulation.[1]

The fortifications of the pre-modern cities were the aspect of urbanisation that most forcefully struck contemporaries, who often tell us more about these walls than about the people who lived within them. Modern scholars have simply perpetuated the notion of enclosure, telling us about the walls and less often emphasising their gates, through which vast numbers of persons and quantities of goods passed daily.

Aristotle realized that the need, not merely the desire, to associate with others in communities is intrinsic to the human condition. There is no more basic question for social scientists to investigate than the motives that cause people to choose to join groups and to associate with specific individuals. The biological argument may work for the family, even the extended family, but it breaks down as an explanation for larger social units. Other criteria of emotional, intellectual, social and economic interdependence are necessary to explain the village, and even more the town and the city. This book is an attempt to explain why some Europeans in the past chose or were forced to live alongside others in a non-agrarian environment, and the means by which they provided a livelihood for most of their number and minimised interpersonal conflicts.

On a less general plane, *Urban Europe* attempts to provide practical applications through examples from history of two interrelated problems posed by geographical theory. First, what central functions did some places fulfil that led to the development of small towns and the subsequent evolution of some small towns into large towns and eventually cities? Second, what attractions did the cities as a group possess that led people to emigrate to them, despite their serious social problems, in sufficient numbers to overcome their extremely high death rates and thus perpetuate settlement?

The central thesis of *Urban Europe*, which is delineated in Chapter 2 and elaborated in the following chapters, is that local conditions created constantly fluctuating regions that came to be centred on towns, and larger regions whose central places were cities. The conditions that typically brought some settlements into existence, performing circumscribed central functions, were very different from those that fostered the evolution of some of those settlements into major cities. The cities developed in but also transformed the rural environment that generated them. Scholars, in their zeal to categorise, have defined the city in rigid terms that emphasise one or more of its functions; yet it is no more valid to describe a city of 1600 purely in terms of its market, or its churches or its government than such an oversimplification would be today.

Another important theme of this book is that the distinction that is commonly made between 'medieval' and 'early modern' is essentially irrelevant in the study of urban history, and indeed is a positive hindrance to our understanding. While all but one of the other existing treatments of European cities use this periodisation, I see an essential continuity of urban economic, social, cultural and governmental forms and ethical structures across these centuries.[2] Important changes inevitably occur during any six-century period, but in this case those after 1500 were of degree rather than of kind. Although some cities changed radically after 1500, most continued in essentially the traditional patterns. As late as 1700 the urban network that had developed in response to changes during the central Middle Ages was still functioning as a catalyst of change in an overwhelmingly rural environment. The urban elites were composed of merchants who avoided work with their hands and of landholders whose social aspirations and ethical framework directed them toward the rural nobility, who controlled political power in the territorial states that had already severely limited urban liberties. These situations would cease to be during the eighteenth century.

The book opens with the first industrial revolution, which transformed economic relations in the cities and their economic and social bonds with their environs: the development of the complex mechanical loom for weaving cloth made an industry that previously had been rural into one that was partly urban. The account ends just before the more famous industrial revolution of the century after 1700, when technological innovations facilitated the concentration of large-scale production in factories which, given their labour requirements, had to be in major population centres. This second industrial revolution also brought the mass production of inexpensive consumer goods and weakened the household unit of production, based on simpler tools and machines, which had characterised the industry of the six centuries after 1100.

Before 1700 most cities and towns had little exportable industry, for their products were sold locally and regionally, a fact that in itself is an aspect of regional economic integration under the aegis of the cities. Historians have tended since the second industrial revolution to equate industrialisation with urbanisation, or at least to see large-scale industry as the essential characteristic of cities, specifically defining large cities in terms of exportable industry. But although delimited here in terms of industrial criteria, the six centuries after 1100 were, far from being pre-capitalist as some have argued, an age of commercial capitalism. The nature of capitalism, in which exchangeable goods and services are assigned an abstract monetary value, and money is used to make more money, fosters interdependence and leads to the need for exports and imports, optimally in balance or favouring exports. This in turn means the dependence of the more complex urban economies on distant areas, even as the smaller towns were restricted to their own regions.

The city is too complex a living phenomenon to be left solely to historians. I have tried in this book to apply the theories of political economists, sociologists and particularly geographers to my essentially environment-driven view of premodern urbanisation. I pay particular attention to the work of Max Weber, the profundity of whose observations on the nature of the urbanisation process continues to impress me nearly a century after his death.

Chapter 1 of *Urban Europe* establishes essential themes that will be followed in the rest of the book and provides a demographic and political summary of the rise and fall of the leading cities of Europe during the six centuries under discussion. Chapter 2 is economic and geographical, discussing the evolution of cities within their regions and the external forces, most of them political or economic, that conditioned their success or failure. The competing interests of interlocking cities and regions together formed a symbiosis that had established a coherent European urban-economic region by 1700.

With the physical environment framed in terms of land use, Chapters 3–6 concern the city from within. Competition continued between old and new elites, merchants and artisans, and geographical sectors of the towns, but the comparative rarity of armed urban revolt after 1400 is testimony to the success and essential rationality of the social and institutional framework that had been developed. Chapter 3 is topographical, analysing city plans from the standpoint of typology and functionality: even the irregular street plans of the older 'nuclear' cities of the Middle Ages fulfilled what Max Weber would have called 'rational' intents. Chapter 4 describes city government, while Chapter 5 discusses social relations as a counterpoise to the economic characteristics of the city that were delineated in Chapter 2. Given that high death rates in the pre-modern city meant that it could not survive without large-scale immigration, Chapter 5 also discusses what it was that made the cities desirable and enticed outsiders to them. Chapter 6 combines a discussion of the cultural functions, 'civility' and attractions of the cities with a 'sights and smells' description of urban life as contemporaries experienced it. The notion of central place is basic to all chapters, for the city provides cultural, governmental, social and economic goods and services that could not be found, at least to the same degree, in other locales.

A book that surveys six centuries of urban development must cope with an immense documentation and a vast secondary literature. All scholars must use their material selectively, and this is particularly true of broadly conceived works such as this one. I have cited works that I have used consciously; but if I have inadvertently omitted something I read 40 years ago that has simply become part of my subconscious arsenal of fact or theory, as I have probably done, or omitted through ignorance works of which I should have known, which I am quite sure that I have done, I beg their authors' and my readers' indulgence.

The 'vast scholarly literature' referred to above contains quite a bit for which I bear personal responsibility. In addition to my specialised studies of the Flemish cities, in 1997 I published a two-volume history of medieval urbanisation, and readers of this book may legitimately wonder what I have to say that is new.[3] The first difference is that the two earlier volumes operated within a much narrower chronological framework than this one. The format of the series in which they appeared necessitated a perpetuation of the 'medieval' and 'early modern' stereotypes. Second, this book attempts to rectify the relative absence of urban theory that characterised its predecessors. Some factual material has inevitably been re-used, but the facts are less dense and the analytical framework correspondingly stronger.

Urban Europe owes a great deal to the support of professional colleagues. To Bernard Bachrach, Marc Boone, Richard Britnell, Beth Carney, Bill Jordan, Bryce Lyon, Andrew MacLennan, Steve Marks, Don McKale, Ed Moïse, John Munro, Jim Murray, Walter Prevenier and Kay Reyerson I extend my sincere gratitude. Jim Miller and Criss Smith, both geographers at Clemson University, read the first three chapters and gave me the benefit of their expertise. To Alexander Cowan, who read the manuscript before publication and made numerous suggestions for its improvement, particularly for the post-1500 sections, my debt is incalculable. I have had the good fortune to work under two superbly cooperative department chairs, Roger Grant and Tom Kuehn, both gentlemen and scholars in the best sense of that hackneyed expression.

Finally, I would be remiss if I did not acknowledge the support of the family of the late Kathryn and Calhoun Lemon, the donors of the professorship that I hold at Clemson. The Lemon chair has provided me with the means to acquire essential books, together with the time for research and reflection that is the *sine qua non* of scholarship.

Acknowledgements

Figure 1.1. Norman J. G. Pounds, *An Economic History of Medieval Europe*, 2nd edn. (London: Longman, 1994), p. 254. Reproduced by permission of Pearson Education Ltd.

Figure 1.2. Norman J. G. Pounds, *An Historical Geography of Europe, 450 BC–AD 1330* (Cambridge: Cambridge University Press, 1973), p. 348. Reprinted with the permission of Cambridge University Press.

Figure 1.3. Adapted from Carlo M. Cipolla, *Before the Industrial Revolution: Urban Society and Economy, 1000–1700*, 3rd edn. (New York: W. W. Norton, 1994), pp. 302–4; Jan de Vries, *European Urbanization, 1500–1800* (Cambridge, Mass.: Harvard University Press, 1984); John U. Marshall, *The Structure of Urban Systems* (Toronto: University of Toronto Press, 1989); Peter Clark (ed.), *The Early Modern Town: A Reader* (London: Longman, 1976); monographs on individual cities.

Figure 2.1. Peter Stabel, *Dwarfs among Giants: The Flemish Urban Network in the Late Middle Ages* (Leuven-Apeldoorn: Garant, 1997), p. 66, Figure 5. Reprinted with permission of the publisher and the author.

Figure 2.3. From Tom Scott and Bob Scribner, 'Urban Networks', in Bob Scribner, *Germany: A New Social and Economic History*, Vol. I (London: Edward Arnold, 1995), Map 5.1. Reproduced by permission of Hodder Arnold.

Figure 2.4. From Franz Irsigler, 'L'Approvisionnement des villes de l'Allemagne occidentale jusqu'au XVIe siècle', in *L'Approvisionnement des villes de l'Europe occidentale au Moyen Age et aux Temps modernes*. Centre Culturel de l'Abbaye de Flaran. Cinquièmes Journées internationals d'histoire, 16–18 septembre 1983. (Auch: Abbaye de Flaran, 1985), Carte 1 at p. 138, with key p. 139. Reprinted with the permission of the author and of the Abbaye de Flaran.

Figure 2.5. From Franz Irsigler, 'Stadt und Umland im Spätmittelalter: zur zentralitätsfördernden Kraft von Fernhandel und Exportgewerbe', in Emil Meynen (ed.), *Zentralität als Problem der mittelalterlichen Stadtgeschichtsforschung* (Cologne and Vienna: Böhlau, 1979), p. 14. Reprinted with permission of the author and of Böhlau Verlag.

Figure 2.6. Peter Moraw, *Von offener Verfassung zu gestalteter Verdichtung. Das Reich im späten Mittelalter*, Propyläen Geschichte Deutschlands 3 (Berlin: Propyläen Verlag, 1985), pp. 112–13. Reprinted with the permission of Propyläen Verlag in der Ullstein Heyne List GmbH & Co.

Figure 3.1. David A. Hinton, 'The Large Towns, 600–1300'. In D. M. Palliser (ed.), *The Cambridge Urban History of Britain*, I. *600 to 1450* (Cambridge: Cambridge University Press, 2000), p. 242. Reprinted with the permission of the Cambridge University Press.

Figure 3.2. From David Nicholas, *The Growth of the Medieval City* (London: Longman, 1997). Reprinted with permission of Pearson Education Ltd.

Figure 3.3. Redrawn after Robert E. Dickinson, *The West European City: A Geographical Interpretation*. (London: Routledge & Kegan Paul, 1951) and F. L. Ganshof, *Étude sur le développement des villes entre Loire et Rhin au Moyen Âge* (Paris: Presses Universitaires de France, 1943).

Figure 3.4. Drawn from Martha D. Pollak, *Turin 1564–1680. Urban Design, Military Culture, and the Creation of an Absolutist Capital* (Chicago: University of Chicago Press, 1991). Adapted with permission of the University of Chicago Press.

Figure 3.5. Archives Générales du Royaume, Bruxelles, Topografisch-historische atlas no. 1071. Reprinted with permission of the Archives Générales du Royaume.

Chapter 1 . . . .

Urban Europe Between the Industrial Revolutions

The essence of the city is a permanent population, plus a marketplace, and a shift from human relations based on status to those based on free contract.[1]
(Fernand Braudel)

The City and Max Weber

Since the cities of Europe took form in a political, social and economic environment that remained overwhelmingly rural and agrarian even in the early eighteenth century, it is clear that the early development of European urbanisation was conditioned by political and economic structures that transcended the city proper. The German sociologist and political economist Max Weber (1864–1920) is best known for the distortion of his views by the English economic historian R. H. Tawney, who tried to explain economic growth as the result of aspects of Protestant religious doctrine.[2] This is most unfortunate, for the heart of Weber's work, which was once dismissed by historians who were wedded to Henri Pirenne's idea of the city as a purely economic creation, has profound insights that provide an indispensable reference for any student of comparative urbanisation.

Weber argued that the city was the catalyst of a 'trend toward rationality' that distinguished western European institutions from the patriarchal and 'charismatic' regimes of other parts of the world. 'Rational' denotes an attitude that is more receptive to innovation and the interplay of competing ideas than the 'traditional' mentality, to which it is contrasted. Legal institutions that guaranteed individuals' rights against the state were a crucial aspect of Weberian rationality. The development of an interregional market network and sophisticated commercial techniques pioneered intellectual innovation, notably calculation in both the specific and abstract senses. In purely economic terms, all cities are market oriented, particularly toward consumption of goods, but those of the West were

1

unique in having partial autonomy from regional authorities and in their development of an urban law that was distinct from that of the territorial state in which the city nested. Weber did not think that fully autonomous cities were a necessary component of urban growth or capitalism, for he realised that the privileges that princes granted to favoured towns were instrumental in the prosperity of some places and the decline of others. He spoke of 'politically oriented capitalism' and thought that the Italians eventually lost economic primacy to the north Europeans because of an irrational political naïveté that was illustrated by their enormous loans to princes who were poor credit risks. But Weber also defined the city in terms of social and cultural characteristics and values, which included tradition.[3]

In this book I am incorporating receptivity to competition into a neo-Weberian notion of rationality. Competition for markets and resources became apparent when the city first began differentiating itself as a type from rural Europe around 1100. Between about 1275 and the early seventeenth century, competition for markets and resources was intense, although there were decelerating forces that fostered conformity. It is undeniable, for example, that many nominally occupational guilds, when they gained control of city governments, tried to stifle competition among masters and create monopolies for their masters. But the consequences of this were felt mainly in industrial conservatism and protectionism, which had less impact than was once thought on capital formation in the cities. Furthermore, competition existed within the guilds themselves, both among masters who vied for the same markets and between guild elites and the rank and file membership for supplies, markets and honours.

The earliest medieval cities were local markets, particularly for agricultural goods. The inhabitants obtained what they needed without leaving their homes; rather the professional merchant brought goods from distant places. The growth of long-distance trade, in many cases accompanied by the development of manufacturing, led urban elites, most of whose members had originated as local landholders trading in the agricultural products that were grown on their estates, to seek new markets. The city was thus the primary agent of commercial capitalism, which dominated the European economy in the period covered by this book. 'Fixed capital' such as land and buildings was very important in the rural economy but was less critical in the cities, especially in manufacturing, since (except for mining) most industrial technology was simple and did not require substantial capital investment. Persons who had money to invest tended to put it into goods and services for themselves, thus generating local demand.[4]

Commercial functions were thus more instrumental than industrial ones in fixing the urban map of Europe during these centuries, for industrial goods must have a demand market created through the infrastructure of a commercial network: craftsmen could not make large quantities of shoes, pots or cloth without having some reason to assume that someone would buy them. Many cities, such as those of northern Italy, were already large before they developed exportable industry, while others, such as Metz, never developed such industries but nonetheless became large regional market centres. The fact that most wealth was created by trade does not, however, mean that industrial production was insignificant. Important technological changes provided Europeans with exportable goods that were exchanged for the exotic products of the east. On the eve of the Industrial Revolution of the eighteenth century, Europe already had the world's strongest industrial capacity.[5]

By 1100 a market economy was firmly in place: all settlements were at least farm markets and had some basic utilitarian manufacture of consumer goods. While the town obviously depended on its rural environs for its food and industrial raw materials, the countryside depended on the town for exchange and manufactured goods. As the townspeople gained control of their own market mechanisms, they tried to reduce the cost of goods that they bought from country-dwellers. Although greater per capita profits, as well as higher risks, were to be had in long-distance trade than in local exchange, the long-distance profit argument becomes much stronger after 1300 and particularly with the onset of the colonial movements in the fifteenth century.[6]

The plethora of small, internally decentralised states, together with the presence of cities with rights that could not be violated by the central or territorial state, was critical to the development of competition and also of the regional interdependence that is still characteristic of Europe. Competition involves vying for resources within a recognised framework of contract and law. Acquisition and concentration, and also alienation of property, were easier under urban than under rural law, particularly as most values came to be expressed in monetary terms. But the European urban system was flexible enough to survive the transition to industrial capitalism and even to facilitate that transition. Before the Industrial Revolution, both large cities and small towns had highly differentiated occupational structures: but in the small towns this consisted of a larger number of crafts than was found in villages, while the diversity in the economies of the larger cities was in types of goods sold and services provided.[7]

Some scholars have built on Weber's idea to argue that the city was the driving force behind the commercial capitalism that made possible European domination of a 'modern world economy' in the late fifteenth and early sixteenth centuries, with the major cities functioning as a 'core' whose continuing contacts with one another served to integrate the peripheries. This view is associated particularly with Immanuel Wallerstein, who saw rural agricultural and industrial production as responding to urban demand, which provided the local linkage of the region into the world market. Yet there is a logical problem with the chronology of Wallerstein's thesis: both urban networks and commercial capitalism had existed in the medieval period. The developments that Wallerstein saw beginning in the sixteenth century could at most have accelerated trends that were already structurally in place.[8]

Urban Europe c. 1100

Europe had few large cities in the late eleventh century, but even then there was a tremendous disparity between the number of persons actually living in urban

3

centres and their importance to the economy and to political and cultural institutions. By 1100 most major cities of Europe, although small, were established communities that accordingly functioned as markets. The few that have originated since then are associated with a deliberate act of foundation. Fortunately, the arid historiography of urban origins is outside the chronological limits of this book. Despite the ferocity with which their proponents advocate them, the theories of why cities came into existence are not irreconcilable; the diverse cityscape of Europe has numerous examples of each type. Furthermore, while a single function can bring a settlement into existence, the characteristics that originate it are not always the same as those that foster its growth. The essence of urbanisation is plurality of functions, which can only come through sustained evolution.

The market – and hence the city – develops at the intersection of supply and demand. This is a far more complex matter than simply one place having a stock of goods for which a market exists somewhere else. There can be shortages and surpluses of labour as well as property. As examples, the two most important urban concentrations of pre-modern Europe developed on economic frontiers. The Italian cities originated in local trade, but their great prosperity was caused by geography: Italian merchants were the natural middlemen for the goods of the Levant, which were in high demand in the west. The second great urban pole, the southern Low Countries and northern France, is less obviously a frontier. Flanders was a poor coastal region whose western part was mainly pastoral until the swamps were reclaimed in the twelfth century. Ghent, Flanders' largest city, began as a transshipment point between northern France, which produced surpluses of food, and agriculturally poor northern Flanders.[9] Forced to trade, the Flemings began manufacturing cloth with native wool, then specialised in luxury cloths made from finer English wool that had to be imported. The exhaustion of strategic natural resources in the rural environs of Flanders thus led to importing and hence an expansion of the economic region. In Italy this occurred too, but chiefly when the grain supply of the environs of the great cities became unable to feed them. The resulting exchange, not a natural surplus, made both regions great.[10]

Cities originated to meet simple needs, but then they attracted trade, political functions and educational facilities. Roads were diverted to the cities, canals were built, and princes naturally sought major population concentrations for their governments and gave privileges only to selected towns. Urban systems also tend to be stable also because urban capital is a constant. Considerable resources are invested in the infrastructure of the city itself: buildings, roads and governing apparatus, not to mention the activities of city people in moneylending and employment. Large cities, with more capital, thus have more jobs, and production and will grow faster absolutely, but not necessarily relatively, than in smaller places. The complexity of operations found among late medieval merchants was simply not feasible in small places with less differentiated labour forces.

England had had the highest urban density of northwestern Europe before the Norman Conquest, but thereafter punitive taxation, the destruction of houses in the larger cities to make way for castles, and the reorientation of trading links from Scandinavia and Germany toward Normandy and France provoked urban decline. The Flemish cities grew in response in the decades around 1100. France was a kingdom only in theory in 1100, and the varieties of early urbanisation there reflect its territorial diversity. Paris was still considerably smaller and less sophisticated in function than such places as Toulouse, whose enormous Roman wall was only then being repopulated. More typical were Roman centres such as Troyes, where the truncated Roman wall of the third century, enclosing the *civitas* or the 'city' proper, sheltered the bishop, the count if he had not been excluded from the town in conflicts with the bishop, and sometimes a few artisans and merchants. Germany had numerous markets, but the only large cities were either repopulated Roman centres along the Rhine, bishoprics or settlements where a castle had preceded the establishment of a bishopric. Farther east, places founded in and after the ninth century as bulwarks of conversion and administration against the Danes and Slavs, such as Hildesheim, Hamburg and above all the border bishopric of Magdeburg, became nuclei of colonisation and conversion.

Italy south of Rome had the largest concentration of large cities in Europe in 1100, but northern Italy quickly overtook the south in the twelfth century. Venice controlled most of the European trade in oriental luxuries, notably edible spices, dyes and cloth, which were imported through the Byzantine Empire, the caravan routes across Asia, and in the twelfth century the crusader states and the islands of the eastern Mediterranean. Genoa would become the great rival of Venice for near eastern markets, but the Genoese concentrated more on forging trading links with the Muslim states of North Africa and Iberia, and the Christian kingdoms that were extending their borders southward at the expense of the caliphate. Florence was still considerably smaller than other Tuscan towns, notably Siena and then-coastal Pisa. In Lombardy Milan rapidly achieved domination in the early twelfth century through its control of land routes across the Alps and southward into Italy.

The Low Countries were the last great urban region of western Europe to develop, but they quickly became the most important concentration of towns north of the Alps. Flanders, in the southwest, was the most precocious part. Ghent and Bruges developed on sites that had been abandoned by the Romans, but in each case the nucleus from which the later town evolved was a fortification of the count of Flanders. Ypres, the third great Flemish city, developed at the point where the Yser river ceases to be navigable, a common feature of the early history of medieval cities. Little of the Flemish towns' early history suggests their later greatness, but the chronicle of Galbert of Bruges (1128) shows the larger ones had considerable power, which they used to extract charters from the two contenders for the Flemish countship. From a base in local trade, Ghent and Ypres developed important textile industries. Bruges also manufactured cloth, but its great prosperity came from the fact that in the eleventh century the high sea level made it a coastal port. As the waters receded, Bruges, although inland, became the most considerable port city of northern Europe by founding new towns on its canal links to the sea, then relentlessly suppressing their attempts to free themselves.

What Is a Town?

Several features were shared by virtually all major towns of the twelfth century, and still characterised European urbanisation into the late seventeenth. First, the cities grew up around markets, primarily although not exclusively where food and other raw materials were exchanged. With rare exceptions trade was more important than industry in creating urban wealth. This involved more than simply providing a place where farmers could sell their goods and reselling locally produced or grown items on a wider market outside the region. The demand market in the cities for luxuries, initially from princes and prelates but soon from the urban elites themselves, was a critical element in early exchange. The cities were always dependent on the agrarian economy of their environs, most obviously for food but also for exportable goods such as wine, which was generally taken to the city, taxed, then re-exported. By 1700 about 10 per cent of the population of France was involved in some aspect of wine production and distribution, and it was only at this late date that rural brokers and shippers began to challenge significantly the stranglehold of the merchants of the port towns on wine exports.[11]

Second, cities that were solely industrial were highly exceptional before 1700, and most of them did not prosper. Industry was usually site-based and thus was less likely than trade to attract capital. But north European urbanisation was transformed in the late eleventh century by the first of two industrial revolutions that fundamentally altered internal relations in many cities and their economic and social bonds with their environs. The development in northern France of the complex mechanical loom for weaving heavy woollen cloth urbanised an industry that had previously been rural and gave northwestern Europe an exportable commodity for the first time. Textile manufacturing added immensely to the population base of the principal cities, but most urban centres made little if any cloth for export: rather, they produced coarser cloth for local consumption. Industry did, however, contribute to the formation of city-centred trading regions. It also fostered interregional trade, for although the cities had the labour necessary for operating the looms and to provide diversification and specialisation of the workforce, they had to import the wool, dyes and other raw materials. Specialisation is often seen as characteristic of industrial towns, and this is probably more true of modern cities than of medieval ones. But it is necessary for an economy to advance beyond subsistence level, and the specialists cannot be isolated from one another. The city provides a locale where they can be roughly co-residential and thus interact with maximum efficiency.[12]

Thus a high level of occupational differentiation in both trade and industry is a third characteristic of the pre-modern city. Urban labouring populations can be categorised very roughly into 'basic' and 'non-basic' producers. The 'basic' producer brings income into the community. Examples are monks or priests, whose income comes from rents from their rural estates, or officials of a territorial government based in the town, or artisans who produce for export or the draper who 'puts out' work to various artisans, then sells the finished product. The 'non-basic' producers derive their income from the locality itself and satisfy the needs of the basic producers: examples are purveyors of food and drink, construction workers and shoemakers. These categories clearly cannot be adhered to rigidly: weavers, for example, produced different grades of cloth, some exportable and some not. Furthermore, many persons had sidelines to their major occupations. Still, demographic models suggest that pre-industrial urban populations are divided roughly evenly between basic and non-basic producers.[13] The occupational diversity of the city thus involves persons in legally regulated competition for the same and diverse markets that are interconnected and produce a market network that may be site-based initially but has the resources to expand.

This in turn means that as cities develop more exportable industries and/or skills, and as their populations increase accordingly, persons in service occupations will be attracted by the job opportunities that the city offers. Yet in most cities whose occupational structure can be delineated from surviving sources, the service sector of non-basic producers is too large for the model. The total population of the city includes the families of the basic and non-basic producers; but most basic producers who moved to the city did not come with their families, but rather were single and eventually took spouses who were already domiciled there. The non-basic population thus tends to grow more rapidly than the basic and creates a demand for still more locally produced goods and services, which in turn become a major part of the central function that the town provides.

The basic/non-basic model can help us to understand why exportable industry was much less important than commerce as a generator of wealth in the pre-modern city. A new factory/industry will increase the number of basic economic activities, add to the permanent population and generate income for the town, but it does not attract people directly to the town's market, since the consumers of the goods that are manufactured there may live in some distant place. This is particularly important with the smaller places, whose regional importance may depend on their markets, which characteristically are held only at intervals, more than on total permanent population. There is a tendency for a place to become more industrial the larger it gets, although an absolute correlation cannot be made. Medieval industry was almost without exception labour-intensive; thus the more industry a place had, the more labourers it required. The other correlation is with a large region that the city dominated for basic market exchanges, including food: a large city with a small region would have to have considerable industry, but a large city developing in a large region might not have much industry.

Cities are thus by their nature multifunctional. Even if one general line of work dominates, such as education or trade, all are present and will have some weight in determining the city's role in its region. Probably no pre-modern city was as functionally specialised as modern industrial cities tend to be. John Marshall speaks of a 'principle of vulnerability':

> the likelihood of a city's falling on hard times is inversely proportional to the diversification of its economy: the more diversified the city, the more

7

easily it should be able to survive regional or national recession or depression. Conversely, the more specialised the city, the more vulnerable its residents will be to economic hardship in times of stress.[14]

The cities of late medieval Flanders, whose dependence on English wool for their export-grade textiles limited their diplomatic options, are an excellent example.

A fourth aspect of pre-modern cities is that they were important as centres of religion and eventually of secular culture. The presence of the bishopric in the repopulated Roman 'city' was an important element of topographic and, to a lesser extent, functional continuity with Roman urbanisation, as we shall see in Chapter 3. The close link between religious institutions and the growth of urbanisation is especially strong in England where, in contrast to the continent, the first cathedrals were often rural or built in towns that did not flourish. From the late eleventh century, however, some bishoprics were being moved into places that were developing into towns, either situating just inside the walls or distorting the street plan by clearing away previous tenements to make room for the church.[15]

Fifth, the pre-modern city had good communications, which conditioned the quantity and variety of raw materials that it could import, and thus affected the nature of its industrial products and the consumer goods it could offer to its inhabitants. The earliest population growth in most cities developed along the artery from which their food came, even when this was the smaller of the routes that led into the city. Yet while a decent land route could suffice for this purpose, cities that developed significant export industry or re-sold the raw materials of their environs over large distances required better links. Thus most cities

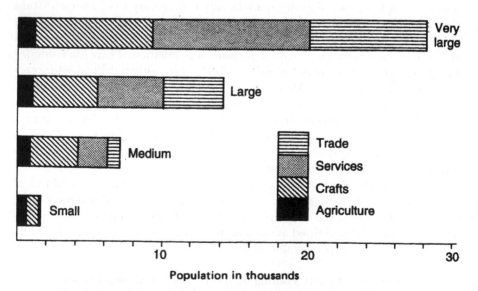

Figure 1.1   Functional differentiation and urban population: a model

that became large after 1100 were located on navigable interior waterways that provided easy communication and were well suited to the large-scale transport of goods. The major exceptions among cities that were significant by 1100 were Venice, on the Adriatic coast, and landlocked Milan, which developed as a bishopric and agricultural market. Milan and Nuremberg, which developed later on land routes, both undertook an intense program of canal building.[16] Yet the importance of overland traffic cannot be discounted: the Champagne fairs, the most important depots for interregional trade for much of the twelfth and thirteenth centuries, could not be reached except by combining water and overland travel.

Sixth, pre-modern urban populations were highly mobile. Urban fertility was generally lower than rural, and death rates were always higher. Thus the city could grow only through substantial immigration, most of it from the rural environs, although the extent to which this was true diminished as the city became larger and its region wider. Since the city must attract immigrants in order to survive, its population will be more diverse than that of rural villages, even if most immigrants come from nearby. In practice this meant that most cities developed in areas of high rural population density.[17]

A seventh feature common to west European cities during this period is a close link to their seigniorial antecedents, which in turn involved social and economic bonds with their rural environs. The cities of northern Europe, although not those of Italy, were once thought to have developed through the growth of long-distance trade, essentially independently of the countryside. This view, which is associated with the great Belgian urban historian Henri Pirenne, is now rejected by most scholars in favour of an organic approach that sees city and village as different degrees of the same phenomenon of settlement growth.[18]

By 1100 most cities of western Europe were making the transition 'from seigniorial to economic urbanisation' and were market centres with recognised legal rights.[19] Those of Germany east of the Elbe and Scandinavia were exceptions, only developing a significant urban merchant class in the twelfth and thirteenth centuries. Yet virtually all towns originated on the domain of a lord, who generally kept substantial rights in them even after some measure of local autonomy was granted in the twelfth and thirteenth centuries. The urban markets depended on the presence of country-based lords and clergy who bought the luxuries that the city merchants imported and whose fortifications protected the settlement. The cities were always foci of local administration, and from the fifteenth century, with the centring of the bureaucratic state in provincial and national capitals, the 'basic' category of officeholders who were paid from sources extraneous to the city of their residence grew immensely. This constitutes a major distinction between the medieval and early modern town, except perhaps in France, where upper bourgeoisie and princely office-holding had always been closely linked.

In Italy and northern Europe alike, many leading families of the cities originated as domain officials of the cathedral chapter or the prince who was the town lord. Not surprisingly, landownership in both the city and its rural environs was the most significant component of the 'portfolio' of these people, a development that was considerably accelerated from the late thirteenth century. Pirenne's idea that the urban patriciates were composed mainly of long-distance merchants has been revised in favour of the notion associated with Werner Sombart that the basis of their wealth was often in rents and finance. The early urban patricians lived from the profits of their rents, which were increasing considerably in the twelfth century as heavy immigration into the cities intensified demand for land and housing. In both Italy and the north, only in the thirteenth century did a clear demarcation emerge between the old landowning families, which by then were branching into merchandising, and a newer elite of purely merchant origins.[20]

The production of goods and delivery of services grew substantially during the early twelfth century, but particularly after the 1160s. As the rural economy expanded and diversified, and as some urban industry developed, town populations grew considerably faster relatively than the farming sector until the late thirteenth century. Just as the demographic base for massive urbanisation was being established, the supply of bullion in the European economy was increased tremendously, as new silver mines were discovered and exploited, and as Italian control of the Mediterranean carrying trade and exports of grain to Africa brought gold into Europe. The amount of coin in circulation in England increased almost ninefold between 1180 and 1310, a period when population may at most have tripled.[21] Larger denominations of silver coin were minted, and gold coins were introduced, facilitating interregional trade, while lesser coins for the first time were used to a significant degree for small consumer items and for wages, both of which contributed to occupational diversification within the city. It was now more feasible to bring small quantities of both raw materials and manufactured goods to market than in an earlier period when barter played a significant role in exchange. The use of money for wages for the first time made possible the service occupations that are so characteristic of the urban economy and also facilitated industrial specialisation, for example in the textile industry, where the labour of many persons went into the making of the finished, marketable product.[22]

Urban life in the centuries covered by this book, a period that bridges the traditional notion of 'medieval' and 'modern', was thus primarily market oriented. Trade was more important for most towns than industry, and the cities functioned more as centres of demand than of commodity production. They had a high level of occupational and functional differentiation and a mobile population. Finally, the cities had good communications, often at the intersection of a land route and a river, and had intimate links with the economies, social structures and rulers of their rural environs.

Colonialism, Foundation of Settlements and Urbanisation

In the age of seigniorial urbanisation, a city was a place with a fortified inner core, with or without suburbs, and the site of a bishopric or at least several parish churches, or a monastery. In terms of their functions, all other settlements, even those with markets, were agrarian villages.

But the late eleventh century brings us for the first time against a problem of defining 'urban'. Most historians trained in the German tradition consider any settlement to be a town if it had a market or a charter that distinguished it legally from its environs. In Germany some three thousand 'towns' were founded in the thirteenth century alone, and virtually all of them always remained small. Since they had privileges that other places did not, they were technically 'urban' settlements. English, American and Belgian scholars, by contrast, tend to use modern economic criteria, but they often take the presence of any non-agricultural occupation as a sign of urbanisation. Yet, while we cannot deny that the 'dwarf towns' had some urban characteristics, usually the right to hold a weekly market and a slightly more differentiated workforce than purely farm villages, lumping Milan and Saltash together as 'urban' creates a category that is too broad to be a useful analytical tool. Whether a region has a low or high urban index thus hinges on how far down the demographic scale one defines 'urban'.

The human landscape was transformed in the two centuries after 1100 by the foundation of thousands of new 'towns', and even more by the physical expansion of existing settlements. The establishment of new towns in the interior of Europe accompanied the reclamation and colonisation of new agricultural land and the military occupation of territory. Lords began giving liberties to places that they were founding or to already existing small settlements whose growth they hoped to encourage. These 'elementary liberties of the bourg' typically gave to the 'burgesses' privileges that included freedom from toll, the right to hold a market, fixed ground rents and the right to justice in the locality, before the lord's representative if no separate town court existed. Most medieval planned towns were established along trade routes. The junction of a river and a road was especially favourable. Some of the new foundations had a glorious future. Ypres, founded in 1066, was already one of the great cities of Flanders by the early twelfth century. The most famous town plantation is Lübeck, re-founded in 1159 and endowed with its own law and government by Henry the Lion, duke of Saxony. Lübeck became one of the great ports of medieval Europe and a leading town of the German Hanse, the league of north German cities. Newcastle-upon-Tyne and Salisbury are obvious examples of the very different directions that such foundations could take: the former became one of the great ports of England, while the latter simply replaced the existing city of the bishop of Salisbury, Old Sarum, which had only ten inhabitants over age 16 in 1377.[23]

Urban foundations, particularly those that received fortifications, were an important means by which newcomers could gain legal and defensive footholds in areas where they were an unwanted minority. The Norman conquerors established French settlements in England, in some cases adjacent to an older Anglo-Saxon town. A century later their Angevin successors were founding English towns in Ireland. In the Iberian peninsula, as the Muslims were pushed southward, towns founded by the conquering Christians became cultural and military outposts. In Gascony the English and French established small 'bastides' as

11

population centres and strongholds. Edward I's Welsh bastides from the 1280s were settled largely by foreigners to keep the natives in check, as was also true of the German plantations east of the Elbe. The English conquerors frankly admitted that civilising the natives by Anglicising them was the intent of town plantation in Wales. After the Welsh revolt of 1295 the Welsh were forbidden to live in English boroughs such as Caernarfon and Conwy. The French bastides, by contrast, were also intended as farm markets and were not completely new settlements, for they often simply regrouped people who lived in the area.[24]

Into the late Middle Ages, and in some cases beyond, Germans were the economic and political elite of colonial east European towns whose populations were mainly Slavic. Although some major Polish towns originated on cult sites or strongholds, genuine urban life was introduced by the bishoprics of the German missionaries, followed by their merchant settlements that brought a German town law, generally that of Lübeck or Magdeburg. The towns founded by the Teutonic Knights, starting with Chelmno and Torun in 1233, are an eastern parallel to the Welsh and French bastides. They were strongly fortified, but traders also moved east, usually attaching themselves to existing Slavic settlements and often establishing a German quarter in them. Although most plantations in the west did not become major cities, this is not true in the east: Berlin and Dresden are really post-medieval in their urban development, but Wroclaw, Poznan, Gdánsk, Frankfurt-on-the-Oder, Rostock and Stettin had all become major cities by 1400.[25]

But these are atypical cases. The conditions that bring a settlement into existence are not necessarily the same as those that will foster growth, and planned and planted towns (which are not always the same thing) developed in an already partly – and in some regions densely – urbanised landscape. Towns that had ancient antecedents had a tremendous advantage. All but five of the 24 greater English provincial towns of the late Middle Ages had walls, and ten of the remaining 19 had Roman walls. All but five had a castle. All but nine were significant before 1066, and all but eight were the site of a bishopric at some time. Domesday Book mentioned 15 as boroughs in 1086.[26] Few places founded after 1200 west of the Elbe evolved into cities, and most of them were patterned on existing towns, topographically, or in their law, or both. The impact of town plantations on the urban network in the west was thus minimal, unless one defines 'urban' very broadly. The German/Slavic East is another matter. While in the early thirteenth century virtually all German towns, even by the extended definition, were west of the Elbe, by 1400 there were about 1500 west and 1500 east of that natural frontier. This, however, involves the establishment of numerous small towns in the older settled parts of Germany, as well as eastern colonisation. Southern Germany, in particular, has numerous small towns, the result of lords founding too many settlements for many of them to be successful.[27]

This is not to say that the new towns had no significant functions in the commercial life of Europe. Transportation of goods was much slower and more dangerous than now. If the small towns were only four or five hours apart by foot or pack animal, as was often true in Germany and England, they served not only as markets of their own environs, but also as overnight or relay stations between the major central places. In addition to territorial lords, some large cities founded towns. Florence established two, Scarperia and Firenzuola, on opposite slopes of the Apennines on the road between Florence and Bologna. They served as defensive outposts against magnates who were hostile to the city, and most merchants en route between Florence and Bologna, a distance of 110 km, stopped overnight at one or both of them.[28]

From Medieval to Modern Urbanisation

By 1300 the urban map of Europe was virtually complete except for the great political capitals that would develop in the early modern period. As population growth in the towns outstripped that of rural Europe, a place of 5000 souls in 1100 occupied roughly the same rank in the urban hierarchy as one of 20,000 in 1300. Paris was the largest city of Europe, with a population of some 200,000 in the early fourteenth century, but it was the only metropolis of France. Montpellier, Rouen, Toulouse and Tours had between 30,000 and 40,000 souls. The next largest cities in the north after Paris were London and Ghent, each at about 80,000, followed by Cologne at about 50,000. Bruges, only 40 km from Ghent, probably had some 50,000 persons. In the Mediterranean, Granada was the largest city of Muslim Spain, with a population of over 100,000, while Seville, at about 80,000, Barcelona at 50,000, and the religious capital of Toledo at 40,000 were the largest Christian communities. Northern Italy had a large concentration of cities, with Venice, Genoa and Milan having populations of between 100,000 and 150,000. The interior cities of Tuscany were a second tier, with Florence and Siena between 50,000 and 95,000.

These populations, however, were high points until the modern period. Europe experienced severe economic dislocation and political disorder in the late Middle Ages. After peaking in the 1290s, the foundation of new towns virtually stopped until the early modern period. The established cities also underwent massive shocks in the half-century between 1275 and 1325. Most of them had absorbed more immigrants during the population expansion of the central Middle Ages than could be supported by existing jobs and markets. Although Italian merchants were making direct voyages to the North Sea ports after 1277, a development that would revolutionise commercial relations in the long term, the economic impact of this change was only slowly felt. Problems of unemployment loomed, and poverty began to be a serious problem for city officials. Occupational guilds that were named for crafts had developed in many cities, and during this period some of them, particularly those that were controlled by an oligarchy of merchants, began demanding the right to seats on town councils; we will explore these developments more fully in Chapters 4 and 5.

Often conditions that originated in the rural areas spilled over into the cities. Family feuds, sometimes involving a political alliance but sometimes

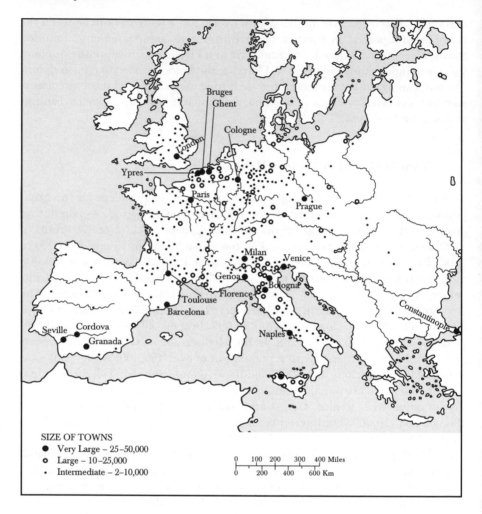

Figure 1.2   The distribution of the larger towns of Europe, *c.* 1300

not, paralysed many larger cities. The Italian towns were racked by vendettas
between family-based factions favouring the territorial aspirations of the Holy
Roman Emperor (the Ghibellines) and those preferring the closer but less effec-
tual pope (the Guelfs). There were fundamental shifts of power. During the thirteenth century Florence mastered its environs and became the economic centre of
Tuscany, replacing Pisa, which it would eventually annex. The feuds of the
Colom and Soler factions impeded Bordeaux between the late 1240s and early
1330s and even defied efforts of the French and English kings to pacify the city.
The elites of the Flemish cities were divided into Leliaert and Clauwaert parties,
respectively favouring accommodation with the French crown and relative independence under the count of Flanders.

The fourteenth and fifteenth centuries witnessed virtually constant war and dynastic turmoil that disrupted trade. During the 'Hundred Years War' between England and France, the suburbs of many cities were destroyed and their populations forced inside the walls, where they were often joined by refugees. More importantly from a structural perspective, bad harvests in the early fourteenth century led to a famine in 1315 that decimated the population of the major north European cities. A series of plagues began in 1348 with the 'Great Death' and continued with considerable intensity until 1400, then with diminishing frequency thereafter until the late seventeenth century. Overall population losses from famine and particularly plague seem to have been in the nature of 40 per cent by 1375. But death rates were much higher in the cities, given their congested conditions and the ease with which infection could spread, than in the rural areas.

The demographic and commercial realignments of the fourteenth and fifteenth centuries had a profound impact on urban Europe. Overall loss of population in the major cities of northern Europe was probably about half, but in Italy closer to two-thirds. Political and social conflict, particularly in cities with large industrial populations such as Ghent and Florence and in devastated political capitals such as Paris, also depressed population through violent death and exile. Paris, indeed, may have been the worst case of depopulation among the major cities of Europe, going from nearly a quarter of a million in 1328 to about 30,000 in the 1430s, although it recovered rapidly after the French regained the city from the English in 1437. The countryside was less affected by plague than the cities, but suffered worse damage from marauding troops. There was some recovery in parts of northern Europe during the fifteenth century, but total population only regained its 1300 levels around 1600.

Towns are living organisms that must adapt to changes over which they have no control or decline. The defensive functions of most towns had become less important by 1500 than earlier, and certainly were not as paramount as they had been in the period of urban origins. Service functions, including government, were increasingly important, and the cities continued to be religious capitals after the Protestant movement, as they had before. The most important consideration for the growth of towns in the modern period, as earlier, continued to be the diversity of functions that they could fulfil. Towns that had only a single dominant function, such as defence, declined.

General trends conceal a host of variables. While it was only after the end of the Hundred Years War that most continental towns recovered from the catastrophes, several English towns grew in the half-century after 1375, only to decline thereafter into the sixteenth century. Since war devastation cannot explain this for England, structural considerations are obviously at work. Given that the English economy was growing in the fifteenth and sixteenth centuries, the correlation that is often made between general economic growth and urban expansion works no better for developed England than for the German-Slavic east. Much of the stagnation was due to the diversion toward London of what had been the exporting trades of the provincial towns. Although London was only manufacturing a small portion of the cloth that was exported from England, 93 per cent of the total customs value on cloth export in 1559 was collected at the port of London.[29]

In 1500 there were 30 fewer cities with a population of over 10,000 than there had been in 1300, due to population losses, some concentration of settlement and mortality from plague, which was higher in the cities than in the rural areas.[30] Yet Europe had a higher urban density by 1600 than in 1300, and this requires some explanation. First, roughly a third of the expansion of the urban sector in the sixteenth and seventeenth centuries came from the growth of national and regional capitals. London was the largest city in western Europe by 1700, nearly 20 times the size of the next largest English city, while Paris surpassed the next largest French city, Lyon, by five times. Many older cities stagnated or declined.[31]

After the plagues, heavy immigration into the towns from their economically depressed rural environs meant that in the long term the cities recovered in percentage terms more of their plague losses than the rural areas did. Several explanations contribute to this. First, rural families tended to be larger than urban and thus had more trouble supporting all their members. Second, particularly after 1375, a cycle developed of low grain prices and high labour costs, and the presence of cheap food in the cities attracted people to them.

Overall standards of living were rising after the plagues. Although rural depopulation meant that the demand for urban manufactures would decline in quantitative terms, the growing prosperity of princes and the urban wealthy stimulated demand for luxuries that were the great cities' specialities. A more serious problem was the mutability of long-distance trade, which was conditioned not only by demand for town manufactures and the locally produced raw materials that were exported through the cities, but also by war disorders.[32] Thus population declined and the standard of living for most city-dwellers rose in the late Middle Ages, due in large part to low grain prices. But this situation was reversed in the sixteenth century, as population grew and the standard of living, based on the movement of real wages (the purchasing power of a given wage measured against the prices of staple goods), declined by some 50 per cent.[33]

The fortunes of war and changes in demography and patterns of demand made possible a new prosperity for cities and regions that had remained largely outside the broader currents of interregional trade until the late Middle Ages. The Hanse league of cities continued to dominate the long-distance trade of northern Germany, although this was rarely translated into power over the countryside. In the fifteenth century the cities of Upper (Southern) Germany – Nuremberg, Augsburg, Ravensburg and Ulm – became major centres of commercial capitalism and banking and of newly developing industries, especially printing. They controlled their environs politically to an extent that was unusual among the older German cities. Nuremberg gained a 'staple' or monopoly on goods passing on the roads that intersected its territory, then expanded this into a general regional hegemony, most exceptionally for a north European city. Nuremberg and to a lesser extent Cologne controlled the overland trade over the Brenner Pass to

Venice. Nuremberg investment capital promoted an increase in mining in the Balkans, and the metals and other raw materials of Bohemia and Hungary passed through Nuremberg en route to western markets, as did the western trade into these areas. Nurembergers were also active in the Baltic trade, at the international markets of Bruges, at the fairs of Frankfurt-am-Main and at the Low Country fairs of Antwerp and Bergen-op-Zoom.

The south German cities also transmitted manufactured goods of southeastern Europe westward, and they provided an overland route for Mediterranean goods. This led to a major reorientation of trade patterns in the northwest. From southern Germany, and from the newly important fairs of Geneva and Lyon, goods were shipped by overland routes to the Rhine and thence to Antwerp, which began its rise to preeminence in the fifteenth century. While the Italian galleys continued to visit Bruges, the artificiality of the Flemish city's commercial dominance became painfully apparent. When the Portuguese established their staple on colonial pepper at Antwerp in 1501, the transition was complete.[34]

The late fourteenth and fifteenth centuries also saw the growth of the cities of the southern and western Iberian peninsula, notably Seville, Cadiz and Lisbon. Barcelona, on the eastern coast, was one of the great cities of the early fourteenth century. Italian competition hurt its Mediterranean trade, but the development of a native textile industry prevented a complete collapse. The Castilian ports developed as depots for colonial voyages and trade with the Atlantic islands and Africa, although none of them developed a significant group of native merchants; capital for the colonial ventures was provided by foreigners, particularly Genoese.

Demographic Perspectives on the Early Modern Urban Network

Despite the depopulations of the late Middle Ages, western Europe was thus a much more urbanised place in the early sixteenth century than it had been around 1100. Although there were still clusters of large cities in northern Italy, northern France and the Low Countries, the spatial distribution of the large towns had become more uniform except in Britain and Scandinavia, as smaller centres took form alongside the old metropolitan cities, in some cases providing significant competition to them.

Around 1500 Europe had 154 places of 10,000 or more inhabitants, and four (Paris, Milan, Venice and Naples) of 100,000 or more. Of the 154, 44 were in Italy, another 44 in France and Belgium (using modern borders). This number had grown to 173 by 1550, with the most significant gains coming in Germany and Spain. No general region suffered major losses, and the strongest gains were in central Europe and the Mediterranean. Growth was much more rapid in the second half of the century, with a total of 220 places over 10,000 by 1600. The most notable increases were in Belgium (despite the religious wars), the Netherlands, France, northern Italy and Spain. This pattern was reversed in the first half of the seventeenth century, with the Dutch and French cities growing rapidly, while the Mediterranean declined sharply and central Europe less drastically. Urban population as a percentage of total population was 31.7 by 1650. England, starting with a lower base than the Low Countries and Italy, rose from 5.8 per cent urban in 1600 to 8.8 per cent in 1650. Although the total number of places over 10,000 declined between 1600 and 1650, the total numbers of persons living in cities still rose.[35]

The paradox in the previous sentence is explained by the fact that population was concentrating in the largest cities, while the smaller ones stagnated. The percentage of Europeans living in cities of at least 10,000 souls rose from 5.6 in 1500 to 9.2 in 1700. But when we make 40,000 the lower limit of what we call a 'city', the figure changes to a growth from a miniscule 1.9 per cent in 1500 to 5.2 per cent in 1700. Growth was most rapid in the larger cities, followed by those of medium size; while if 'city' is taken without a demographic qualifier, the total increase is least marked.[36]

Only fragmentary population data survive for the pre-modern cities, and virtually all require considerable imagination on the demographer's part to be useful. Figure 1.3 summarises the current consensus for individual large cities. John Marshall has also compiled a useful table showing the changing relative size of 60 cities and towns, although he omits such notable places as Cologne and Nuremberg. Among the cities included in Marshall's list, London was the 24th largest in 1500, fourth in 1600 and first after Constantinople in 1700. Paris was eighth in 1500, third in 1600 and second in 1700. Naples was second in 1500 and 1600, fourth in 1700. Moscow rose from 44th in 1500 to ninth in 1700. Lisbon and Prague and Florence shared the twelfth position in 1500; but Lisbon rose to fifth in 1700, while Florence dropped to 21st in 1600 and 23rd in 1700. Vienna is a spectacular case: although the political capital of Habsburg Austria, it was only the 32nd largest city of Europe in 1500 and dropped further to 72nd in 1600 with the Turkish wars, but it rose to 13th place in 1700. Amsterdam was a small place as late as 1500 but rose to 38th place by 1600, then experienced a spectacular growth to sixth place by 1700. Madrid mushroomed as a political capital at the expense of Toledo, to 18th place in 1600 and 12th in 1700. Venice and Milan declined relatively, but they were still in the top score of cities in 1700. Hamburg rose dramatically, while Lyon declined: in the former case from 78th place in 1500 to 21st in 1700, in the latter from eighth in 1500 to 19th in 1700. Seville grew from 24th in 1500 to seventh in 1600, due to its privileges in the colonial trade granted by the Castilian crown; but with the decline of the colonies, it dropped to sixteenth in 1700. Rotterdam, Stockholm, Warsaw and Liverpool all grew significantly in the seventeenth century, in Liverpool's case at the expense of Chester, as the silting of the Dee estuary made access to the older centre difficult, while Manchester and Birmingham were mainly creatures of the eighteenth.[37]

These figures show the considerable decline of many of the great medieval centres in the early modern period, although some of them recovered after the religious wars, particularly those of the southern Low Countries: despite being the *de facto* capital of the Burgundian/Spanish Netherlands, Brussels was only

I. Italy

	c. 1300	c. 1400	c. 1500	c. 1550	c. 1600	c. 1650	c. 1700
Bologna	40	25	55	55	63	58	63
Brescia	45	25	50	40	50	40	35
Cremona	40			37	40	17	
Florence	90	35	70	60	80	70	80
Genoa	100	60			63	70	
Milan	100		100	50	110	95	100
Naples	40			210	250		215
Padua	30		27	32	35	25	
Palermo	60	40	50	80	100		100
Rome	40	40	50	45	110	126	135
Turin		4		14	20		42
Venice	120		115	160	150	120	140
Verona	40	20	40	46	55	25	

II. Holy Roman Empire

	c. 1300	c. 1400	c. 1500	c. 1550	c. 1600	c. 1650	c. 1700
Cologne	80	30	40	35			
Frankfurt		10			25	15	25
Gdánsk			30		40	100	
Hamburg	5	10	20		20	50	
Leipzig				7	15	15	22
Lübeck	25	30	30				31
Nuremberg		20	50				
Prague		40	30				
Vienna			20		60		

III. France

	c. 1300	c. 1400	c. 1500	c. 1550	c. 1600	c. 1650	c. 1700
Lyon		15	40	70			90
Paris	200	100		250	250		300
Rouen	40	20		75	80		65
Toulouse		23	35	50		42	43

Figure 1.3 European urban populations (in thousands)

the 52nd largest city of Europe in 1500, but it had grown to 21st by 1700. Antwerp's population shrank from a high of 100,000 around 1565 to 42,000 after the blockade of the Scheldt in 1585, but it revived in the early seventeenth

IV. Low Countries

	c. 1300	*c. 1400*	*c. 1500*	*c. 1550*	*c. 1600*	*c. 1650*	*c. 1700*
Amsterdam			15	35	100	135	180
Antwerp			40	100		57	
Bruges	50	35	30	35		34	
Brussels			37		50		60
Ghent	80	40	40	45	30		40
Liège						50	55

V. England

	c. 1300	*c. 1400*	*c. 1500*	*c. 1550*	*c. 1600*	*c. 1650*	*c. 1700*
Bristol			10				20
London	80	35	70	80	250	400	500
Norwich			13		13		30

VI. Spain

	c. 1300	*c. 1400*	*c. 1500*	*c. 1550*	*c. 1600*	*c. 1650*	*c. 1700*
Barcelona						64	
Madrid					65	75	120
Seville				100	150	125	

Figure 1.3 *(continued)*

century. Ghent declined from eighth largest in 1500 to 36th in 1700. The case of Lübeck is indicative. Its commercial privileges had virtually ended by 1600 with increased competition from the English and Dutch in the Baltic trade. Lübeck's population was around 31,000 in 1650, which was probably about its fourteenth-century size; but this made it a secondary city in the urban framework of the seventeenth century.[38]

The highest relative growth through 1700 was in two types of city. The first comprised political capitals: Copenhagen, Madrid, Moscow and Paris in the sixteenth century, and Lisbon, Stockholm and Vienna in the seventeenth; London's situation as a political capital contributed to its growth but was not its fundamental cause. Ports made up the second group: Amsterdam, Cadiz, Hamburg, Oporto, Lisbon and Rotterdam, all of which had colonial involvements, and Bordeaux, Marseille, Nantes, Bristol, Glasgow and Liverpool. All of these except Marseille were Atlantic or North Sea ports, showing the shift of commercial pre-eminence away from the Mediterranean. Amsterdam, Copenhagen, Lisbon and London were both ports and political capitals. Not until the eighteenth century would a third category of towns, manufacturing centres, begin to experience a significant relative growth. Even then it remained the smallest group of the three, and until after 1800 rapidly growing manufacturing cities were found only in the British Isles.[39]

The cities of the Holy Roman Empire illustrate regional mutations behind the total population figures. In contrast to the western monarchies, the decentralised Empire did not have a capital. Vienna developed later, and it was too geographically peripheral to become a German capital when it did. In purely demographic terms there was little change in the rank order of the cities of the Empire between 1500 and about 1630: Cologne, Nuremberg, Gdánsk, Augsburg, Prague and Lübeck – all of them commercial centres except Prague – remained the largest. The great changes after 1630 are associated with the rise of political capitals. There were also changes in regional distribution. As late as 1600 the most urbanised part of Germany was within the old Roman frontier in the south and west, but thereafter this region declined in favour of the towns of the north and east, particularly the local administrative centres of the interior, which grew as some of the ports declined. The German urban network was polycentric, with a large number of medium-sized towns of comparable populations, which served as centres of regions that were largely autonomous. The greatest growth occurred at Hamburg, Königsberg, Breslau, Frankfurt and Leipzig, which slightly more than doubled in size. But the political capitals, Vienna, Berlin and Dresden, grew even more rapidly; while Leipzig, the economic centre of Saxony, doubled in size between 1500 and 1700, the princely residence of Dresden quadrupled, an evolution that left the two Saxon towns of comparable size (*c.* 15,000) at the end of our period. The growing political domination of Prussia and Austria led to the rise of Berlin and Vienna, but it did not do violence to local networks.[40]

The great Italian cities were once thought to have lost much of their trade after the Turkish capture of Constantinople in 1453, which disrupted their eastern sources of supply, but this has been exaggerated. The definitive loss for Italy and its cities only occurs in the seventeenth century, and particularly after 1630, as they lost their monopoly of shipping in the Mediterranean to the English and Dutch and as their highly priced luxury manufactures were supplanted by cheaper competitors from the north. Five of the eight cities of Europe with populations of over 100,000 in 1600 – Venice, Palermo, Messina, Naples and Rome – were in Italy or Sicily. Venice and Genoa continued to dominate Mediterranean trade, and Genoese bankers financed much more of Spain's colonial endeavour than did native Castilians. Florence was still important for banking and its textile industry, but its population was truncated. The other Mediterranean cities remained large, but they were becoming more consumer cities on the ancient model as they lost banking and industrial functions. Italy had a high urban index but was not prosperous. The fact that there were so many large cities, with rentiers residing in them while living off the income of their peasant tenants, depressed Italy still further. The positive correlation between economic growth and urbanisation, which as we have seen does not always work for northern Europe, had also become inverse in the Mediterranean basin by 1650.[41]

The Early Eighteenth Century: The Transition to Industrial Urbanisation

Except for the heavily industrialised cities, the modern urban map of Europe was thus established between 1100 and 1700. Market networks with pre-existing cities as their nodal points had been superimposed on the locally-based cult and princely centres of the early Middle Ages. These cities had some industry, most of it based on satisfaction of basic consumer needs of the local market. Europe had also developed some exportable manufactured goods, particularly textiles, most of which were either made or at least finished in the cities or financed with urban capital.

No fundamental change occurs suddenly, and antecedents of the modern factory system developed before the Industrial Revolution. An important distinction between industrial production before and after about 1700 is that, given the prevalence of putting-out and of household production (see Chapter 2), few medieval industries had large fixed capital. Although city governments fostered competition, it was not unbridled, and the cities regulated strategic goods. Mills were too expensive for individual millers and were often taken over by town governments. By the sixteenth century in England, workshops for coarse cloth working amounted to small factories, with numerous persons in a single small room. Factories for armaments, which did require a substantial capital outlay, are found in early modern France, northern Italy and the Low Countries. Several German cities had factories in the sixteenth century, usually with privileges given by the city government. Huguenot exiles established a factory for silks and brocades at Zürich; in 1592 a brocade factory was established at Antwerp, and a soap factory at Nuremberg in 1593. In places that had shipyards, the city government usually owned them and leased them to guilds or to syndicates for actual operation.[42]

Apart from printing and metalworking, there were few fundamental changes in industrial technology before the Industrial Revolution. Some changes were made to the spinning wheel, and the gig-mill was now used in cloth finishing. There were improvements in bellows and furnaces, especially the development of the blast furnace. Better pumps and ventilation systems made it possible to dig deeper mining shafts. But most of this occurred outside the towns; even their iron-workers finished iron and other metals that had been smelted outside the town. Thus the major improvements were in the organisation of industry, particularly the increasing direction of industry by merchant capitalists through the putting-out system. Woollens, the staple of the greatest industrial cities of the Middle Ages, were largely urban this late only in Spain, except for the highly skilled finishing processes. Even the prosperous English export textile trade was in unfinished cloth, which was dyed at Antwerp.[43]

The technology that created the breakthrough to the second Industrial Revolution established a new set of circumstances that changed the pattern of urbanisation, which previously had been primarily commercial but now became mainly industrial, and brought with it the rise in the eighteenth century of such places as

Roubaix, Manchester, Liverpool and Birmingham. In this chapter we have indicated the most important cities and trends at work in the period of incipient urbanisation. But the rise and decline of cities was determined by a complex and evolving interaction of circumstances and characteristics. To those issues we now turn.

Chapter 2 . . . .

City and Region

A town never exists unaccompanied by other towns.[1]
(J. K. Hyde)

The Region

Urban regions were defined initially in terms of a localised market radius or by
political privileges that gave a city institutional control over its environs. But as
economic regions became characterised by speciality goods or services, access to
the interlinked commodity and labour markets could be had only through the
cities, which had the infrastructure and capital base necessary to convey the
region's surpluses to more distant places. Whatever was unavailable in one
place could be obtained elsewhere through the urban network. Specialisation
developed not only between regions, but also within smaller territories that
served as catchment areas of the major cities. All urban places had to provide
basic support and sustenance to their inhabitants; the major distinctions between
cities thus arose in the basic rather than non-basic sectors of the labour force.
Competition sometimes degenerated into violence, particularly at the level of
the territorial state, but it also fostered inventiveness, an ability to produce or
acquire what was better or cheaper than what rivals could do.[2] The development
of cities was thus one element of a broader diffusion of market relationships,
which by their nature involved competition.

Definition of the urban region must also be in terms of the functions that the
city provides to its environs. Some urban regions were small territories, others
quite large. The two peripheral areas of Europe − northern Italy, and the southern Low Countries with northern France − had large cities that were centres of
regions that were much smaller in area, but not population, than was the norm
elsewhere: for while a region normally has only one higher order centre, it can
have more if it has a high population concentration and corresponding degree of
functional differentiation.[3] Nor are urban regions mutually exclusive. The more
economically developed the metropolitan area, the more likely the spheres of
influence of individual cities are to overlap. A gateway city such as Bristol serves
at least two areas. Bristol is really part of three regions: Wales, southwest England

excluding Cornwall, and Cornwall. Being at the wrong gateway could cost a place dearly. Carlisle, on the border of the north English region, at the junction of three rivers and two Roman roads, suffered through its location on the border with Scotland.[4]

Within the region, hierarchies also developed among the towns. The fact that the labour forces of small places were relatively undifferentiated generally meant that, for goods or services that they could not provide for themselves, they were more likely to have recourse to a larger central place than to a place of comparable size to themselves. Yet while population is the most commonly used indicator of rank within the region, it is not the only one and can be misleading. The most obvious definition of hierarchy within regions is through central-place theory. Local trade relations generally make a central place. But as regions became interdependent and exchanged goods and to some extent populations, many 'central places' of regions were not geographically central, and cities that developed along traffic corridors or functioned as gateway cities or points of entry became large. Even in most of the greatest cities, long-distance trade generated less wealth than internal markets, but it had a disproportionate impact on the standing of the city within the regional hierarchy; for critical luxuries and industrial raw materials (and from the late Middle Ages also food) came through the city within the region – usually no more than one – that had access to interregional trading currents.[5] The Flemish urban region in the late Middle Ages contained three cities of over 20,000 persons, and the most economically powerful of them was probably Bruges, the second in size, through which most exports passed.

Over time, rank order within urban regions tends to vary less at the top than at the intermediate and, especially, lower levels. When a great change occurs, it usually reflects the growing importance of some new criterion for city power, such as politics, education, the development of a new trade route or the breakthrough of a commercial technique or transportation facility. This in turn means that historical development is important, for the earliest founded places *tend* to dominate but will not always do so. After 1450 there was, for example, a major restructuring. Tuscany and the Low Countries remained the most densely urbanised parts of Europe, but within regions one metropolis might succeed another (Antwerp took on many of the functions of Bruges), and slightly later political conditions and changes in rural purchasing power could cause a shift at the secondary level (as with the decline of Flanders in favour of Holland within the Low Country region).[6]

Power in the interregional economy could not be obtained until a city dominated its local economic region; but the characteristics that are needed for a city to achieve local hegemony are not always the same as those needed for European preeminence. Before 1300, the regions of most cities were defined largely in terms of the territory that the urban militia could control. A second factor that usually defined pre-modern urban regions related to the ability of the rural environs to feed the city and provide raw materials that could be converted into exportable goods. Most urban regions originated through the interaction of agricultural productivity, population density and the potential of the local labour market and distribution facilities. Before the thirteenth century transport facilities were inadequate for the long-distance transport of bulk goods such as grain. Even after the great population growth of the thirteenth century, most Italian cities could still be fed by supplementing local grain with imports from southern Italy, Sicily and northern Africa. The fairs of Champagne were held throughout the year to permit merchants to return home to visit their local fairs and bring exportable goods of high value to the next fair. But this changed when galleys from Italy began making direct voyages to the North Sea ports in the late thirteenth century. Not only were they bringing what had previously been luxury goods in greater quantities to the north, but the northern cities were also able to import grain and forest products from northern Germany through the German inter-urban league, the Hanse. What had previously been restricted networks of distribution thus assumed a more interregional context after 1300, as the cities, which had earlier channelled the goods of their environs to the fairs, now themselves succeeded the fairs as direct nodal points for the re-export of goods from their immediate regions to a wider consuming public.

Admittedly, the volume of port trade was still quite small. The port of Lübeck, the leading city of the German Hanse, had 430 ships entering and 870 departing in 1368. Sluis, the outport of Bruges, probably saw about 850 vessels in 1371, but many of them were small fishing craft. A century later, when boats were much larger, the port of London had 224 entries and 215 departures. But while cargoes were small, commodity value was high. The turnover of all Baltic ports in 1368 in terms of silver was triple the state revenues of the English king, and values in Italy were even higher. Although the volume of interregional trade grew as conditions became more peaceful after 1450, the cities remained dependent on their environs.[7]

This chapter will consider the applicability of several theories of regionalism propounded by geographers, historians and sociologists to pre-modern urban development in Europe. The weakness of these theories is their assumption that natural forces, particularly economic considerations, operate without constraint. These models are not mutually exclusive. Depending on function and on stage of development, central-place, rank-size, or network theory can provide the most satisfactory explanation of the urban characteristics of different places. The theories furthermore presume a static condition; if one can only eliminate all variables, the result will be certain, but this never occurs in history. The urban region as such is a moving target, and it would be foolhardy to attempt to construct a single map that works for the six centuries under discussion in this book. Urban regions are the products of disparate forces and situations, each unique in time, and their structure and dimensions were thus subject to change. A town's first development was usually due to circumstances that were transitory. How rationally its elite adapted to changes determined whether it evolved into a major city. But even if the city's growth was stunted, it was likely for demographic reasons to continue to exist as a secondary centre, while other places that initially were less significant surpassed it.

Gateway Cities

Even the smallest town had to develop at the intersection of supply and demand. The more comprehensive that intersection was, the larger the city was likely to be and become. Cities developed on frontiers, not only of supply and demand, but also of broad currents of trade, or at ethnic meeting points and topographical boundaries. Cities that controlled the import of food or strategic industrial raw materials for a large region, or of luxuries that reached a narrow market in many different places, tended to fulfil a gateway function for their regions or even for Europe as a whole, as was the case with Venice for Levantine luxury goods.

Gateways link regions that are dominated by cities, most often one central place or, less often, several substantial cities that develop in a rank-size pattern. Not every region has an urban gateway, and gateways are not always on the geographical peripheries of their regions. Towns that are centrally located within their regions can also be gateways. For example, if the Low Countries constitute a region, Bruges, which was definitely the gateway in the fourteenth and fifteenth centuries, was at its edge, while Ghent was its central place. The same is true of Antwerp in the sixteenth and Amsterdam in the seventeenth centuries. But if the entire Low Countries and Northern France are defined as a single region, Bruges was central geographically. Smaller sub-regions also had gateways. The customs headports of England, most of which were wealthy and prosperous, served as gateways to locally-defined regions, which in turn fed into the larger English region dominated by London.[8]

The Primate City

As Max Weber recognised, when an agricultural region produced too much for the local market to absorb, large estates developed which exported their grain through the few cities of the region, most of them coastal. This type of colonial economy produces 'primate' cities, often at the gateway to the region, in which administrative and economic functions are centred. Primate cities are typically endowed with special privileges by territorial rulers. Many gateway cities, which tend to become primate, were founded before the land was settled thoroughly. Access to the interior was typically along a series of long-distance routes leading from the coastal primate city, along which smaller towns developed to handle regional distribution of imported goods.[9] Densely urbanised western Europe exported manufactured goods to the colonial areas in the east, which exported raw materials through the cities that had been founded as coastal or regional emporia and thus controlled their hinterlands' access to distant markets. Primate cities thus tend to be characteristic of an economy that is closely linked to exports. When state growth preceded economic expansion, and in effect required economic growth to take care of the needs of the state, the result was more often an administrative primate city pattern.

Primate cities are so enormous that they depress normal market relationships and hinder the formation of secondary centres within a large area. Gdánsk and other east European colonial cities are excellent examples of such places. By 1500 Gdánsk controlled about three-quarters of Poland's exports, two-thirds of its imports, and most banking and manufacturing. With a population that grew from 40,000 in 1600 to 100,000 in 1650, Gdánsk depended for its prosperity on the backwardness of the rest of the Polish economy.[10] Southern Europe offers two further conspicuous examples: Granada in Muslim Spain before the Christian conquest, and the overwhelming domination of southern Italy by Naples in the modern period. Some political capitals, such as Madrid, in effect functioned as primate cities; others, such as London, did not. Thus whether urbanisation contributed to economic growth in the colonial areas of Europe is highly problematical.

Within the Urban Region: The Development of Rank-size Patterns

The rank-size explanation of the spatial distribution of cities was formulated in 1941 by George K. Zipf, then subsequently refined.[11] When P is the population of a given city, A the population of the largest city of the region, and r is the city's ranking in the regional hierarchy, $P = A/r$. By this formula, the second largest city of a region should have half the population of the largest city, the third ranking city one-third of the largest, and so on. Thus, if the population of one city is known with certainty as well as (usually by more qualitative criteria) the ranks of the component cities in the regional hierarchy, the population distribution of the urban region can be calculated. Rank-size is more numbers- or population-driven than central-place theory, since the region must have a predictable pattern of sizes of towns. Scholars have complained of a 'flat' top of the graph of city sizes before 1700 and an incomplete rank-size order, and have called regions whose largest cities are smaller than would be predicted by the rank-size formula 'immature', an unfortunate term that implies impatience that people do not behave the way the model says they should.[12]

The most comprehensive attempt to analyse pre-modern city populations by a rank-size method was made by Josiah C. Russell.[13] He was using mainly figures from the period before 1400, which are notoriously unreliable. To take account of the fact that all his chief cities were too small for the model, Russell changed the mathematical basis of the formula, reducing the numerator to produce smaller second-rank cities. When he did not have the correct number of cities of a given population, he simply altered the borders of the 18 urban regions into which he divided Europe, without regard to economic ties, culture or language. He also failed to explain urban regions that had no metropolis but rather several medium-sized cities of similar size, or particularly the fact that, since he had to draw his regions without regard to internal cohesion to get the right numbers, many of his metropolitan cities were near the borders of their regions and thus assume the character of gateways, for example Cologne, Toledo, Prague,

London and Barcelona.[14] Yet for all its faults, Russell's formulation has been the model to which most later scholars have referred. Jan de Vries, perhaps the most profound demographer of early modern urbanisation, prefers the rank-size model to central place, although he does not reject central place completely. Russell and de Vries have very similar population figures for the cities of Europe in 1500, with the major variant consisting of Russell's number of cities of 10,000–20,000 inhabitants. De Vries agrees with Russell's conclusion that the urban system was 'immature' because of low agricultural productivity, but he obviated the problem by defining larger regions than Russell had done and starting with a higher urban threshold than Russell, considering as urban only 378 cities that had populations of 10,000 or above at some point between 1500 and 1800.[15] The rank-size model clearly works better for urban systems that are at a late or mature stage of development. Thus a region may originate around a single dominant primate city, then develop a network with a hierarchy of towns that are economically and culturally integrated with one another.

The Low Countries provide the best example of a rank-size ordering of pre-modern cities, reflecting the region's high level of economic development. Flanders had the highest population density in Europe in 1469, with over 36 per cent of the inhabitants living in towns. Central-place theory does not work well there, even in comparison to Italy. The region does have elements of a gateway structure, with most imports passing through first Bruges and later Antwerp.

Flanders had two clearly defined urban regions. Bruges dominated the northern coastal areas, which had numerous 'dwarf' towns. Ghent's size and political power dominated eastern Flanders and repressed the small centres around it, but most of the Flemish towns in the 3000–6000 range were in the 'quarter' of Ghent. Ypres, the third great Flemish city, briefly became the centre of an urban region on the basis of its credit network in the late thirteenth century, but it declined sharply in the fourteenth and particularly the fifteenth centuries. The Flemish cities were distributed unevenly from the perspective of forming a network on purely demographic grounds. Ghent had about 80,000 inhabitants in the early fourteenth century, perhaps declining to as low as 30,000 by 1385 before recovering in the fifteenth century. Bruges had 40,000 souls, Ypres about 20,000. 'Quarters', which were recognised in Flanders by the 1340s as the spheres of influence of the three great cities, in a sense encapsulate their immediate regions together with the secondary regions that composed the greater ones. The most serious quarrels between the cities and the central regime concerned the privileges of the city in its quarter, which was a political extension outside the town corporate limits of its economic influence.

The most singular feature of urban distribution in Flanders was the absence of middle-sized towns of from 10,000 to 40,000 inhabitants (although Ypres was barely above 10,000 by 1469). In terms of the rank-size model, there was a flat top: Bruges was too big in relation to Ghent, the largest city. A census of 1469 shows seven other major towns between 5000 and 10,000 inhabitants, eleven smaller ones between 2000 and 5000, 14 between 1000 and 2000, and numerous others under 1000. The few towns within a 25 kilometre radius of Ghent or

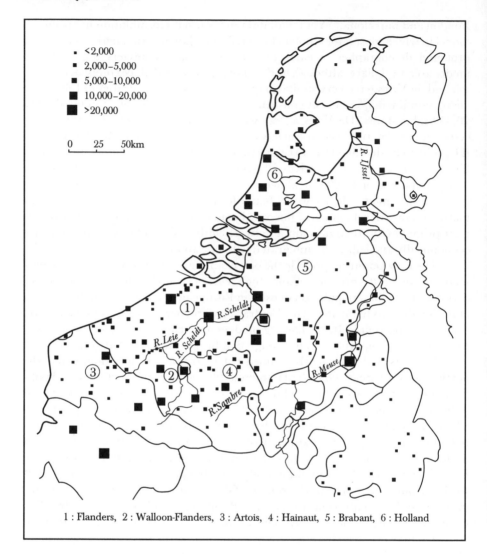

1 : Flanders, 2 : Walloon-Flanders, 3 : Artois, 4 : Hainaut, 5 : Brabant, 6 : Holland

Figure 2.1   The urban network in the Low Countries

Bruges were completely dominated by the two metropoles. Peter Stabel identifies 15 urban functions, of which all were fulfilled in the fourteenth century by Bruges and Ghent, 14 by Ypres, and between nine and 11 by the next three towns in the demographic hierarchy, the largest of which (Dendermonde) was three-quarters the size of Ypres.[16]

The Flemish case illustrates the difficulty of applying rigid models, and also the problems of a demographic rather than functional approach. Stabel sees Bruges as the chief place of the Flemish urban system; for although Ghent was more centrally located within Flanders and had a population at least 30 per cent larger, the diversified commerce and industry and the international connections of Bruges were more sophisticated than in Ghent. Stabel's arguments are persuasive; yet it is unusual for the chief town to be second in population, and Ghent did supplant Bruges in functional terms by the early sixteenth century.[17]

A further problem is that the urban networks of Walloon Flanders, Brabant and Holland, which bordered Flanders on three sides, were displacing the Flemish from regional leadership. The economic region was being widened, and concentrating on Flanders misses this essential point of dynamism. Antwerp, rather than Bruges, became the gateway to the Low Countries in the late fifteenth century, as the economic region came to be defined in contemporary political terms: Brabant and Flanders were under the same government in 1500 and 1600 but not in 1400.[18]

Similarly, the northern Low Countries developed economically considerably later than the southern provinces. As was true of Brabant in the late fourteenth century – but less so by 1500 – Holland, the most urbanised province of the north, in the late fifteenth century had several cities of medium and comparable size, and thus in no discernible rank order: Haarlem, Delft, Gouda, Leiden, Amsterdam and Dordrecht had between 10,000 and 15,000 inhabitants. In the early sixteenth century Amsterdam emerged as the major port, with exports perhaps ten times the value of Dordrecht's, while Leiden was the chief industrial centre.[19]

The exponential growth of Amsterdam in the seventeenth century as the successor to Antwerp, which had been ruined in the religious wars, led to a more hierarchical system. Yet the Netherlands still fits a rank-size scheme rather well in the seventeenth century. Amsterdam grew from 30,000 in 1550 to 175,000 in 1650; Leiden, the second city, had 67,000, and Haarlem, the third, had 38,000: thus the second city was double the population of the third, and first was double the population of the second. Despite its domination of long-distance trade and finance, Amsterdam was not able to overpower the other cities. In the early modern United Provinces, while each city of Holland and Zeeland had such staples as textiles and brewing, local markets and some bureaucracy, they also developed specialities that made them regionally interdependent and less competitive with one another than might have been the case had the entire area been devoted to one type of activity, as had happened earlier in Flanders with luxury woollen textiles. Thus Amsterdam dominated Mediterranean and Baltic trade, but Rotterdam and Middelburg surpassed it in trade with England. Leiden and Haarlem were industrial, and Leiden had the first Dutch university. Dordrecht remained bound mainly to river trade, Gouda to overland traffic. The Hague was the centre of government. Rotterdam was primarily a fisheries centre but also had river and sea trade. Delft's importance was for beer and dairy goods; Utrecht was a cult centre; Middelburg dominated the French trade. This gave the cities of the Netherlands a sort of collective gateway pattern by the early seventeenth century that is highly original. What is now called the Randstad (Rim City), the 'great circle of cities Amsterdam–Haarlem–Leiden–The Hague–Delft–Rotterdam–Gouda–Utrecht–Amsterdam', was already present.[20]

There are important parallels between the urban networks of the Low Countries and northern Italy. Each region was politically fragmented, had a prosperous agriculture that supported a dense rural population, several large cities, and a lack of medium-sized towns. The north Italian cities controlled their rural environs (*contadi*) much more thoroughly than the Flemish cities ever controlled their quarters. For its size, northern Italy had fewer large cities, but those that did exist were larger than the Flemish, and their hinterlands were also larger than the Flemish urban quarters. The metropolis dominated to an extent unknown in the Low Countries: Florence, with 38,000 persons in 1427,

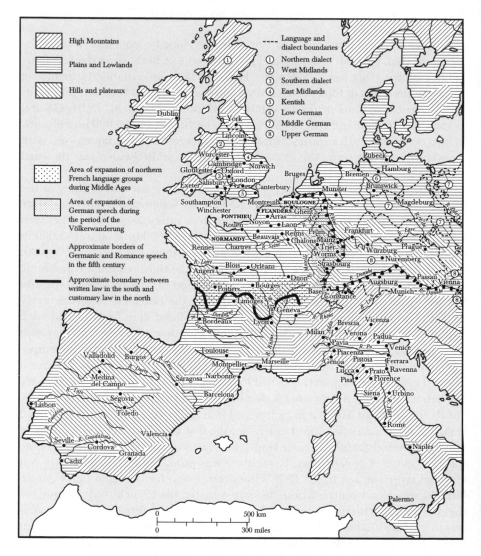

Figure 2.2   Relief, topography, language and urbanisation

was more than five times the size of Pisa (7300), which was in its state and the second city of Tuscany.[21]

Germany in the sixteenth century had numerous middle-sized and small towns. The Holy Roman Empire had about 25 cities with populations over 10,000, if one includes Gdánsk and Prague, with were partly Polish and Bohemian respectively. Cologne was the largest with 40,000. Lübeck, Gdánsk, Magdeburg, Nuremberg, Prague, Strasbourg and Augsburg had populations between 20,000 and 40,000. Between 10,000 and 20,000 were commercial cities such as Hamburg, Lüneberg, Brunswick, Aachen, Frankfurt and Ulm; while residence-cities such as Vienna, Munich, Würzburg, Berlin, Leipzig and Dresden were still small. By the beginning of the Thirty Years War in 1618, however, the number of cities had grown to 32, including seven over 40,000. After 1650 the number declined again to roughly the level of 1500, then grew again in the eighteenth century. During the centuries 1500–1800, the number of cities over 10,000 in Germany thus roughly doubled, from 30 to 60.[22]

There were four main economic regions: the North, dominated by the Hanse towns; the Bavarian south, centring on Nuremberg and Augsburg; the Rhineland; and a less defined east-central area around Leipzig. There were some 3000 towns of more than 800 persons, but even with this low threshold only the south and the Rhineland, the most economically advanced areas, had urban ratios as high as 75 per cent. Except around Prague, middle-sized towns dominated.[23]

The City as Central Place

Geographers have long been concerned with problems of central place and settlement distribution. J. H. Von Thünen noted in 1826 that areas nearest the city walls were dominated by gardens and small farms, but generally not large estates; for vegetable growers had to be near the consumer in view of the perishability of their products. Demand from the cities made small farms profitable. Von Thünen also noted that the higher the transportation costs to market, the lower the amount of rent a farmer would be willing to pay to use land. Land values thus generally decline as distance from the market increases. Wine, honey, salt, wax and grain, by contrast, had a much larger trading radius. Meat was the food trade least bound to the urban region, for no cartage was involved since the animals were generally driven live to the point of slaughter. Von Thünen's ideas are particularly applicable to pre-modern urbanisation in view of improvements in techniques of carting and transportation from the thirteenth century, which made farmers less bound to regional markets. They could now go to the central place more easily, the transaction cost of maintaining the central place was diminished, and the range of the central place was correspondingly increased.[24]

Central-place theory is associated with the German geographer Walter Christaller. Since population is usually distributed unevenly, the demographic centre of an area is normally its central place, but only if it also performs central

33

functions. Identifying these functions is relatively simple, but the relative importance of each function varies with the town. Implicit in central-place theory is that a locality must have a minimum population to provide the goods and services needed to make it central. Central professions are site-bound to the central place and can be performed nowhere else, or at least not as effectively. Both central goods and central services are generated at central places but consumed or used throughout the region.[25] Central-place theory deals primarily with local trade. Industry and long-distance trade play minor roles; but since local trade dominated the economy of most towns in the period covered by this book, central-place works better as a comprehensive explanation of the spatial pattern of the cities of pre-modern Europe than the other theories that we have discussed.[26]

Christaller's model was far more sophisticated than its critics admit. He never considered centrality purely as a function of population. Indeed, his seven categories of central places are defined in terms of political position within the region; Gilbert Rozman's complex scheme of two criteria or variants of urbanisation, each with seven levels, virtually replicates it.[27] Christaller recognised further that since cities are consumers, their fortunes are conditioned by high demand for their goods and services. In places that are not central, supply can meet demand, but a central place will usually have greater demand than can be supplied, and it thus continues to attract increasing amounts of food or other consumer goods, or of labour. Thus a central place will tend to grow, while dispersed places will stagnate at a given level.[28] Since functions change as some places prosper while others languish, city populations should theoretically react accordingly; yet this is impossible, for a city may acquire new functions, for example becoming an administrative centre after initially developing as a market. Furthermore, an entire city, in contrast to a village, cannot simply be moved to accommodate a change in function; Salisbury, the only case I am aware of where this occurred, involved an *anticipated* change of function (for Salisbury, see Chapters 1 and 3).

The city had to provide goods and services for its environs in return for the raw materials and human capital that it demanded. The central place thus furnished retail trade and political administration for the adjacent areas, which are variously called service areas, hinterlands or environs. Christaller also noted that at some point customers of the central place will go to a closer place to get what they want, or simply take something less intrinsically desirable to avoid the bother and expense of the trip. The more specialised and unique the goods and services provided by the central place, and thus the larger and more diverse its 'basic' producing population, the wider its radius will be.[29]

Large economic regions are composed of a network of interlocking and overlapping smaller ones. In each of the sub-regions, one town will perform central-place functions, in effect 'nesting' within the areas of the central places of higher order in a 'hierarchy of central places. ... Each higher-order centre performs all the functions that lower-order centres perform for lower-order hinterlands, plus a group of more complex functions for a larger hinterland that encompasses several lower-order centres and their immediate hinterlands.'[30] Thus, for example, basic foodstuffs could be obtained on the regional market of

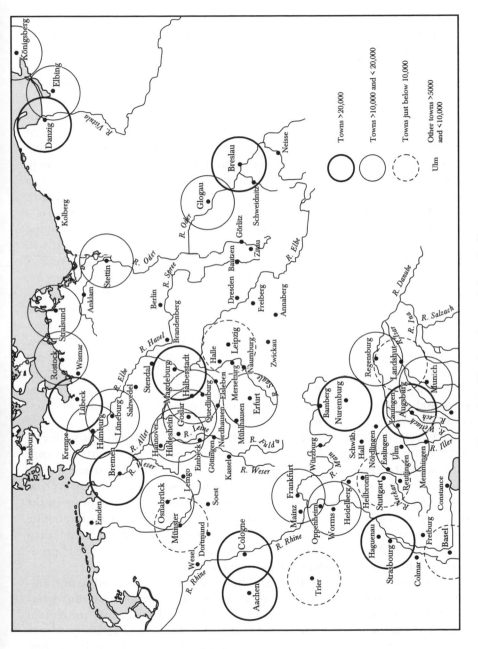

Figure 2.3 Nesting of central places in Germany

Towns >20,000

Towns >10,000 and < 20,000

Towns just below 10,000

Other towns >5000 and <10,000

Ulm

35

Julich, and a loan for purchase of a house or plough could be arranged through a local creditor. The consumer who wanted almonds or dried Mediterranean fruits or who needed credit to finance a cargo destined for Bruges would have to go to Cologne.

The gradual evolution of England into a national market dependent on London illustrates the process. Differences among the secondary towns of England diminished between 1377 and 1524–5, as the larger towns lost ground as a group – and in most cases individually – to London, while the medium-sized towns gained. But the relative standing of many towns in the hierarchy was disastrously compromised. The persistence of long-distance trade is the most important criterion, but the major success stories – Exeter, Colchester, Bury St Edmunds, Lavenham and Totnes – all owe their changing fortunes to developing cloth manufacture. The declining towns were affected adversely by the drop in wool exports while not benefiting from the rise in cloth exports. Thus they remained markets, but only for wool, rather than developing manufacturing or becoming exchange centres for cloth made in the rural areas. The rise or fall of a town thus depends on the economic fate of its region: if total production in the region is declining, for whatever reason, the central place that serves it will decline, and the decline of the chief town will entail a decline of the smaller centres in its network. Thus York declined with Yorkshire and the smaller places nearby, while Exeter rose with the general increase in prosperity of the southwest.[31]

Central-place theory thus presumes that urban growth is ultimately the outcome of rural development, with the city gradually taking over functions from local markets. Central places tend to be distributed relatively evenly, although rural population density and productivity will have an obvious impact on the extent to which centralised services are needed in a given area. The access of the central place to settlements within the region from which it derives trading goods and population is along important roads, and secondary 'transport cities' typically develop along them.

A variant on central-place theory is the 'dendritic' model, in which the city acts figuratively as the trunk of a tree. It takes in goods from the countryside, consumes some of them, then re-exports the rest to branches elsewhere in the system. This model is less oriented toward a single centre than central-place theory and thus involves more secondary towns. Political elites tend to concentrate in the highest-level centre of the region, which is the central place for both retailing and wholesaling. This model may work better for the early modern period than for the Middle Ages, but it certainly is applicable to towns with 'staple' privileges, which required transhipment in the staple town.[32]

Transaction costs, 'the direct and indirect outlays associated with transporting, distributing, and marketing goods and services', are an important determinant of how central places develop within regions.[33] They include the costs of brokerage and contract enforcement. The distance of merchant and/or producer from the town market, ease of access (for example location on a river in addition to a land route), and whether the market is on the geographical extremity of its attraction range are also involved. For example, Taunton importers came to

Exeter, 27 miles away, rather than to Bridgwater, less than ten miles to the north: Bridgwater was harder to reach down a small, winding river, and goods accordingly cost more there for Taunton merchants than at Exeter, whose larger size and easier access to Southampton drove down prices and made more goods available. Local authorities needed to lower transaction costs to draw trade, but some of their activities raised them: taxes, tolls, fees, and monopolies and privileges that hindered the operation of the free market. Many of these regulations were designed to ensure that consumers would get what they paid for – for example the requirements of transacting in daylight or on open markets – but they raised costs. Most towns legislated against forestalling (selling goods that were destined for the town market before they arrived there), a practice that increased costs to the consumer, but the fines were so low that most who did it simply paid the fee and went ahead.[34]

Transaction costs affect the central place in both its commercial and industrial capacities. Urban industry, made possible by the concentration in one place of a large workforce, can make more specialised goods than are possible in smaller places, and demand for them widens the attractive radius of the central place. The purchasing power of the customer is involved in the establishment of central places. The wealthier or higher-status the buyer, the farther from home he would go for specialised items, but not for ordinary goods; there is a point where one's desire to have the very best cloth will yield to a willingness to take something almost as good but available more cheaply in a nearer place. Small-scale transactions dominated local town markets, whereas many large institutions and wealthy individuals who needed large quantities even of basic goods bought them at major central places rather than on their local markets. For example, King's College Cambridge in the fifteenth century bought at Salisbury, Winchester, Stourbridge fair and London, but not on the local market at Cambridge. The household account of 1406–7 of Richard Mitford, Bishop of Salisbury, shows expenditure of £143, of which 41 per cent occurred in London, and 39 per cent in the larger towns of Bristol, Southampton and Salisbury combined; but Salisbury's share was less than £5, or 3.5 per cent of the total. The other 20 per cent went for local purchases or specialised goods in distant places, notably medicines at Oxford. Mitford bought preserved fish, wax, jewellery and spices in London, wine, fish, spices and imported iron at Southampton and Bristol, fresh fish and horseshoes at Salisbury, and perishables on village markets. Although Wiltshire contained twenty-six boroughs, Mitford made purchases at only three.[35]

Transaction costs tended to hamper urban industry, particularly in periods of warfare, and forced the towns to concentrate on luxury goods for export. They could serve adequately as central places for a relatively restricted region, and their own less wealthy citizens were a market for the local city manufacture of utilitarian items. The tendency of the cities to concentrate on luxuries was facilitated by the level of specialisation and quality control in the cities, together with infrastructure and access to money markets. This in turn explains why, unless a rural place was able to find direct access to international markets, it was

37

dependent on pre-existing cities that did have such access. Thus the growth of rural industry benefited the cities, unless that rural industry either produced goods that were too mediocre to be exportable and thus suitable only for a purely local market, or was so good that the city's artisans saw it as a threat and imposed protectionist controls. Rural industry needed city traders if it was to reach a distant market. Thus Thaxted, 60 km north of London, developed a cutlery trade, already renowned by the mid-thirteenth century, whose products were exported through London. The small textile towns of East Anglia in the fourteenth and fifteenth centuries also produced for the London export market.[36]

The Grain Trade and the Central Place

Food marketing was critical in the establishment of central-place function at the beginning of urbanisation, since virtually all towns originated as farm markets. Towns such as Amiens, with a population of about 20,000 in the thirteenth century, needed 8000 tons of grain per year, which – taking account of technology and consumption by local peasants and in the small towns before sale on the city market – would require as many as 20,000 hectares of land given over solely to the needs of the urban market. Thus, unless a town of this size could import cheaply over a considerable distance, for example by boat, it would require a minimal radius of 15–18 kilometres in order to be supported from grain of the region; and this does not take account of other foods, which would extend the size of the region still further. Many city people maintained gardens in their back yards, but mainly for raising vegetables and poultry. Grain required extensive acreage and, as the least perishable food and the main source of carbohydrates before the introduction of the potato from the Americas, it had to be imported. Some cities became so large, and the fertility of their hinterlands was so low, that they had to import grain from outside the immediate area. But other cities managed to enlarge their grain areas gradually, and this process illustrates the changing nature of central function without (necessarily) having a political component.

The presence of ecclesiastical establishments in the towns, and the extent of rural landownership by townspeople, were important in the grain supplies of some cities: as late as the seventeenth century almost a quarter of Paris' grain came in rents in kind that were paid to the city's religious houses and thus bypassed the market. This undoubtedly explains how most cities were fed in their early stages, but by the thirteenth century the larger places were being provisioned by a market mechanism. This is particularly true of England, which had few internal tolls, convenient transport facilities and a large number of small markets.[37]

The study of London's grain market by Bruce M. S. Campbell shows the continued relevance of Von Thünen's theories for the process of urbanisation. London around 1300 had a population of perhaps 80,000, against Paris's 200,000. It was thus far less large in relation to the rest of England than Paris was even to its immediate environs of northern France. A city of London's size required some 165,000 quarters of grain per year, a figure that is in rough agreement with conclusions reached in studies of Florence, Paris and Cologne. Within a ten-county region surrounding London, the metropolis had to compete for grain with several medium-sized cities, notably Oxford and Canterbury. The region contained 3.8 million acres of arable that could be under cultivation at any one time. Given normal yields, this could feed a population the size of London's and accommodate the smaller towns. The northern part of the region was too far away to be much involved in feeding London normally, but higher prices in years of scarcity did make it worth the farmers' while to sell to London cornmongers. London rarely had to import grain from overseas, and in that way it is not typical of cities of its size. The city government of London rarely involved itself in provisioning the city: until 1440 London had no public granary or grain staple of the sort found in many continental cities.

As Von Thünen knew, market considerations determined crops grown in particular localities. Wheat and rye were grown at some distance from London, for prices on these grains were high enough to bear the higher transport costs. The regions immediately around London were given over to oats, which were even more necessary for animals than for humans but had too low a price to absorb much transport cost. Henley-on-Thames in Oxfordshire, at the point where the Thames ceased to be navigable, was much patronised by London cornmongers, who had warehouses there; it became a depot through which grain was channelled through the local markets that were so abundant in England to a London destination.[38]

Campbell also compares the situation of London with Paris in 1304, a year of scarcity when grain merchants were searching for supplies up to 200 kilometres from the city, although in normal years the radius of the grain supply was probably no more than 65 kilometres. In the late seventeenth century, when Paris was five or more times larger than London had been in 1300, the city was obtaining grain through market towns that were as much as 60 kilometres by road from the city, but if the subordinate markets were accessible by river the urban region was enlarged by 50 per cent to 90 kilometres. Given differences in agricultural technology and farming regimes, these figures seem congruent with the London example.[39]

There is a strong correlation between the fertility of the soil and the density of the urban network. Small towns tended to be located slightly off-centre within the territories from which they imported their food, for their location would be determined by supply and transport considerations. This is generally but less invariably the case with larger towns, which also have facilities to import comestibles from outside the region (as the smaller ones do not). Cologne was on the edge of some of the most fertile land in the Rhineland, but because of its size it had to get food from a large area. Yet its provisioning area was comparable to that of Trier, a city about one-quarter Cologne's size, because Trier's hinterland was dominated by the vineyards of the Mosel valley, which provided wine for export through the central town.

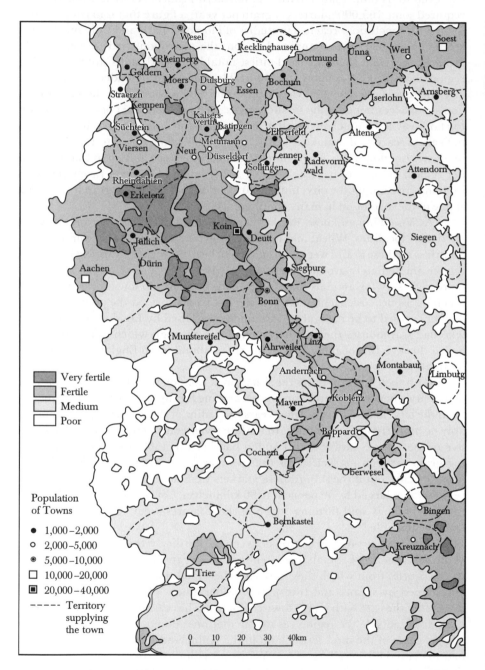

Figure 2.4 Soil fertility and food supply in the Rhineland at the end of the Middle Ages

Political pressure through 'staple' (monopoly) privileges could sometimes create centrality where none would exist on the open market. Even with the depression of grain prices during the late Middle Ages, retail prices were still much higher in the cities than on village markets, partly because much of the city's income – in many places the major source of it – came from taxes on goods that passed through the city's gates. To make certain that their city populations would have enough food, princes required the peasants of the environs to bring their food to the city possessing the 'staple', where it could be taxed centrally. As staple rights were initiated to guarantee the food supply of the cities, so the cities became collection points for grain and made a considerable profit re-exporting it after the basic needs of the town had been met. Ghent made enormous profits by requiring grain coming down the Leie and Scheldt rivers to pass through the city's grain market and pay toll. Whatever was not consumed locally was then re-exported downstream on the Scheldt to Antwerp, where the price on French grain was often 50 per cent higher than in Ghent. The town council of Paderborn was able in the fourteenth century to prevent grain brought into the town from being re-exported until demand at Paderborn had been satisfied. Augsburg and other German towns pursued similar grain policies. A flagrant example is the staple of Dordrecht, which began in 1299 as a requirement by the count of Holland that certain items in transit on the Lek, Merwede and Meuse rivers be unloaded at Dordrecht; by 1355 this had been extended to force most river cargoes in South Holland to come to the city. The regional importance of the Dordrecht staple was only reduced in the late fifteenth century. Staples were also given to centralise international trade. The growth of Bruges was favoured by privileges granted by the Flemish counts to foreign merchants who would settle there, but also to the brokers of Bruges, who were thus able to control the trade between the different foreign groups.[40]

The larger Italian cities were trying to force farmers of their *contadi* to sell on the town market at fixed prices in the thirteenth century, but the turn of the fourteenth saw a critical transition. Some cities of medium size, such as Siena, Pisa, Lucca, Perugia, Orvieto and Verona, could still be fed in normal years by grain produced in their *contadi*, and even export some in good years. But the great metropoles – Florence, Venice and Genoa – always had to import from outside the *contado*, and in bad years so did the medium-sized cities. With depopulations after 1348, there was some amelioration, and even Florence could be fed by its *contado* in good years. But the cities still had to import during scarcities, and the infrastructure for imports had to be in place for emergencies even if it was not used regularly. The great urban banking houses, notably the Bardi and Acciaiuoli, controlled the grain trade toward the Italian cities in the early fourteenth century, organising convoys and dealing with middlemen.[41]

Granaries were maintained in the town halls and other public buildings to ensure that the city could not be starved out. After the famine of 1437 some German towns, including Nuremberg and Cologne, built new and larger granaries. Cologne's *Kornhaus* could store enough to feed the entire population for up to two months. Hospitals, churches and abbeys also had granaries that were stocked by rents in kind from their rural estates, which were generally in the environs of the central place. Strasbourg built one of the largest public granaries of the Holy Roman Empire: five storeys, capable of storing 50,000 sacks (about 5.5 million litres) of grain and flour, which could have fed the city for half a year. When the stocks of individual citizens are added, Strasbourg may have had 300,000 sacks at one time. Although grain was the major item, other foods were collected. Faced with a siege in 1538, Strasbourg bought between 500 and 600 cows, hams and pork from Westphalia, as well as fish.[42]

Hoarding was always a problem. Faced with a military emergency in 1444, Strasbourg made a city-wide survey of the number of inhabitants and the amount of food in their possession. Thus

> Herr Hanns Hiltebrant von Mülnheim and Hanss Renner have listed for their district [in the city centre] 1346 townspeople, of whom 550 have no grain; but the others have 10,557 quarters of rye, 48,028 quarters of white corn, 759 quarters of barley, 1881 quarters of oats, 76 quarters of lintels, peas and beans. . . . Herr Hanns Conrad Bock and Wilhelm Rotschilt have listed for their district 2877 persons, burghers and country folk together, of whom 1352 have no grain; but the others have 1066 quarters of rye, 3369 quarters of white corn, 628 quarters of barley, and 1845 quarters of oats.[43]

The trade in foodstuffs was so critical that city governments interfered with the mechanisms of the free market. Some tried to prevent food purveyors such as butchers and bakers from forming guilds, for fear that they would raise prices. In some years of scarcity, city governments would subsidise grain merchants to guarantee them against loss. Bruges took over direct administration of the grain trade 16 times in the fifteenth century, and Ypres 13 times. During the crisis years 1436–8, Bruges bought 56 litres of grain per inhabitant, Ypres 17.2 litres and Deventer 27 litres. Bruges even proposed a scheme to centralise grain imports for all of Flanders, bringing them through Bruges, whose merchants could then distribute them to other communities. Bruges gave enormous subsidies in 1488 to merchants who would guarantee to bring 500 bushels of wheat or rye to the town market. In periods of scarcity prosperous burghers were expected to maintain stocks that they could release on the market to help tide over the shortages. Leiden in 1477 required all burgesses with property worth more than 50 nobles to obtain a stock of 227 litres of grain.[44]

Most Italian cities had offices to handle the food supply. Milan from 1215 issued 'food laws' concerning grain imports. Bologna and Verona established grain offices in the fourteenth century. That of Florence, established in 1274, was called the *abbondanza*, and from there this name for the position became usual. These offices were ad hoc in the beginning, but they soon handled such matters as price and supply, making contact with growers and arranging convoys. Given the threat that bread shortages posed to public order, the cities were willing to suffer financial losses to ensure the supply. In 1295 Siena spent a third of its budget on grain and its transport. Rural depopulation after the plagues deepened the agrarian crisis in Italy, as there were too few farmers to produce the desired quantities. By 1500 most city governments in Italy were often managing their food supplies under the supervision of territorial officials. Even so, the possibilities of great loss – for example, if the city bought a large amount of grain and found that there was no scarcity – were such that the city governments still worked through private merchants much of the time. With the population decline of the seventeenth century, the cities became smaller and thus more able to be provisioned by their *contadi*, with much of the grain coming from estates owned by townspeople. Rural land became not only a safe investment, but as profitable an investment as one would be likely to make with the decline of north Italian manufactures and trade. In the mid-sixteenth century Venice imported about 21,000 tons of grain yearly from the Levant, but by 1600 one-third of the grain that its people consumed was grown on the estates of Venetian citizens. Florence had encouraged sharecropping in its *contado* from the late fourteenth century, and this brought more food directly to citizens.[45]

The Central Place and Population Movement

Thus, although the primitive urban region can be defined best as the territory that was required to feed the town, the cities' growing populations forced them to seek more distant sources of food. Similarly, the cities drew most of their immigrants from their immediate environs, but this was much smaller than the grain radius, in most cases no more than 20 miles for the vast majority of immigrants until the late Middle Ages. Exeter's radius for immigrants was 20 miles, similar those of Leicester, Norwich and Nottingham and also to that of York, which was a much larger town. Most of Exeter's new freemen came from Devon, and immigration was sufficient to cause a growth from 3000 in 1377 to 7000 in the 1520s, making it the fourth largest provincial town in England. More than three-quarters of the new apprentices enrolled at Norwich in the early sixteenth century were from Norfolk, and only 17 per cent were from outside East Anglia. In most cities about two-thirds of the newcomers came from a radius of 20 kilometres of the town, but within that group the percentage of women was about twice as high as that of men. Generally the larger the town, the wider its attractive power: while three-quarters of Beauvais' immigrants came from within 20 kilometres of the town in the sixteenth century, Lyon drew many from Normandy, the Paris Basin and the Loire valley. The larger the city, the more diversified and specialised its labour force was, and accordingly the large cities attracted immigrants from a much wider area. Nearly half of London's new apprentices in the sixteenth century came from more than 90 miles away.[46]

Immigration into the city was fundamentally different from rural immigration. First, it was much more extensive. Although there was substantial circulation of workers seeking wages, few would leave one farm village to try their luck in another except in cases when a new village was being founded, where they might hope to clear land and hold it. People came to the city in search of jobs, preferably skilled ones where available. The comparative immobility of rural land that descended mainly by inheritance – granted that the land market was much more vital after 1200 than before – meant that the city attracted uprooted people who possessed skills.[47]

Pre-modern urban death rates always exceeded birth rates, which meant that all urban population growth had to come from immigration.[48] Every city has horrific examples of families that died out even though they produced numerous children. Quite apart from the question of colonial towns, first-generation immigrants made up a third or more of most town populations that were either growing moderately or stagnating, with a tendency toward the end of the seventeenth century for the percentage of immigrants to decline. In places that were growing significantly, they often made up more than half the inhabitants. In the sixteenth and seventeenth centuries, immigration rates were considerably higher among men than women, for men came from all social strata while the women were mainly domestic servants, by that time the only occupation available to most women.

Not all of the immigrants became citizens, for that status rarely came automatically with residence (see Chapter 4). We know little about most of them; for most cities we can simply say, on the basis of a variety of indices, that heavy immigration occurred. All cities contained numerous 'residents' and other foreigners. Between 1100 and 1300, when urban and rural growth seem to have been in rough symbiosis, immigrants to the cities were more often skilled than after the plagues, when more persons immigrated into the cities than could be accommodated easily. Some occupational guilds tried to hinder newcomers from matriculating as masters. War refugees were a problem for many cities. As most immigrants had not come a great distance to the host city, many maintained family or property in their native villages.

Contemporaries recognised the importance of immigrants to the city. In a letter of 1438, Aeneas Silvius Piccolomini, the future Pope Pius II, commented that 'there are only a few people living in the city [Vienna] whose ancestors are known to the neighbours'. The most easily documented immigrants are obviously those who entered the governing elite, or whose descendants did. Of members of the city council of Vienna between 1396–1526, about a quarter originated in the city proper, while 37 per cent came from the hereditary lands of the Habsburg dynasty, 18 per cent from the rest of the Empire, 5 per cent from the Hungarian crown lands and 2.3 per cent from Bohemia, Moravia and Silesia. Nearly half the mayors between 1400 and 1600, and 40.5 per cent in the seventeenth century, were not natives of Vienna.[49] London's elite shows a similar pattern, and the turnover of population became more intense with the demographic disasters after 1300. In the thirteenth century dynasties of leading families produced many of the city's mayors and aldermen, but after 1300:

> no family produced an alderman in two successive generations, let alone a mayor. New men, like Adam Franceys from Yorkshire, John Pyel

from Northampton, Richard Whittington from Gloucestershire, Simon Eyre from Suffolk, came from the counties of England to people and rule London.[50]

Religion, Migration, and Ethnic Quarters

The wars of the sixteenth and seventeenth centuries created a new category of immigrant, the religious refugee. The destruction of Antwerp by the Spaniards, although temporary, caused many of its elite to move to Amsterdam. Colonies of foreigners at Frankfurt and Aachen numbered 20 per cent of the total agglomeration, and at Cologne 5 per cent, while in some smaller cities the figure approached half of the total population of the settlement.[51] But except at Amsterdam the increase was not long-term. There were 5450 aliens in London and its environs in 1593 – up 2.5 per cent from 1573 – but the alien share in the population had actually decreased, since city's total population grew from 152,000 to 186,000 between these dates.[52]

Yet there is continuity between the movement of merchants between cities in the late Middle Ages and the migration of the same sorts of people in the sixteenth century; for even if the immediate cause was religion, they would usually go where they had personal or business contacts, or shared language and/or religion. Assimilation was frequently incomplete. Foreigners often had their own fraternities. The clubs sometimes formed around foreign national groups in an overseas city, such as the Germans in Florence and London. The case of Jacob/Giacomo Strycker is very revealing. His business caused him to move in 1647 from Amsterdam, where his family had been prominent economically and politically, to Venice. Once there, Strycker quickly converted to Catholicism. Since his wife was Dutch, he could not intermarry with Venetians of his economic standing. He tended to associate with Dutchmen in Venice.[53]

The Jews were a largely urban group everywhere. Jewish capital had been important in the formation of the early cities, but the growth of moneylending among Christians marginalised them. Persecutions from the late twelfth century led to their expulsion from England and the French royal domain – which did not include most cities in France – by the early fourteenth century, although a few eventually returned. Although territorial princes usually gave the order, this followed local agitation against the Jews. The Iberian peninsula saw little anti-Semitism against the large Jewish community until the late fourteenth century, but thereafter hostilities toward Jews and *conversos* (Christians of Jewish ancestry) reached a fever pitch that culminated in their expulsion in 1492. Although many went to Africa and eastern Europe, Antwerp and eventually Amsterdam developed large colonies of Jews of Iberian ancestry. The attitude of the Spaniards toward Jews was unusually harsh even in the Mediterranean: Lisbon had several Jewish quarters, although they were too small to make a ghetto feasible.[54]

The Jews in Germany and eastern Europe suffered less, but their situation was still parlous. They were placed under imperial protection, but this amounted in practice to the emperors selling to cities and territorial princes the right to extort money from them. The Jews of several cities in the Empire were blamed for the Great Death, and riots resulted. In 1349 the emperor Charles IV permitted Nuremberg to destroy the Jewish quarter; the vacated land was used to enlarge the market. Similarly, the Jews of Frankfurt am Main were blamed for the plague, and the whole community was killed. In 1462 they were transferred to a specially constructed street, the Judengasse, on a sparsely inhabited part of the dried-up moat that ran along the wall dividing the old from the new city. It was enclosed by walls and entered through gates. There were 110 inhabitants in 1463, 900 by 1569, 3000 by 1610. The Jews accounted for more than ten per cent of Frankfurt's population by that time. Other cities in the Empire also had large Jewish communities, particularly Prague, whose Jewry was even larger than Amsterdam's.

The Jewish areas of most cities were walled by 1300. In the north the separation was generally done because the Christian authorities feared Jewish 'pollution'. In the Mediterranean the cause was more often that the Jews found it easier to enforce religious rituals and prevent intermarriage with Christians. Venice actually had three ghettoes, linked to one another but physically distinct, by the sixteenth century. The 'New Ghetto' of 1516 was definitely enclosed to protect the Jews from Christians.[55] When the ghetto was formed, Christians had to move. Many areas that previously had had substantial numbers of Jews were simply transformed into firmly segregated areas. Ghettos were established in Rome in 1556, Florence in 1570, Siena in 1567 and Ferrara and Modena in the early seventeenth century. The Jews of Rome had lived in a commercial district near the Tiber since the fourteenth century, but Pope Paul IV simply moved them into an enclosure in 1555, manned by Christian guards, in houses owned by Christians but held at fixed rent; they were allowed only one synagogue. Although a slight enlargement was permitted at century's end, the rapid increase in population, including some by migration, forced the Jews to build their houses upward rather than out and led to horrible conditions and overcrowding. As populations grew, the ghettoes became impossibly overcrowded, since their walls prevented spatial expansion.

The settlements of Jews in Tuscany were near the markets, where they could be moneylenders. In Pisa and Livorno the Jews were originally more dispersed through the city than elsewhere, but in the seventeenth century they were forced to live in undesirable quarters, variously near abattoirs and prostitutes' streets. In Florence, however, these occupations were removed to make room for the Jews. Duke Ferdinand of Tuscany himself bought the buildings to be converted into housing for the Jews and commissioned an architect to redesign the quarter. Venice and Palermo were unusual in having the Jews on the outskirts; elsewhere they were given central locations. Another important characteristic of the Jewish ghettos in Italy, and to some extent those in France, was the extent of public services: cultural and ritual institutions, but also drinking water, garbage disposal, baths, and speciality shops. A central square normally provided a social link for the community.[56]

Capital and Industry in the Central Place

Only the largest cities were centres of international banking, but most medium-sized towns had important financial functions. While many peasants and nobles obtained credit from villagers, regional hierarchies developed. Most customers of Worcester's market in the sixteenth century came from no more than 15 miles away on a north–south line, and 25 miles east–west. Distance was a factor, as was the presence of other markets within the larger city's area. Most debtors of merchants of Exeter were from Devon and other places in western England. But even before the great expansion of London, its financial market was dominant: a sample of 7806 cases around 1400 shows that most of the debtors to Londoners were from York, Bristol, Coventry, Norwich, Salisbury, Oxford and Canterbury, who in turn were creditors of the villagers of their environs.[57]

Before the eleventh century 'there were practically no financial mechanisms to facilitate the transformation of saving into investment. Those who saved either invested directly or hoarded'.[58] Partnerships, not always between merchants of the same city, involved the extension of credit. The money supply was growing after the late twelfth century, but supplies of bullion became inadequate to handle the increased volume of commercial activity after 1300. This enhanced the central function of capital and credit. Transactions on credit became the norm rather than the exception, and the result was an enormous increase in the amount of debt litigation before the city courts. The problem led to more use of payments in kind, as when a butcher would repay a draper by furnishing him with meat. Debt arrangements, even in the short term, were guaranteed by pledges, who could be liable if the principal debtor defaulted. But the pledges thereby became, if they were not already, business partners of the person for whom they were vouching, and many of these arrangements linked rural and urban businesspeople. In the sixteenth century the amount of coin increased so much that it contributed to inflation, without causing it, but credit in kind continued to be common. As employer–employee ties centred increasingly on the city, and as the largest sums of money were available only there, the central functions of the city were again enhanced.

City people invested heavily in real estate. Rents generally brought a return of about 5 per cent at Marseille in the early fourteenth century.[59] This was less than a spectacularly successful business venture might bring, but many ventures were not successful, and it was above the rate of inflation. Thus it was neither stupidity nor conservatism that caused townspeople to invest in rents and in public debts: it was a good, highly rational way to make money, and much safer than the more speculative ventures. Such investment centred financial markets in the city, which needed capital for its debt and infrastructure. The massive investment by townspeople in rural land extended credit to the countryside. Townspeople also provided cash to farmers in return for annuity rents in grain or other kind. Despite the formal prohibition on usury, straight loans at interest also bound rural people to urban lenders.[60]

City moneylenders had more capital to lend than did their rural counterparts. Given that industry is labour intensive while commerce is not, places with at least some industry, even if only production for a local market, were more likely to become the central places of economic regions than more purely commercial centres. But industry also entailed the development of financial and credit mechanisms in connection with obtaining the raw materials and labour. The central place thus operated as a capital market. With the need to get raw materials from a distance and to produce for a market in which demand was rarely secured by in-advance orders, credit was ubiquitous and operated at all levels of the manufacturing processes. Bankers of Bruges advanced money to drapers, for they had to buy raw materials and pay the wages of as many as 20 artisans needed to produce a finished piece of export-quality cloth; only at the end of the process could the draper sell and make his profit. It was very hard to get credit unless one had a good reputation; all but the largest pre-modern cities were microcosms where people knew much about their neighbours.[61]

Most industry, particularly in trades that required a substantial infusion of capital, was still organised on a 'putting-out' basis: the cloth merchant bought the wool, dyes, mordants and other raw materials, then 'put out' the work to specialists to whom he paid a wage. At the end of the process, the textile belonged to the merchant, who could then sell it. This gave significant employment to workers in the city, for the only processes for which the merchants normally employed rural labourers were the less skilled trades, spinning and fulling. More specialised or skilled operations were generally reserved for the more highly trained craftsmen of the city proper.[62] Beauvais in the mid-seventeenth century is a classic example of a town whose prosperity was based on putting-out a major manufacture, in this case linens, to rural artisans of the environs, including the bleaching, then doing the final operations in the town and marketing the finished product.[63] Putting-out thus became an important aspect of centrality in the late Middle Ages and the early modern period. It involved a division of labour that could be controlled by the city or its merchants, resulting in a division of function between basic/primary manufacture (rural) and finishing (city).

Not all rural industry was financed with urban capital. Some of it was in competition with city interests. The first industrial revolution had concentrated industry and crafts in the cities, but some crafts, particularly those requiring less skill, were moving back to the rural areas from the late Middle Ages. Particularly in densely urbanised areas such as the southern Low Countries, rural 'proto' industries developed, particularly in textiles, that contributed to regional economic integration but to a great extent bypassed the urban capital market. Proto-industrialisation is really a late stage of what had happened to create the major cities of the urban network in the eleventh and twelfth centuries, with the difference that some town governments were in a position to take military action to protect what they deemed the interests of their always volatile craft populations.

Municipal authorities in Italy tried to turn the urban region into a protectionist domain, either prohibiting the import of goods that would compete with those made in the city or subjecting them to punitive taxation. Just as earlier Florence had protected its own industries, by the sixteenth century all of Tuscany, dominated by Florence, was a protectionist area. The cloth production of Florence was mainly exported and was inadequate even to meet demand in the city for cheaper cloth. But in the early modern period this became unfeasible. The city government of Genoa fought a running battle on behalf of its silk weavers with those of overpopulated rural Liguria, for whom weaving was a second income and who were not bound by the urban guild restrictions. By 1576 there were 480 silk looms in the city, some of them idle, against 2064, all of them active, in the countryside. But Genoa continued to benefit as the centre through which the Riviera silk was marketed.[64]

Industrial protectionism also occurred in Flanders, although by the late fifteenth century it was breaking down. Although Cologne seems to have avoided protectionism, it did occur in other German cities, notably Nuremberg, which tried to make the rural areas that were subject to the town into protection zones for the urban artisans and to hinder rural artisanry. Regional industry was thus increasingly dominated in the early modern period by the imperatives of the city governments that needed to protect the supplies and markets for the goods that their volatile artisans made. The interests of merchants and craftsmen did not always correspond. At the turn of the sixteenth century the weavers of Augsburg objected to merchants bringing green yarn in bulk from Prussia, because this upset the livings of urban women and of spinners in rural Bavaria and Swabia. In 1501 the city allowed the new import on condition of strict inspection for quality to make certain that it would hold dyes. As fustian working became important in the city from the mid-fourteenth century, the city fathers of Augsburg tried to force yarn onto their market. By 1546 yarn sales were forbidden within eight miles of Augsburg. By this time the attractive power of the Augsburg market in textiles included all of Middle Swabia and western Upper Bavaria. Elsewhere, however, German merchants saw the possibilities of investment in the rural industries. The famous linen industry of the Lake Constance area was largely financed by urban bankers, as was Westphalian linen, which became an important element of the late medieval prosperity of such places at Cologne, which marketed it in the northwest.[65]

Cologne as a Case Study

Franz Irsigler has provided in several papers a splendid case study of the manifold central-place functions of Cologne, the largest city of Germany in the late Middle Ages and one of the greatest thereafter. Although Cologne was an archbishopric, the market function of the medieval city was primary. Cologne is a particularly interesting case for central-place theory, for long-distance trade and export industry were of roughly equal importance in its total economy, while in most cities local trade predominated and export industry was weak. Even in the thirteenth century Cologne was exporting cloth that had been manufactured in the villages of its environs, but only after ensuring that it measured up to the technical specifications of Cologne cloth; then it was exported as Cologne cloth. In contrast to the Flemish cities, Cologne was not protectionist of its own industry, even after a guild regime took power there in 1396.[66] In the fifteenth century cloth of various places in the Low Countries was being sold alongside that of Cologne in the cloth hall. Based on this criterion of centrality, Cologne's sphere of influence extended west almost to Aachen, then south.

While Cologne's central function in textiles was exercised mainly west of the Rhine, in metalwork it was east-Rhenish, with some extension west. The persons who furnished steel to Cologne merchants came from an area mainly within 110 kilometres of Cologne, east of the Rhine between the small tributary rivers

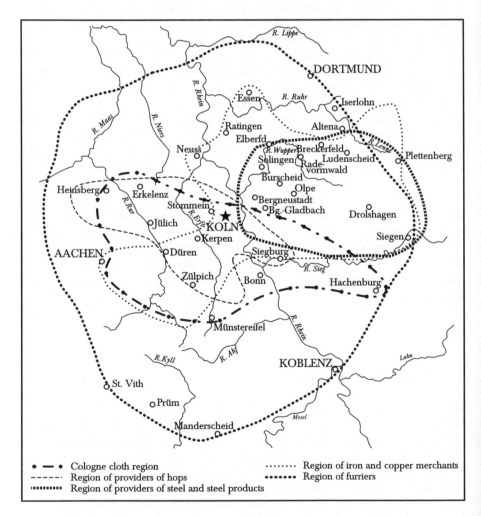

• — • Cologne cloth region	•••••• Region of iron and copper merchants
– – – Region of providers of hops	••••••• Region of furriers
••••••••• Region of providers of steel and steel products	

Figure 2.5 Cologne as regional central place in the fifteenth century

Lenne on the north and Sieg on the south. The same geographical distribution is found for places of origin of persons furnishing iron and copper wares to the city. Furs came mainly from this area, but some also came from west of the Rhine into the Low Countries. Hops came from an area entirely west of the Rhine except for Deutz and Siegburg, mainly within 25 km but with a few more distant. Cologne was thus the centre of an economic region that consisted of numerous different components, both east- and west-Rhenish. The largest area for which Cologne was central was that of furnishers of furs, which was roughly concentric around the city. The region from which Cologne entrepreneurs exported cloth was mainly south, east and west of the city. Due to the importance of Cologne's metal trade, the area of providers of metals was only slightly smaller than that of cloth, including all regions except northwest of the central place.

Irsigler also draws important general principles from the Cologne case that can be applied to other central places. First, an urban export industry can develop when the city maintains over a long period production of an item that is not being produced, at least in the same quantity (leading to low price) or quality (leading to high price) elsewhere within the market area. Second, putting-out is more likely to occur when the raw materials for the industry in question are relatively expensive or are not available near the city, or when the technology of the industry is complex; for in each case, urban capital is required. Capital investment in the rural areas took two forms: payment for goods to be delivered, and start-up costs for production, especially for mills, glassworks and metal foundries. This in turn made the rural areas dependent on the city, a development beginning clearly in the fifteenth century, but over time it gave them independence, since the city depended on rural industry for something to sell overseas. Third, the availability of capital permitted the entrepreneur to expand his operations into production in the environs, integrating its production with that of the city. By escaping urban guild regulations, including high wages for artisans, he lowered costs by using rural labour. Fourth, putting-out facilitated the division of labour between city and environs, especially in textiles and metals. While city export industries up to about 1450 were mainly directed toward luxuries for the wealthy in other cities and for the nobility, thereafter there was more mass production of consumer goods directed at a wider market. Fifth, capital acquired from long-distance trade became the basis for investment in industry. Sixth, expansion of industry, particularly of metals, required capital investment. This helped break down the urban occupational guilds, with their emphasis on small-scale household production. Except for printing, little new urban industry developed after about 1500, but much did in the countryside, and the goods produced there were exported through the infrastructure provided by the network of central places.[67]

But Cologne also illustrates the growth of central functions in a more than local context, albeit at a much later stage of development. Cologne's merchants traded in England, France, Scandinavia, Spain, Italy and the German/Slavic East and served as intermediaries for the interchange of goods among these regions. They bought English wool at Calais, English cloth in England itself and at Antwerp, and finished rough cloth made at Cologne and its environs, and sold it through the city's market network. Cologne became the market through which not only its own cloth but also English textiles passed to southern and eastern Germany, the Frankfurt fairs and Italy. Cologne copper implements were sold throughout Europe and eventually the European colonies overseas; but the raw material, far from originating near Cologne, was bought at Antwerp, Nuremberg and in Spain. Such complexity of operations simply was not feasible in a small place with an undifferentiated labour force.[68]

City-states and Urban Regions

As Weber recognised, political forces were involved in the determination of every urban region. Only within the territorial framework provided either by privileges given by a prince or by rights over the rural areas usurped by urban militias, and under the guarantees that legally binding contracts would be enforced, did the market forces that gave rise to central places and the hierarchical structure of rank-size distributions take effect.

The domination of a *contado* (countryside) by a city provides the classic example of a politically defined network of central places. Northern Italy is the best known case. The vendettas of aristocrats and their clienteles made them obnoxious to the merchants and craftspeople of the cities. Some towns required their nobles to agree contractually to spend part of each year in the town and observe the peace of the community. By 1200 the urban militias had simply taken control of most of rural northern Italy.

Florence in the twelfth century began to enforce the claims of the city's bishops against the magnates and their own tenants, then moved to assume the judicial rights of the bishop himself. The Archbishop of Milan, however, remained powerful as the town lord. By the early twelfth century Milan was the metropolis of a network of cities, each of which was the central place of its own region. The archbishop pursued a vigorous territorial policy against the interests of the bishops of Pavia, Lodi and Cremona. The Po River had small tributaries that were navigable by the small craft of the time. The Milanese linked their extramural territories by building canals.[69] The rise of Milan occurred at the expense of Pavia, which earlier had been the economic centre of the Lombard kingdom. Milan's rivals supported the emperor Frederick Barbarossa rather than the Milan-dominated Lombard League in the war of 1159–83.

Thus political forces in the early and central Middle Ages, including the conquest of the *contado* by force, created the basis for the economic hegemony that the large Italian cities exercised later over regions that were far removed from Italy. Not surprisingly, the cities of northern Italy took the lead in establishing territorial states in the fourteenth and fifteenth centuries. Giangaleazzo Visconti (d. 1402), duke of Milan, was a new type of urban prince bent on territorial expansion at the expense of other cities, and he met vigorous resistance from an urban coalition led by Florence.[70] Most of the Italian cities by 1500 were central places of extended *contadi* that included other large towns. Venice in the early fifteenth century conquered a *terrafirma* that included a number of cities, all of them large by north European standards: Treviso, Vicenza, Verona, Padua, Friuli, Brescia, Bergamo and Crema. The Venetian government sent representatives to govern each of these places, which were ruled under Venetian law and whose native elites saw a considerable interpenetration of Venetians. About half of Venice's income at the beginning of the sixteenth century came from the dependent mainland cities and overseas territories; and as Venice's overseas empire was lost, the city concentrated more on the Italian *terrafirma*. People from all walks of life, including artists and writers, emigrated from the dependent cities and territories to the cosmopolitan metropolis. On balance, it is hard to avoid the impression that Venice was parasitical on its hinterland, particularly after the loss of the overseas empire.[71]

The ability of a city to conquer a rural district usually hinged on the absence of a strong regional prince. Many towns in southern Germany conquered territories, but few did so in the north, where the nobles were stronger. Since the large cities were much farther apart than in Italy, where the border of one city-state reached that of another, the development of a network of city-states that could control the nobles was hindered. When cities gained extensive territories, it was more often the result of individual treaties, foreclosed mortgages and occasionally purchases than military conquest. The ecclesiastical link, although not as important as in Italy, was still significant. Most city governments exercised 'advocacy' over the territories of churches headquartered within their walls. This helped the smaller towns in Swabia, for example Memmingen, to get control of rural territories. Augsburg is a notable case, where the city council's protectorate over the city's hospitals, parish treasuries and abbeys afforded opportunities for jurisdictional footholds in the countryside.[72] Bremen, Hamburg, Lübeck and Brunswick all gained territory by mortgages from impecunious nobles; but mortgages could be redeemed, and most German cities actually lost extramural territory after reaching a high point around 1400; Rothenburg, for example, bought a considerable territory in a relatively brief period, 1383–1406, then was unable to hold it.

Some north German cities also acquired territories for non-commercial reasons: the Wendish cities of Rostock, Greifswald and Stralsund all built up territories that included seigniorial rights over several villages. Erfurt had the largest territory of the north German cities, with at least 610 square kilometres and including over 60 villages. The southern cities had larger states: Nuremberg had the largest in Germany with 1200 square kilometres, then Ulm with 830, followed by Erfurt, Rothenburg-ob-der-Tauber, Schwäbisch Hall and Strasbourg. Of the Swiss cantons, Bern was by far the largest at 9000 square kilometres, followed by Zürich and Lucerne (both of them larger than Nuremberg's state). But even the small towns had territories, at the very least a 'ban mile', a territory outside the walls over which the town had jurisdiction. Some of these were densely populated and added substantially to the town's population and/or economic strength. The size of the territory had no direct relation to economic power: Basel, which in the sixteenth century was the financial capital of the Swiss confederation, had only a small territory. Zürich was probably more important economically, due to commerce and industry, than Bern, whose territory was over five times the size of Zürich's but was agricultural.[73]

City governments in the north also bought land and seigniories, mainly between the fourteenth and sixteenth centuries. Ulm got much of its territory by buying the lands of nobles. Nuremberg's outside territory came mainly through peaceful purchase. The desire to use the territories as a source of grain for the cities was an important motivation, as in Italy, but strategic considerations and defence also played a role; in 1560 Nuremberg's government decided not to buy the distant lordship of Kirchberg because it would have been hard to defend in war, and Ulm also declined to buy Hall in the fifteenth century for this reason. Nuremberg did, however, acquire the Knoblauchland north of the city from rural lords, then turned it into a source of food for the city and also collected the rents owed by peasant tenants to the previous lords. By contrast, although the bishops of Cologne were powerful enough in the environs of the town to prevent the city government from establishing a dependent territory, the city did gain some influence by protecting the property of individual burgesses and churches.[74]

The relatively few cities of northern Europe with extensive rural territories that were integrated administratively with the city were less likely to oppress the rural areas, for example by trying to prevent them from developing industry, than were their neighbours whose territories were smaller, and certainly than the Italians, who carried urban exploitation of the countryside to a fine art. Several north Italian cities tried to restrict immigration from the *contado* for fear of rural depopulation that would compromise the tax base that was so convenient for the urbanites.[75]

Florence is the worst example. By 1406 Florence was the master of an extended *contado* that included not only its immediate environs but also Siena, Pistoia and Pisa, each of which had its own subordinate territories. Thus Florentine-controlled Tuscany was a kind of super-region in which cities that previously had directed production and market functions toward themselves now did the same for Florence. In 1427 the city of Florence had 14 per cent of its state's population and 65 per cent of its taxable wealth. The grand duchy of Tuscany, established in 1569 by the Medici family of Florence, was simply a consolidation of the Florentine city-state of the Middle Ages.[76]

The stifling regulations to which Florence subjected its *contado*, preventing industry and forcing farmers to deliver quotas of grain to the city at below-market value, caused long-term economic stagnation. Tariffs distort the free working of the marketplace and basically protect the inefficient. For specialisation of function to develop, markets must be free of hindrances. This desideratum was never reached in pre-modern Europe, and Tuscan agriculture remained relatively backward, undiversified and with low yields. Food supplies increased in most areas as land fell vacant after the plagues, but before the 1420s this was not true of Tuscany, and as a result Florence still had to import much of its food. Rural textiles were weak in Tuscany, perhaps due to inadequate demand, perhaps due to the institutional stranglehold of Florence over what market did exist. Changes in the *contado* were to benefit Florence. Pisa manufactured soap, which was mainly sold in Florence. The Florentines drained the Pisan plain after 1450 and converted its pastoral economy to grain. Thus Florence's region and soon Florence itself lost relative position, as other regions and their cities adapted better and with less constraint to the changed conditions. The fact that the city was the *de facto* central government benefited the metropolis but hurt the rest of Tuscany.[77]

Virtually everywhere, including places where strong princes prevented the formal establishment of urban territories, the regional grip of the city was strengthened by the extensive purchase of rural lands by townspeople, and in some cases their acquisition of seigniories with jurisdictional power. City people in Italy owned enormous amounts of land in the *contado*. Townspeople owned considerable rural land in England, but strong royal control in the shires prevented the cities from developing Italian-like rural districts.

Burgesses of Ghent and Bruges owned a substantial portion of the rural land in Flanders by the fourteenth century. Virtually all villages had at least one property owned by a person from a great city. Citizens of the great towns were allowed to choose trial in criminal actions either in the town court or at the place where the deed was alleged to have occurred. The idea seems to have been that the town court would protect its own, and rural courts that were not controlled by the Flemish counts would not dare to offend one of the great cities.[78] The extent of ownership of rural land by townspeople in the villages of Holland has been estimated at between 50 and 60 per cent. By the seventeenth century Parisians owned at least half the arable land in the villages south of the French capital, and the picture for Toulouse is comparable. Rural debt and foreclosure was an important avenue by which townspeople acquired rural property. This in turn weakened the peasantry economically and politically, as did the fact that when lands in rural France were bought by 'nobles of the robe', they were withdrawn from the tax base of the communities in which they were located. Beginning with the fourteenth century increasing numbers of urban landowners built country houses and resided in them for part of the year.[79]

The central role of the leading city of a region was also enhanced by the development of families of urban law. When lords founded towns, they generally gave them the law of an existing community. The customs of Bremen and particularly Magdeburg and Lübeck were important in the German-Slavic east, those of Lorris and Soissons in France. Whenever a city founded a daughter town, it extended its own law to it; Dublin had an ancient history, but it received the law of Bristol in 1172 after a group of Bristol merchants settled there. Often this was accompanied by a requirement that doubtful points of law be adjudicated at the court of the home city, sometimes as an appeal, more often as a request for a legal opinion before judgment was rendered. The Flemish cities, which received identical charters of liberties between 1165 and 1177, became judicial 'heads' of most of the smaller communities in this way, and inevitably this involved some

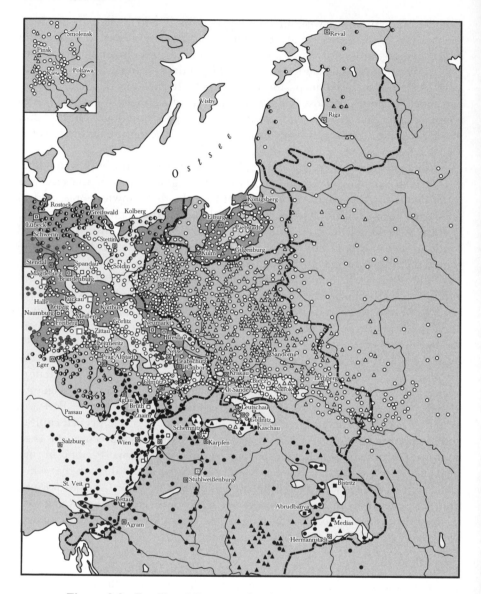

Figure 2.6 Families of German urban law in the east (key overleaf)

extension of urban authority, including in some cases the right to punish the subordinate jurisdiction for failing to adhere to the chief city's verdict.[80]

Another important tool of urban regional centrality in Germanic Europe was 'outburghership' (*bourgeoisie foraine*, *Pfahlbürger*, *buitenpoorterij*). Persons who lived outside the city would purchase citizenship in it. This conferred the right to judgment in the town court and also tax advantages on their rural property.

Places that still exist as towns are marked with circle or square. Modern villages, including places that have been re-founded as towns, are marked with triangles.

○ △   Magdeburg law and affiliates, and laws strongly influenced by Magdeburg
⊙ ◬   Town law families that merge into Magdeburg law or use it substantially in a subsidiary capacity
◑ ◮   Lübeck law and related town laws in the coastal area
⊕ ◭   Other northern and central German town laws of less significance, including the Saxon and Silesian mining towns
◐ ▲   Nuremberg district
● ▲   Southeastern German town laws
▣   Important appeals courts
▣   Appeals courts whose importance extends beyond their territory
▢   Appeals courts that are important for a larger territory
▢   Appeals courts with only local or trasitory importance
▄▄▄   Borders around 1400
▭   Areas of German settlement
▬   Areas of settlement of other peoples
▬   Areas originally of non-German settletment that were changed through German settlement or rule

Figure 2.6   *(continued)*

In 1469 one Fleming in six was an outburgher. Bruges recruited its outburghers mainly within its quarter, but Ghent's came from all parts of Flanders. Rural nobles as well as farmers bought citizenship, and many bought town residences. Lucerne, Bern and Zürich acquired thousands of outburghers, many of them recently emancipated serfs, and they became an important tool for Bern to develop jurisdictional footholds and create its enormous city- state. For obvious reasons the princes disliked outburgership. The imperial Statute in Favour of the Princes of 1231 ordered the cities to expel their outburghers, and Charles IV's Golden Bull in 1356 forbade the practice, but only Nuremberg seems to have observed it strictly. The dukes of Burgundy prohibited outburghership in Flanders in the fifteenth century, but it took some time for it to die out.[81] The legal domination of the Italian countryside by the cities was so complete, with all persons subject to the city court or to local courts that it appointed or confirmed, that outburghership never developed there.

The cases that we have discussed to this point involve city governments using their right to protect their burgesses and churches to involve themselves in conflicts over rural land owned by townspeople and jurisdictional rights of the churches. But it was equally common for the ruler of a settled territory to award privileges to selected towns that gave them commercial or legal advantages over the towns of rival lords or even other places under the jurisdiction of the same ruler. We have seen the economic impact of the grant of staple privileges to favoured towns.

Prague is perhaps our best medieval example of a place that was 'made' by such privileges. Prague had two central functions: it was the residence of the Bohemian kings, some of whom became Holy Roman Emperors, and it was the cult centre of Bohemia, a function that was enhanced when Charles IV built a new cathedral, had its bishopric elevated into an archbishopric and founded its university in 1348. The Czech parliament and the central courts were held at Prague.

Charles gave a new privilege in 1348 to Prague proper, the Old City, and also established a New City, which was to have its own council and serve as the craft centre. Thus, as was true of most large places, Prague was a composite settlement, not a single city. The population at this time was around 40,000 for the entire agglomeration. Although small in comparison to the Italian and Flemish cities and Paris, Prague was by far the largest city of eastern-central Europe and nearly as large as Cologne in Germany, whose central functions were mainly economic.

Economically, however, Prague was the centre of a region of only 20–25 kilometres in the late fourteenth century, and in this respect its attractive power over its environs was much less than that of other cities of comparable size. Surrounded by mountains, and at a distance from the great trade routes, Prague never became a focus of long-distance commerce. There was scarcely any industrial production for export. Although many Prague citizens owned land outside the walls, none of the Prague cities tried to develop a rural district subject to itself. The Praguers who bought rural land generally moved into the lesser nobility and gave up urban affairs. After Charles IV died in 1378, the burgesses tried to build the economic power of the city. The government of the Old City tried to force foreign merchants to sell their goods only to Praguers, as was commonly done in the major cities of the west. In 1393 King Wenzel gave a staple privilege that all foreign merchants had to proceed from the border directly to Prague and sell their goods to Prague merchants. However, the practical impact of this was less than elsewhere. Traffic continued to bypass Prague. Investment in mining, which became a major source of wealth for such cities as Nuremberg and Augsburg, did not occupy the capital of Praguers, although the mines at Kutna Hora had been important even in the thirteenth century. Prague was unable to capitalize on its momentary success during the Hussite wars of the 1420s. Its privileges were slowly whittled away and were totally lost by 1547.[82]

National Capitals and Central Place

Except for England, and to a much lesser degree France, the nations of Europe were too inchoate territorially before 1500 for their centres of government to be considered capitals. Even after the consolidation of state power, at the national level in Spain, France and England, and at the level of the city-duchy and territorial principality in Italy and Germany, the urban region cannot be defined solely in terms of political boundaries. The political capital of a region might not be its economic centre. Even the cities themselves were rarely jurisdictional units before the modern period, and rural villages were often subject to several lords.

However, the importance of territorial government would increase for virtually all towns after 1500. Political rights tend to follow economic development chronologically, although through privileges and the fixing of princely residences they can ossify conditions that are already present organically. But fundamental alterations would occur after 1500 that brought nation and urban-economic region into closer linkage. Much of the urban demographic growth of the sixteenth and seventeenth century was actually absorbed by the capitals. Madrid and Berlin, to use the most obvious examples, were thus superimposed on an urban structure that was already in place and, in the case of Madrid, modified it significantly.[83]

Four highly diverse urban regions developed in late medieval Castile. Villages and small towns dominated Navarre, Galicia and the Basque country in the north. Valladolid, with a population of about 35,000 in 1500, was the chief town of southern Old Castile, followed by three towns about one-third its size. Northern Old Castile had many small towns and a low population density. Toledo, with a population of 20,000, was the only large city, followed by Murcia, which was half its size. Andalusia, by contrast, was highly urbanised. Seville, at over 35,000 in the early sixteenth century, was the largest city, but six others were over 10,000. Seville was the only Castilian city that was active both on international and regional markets, effectively functioning as a gateway to southwestern Spain, as Barcelona in Catalonia was on the east. In the early sixteenth century the five largest cities of Castile grew at four times the rate of population expansion in the country as a whole.[84]

But this pattern of diffused urban growth changed with the decision of King Philip II in 1560 to shift his government to Madrid. This gave the Iberian peninsula a primate city that led to de-urbanisation in other regions. Madrid siphoned economic functions from Toledo, which kept only its archbishopric, and political/administrative functions from Valladolid. In the 1590s the eight other largest towns of Spain contained a population of some 200,000, against Madrid's 65,000. By 1700 Madrid had nearly doubled to 120,000, but the other towns had declined to 78,000. The demand market of Madrid absorbed most of the production of Castilian agriculture. From the 1580s villages around Madrid were forced to provide quotas of bread or wheat to the city at fixed prices; this led to overcropping followed by declining production, which in turn led the regime to extend the radius of obligatory grain staple to 100 kilometres. The city then acquired rights to pasture, cultivation and sale of firewood within this area. These privileges cut into the areas that normally fed other cities, notably Toledo, and thus limited their efficacy as central places of their regions. Further, since peasants could not get fair market prices for their goods, the countryside lost population through emigration, and agricultural production declined. The export of wool, grain, wine and other products from Castile virtually ceased in favour of the fixed Madrid price scheme. Madrid's artificial growth both weakened the rest of the Iberian urban network and imperilled the entire Spanish economy.[85]

Elsewhere the national capitals were much less parasitic. Dublin grew rapidly in the seventeenth century as English authority was expanded throughout Ireland, although it had always been the largest Irish city. The seat of Ireland's only university and the location of all meetings of the Irish Parliament after 1603, Dublin's growth was enhanced as it served as the gateway to colonisation of the interior.[86] Warsaw is a more ambiguous case. Krakow, the medieval capital of Poland, declined in the fifteenth century, although it remained a university city and the site of the coronation and burial of the Polish kings. The port city of

Gdánsk was the economic centre. Warsaw, formerly the chief town of the duchy of Masovia, became Polish in 1526. The treaty of 1569 that linked Poland and Lithuania left Warsaw geographically in the middle of the two. It was on the Vistula and had good overland communications. The Parliament always met at Warsaw. Yet the Polish monarchy was so weak and underinstitutionalised, and the power of the gentry so great, that being a capital meant less in Poland than in the western states. Warsaw was really more a residential centre than a national capital in the sense that Paris and London were. Indeed, construction was Warsaw's major industry in the seventeenth century, as nobles built homes there. The growth of palaces and suburbs spurred demographic growth; by the 1640s Warsaw had a population of 20–30,000 inhabitants, second only to Gdánsk.[87]

Paris seems to have depressed urban development in its environs, although not in France as a whole. Paris was the largest city of northern Europe between 1300 and 1600, except during the English occupation (1421–37). Although not centrally located in France, it was near the geographical centre of its immediate region, which had a high rural population density. Thus the countryside provided enough immigrants to satisfy the needs of the city. Although Paris continued to channel the goods of southern France toward England, the Baltic and particularly Antwerp, Paris had little industry, although its finishing industries were growing, particularly cloth finishing, paper manufacturing and printing.[88]

Accordingly, London began to overtake Paris in the seventeenth century. The university and its supporting population were important components of urbanisation at Paris, with a student population of perhaps 5000 in the fifteenth century. But the centralisation of the increasingly complex court was the basic reason for the continued success of Paris. The French government was much more inefficient and bloated than the English, which meant that the element of political capital was much less important in London's growth than at Paris. Between 1500 and 1700 the old Gallo-Roman cities – Rouen, Amiens, Troyes, Orléans – that were between 80 and 100 kilometres from Paris to some extent escaped the pull of the capital. As provincial capitals and seats of bishoprics, they had significant basic economic factors that were independent of the demand market of Paris. But the smaller towns near Paris declined against the attraction of the central place; by 1700 Versailles, the royal suburb, was the only town of the Paris basin aside from Paris itself with a population over 6500.[89]

England too was becoming a national-urban region in the sixteenth and seventeenth centuries, but London was never an economic parasite. Westminster was the favoured residence of the kings by the thirteenth century, although London only gained economic primacy at the expense of the east coast ports, which controlled much of England's German trade, in the later Middle Ages. By 1334 London had five times the wealth of Bristol, the second ranked city, and more taxable wealth than the next three towns (Bristol, Newcastle and York) combined. It had 2 per cent of the total assessed wealth of the kingdom in 1334 and 10 per cent in the 1520s, by which time it had ten times the wealth of Norwich, which had passed Bristol into second place. London also became the major port of the realm. Its share of overseas trade doubled in the thirteenth century, mainly in the period of Edward I, to 35 per cent; this share remained steady in the fourteenth century, but had nearly doubled again by 1500 to 68 per cent, and in 1540 it was 85 per cent. By 1543 Southwark (the suburb of London across the Thames) alone paid more tax than Bristol. Cloth exports from such diverse places as Devon and Yorkshire were handled by London merchants, who had better access to continental goods to be exchanged than did the regional merchants of Exeter and York.[90] Cloth and its marketing occupied a quarter of London's workforce in the late sixteenth century, and textiles gave employment to more workers than all other trades apart from victualling combined. London was important both for finishing cloth (little cloth was woven in London) and for exporting what was made elsewhere.[91] The English experience shows that when an enormous metropolis develops organically over a long period, and particularly when it offers goods and services that are useful to its region, change is gradual and occasions less shock in the rest of the urban hierarchy than the Spanish case, where all considerations were secondary to the political goal of promoting Madrid. The contrast is the more striking in that London was always much larger in relation to the smaller cities of England than Madrid was in relation to those of Spain.

We have been considering the development of cities in relation to their environments, which naturally included their links to one another. For the rest of this book we will adopt a more internal perspective on the pre-modern city, seeing it in terms of its impact on the persons who lived within its walls. The city plan, to which we now turn, was the basic physical framework within which burgesses interacted with one another.

Chapter 3 . . . .

The Morphology of the Urban Plan

Cities are living organisms that, like the people who inhabit them, mutate over time without altering fundamentally. Despite cycles of growth in the central Middle Ages, contraction in the fourteenth and fifteenth centuries and renewed expansion after 1500, the plans of most cities evolved without fundamental alterations of concept in these six centuries. The functions that a city exercises are conditioned by its physical structure. Buildings and street layouts persisted but were adapted to changing circumstances in an 'endless compromise . . . between form and function. . . . No city ever absolutely denies its past'.[1]
(James G. Vance, Jr.)

Organic and Planned Towns

The street pattern of most pre-modern cities took form in the central and late Middle Ages and underwent only minor modifications in the sixteenth and seventeenth centuries. The city plan included streets of differing sizes and social characteristics, providing the basic framework for social interaction. The plans also incorporated larger areas, such as markets and squares in front of halls and churches, which were initially owned by private persons but came to be recognised as public space during this period. City walls provided defence but also constrained the flow of persons and goods.

The plans of most older cities of Europe evolved organically, with an irregular street layout, particularly in the early stages. Before the tenth century, most leading cities west of the Rhine developed around a nucleus provided by the shrunken Roman wall of the third or early fourth century, in which the bishop resided. Less often an abbey or a princely castle served this function. In Carolingian central Germany the newly founded bishoprics became nuclei of settlements. The walled area was usually small, with a chaotic street plan, broken by the complexes of the public figures. When the fortification was the seat of a bishopric, it was called *civitas* in contemporary Latin documents; to this day it is the *cité* in older French towns, while *ville* refers to the entire agglomeration. As sub-urbs (literally 'under the city') formed around this core, though rarely concentri-cally, they were walled.

Except for the rare cases where planned foundations evolved into major cities, most large medieval and early modern cities were conglomerates of settle-ments that had initially been distinct. The old walls were not torn down, serving instead to mark borders of parishes or quarters of the town. Once what had initi-ally been the suburban area of the town had been walled, the older walls of the *cité* were often allowed to fall into disrepair, since their defensive value was less except as a final stage of resistance.[2]

Churches, monasteries, sanctuaries and hospitals occupied a considerable part of the area of all medieval and early modern towns. In France the bishop's headquarters was always in the *cité*, except for bishoprics that were headquar-tered in newly founded towns. The church is less directly associated with incipi-ent urbanisation in England, probably because Christianity did not long survive the departure of the Romans there. In most English cities the cathedral was, in contrast to the continent, in a 'close', often in a corner of the fortification and always separated physically from secular activities. Archbishop Lanfranc's deci-sion in 1072 to move several bishoprics to larger places meant that the church was more associated with the second stage of urbanisation.[3]

Castle and cathedral were both important in the development of western European cities, but rarely was this true of the same city: either a bishopric would give rise to a settlement to which a nearby castle might be joined, or less frequently a castle, often situated near a monastery, would give rise to a settle-ment in which churches would be built. Castles did not play as great a role in early urban development in Germany as in France; given the 'feudal' chaos of early medieval France – the time when the towns were forming – a castle was often present, particularly in the south. In Germany most urban castles postdate 1150. Thus, especially in places with a strong ecclesiastical lord, who would often have little competition from a secular count, castles were built later and thus tended to be extramural or occasionally distort the interior cityscape. In the colonial areas of eastern Europe, by contrast, castle and city cathedral were often linked in the same walled precinct, due to the danger of invasions. The best example is the Hradcany at Prague.

Large cities have a more marked core than smaller places, and a more com-plex street and neighbourhood pattern that reflects occupational diversity and differentiation. They shared, however, a tendency to concentrate commercial operations in the geographical centre of the settlement, or at least in a district that once had been at or near it, while relegating industry to the periphery. A major distinction between both the large and small pre-modern towns and what the cities have become since the second Industrial Revolution is the conjoining of workplace and residence before 1700, which has become impossible in the age of the factory and the office building.[4]

Access to trade networks was critical for the evolution of a village into a town and eventually a city. Most major cities developed on rivers, particularly those that were well established before land transport became easier in the thirteenth century. Some smaller places started with a single main street along the river, which was then joined by others that ran nearly parallel to the first as the town expanded, usually further from the river on the same side, and only much later on the other side of the river.[5] But important as rivers undeniably were for trade, they were often secondary nuclei of habitation. Huy, which became a major metalworking centre, is on the Meuse, but until the thirteenth century most settlement was not on the river itself but along a small tributary stream, the Hoyoux, and a land route that intersected the Meuse. At Ghent the districts along the Scheldt were suburban until the thirteenth century; most early settlement was on the Leie river, along which the city drew most of its food, and on a canal and a northern street that linked the two rivers. Warehousing and marketing rather than residences more often dominated the river areas of the cities.

Similarly, a location that was favourable for defence was important for the early cities, although this became less important as they received comprehensive walls. The hilltop sites of some towns, such as Besancon, protected them but hindered trade. Contemporary terminology often distinguished the 'high city', which contained the fortification and public buildings, from the commercial and artisanal 'low city'. Marseille is the most conspicuous example: the viscount of Marseille became lord of the upper city, and the bishop of the lower. Brussels was dominated by a lower town centred on the Grande Place, the focus of trade and industry, and an upper city on the Caudenberg. The two parts of the town were linked by the land route that ran between Cologne and Bruges.[6]

Although it was once thought that planned street layouts were confined to 'new towns' and the cities of the Renaissance, completely irregular plans were unusual in fully developed medieval cities. The central nucleus often gave rise to a roughly radial pattern of main streets leading away from the fortification. The side streets that joined the main arteries were unplanned. The main market was often outside the original fortification, at the point where it joined the suburb. In these cases, it often had a triangular shape. Second and later suburbs were often laid out with specific plans for a market. In such cases the market square was often the nucleus of what amounted to a street plan completely separate from that of the fortification except for linkage at the gates. Thus there are elements of street planning. In 'organic' cities that developed in the early Middle Ages, the successive suburbs are typically more planned and grid-formed than the primitive *cité*, but there are plenty of exceptions. At Metz the *cité* had a more regular plan than did the suburb immediately outside it. Suburbs that developed later, however, were more carefully planned. Reims is the most famous case, where an industrial suburb with a regular street plan was established at the turn of the thirteenth century on the southern extremity of the *cité*, in effect a 'new town'.[7]

Virtually all large cities were polynuclear, and the nuclei developed their own social or economic singularities. Long before 1100 suburban settlements had developed outside the original centres. As town populations grew and suburban settlements were walled, the *cité*, which had originally been the nucleus of the agglomeration, often came to be on the periphery of the mature city, and the suburbs housed the major markets and most of the population. Scholars, particularly those in Pirenne's tradition, once concluded from this that in the towns of northern Europe the *cité* was economically passive, with most activity centring in the commercial and industrial suburbs. This distinction is vastly overdrawn, particularly given the concentration of wealth among the clergy and secular potentates who inhabited the 'city' proper. The demand for labour, goods and services from these consumers was at least as strong an impulse as supply toward the development of urbanisation. Demand for luxuries by those leading accumulators of capital–bishops and secular rulers – has explained the numerous cases in which the economic centre of the total agglomeration remained in the older part. Although most of Barcelona's wealth came from overseas trade, the centre of activity was not in the port, but rather inland in the original Roman settlement of Barcino, now called the 'Gothic Quarter', which included virtually all government buildings, the cathedral and other churches, and had a high population density.[8] Furthermore, the dichotomy of fortification and suburb is found mainly in the once-Roman centres of France and Germany along the Rhine and Danube and in the towns of Flanders. This form was not universal even in these areas, and it was unusual in eastern Germany, rare in England, and non-existent in Italy.

The bastides and 'new towns' generally had much more regular street plans than did cities that evolved organically. Most south German small towns have a simple street plan, established in the thirteenth century, with one or two main streets that intersected. Nördlingen is the main example of a rare concentric-radial plan. Virtually all colonial cities of the German/Slavic east have a rectilinear plan. Posen (Poznán) was founded in 1253 as a German town across the river from a settlement that had contained the bishop's quarter and the cathedral since the early eleventh century. In 1257 Krakow was founded adjacent to the native Polish castle, the Wavel. In the colonial areas an oval nucleus, the shape of the fortification, often determined the town plan. The market was usually inside this or just outside its wall, and the streets led to it. Rectangular plans are also numerous; Greifswald, Rostock and to a lesser extent Thorn are examples.[9] The plan of Salisbury is almost perfectly rectangular, with allowance made for the Avon. The market served as the nucleus around which the blocks were centred. The other major churches were on the peripheries of the city as originally laid out, and the cathedral was in a distinct close near to but not crowding the market, as is characteristic of English cities. The major north–south road was diverted around the close. The town was planned in three phases, each with its own characteristics.[10]

The term 'planned' means different things to different people. Lübeck, the most famous of the 'planned' foundations, was destroyed, then refounded in 1159 on a Wendish site by the Saxon duke Henry the Lion. He moved the centre of settlement farther inland, away from the junction of the Trave and the Wakenitz rivers, and planned a central square with the church of St Mary and the market as the nucleus of settlement. Lübeck received a charter, and its law became the model for that of many colonial cities. Its grid plan, with rectangular city blocks

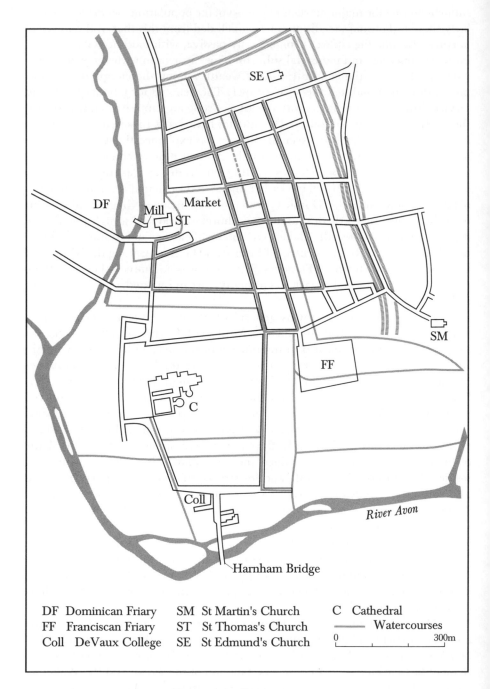

Figure 3.1   Salisbury *c.* 1300

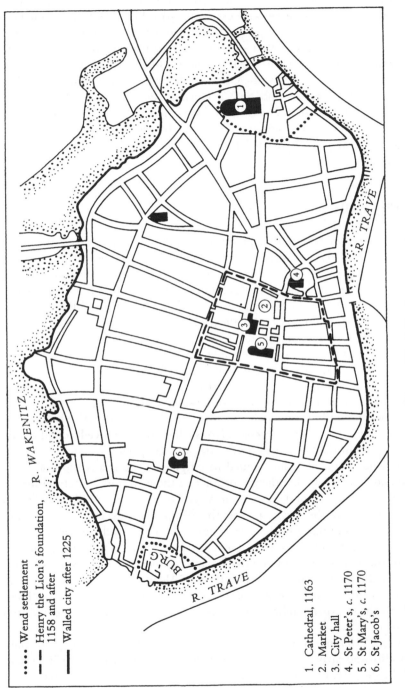

Figure 3.2 Lübeck

..... Wend settlement

- - Henry the Lion's foundation, 1158 and after

— Walled city after 1225

1. Cathedral, 1163
2. Market
3. City hall
4. St Peter's, c. 1170
5. St Mary's, c. 1170
6. St Jacob's

(insofar as local topography permitted) containing regular plots of land around the central market square, became characteristic of the German founded cities. The development of the city plans of Magdeburg and Breslau (Wroclaw) are remarkably similar, given that some three centuries separated their origins. While Magdeburg was established as a bishopric on the Elbe in the tenth century, Breslau was at a bridge across the Oder. A Slavic fortress existed on a mid-river island, and first a Slavic and then a German merchant settlement grew up around it on other islands. The cathedral was then added, integrating the settlement. This island town was destroyed in 1241 by the Mongols, then rebuilt and walled in the early 1260s on the left bank of the river, in an almost rectangular street plan.[11]

City Walls

A major difference between the pre-modern and the modern city is the presence in the former of high defensive walls. Those of Montpellier, for example, were about two metres wide and seven to eight metres high, with eight gates originally and another three added after 1200, and more than 20 towers.[12] Only in England were most towns unwalled; the main exceptions were those of Roman or early medieval ancestry and coastal fortifications. The English town walls generally served as toll stations rather than defensive bastions, for except during the Hundred Years War the towns did not experience the danger of foreign attack, and then only in coastal areas. Coventry constructed its wall over nearly two centuries after 1355, but even then managed only to enclose part of the town area. Norwich was unusual in having a 2.5-mile wall with twelve gates and numerous towers, but the walls were only 3.7 metres high. Not surprisingly, English towns often let their walls fall into disrepair. Houses had to be removed from the walls at Southampton in 1338, when a French attack was expected.[13]

Recent scholarship has tended to emphasise the integration of city and countryside and downplay the importance of the wall, but contemporaries saw the wall as an important demarcation, a symbol of municipal liberty. The walls fostered a sense of the corporate identity of the town even when they did not contribute substantially to defence. They were portrayed frequently on town seals as a symbol of the city's independence. Westerners writing about the cities of the Levant in the late fifteenth and sixteenth centuries almost always emphasised the fortifications. Descriptions of Alexandria contrasted the magnificent fortifications with the number of ruined buildings inside the city. The fact that Beirut was largely unfortified struck the Genoese observer Anselmo Adorno in 1470–1.[14]

Until 1100 most towns on the continent were unwalled except for the *cité*. The twelfth and early thirteenth centuries, however, were a period of intense walling of the suburbs, with population growth so rapid that some cities received several separate enclosures. Florence built five new walls between 1078 and 1333, Strasbourg three (and a fourth in the late fourteenth century) and Bruges two

(1127 and 1270–98).[15] The walls provided defence, and they demarcated the jurisdictional area of the town, as most large cities controlled a 'ban mile' beyond the walls.

Harold Carter distinguishes five types of medieval suburb. The most characteristic was the 'portal suburb', which developed at a city gate where traffic was blocked as it tried to enter the city. This occurs most often when settlement developed outside a Roman wall, church or fortification. Roads often intersected in the suburbs with extensions of streets that went on into the town. The 'ribbon suburb' is a prolongation of a single street leading into the town; Lincoln is a fine example. Settlements sometimes developed around suburban churches and sanctuaries. The 'bridgehead suburb' was a type of the portal suburb but at a bridge, such as Southwark, across the Thames from the City of London. Finally, the 'marginal suburb' developed as a zone surrounding the walls, usually occurring in places where the inner city was walled in stages. Many larger cities had a mixture of suburb types.[16] The gates in the walls were also points of control through which outsiders had to enter and (usually) deposit their weapons, and through which imported goods had to pass and pay toll.

The population of the suburbs in relation to the walled area within the town varied. At Rouen 9 per cent of the total inhabitants lived in the suburbs in the thirteenth century and still did so in 1700, but Rouen was unusual in having only one wall beyond the Roman *cité*, and that rather late, from the thirteenth century.[17] Much depended on how much of the total agglomeration was walled during the population growth of the central Middle Ages. Ypres is the contrary example to Rouen, with a small walled city and enormous industrial suburbs. Disorders among the artisans in 1280 prompted the Flemish counts to keep the suburbs unwalled to keep agitators out of the central city; the English siege of 1383 destroyed the suburbs, and Ypres, already in decline, never recovered from this catastrophe.

The 'new towns' were bastions as well as trading centres, and accordingly most of them had at least some defences. Most of even the smaller places that were founded in the east in the thirteenth and fourteenth centuries, for example by the Teutonic Knights, were walled. On the continent, cities that had charters were much more likely to be walled than those that did not. Of German cities for which we have demographic information from the three centuries after 1200, all with populations over 3000 had walls, and 90 per cent of those between 1000 and 3000 did. The proportion drops to 43 per cent for places of under 1000 inhabitants. Given the expense of walls, the extent of walling diminished in the modern period. Between 1500 and 1700 all towns of over 5000 persons were walled, 83 per cent of those with 3000–5000 inhabitants, and 84 per cent of those with 1000–3000, and only 39 per cent of places with less than 1000; and of course, many of these were old walls, not new ones.[18]

The pattern of walling in the west after 1200 is uneven. The once-suburban individual settlements were walled individually, but they were in turn bound together by a separate wall, generally in the twelfth century but occasionally later. The thirteenth century was relatively peaceful, and accordingly many town walls in France were never extended then, although fortification continued in Germany, the Low Countries and Italy. Since population growth continued, the substantial later suburbs remained unwalled. By the fourteenth century, only for the most powerful and politically independent cities were they built and maintained largely with local resources. The outbreak of the Hundred Years War between England and France was a disaster for French civilian populations, for numerous cities were completely unprepared to defend themselves. Some of them, including Saint-Omer and Lille, destroyed and desolated their own suburbs in order to refortify the inner core; the English invaders did the work elsewhere, including the suburbs of Paris. The French capital was rewalled under Charles V (1364–1380), but the new trace excluded a considerable space on the south that had been inhabited in 1300. Towers were added, and moats were extended. Some of the late medieval cities had 'no building zones', although they were much smaller than those that developed in the modern period. Bridges were destroyed, hindering hostile approaches to the towns but of course striking at their market infrastructures. The French kings remitted the *taille* for the 'good towns', which were to use the money to take charge of their own fortifications, while in England some cities were granted the right to take murage, an indirect tax on goods passing the gates, to pay for their fortifications. The practice was ended when they diverted the money to other uses.[19]

The gates in the walls were anomalies in a sense. They controlled access to the city and served as toll stations. Posterns in the walls gave access to wells where fresh water was collected. The city arsenal was often in the gates. Even in the twelfth century there were shacks on some town walls. Two of London's gates (Newgate and Ludgate) served as prisons. But since the cities were not constantly under siege, they sometimes rented living space in the gates and towers of the walls, particularly in the late Middle Ages, on condition that the inhabitants turn them over to the city when they were needed. Geoffrey Chaucer's salary as controller of the wool custom of London included an apartment over Aldgate. At Montpellier the towers and half-towers on the wall were granted to citizens who maintained them for defence and lived in them. City officials controlled rentals of property along the walls and adjacent paths, and levied fines for damage to the walls, use of their masonry for constructing private homes and building latrines in unauthorised places.[20]

Markets and Public Squares

The *cité* contained the oldest churches and the castle of the secular lord of the place, if it had one. But as city governments from the late twelfth century assumed control over most aspects of public policy (Chapter 4), the public buildings of the town corporations, such as town halls and guildhalls, and the major marketplaces are generally found outside the *cité*, most often in the earliest suburb to be walled. The most famous example of a market at the edge of a *cité* is the Rhine

Suburb of Cologne, the area between the Roman wall and the river; it was the first suburb in Europe to receive its own wall, in the late tenth century.

The large parvis (squares in front of churches) of most cities are the result of modern razing; they were not that way in the Middle Ages. The parvis was usually so small and irregular in shape, with side streets entering it at all angles, that there was barely enough space for a visitor to see the great façade, and certainly not enough to step back for a good view. Open space was desired in ancient city planning, particularly Roman, and this ideal was revived in architectural work of the Renaissance. Rome itself, however, and indeed most unplanned cities of antiquity, more approximated the plan of the organic or nuclear medieval cities. The medieval city, with walls almost from the beginning, was an enclosed, tightly constructed space, and the streets and alleys produced more often the unpleasant surprise than the untrammelled vista.[21]

As was true of the main market, the town hall was often in the first suburb to be walled rather than in the 'city' proper. Most places did not have separate town halls until the fourteenth century unless political confiscation freed land within the walls. Poitiers got a self-governing commune in 1199, but it had no town hall until the early fourteenth century, when one was built at a distance of some 600 metres from the cathedral of Sainte-Radegonde, the primitive nucleus. The Old Market (Vieux Marché) is slightly farther from the cathedral. Montpellier used the opportunity of numerous vacant buildings behind the chief cathedral to build a new town hall in 1364.[22]

The effort by city governments to distinguish municipal from ecclesiastical space is most apparent in Italy. Florence used the enormous properties confiscated from political exiles in the thirteenth century to construct new public buildings. Bologna, faced with the same source of vacant land, razed old buildings to construct the new town square, the Piazza Maggiore, with a new town hall nearby on the Piazza del Comune. The government also forbade new towers, improved access to and on the new squares, and standardised heights and architectural styles of new buildings on them.[23] The town hall housed the municipal bell, which tolled hourly rather than according to the canonical hours of the mass, and moulds for the official weights and measures. Important ceremonies such as the rotation of the council were held there. The council met at the town hall, and court sessions were held there. Town halls sometimes housed the treasury and always the accounting office, where citizens paid their taxes. Statutes were proclaimed from a balustrade of the town hall; before the development of printing, few could read them, and thereafter few wished to. Sometimes the town hall had an arcaded area on the ground floor that could serve as a market hall.[24]

The market was often the main town square, but the parvis and the area in front of the town hall were also important public spaces. Paul Zucker has distinguished several principal types of town square; the exceptions are mainly in Italy. Some small organic settlements, but more often the planned foundations, had a market square that was simply an extraordinarily broad main street: Bern, Augsburg and Innsbruck are examples. But this is also true of large cities, including no less a case than London, whose main market was not a square, but rather Cheapside.[25] Some market squares were lateral extensions of a street. Public buildings were often erected on one side of such an expanded street, but always so that they would not impede traffic. Some markets involve splitting the main thoroughfare into two almost parallel streets, as happened at Reutlingen. Some squares were at the town gate, with two or three streets radiating into the town. Other town squares were centrally located; this is usual in planned communities, such as Lübeck. In the Slavic areas the location of this square or rectangular market was often determined by the previous round Slavic settlement. The parvis might serve as a market. Finally, grouped squares are found most often in Germany, with the separation of distinct church and market squares. The Hanse towns of Rostock and Stralsund are examples. In the Old City of Brunswick the market was an almost closed square, but the square around the Marienkirche leads off it on one end but then expands into a separate but non-continuous square.[26]

As the larger cities acquired more suburbs, this was accompanied by a proliferation of markets. Larger towns are characterised by multiple markets, in different parts of the town. As urban populations expanded in the late eleventh century, the total value of the goods needed by the artisans and small farmers of the suburbs was beginning in some places to outweigh that of the *cité*. Ghent had four major market squares, several smaller street markets, and squares in front of the major churches and the town hall. York had three markets. The city differs from the small town in that the inhabitants can buy and sell more or less constantly. Meat, fish and bread halls were open every working day, and others less frequently. They even stayed open on Sunday in some places. Specialised markets, some of which were only for certain types of goods, were usually open only part-time, but exchange could be done anywhere in the city except on holidays, and sometimes even then. Thus retail sales were higher both in quantity and in terms of differentiation in city than in town.[27]

The greater markets came to be dominated by guildhalls, warehouses and other places for inspection of goods, as municipal regulation of trade became more exacting (Chapter 4). Most notable among these are the cloth halls and, in the largest cities, the merchant halls. The specialised market halls were most often for the main export product (the cloth halls of the Flemish and northern French cities are famous) or for grain. Orsanmichele, the grain market of Florence, from the fourteenth century was an arcaded structure occupying a small city block. The Halles at Paris, going back to the late twelfth century, formed a huge covered market with numerous buildings and a complex trading organisation. The process continued into the modern period, with the spread of covered markets, sometimes with an open market outside. Leadenhall, the closest London equivalent to the Paris Halles, originally had four buildings, then after the 1666 fire absorbed four other street markets nearby. There were hundreds of stalls, but by 1700 they were spilling out onto the streets. These were retail markets where foreigners could buy the town's industrial products from local brokers after inspection by the guild leaders.[28] Exeter in 1533 established a location in the Guildhall where foreigners would transact their business. From 1538 the city was building and leasing other halls for cloth and wool, and the result was a network of wholesale markets at which merchants from outside Exeter sold wholesale – not retail – to merchants who were freemen of the town. The market hall, open for two or more days per week, was thus an intermediate stage between the home-based crafts and the temporary stalls on the main marketplaces of the Middle Ages and the modern retail shops, which are permanently open.[29]

The markets were the scene of frenetic activity. Antonio Pucci gave a vibrant description of the Mercato Vecchio (Old Market) of Florence in the mid-fourteenth century:

> The Mercato Vecchio feeds the whole world and takes the prize from other markets. . . . It has four churches at its four corners, and at each corner two salient roads. Around the market artisans and traders of each and every kind. . . . It has medical doctors for all ailments, and sellers of woollen cloth and linen, grocers and traders in spices. There are sellers of glasses and jars, and those who give food, drink and lodging to all sorts of miserable youths. . . . And always great wheeling and dealing: the hustlers are in their element, for the market is full of their types.[30]

On market days, merchants would often come from outside the town with their portable prefabricated shops on their backs, display their goods, then return home with the stand at the end of the day. Elsewhere the confused markets of the early Middle Ages gave way in the fourteenth century to statutorily demarcated areas where practitioners of each craft could display their goods, often with physical barriers on the greater markets, which were thus being subdivided. Yet retailing on the market usually spilled over into adjacent streets and lanes. Ghent, for example, had an enormous open space in the city centre, initially without physical barriers, but given separate names in contemporary descriptions. In 1366 the council ordered barriers built to separate the Grain Market, the Short Mint and the Fish Market. Sellers of spices, dairy products and fruit were prohibited from spilling over into the Grain Market. Sellers of poultry, vegetables and cheese set up their stalls wherever they could find space.[31] Other cities, including Venice at the Rialto bridge, set up a rotation, so that the same trades would not always get the most desirable sections of the market. Most cities became more vigilant in restricting trade to predetermined places in the late thirteenth and fourteenth centuries than before.

Numerous examples illustrate these general features of the medieval city plan. Basel developed on the site of a Roman fortification in a great bend of the Rhine where several land routes converge. But the medieval settlement and the first wall centred on the Birsig, a small stream that intersected the Rhine south of the Roman settlement. Thus, as often happened in the origin of towns farther north, settlement developed on the lesser of two intersecting streams. The primal city, the *Altstadt*, grew on a hill between the Birsig and the Rhine. It contained the cathedral, bishop's palace, eventually the university that was founded in 1460, and St Martin's Church. The industrial suburb of Kleinbasel was settled on the right bank of the Rhine by the thirteenth century, when a channel was made in the river to power mills for bleaching and dyeing cloth. The only medieval bridge, built in the thirteenth century, linked Kleinbasel with the Altstadt. The Kornmarkt, the main medieval market, was on the Birsig near the Rhine. Basel's great age was the fifteenth century, when it reached 20,000 inhabitants. Despite the university, which made Basel an intellectual centre that attracted no less a figure than Desiderius Erasmus, and its printing and

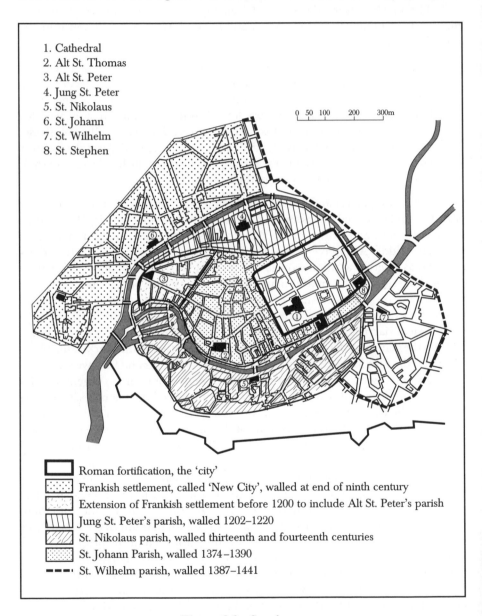

1. Cathedral
2. Alt St. Thomas
3. Alt St. Peter
4. Jung St. Peter
5. St. Nikolaus
6. St. Johann
7. St. Wilhelm
8. St. Stephen

0 50 100   200   300m

- ☐ Roman fortification, the 'city'
- ▦ Frankish settlement, called 'New City', walled at end of ninth century
- ▦ Extension of Frankish settlement before 1200 to include Alt St. Peter's parish
- ▥ Jung St. Peter's parish, walled 1202–1220
- ▨ St. Nikolaus parish, walled thirteenth and fourteenth centuries
- ▦ St. Johann Parish, walled 1374–1390
- ▪▪▪ St. Wilhelm parish, walled 1387–1441

Figure 3.3 Strasbourg

paper manufacturing, Basel did not become more than a medium-sized city, evidently because of its location at three political frontiers.[32]

The example of Strasbourg complements Basel, but with the difference that it was not on a major river. Although the outskirts of modern Strasbourg are on the Rhine, the early city grew up around a Roman fort on the Ill, a tributary of the Rhine at the edge of its flood plain. The reoccupied Roman *cité* became the centre of the medieval town, with a layout determined by the two main Roman streets. Strasbourg grew up around the cathedral on domains of the bishop and king. A 'new town' developed as a suburb west of this nucleus in the ninth century and received a common wall with the old 'city'. Its market was the site of the later Gutenberg Square, where the town hall was eventually built. A new wall of 1202–20 nearly doubled the enclosed area, and a final wall in the late fourteenth century enclosed the two earlier ones. More than with most cities, where the 'city' became peripheral, Strasbourg's growth was roughly concentric on three sides; only on the north was there no expansion.[33]

Occupational Geography of the Pre-modern City

While wealth is generally an indicator of social status, the correlation was less strong in the Middle Ages than now. Ancestry, positions occupied, properties held and under what conditions of tenure, and obligations owed, all played a role in determining the esteem in which one was held by others. Not surprisingly, most persons of high status in the early towns – clergy, nobles and their officials – lived in the original nucleus, the 'city' proper. Possession of land in this original town area carried prestige. Many members of the sworn associations that gave rise to town governments (Chapter 4) were officials of the town lords whose headquarters were in the city. They owned prime land, particularly around the markets, and made considerable sums through rents.

But even the earliest cities also had a support personnel. Initially they seem to have settled rather evenly through the agglomeration: every parish or neighbourhood had bakeries and taverns, and every several neighbourhoods a butchery and a brewery. As the settlement became more complex, the neighbourhoods became more interdependent, given the uneven distribution of food and wine shops, wells and squares. Since the population of the suburbs was larger, more of the non-basic (Chapter 1) producers lived there than in the 'city', but they were present everywhere.

The major change in social geography comes with the great population expansion of the cities after 1100, with the development a highly diverse labour force with numerous specialists, and particularly the fixing of exportable industry in some towns. Proximity to the raw materials of the trade determined the sites of breweries and dyeries, for example, since they needed fresh water, but in the early stages there were also occupational groupings determined by chronology, particularly as weavers, fullers and other artisans came to cities that had already made their fortunes through local trade (see Chapter 2).

The old city generally had the highest density of population, much more than the suburbs, although total figures are distorted by the large concentration of churches and public buildings there, which lowered the area available for habitation. The result was a large number of tiny, winding streets in the old city. The common practice of renting out attics and outbuildings, the less desirable parts of the house (see Chapter 6), meant that virtually all cities had more taxpayers than houses; the ratio was nearly 3 : 1 at Constance in the early fifteenth century.[34] When topography prevented suburbs from forming, inner city populations had no place to go but up. The houses of Genoa were famed for their height, since the city was caught between the mountain and the sea. Some of them had as many as six taxpaying families.[35]

Spaces became more open as one proceeded through successive suburbs to the final outer wall. Cities since the second Industrial Revolution have generally had clearly defined commercial and residential areas, sometimes formalised by zoning. Some overlap between the two is provided by neighbourhood groceries, hardware stores and the like. In most parts of the pre-modern city, by contrast, it is impossible to separate retail from residential districts, since most craftsmen worked in their residences and sold their goods retail. There are some exceptions: even before 1300 Cheapside amounted to the shopping district of London, with West Cheap's shops specialising in luxury items and East Cheap in utilitarian goods. This area still has names for small streets that reflect the types of goods sold there: Bread, Milk, Wood and Friday Streets, Poultry and Ironmonger Lane and Fishmarket.[36]

Cheapside was immortalised in 'London Lickpenny', a poem of the early fifteenth century:

> Then unto London I did me hie; Of all the land it beareth the prize. 'Hot peascods,' one began to cry, 'Strawberries ripe' and 'fresh cherries'. One bade me come near and buy some spice; Pepper and saffron they offered me. But for lack of money I might not spend. Then on to Cheapside I went, Where many people I saw standing around. One offered me velvet, silk, and lawn; Another took me by the hand, 'Here is Paris thread, the finest in the land'. I never was used to such things indeed, and wanting money, I might not spend. . . . Then I hied me into Eastcheap. One cried, 'Ribs of beef and many a pie!' Pewter pots they clattered on a heap; There was harp, pipe and minstrelsy.[37]

Artisans practising the same trade had a tendency to occupy the same part of town in the early stages of urbanisation, when a single street might suffice to house the shoemakers who served 5000 persons. Many cities had Jewries or Jew Streets. Even before 1100 Winchester had streets named after the tanners, shoemakers, shield-makers, goldsmiths and butchers. But at no time were other occupations kept out of such streets; adjacent houses were used for quite different occupations. More importantly, as the town became larger, the service occupations tended to become more diffused and closer to the markets.[38] The process can occasionally be discerned. In the late thirteenth century the Alwarnestret of Winchester was renamed Flesmangerestret, ossifying a situation that was by then obsolete, since the butchers (*Flesmangeres*) had already moved to the west end of the High Street by the early twelfth century. Not a single fuller can be shown to have lived in the Fullers' Street of Ghent during the fourteenth century, and only one currier lived in the street named for his trade in Paris in 1300. The black-smiths, given the need for horseshoes, were near the city gates. Goldsmiths and moneyers were centrally located, near the houses of nobles and royal officials. In the late Middle Ages the street markets tended to segment. The foodmongers and retailers of specialities were usually in the inner sectors of the main street, while industry, including clothmaking, was farther out. Although such differentiation was developing, it does not warrant describing the city centres as retail areas and the suburbs as industrial. Even in Ghent, where the suburbs did have an industrial character, so too did many districts in the city.[39]

Occupational segregation persisted longer in the south than in northern Europe. As late as 1204–5 the city council of Montpellier was legislating to forbid craftsmen from moving away from the streets and squares named for their trades and those adjacent to them. Although the extent to which this was actually a matter of practice is debatable, 42 of 62 houses in the rue des Fustiers (carpenters) in the Old Port quarter of Marseille belonged to carpenters, joiners and other woodworkers as late as 1405.[40]

The pattern in the thirteenth century, as population continued to grow and the land market became more fluid, was for smaller concentrations of artisans practising the same trade to develop: for example a handful of bakers, cord-wainers and drayers in the same street.[41] As export industry continued to develop, and as the internal market broadened and diversified, multiple nuclei of settlement thus arose.

As the trades lost political power in the cities of the French Midi in the thirteenth and fourteenth centuries, collective terms that were used for their quarters tended to disappear or become restricted. For example, in the thirteenth century the smiths of Marseille often identified their residences in terms of a vicinity, the Smithery. When notaries recorded property transactions, they usually separated this neighbourhood into several streets, with one bearing the name of the trade. The notaries' usage reflects a changing social geography; for while through the thirteenth century many urban occupational guilds – particularly the smaller or more restrictive of them – could concentrate their members' residences in a specific part of town, their houses became much more dispersed in most cities from the mid-thirteenth century. Thus identifying an entire area as the 'Smithery', at a time when smiths were living throughout the city, simply made more sense.[42]

By the fourteenth century many trades had an elite of persons who imported the raw materials on which the artisans depended (for example, wool merchants at the apex of a weavers' guild). Often they were persons whose ancestors had been in the town and practised the trade in question. Thus, as more persons streamed into the sprawling suburbs, the older streets with occupational names became aristocratic and connected only to the merchandising side of the trade. At Paris, Drapers Old Street (rue de la Vieille-Draperie) was the new name given to Jewry Street (rue de la Juiverie) after Philip Augustus destroyed the centrally-located Jewry in 1182 and tried to attract textile artisans to his capital. The wholesalers who were leaders of the trade lived there.

In the north there are four major exceptions to the pattern of increased diffusion of the work force. First, recent immigrants tended to congregate with others from the same natal locality, usually on the outskirts, and higher-status foreigners, usually merchants, lived in proximity to one another nearer the centre. In Italy a sense of identity with the ancestral home may have been a more powerful force in fixing patterns of residence than occupational groupings, contrary to the case in northern Europe.[43] Second, particularly after 1300, tradesmen whose work caused environmental problems or noise were sometimes relegated to the edge of town. Butchers and fishmongers were characteristically segregated on the downwind side of markets because of the offal and odours associated with their trades. The Butchers' Hall in Strasbourg was at the foot of the bridge crossing the Ill River into the suburbs, on the city side. The animals were slaughtered on the bridge once a week, the offal discarded into the river, and the meat sold on a big open-air market on the other side of the bridge, away from the central city.

Finally, groups that were politically powerful or controversial lived in concentrations, but almost always intermingled with the dwellings of other artisans. At Ghent, over half of whose population was supported by textile manufacturing in the mid-fourteenth century, the weavers (who included most of the wealthy drapers) and fullers (who worked for the drapers for wages) were the great antagonists. In the wealthy parish of St John, in the central city, the two were of nearly equal strength. But most of the other weavers lived south of the town, both within the walls and in a suburb controlled by an abbey, while most fullers, the smaller group, lived on the north side of town within the wall.[44]

While the Industrial Revolution began a deterioration of the inner city that has accelerated since 1900, before 1700 the wealthier quarters tended to be centrally located, particularly in proximity to the markets. The earliest citizens were most often those with property around the markets. Given the primacy of trade in most cities, this is hardly surprising. There was, however, also a high concentration in the central city of persons in non-basic productive activities, particularly food preparation and other service professions. Furthermore, the fact that the residence and the place of business were the same for most persons meant that most neighbourhoods were extremely variegated. Virtually all had some bakers, and in the southern cities notaries, and in general workers in site-bound occupations. Although the central districts of most cities had more taxable wealth than the peripheral parishes, the rich lived alongside the poor throughout the city in a kind of unofficial 'vertical zoning': the lower stories and street fronts of houses were occupied by the more well-to-do, and the upper storeys and rear courtyards rented to the poor or used by service personnel, the apprentices and journeymen. Thus the higher above ground one lived, the lower one's social standing was likely to be.[45]

Thus, although tax records permit us to reconstruct the overall wealth of specific districts of many towns, the average figures conceal the fact that even the same street often housed extremes of wealth and poverty. Given that exportable industry tended to develop in a city only after it had achieved a central position through trade, and by that time most desirable land in the central city was occupied, persons such as clothworkers tended to settle in the suburbs and thus were more distant from the sources of wealth. There was also considerable variation among the suburbs of individual cities. The southern suburban Raval quarter at Barcelona was the poorest section of town, with many clothworkers and apprentices. The northern suburb, the Ribera, was the specialised commercial and artisan district. Although it included the palaces of many merchants, it also had the Marina, with the dock population, and thus was prone to riots. London's suburbs of Southwark and Westminster, which were not covered by the jurisdiction of the city, had a higher tax valuation than Southampton in 1334.[46]

Yet the mixture of owned and rented properties gives a distorted perspective. When house ownership is considered apart from place of residence, the city centres were occupied by the wealthy, while poor persons who managed to own a free-standing home more often had shacks nearer the wall. With the depopulations of the fourteenth and fifteenth centuries and the rise of the single-family dwelling, with differentiated rooms and more outbuildings, the poor were gradually relegated to separate quarters away from the central city. Thus at the end of the Middle Ages and in the early modern period, the mixture of rich and poor within the same quarter that had characterised many medieval cities was breaking down, and tax records show substantial differences in wealth between parishes and quarters.[47] Segregation by wealth was thus more common in the early modern city than in its medieval ancestor, but this also corresponds to a difference of function. Merchants and craftsmen generally lived in different areas from clerics and administrators, particularly in the central European towns. At London the two nuclei of wealth and status were Westminster and the City proper, the preferred residences of government officials and merchants respectively.

The nature of the real estate market also helped keep the central cities as preserves for the wealthy. The land market was much less mobile than now. First, although mortgages did exist, most houses were sold for payment of the entire purchase price. Not surprisingly, most properties were transmitted by inheritance, and inner city properties thus tended to stay in the same family. Even when such a place was sold, the price was often prohibitively high. But in some cases the natural forces of the market were aided by policy. Probably no urban elite was as zealous in this regard as that of Nuremberg, whose council from 1382 divided citizens into three categories based on parish of residence, and allowed only immigrants who could meet a stringent property qualification to move into the two central parishes of St Sebald and St Lorenz. Master artisans and tradesmen who had less than this minimum wealth had to pay a still higher entry fee and reside in one of the fortified suburban parishes for five years before being allowed to move into the inner city, even if they could afford it. Similarly, in 1306 the lineages of Brussels forbade weavers and fullers to live within the walls.[48]

Urban Morphology in the Later Middle Ages and the Renaissance

Most cities had reached population levels by 1300 that they would not attain again before 1600 or even later. But the plagues, famines and wars of the fourteenth and fifteenth centuries, together with the fact that by 1300 Europe had too many persons to be fed using the existing agricultural technology, caused a massive population decline. The losses were most severe in Italy, where Florence declined from about 90,000 in 1338 (according to the chronicler Giovanni Villani, even this represented a decline since 1300) to 38,000 in 1427. Over the same period, the populations of Venice and Siena declined by at least 50 per cent. Between 1300 and 1500 the relative position of most cities did not change drastically, simply because the larger places could sustain a greater relative population loss than the smaller ones. Lucca, for example, went from about 15,000 in 1331 to 10,000 in 1369. Losses in the north were less severe, generally between a quarter and a half of the pre-1300 populations. London declined from 80–100,000 to 60,000 in 1349 to 35,000 in 1377.[49]

For reasons discussed in Chapter 1, the cities made up some of their losses through higher rates of immigration from the depressed rural areas, but the occupied area of virtually all cities shrank. Many suburbs were virtually abandoned, and the less desirable real estate inside but nearest the walls fell vacant as more houses became available in the more prestigious inner cities. Older patterns of occupational and status segregation were breaking down. There were important changes of land use in the two centuries after 1300, much but not all of it for purposes of conspicuous consumption. Winchester illustrates the process graphically. Already in decline since the twelfth century, when it was the preferred residence of the English kings, Winchester witnessed a virtual abandonment of the areas nearest the walls. Even before 1300 shops and residences were moving from the side streets perpendicular to the High into the main street, but the process was accelerated with the late medieval depopulations. By 1400, there were still 19 parish churches surviving within the wall, eleven of them on the High or within a short block of it, but ten others that had existed in 1300 were gone. Winchester had virtually become a single-street settlement.[50]

Given the magnitude of the changes, the fact that most town plans underwent little fundamental alteration in the three centuries after 1348 illustrates the essential rationality of their designs. They served the needs of settlements that were still primarily commercial but increasingly industrial. Although some cases of destruction of a town led to improvement of the city plan, this did not always happen. When much of Toulouse was destroyed by fire in 1463, the gutted buildings were simply replaced by open squares that left the street plan intact.[51] In 1540 the troops of the emperor Charles V destroyed Ghent, but it was rebuilt into its modern form with scarcely any alteration of the street pattern shown by the anonymous artist who drew a detailed street plan of the city, from a vista east of the city, in 1534.[52]

Yet changes there were. Most of them were driven by military and strategic needs and by the vanity of princes. Depopulation gave rise to more diverse land use. The suburbs continued to be used for activities that were environmentally noxious, such as tanning, and for linen bleaching, which required open space. At Montpellier wood merchants used the area of the *Douve*, the trench outside the wall, for storage. Cordmakers also used the suburban space for stretching their ropes. Leather workers were also outside the walls.[53] At Venice the arsenal, glassmaking and gunpowder manufacturing were segregated from the main areas on their own islands.

Such 'environmental zoning' was never comprehensive, but it did have the practical effect of moving pollution away from the homes of the elite. Yet there are problems in interpreting it as 'class' legislation. At Winchester in the fourteenth century, the dyers and fullers did move to quarters that the tanners had previously vacated; but this may have been to get closer to water, for no statute ordered them to move. Indeed, such a measure would not have been enforceable: they could not have shifted quarters of town unless real estate had been available. Butchers, who were notoriously disorderly (their jobs made it necessary to permit them to carry long knives) as well as dirty, were the exception, for strict requirements for meat inspection required them to slaughter their animals in the central city. From 1302 the butchers of Ghent had a charter making mastership in the guild hereditary in the male line. Shortly thereafter numerous members of the guild bought property in the Drabstraat, which exited across a bridge from the main Meat Hall.[54]

Particularly in the fifteenth century, more peaceful conditions led nobles to build town houses nearer the walls or even outside them, paradoxically thus coming closer to the pollution. After the plagues the urban land market became much more fluid. As properties fell vacant or became burdened with debt, speculators could consolidate smaller tenements into larger blocks, which could house impressive *hôtels*. This made some street plans nearer the walls less regular than before. Paris, which had as many as 24,000 vacant houses in 1423, is the best example of this process at work. The areas around the Louvre and the Hôtel-Saint-Pol were the preferred spots, with officials and lawyers moving nearer the sources of power. The great accumulation of wealth and depopulation of tenements permitted the elite of Florence to build ornate palaces, almost entirely in the central city rather than the suburbs.[55]

City Walls in the Late Middle Ages and the Renaissance

The walls had always figured largely as the most tactile and visual representation of citizens' feelings of corporate civic identity. The argument that the old city walls were made obsolete by gunpowder and artillery is probably overdrawn, for cities were now the focal points of sieges that earlier had focused on castles, but it is undeniable that they were much less effective against cannon than against crossbows and trebuchets.

Most importantly from the standpoint of urban morphology, medieval city walls had not hindered expansion of the city plan. When population settled outside an older wall, a new one was built and joined to its predecessor. But in the late

Middle Ages the walls often became a barrier to continued growth. In the late fifteenth century Italian military engineers began using the 'bastioned trace', called *trace italienne* by its northern imitators; an incomplete example is shown on Guicciardini's plan of Antwerp in 1568 (see Figure 3.5 in the discussion of Antwerp later in this chapter). It replaced the high medieval wall, which was often torn down, with a low rampart that was better able to withstand the flat trajectory of cannon balls. A variant on this was to keep the old wall but demolish the suburbs and/or the buildings near the inside the wall in order to allow construction of a separate rampart. The medieval urban wall had emphasised verticality, while the bastioned trace, which extended horizontally, used land that otherwise would have been civilian.

> A fully built bastioned trace could take up as much ground as the area occupied by the city itself. The city as a form of human society was apparently not well adapted to enclosure within such a massive girdle: new fortress-cities would eventually be built in the *alla moderna* style, but none ever attained the population level envisioned by its builders.[56]

As the cities recovered population in the sixteenth and seventeenth centuries, they were thus actually being enclosed in a smaller space than before. The result was a less planned layout of streets than the original medieval suburbs had displayed. Given that most towns had expanded beyond their late medieval walls by the time it became desirable to build a *trace italienne*, the new defences involved destroying suburban buildings, which often meant hospitals, religious houses, mills and furnaces. The fact that Renaissance fortifications were so extensive meant that it was not feasible to build adjacent to them, for defenders would need a line of fire, and attackers would simply raze the suburbs. Thus the existing walls were generally extended, rather than building bastioned traces and allowing new suburbs to develop in unplanned fashion outside. Some of the most rapidly growing cities, such as Madrid, had only fragmentary defences.

Although generally the fortifications were completely rebuilt only for towns in strategic locations, or those such as Ghent that were dangerous to their lords, they were provided with bastions and cannon mounts. The new-style fortifications were extremely expensive and were rarely built, certainly not by townsmen; for princes expected their towns to pay for fortifications that could be used to limit their own independence (see Chapter 4). They were so formidable that suburbs simply did not develop outside them, in contrast to the form that medieval town expansion had occurred. Thus, in places whose population was continuing to grow, buildings went to more storeys, and population density inside the towns rose. On balance, the new style of fortification worked best at opposite extremes of the urban spectrum: new towns that were planned as fortifications, and some of the largest cities that had plenty of space, but elsewhere the bastioned trace was a burden.

Naturally, the new design was most common in Italy, where the older cities, constantly warring among themselves, needed them, and the territorial princes fortified the smaller towns, especially those on the frontiers. The most impressive example of the *trace italienne* is late and involves the transformation of a major city. Turin was still contained within its Roman wall and had a medieval street plan in the 1560s, when Duke Emanuele Filiberto of Savoy decided to make it his capital. Although he built a massive pentagonal citadel, he did not make many changes to the street plan of the inner city, but his successors did. Military designs gave rise to regular streets and open spaces. While in medieval cities the market square and/ or the cathedral square were usually the *foci* of urban development, at Turin the central square was used for military parades and musters. Duke Carlo Emanuele I began a palace compound, diagonally across Turin from the fortress. A network of streets radiated from this to other ducal power complexes. He established a build- ing agency to supervise the expansion into the New City (Città Nuova) that he planned outside the walls and to coordinate changes in the inside of the city. An idealised drawing of 1674 shows old Turin, inside its Roman wall, with a regular street plan, with roughly square blocks in the centre but rectangular blocks on the outskirts toward the wall. Many of the rectangular blocks were bisected by side streets at right angles to the main street network created by the Roman sector. The New City was a seventeen-block addition on the southeast, directly across town from the Citadel, with rectangular blocks. The old and new city streets did not meet exactly; and the link between the two became a new square, the Piazza Reale.[57]

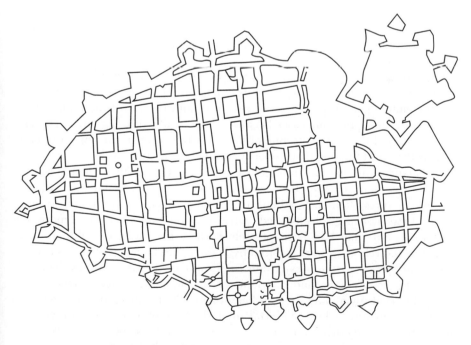

Figure 3.4   Turin in the late seventeenth century

By 1700 the walls had no practical utility for many towns: they were no longer a town–country barrier, and most of them were so dilapidated that they could serve no police function, however annoying they might be to transients. Many towns simply allowed their fortifications to decay, since the town government had to maintain them but had little use for them. Through its engineers and architects, the French royal government handled some reworkings of town walls, especially the introduction of the *trace italienne* in the 1540s. Between 1520 and 1560 about 20 French cities, including Tours, Marseilles, Toulouse and Poitiers, had their walls rebuilt and strengthened, often by Italian engineers. This usually involved substantial destruction in the older part of the city and the building of boulevards and large plazas. The Spaniards extended the *trace italienne* into the Low Countries, which they controlled through the sixteenth century, and the northern French towns became a defensive line against them.[58]

Urban Evolution and Planning in the Renaissance

The extent of open area within the walls of most towns, particularly after the late medieval depopulations, meant that (unless new fortifications were built) a considerable population growth could be accommodated as population recovered in the sixteenth and seventeenth centuries. Except for the rapidly growing ports and national capitals, modifications in the urban plan were much less drastic in the early modern period than the changes of the central Middle Ages had been for the primitive cities. The medieval street plan of most cities was ossified in a sense, as city governments began using more precise designations for addresses and property descriptions, and it rarely underwent fundamental alteration. Furthermore, the greatest cities of 1700 were not the greatest cities of 1400 (Chapter 1). Many of the largest medieval cities stabilised in the modern period at something approaching their medieval high points of population. Some cities, like London, saw the building of aristocratic estates outside, but this is hardly a 'suburb' in the traditional sense. In some cases because of the walls, in others not, the early modern period thus saw a decline of the suburb, except in the few older cities such as Paris and London that were expanding beyond their walls.[59]

Changes in domestic architecture in Renaissance Italy – the big palaces with their gardens (Chapter 6) – began to have an impact on overall city plans. These structures often enclosed courtyards that effectively promoted straightening of streets and gridiron-based districts, as the house became a more self-contained unit than had been possible earlier. Renaissance buildings, both domestic and religious, were inspired by Roman and Greek models and accordingly had more horizontal extension than most medieval buildings. This was occurring precisely at the time when land was becoming scarce again in the cities.[60]

Medieval town planning had been the work of princes and, less often, of town governments, and was undertaken on the basis of practical considerations of topography and function. In the Renaissance, academic planners were acting under classical inspiration, and planning accordingly became more abstract.

For, absent confiscations or war devastation – both of which, admittedly, did free some tenements in the clogged city centres – governments could not simply raze entire populated quarters. The revival of Roman architecture, particularly the study of Vitruvius, led to the development of a kind of urban theory among architects. Planners such as Leon Battista Alberti wanted the town to be pleasing visually, an aesthetic experience, in which also perspective of view could be fostered. Although radial plans are found in the suburbs of some organic cities of the Middle Ages, only during the Renaissance did newly planned towns and suburban extensions take this form, as at Versailles and Karlsruhe, and then in places that were intended as fortresses. Alberti preferred radial–concentric schemes of urban planning and urged that towns be planned as an organic unity. Important architectural innovations at Florence included Brunelleschi's Foundling Hospital, with an arched arcade, which led to buildings in a similar style around the square. While in the Middle Ages the arcade was generally confined to a single building, Renaissance arcades were extended around the square.

Thus the notions of the Renaissance theoreticians of urbanisation, such as Alberti, Antonio Filarete and Albrecht Dürer, were feasible in completely new towns, but could be implemented only piecemeal in older places, for example by condemning buildings around a market square and rebuilding the whole area more symmetrically and with arcades, or doing the same with existing buildings along a major thoroughfare. The urban landscape was largely fixed by 1400. Since the large fortifications and in many cases population stagnation precluded continued expansion into suburbs, improvements such as widened streets were usually possible only after a disaster. Thus individual streets and squares were widened and straightened, but entire sectors, let alone the city plan as a whole, could not change fundamentally in the older places.[61]

Rome is perhaps the best example of thorough renewal of an older city, but much of it was already in ruins, it was further depopulated in the late fourteenth century, and the popes' powers over the city, probably more extensive than even those of the kings over their capitals, were at their height in the sixteenth and seventeenth centuries. Julius II (1503–1513) undertook considerable new construction. The popes planned the Piazza del Popolo in the sixteenth century to give grandeur to the northern edge of the city, through which most visitors passed, and particularly St Peter's Square, designed at Alexander VII's instigation by Gian Lorenzo Bernini in 1656–7.[62]

Italian advances in architecture also spread to the north, but no northern city was able to undertake a comprehensive 'urban renewal'. At Antwerp some new merchant homes and warehouses were designed as *palazzi*, notably the Great House of the Easterlings, built 1564–8 for the Hanse merchants as residence, office and warehouse, designed around a courtyard and with the main facade decorated. The city built the New Bourse in 1531, with an Italianate inner courtyard, somewhat away from the main business centre but still easily accessible. Thomas Gresham used Antwerp architects to build the London Exchange (renamed the Royal Exchange in 1571). The inner courtyard type was also used for some private houses at Antwerp. Greater attention was paid to the visual impact of buildings. The town hall of Antwerp was initially on the south side of the Great Market, but it was destroyed by a fire in 1541, then rebuilt in stone on the western side, where it could be seen from all sides. Similar considerations governed the building of the new town hall of Amsterdam, designed in 1648.[63]

While Italian urban planners used the radial-concentric plan, French architects preferred squared layouts with some variation. Renaissance town development in France shows the combination of planning and emphasis on elaborate fortification. New towns included Le Havre and fortresses such as Mariembourg, Philippeville and Henrichemont. Cardinal Richelieu planned a small town with a grid plan around his eponymous castle. Lyon and Dijon underwent substantial renewal and redevelopment. The main 'new towns' of the French-speaking area in the sixteenth century were Nancy and Charleville. Nancy had a small medieval core, to which a planned rectangular suburb was added in 1588. Charleville was founded in 1608, with a gridiron plan encompassing a main central square and six secondary squares, all within an up-to-date fortification.[64]

Urban planning was obviously much harder in the large cities. Public space was at a premium in Paris. The nerve centre of the city was still the *Ile-de-la-Cité*, but access was difficult. The Pont Neuf was built between 1578 and 1604 at the southern end of the island, to link both banks of the Seine. Until the seventeenth century even the *places* of Paris were small. There were considerable open private spaces in gardens, courtyards and stables. Paris' change from a medieval layout began in the late sixteenth century under Henry IV and continued under Louis XIV, but a comprehensive redesign only came later. Occasionally something was done to regularise the internal street plan. The Place Royale (later Place des Vosges) was built between 1605 and 1612 on Henry IV's orders on land in north-eastern Paris that was being used as a horse market. Buildings on the square were to be in a standard architectural form, linked by an arcade; persons who bought land on the *place* promised to build their palaces in this way. But this was helped by the fact that the property had a single owner until the plots were sold by the crown; multiple ownership hindered such things in most large cities. Henry IV also planned the place Dauphine, on the south end of the *Île*, but space limitations minimised its influence on the rest of the city plan. On balance, before the end of the eighteenth century little was done to change the medieval core of Paris, except for constructing the Champs Elysées as a straight western axis and laying out several squares whose original justification was to hold a statue of a king: the Place Louis XV (now Place de la Concorde), Place des Victoires and Place Vendôme. Before the eighteenth century such 'statue squares' were the main features of Renaissance urban design to reach the provincial towns of France.[65]

Most of the older towns of Germany did not outgrow their medieval walls. Thus there is less alteration of city plans there than in France. Stuttgart added a suburb in the sixteenth century. The best examples of Baroque town planning in Germany are Mannheim and Karlsruhe. Mannheim was founded in 1607 by Elector Frederick IV of the Palatinate. A castle-residence, the Friedrichs-burg, was built at the junction of the Rhine and the Neckar. Adjacent to it was a town intended as a refuge for Protestant refugees. Mannheim's plan was hardly revolutionary: a central marketplace was the linchpin of a regular grid. The town was razed subsequently, and the present city dates from 1720, but it simply extended the principles of the earlier design. Karlsruhe was built for the Margrave of Baden in 1715.[66]

Amsterdam was small enough when it began its period of rapid expansion for concepts of urban planning to be instrumental in its evolution. The city is a classic example of the 'characteristic Dutch form of urban settlement': the Amstel river was dammed in 1240, and several channels led to the sea, separated by dikes. These became streets that served as the main arteries for land traffic and intersected the larger dam in a radial pattern. The dam itself, the Damrak, amounting to a headland, became the central square where most public buildings were located. As new canals were added, they were equidistant from the core settlement. Amsterdam was unusual in that the guiding genius behind the urban plan was the city government. In 1607 it adopted the 'Plan of the Three Canals' (Heren, Keizers and Prinsengrachten). The three main canals were linked in turn by radial waterways and numerous bridges. They were joined to the Singel, a canal that encircled the city, and extensions beyond the Singel simply replicated the radial form of the inner city. On the western side of Amsterdam, the Jordaan became an industrial suburb.[67]

Except for Amsterdam, city regimes in northern Europe did not intervene much in building projects in the older quarters, although some were involved in planning suburbs. Antwerp's government made the changes ordered by the Spanish rulers in the sixteenth century, mainly in improving the fortifications, for which the city council enlisted the help of Albrecht Dürer in 1519. The phenomenal population growth of sixteenth-century Antwerp was handled by developing the suburbs, where there was considerable building in the private sector. A New City (Nieuwe Stad) north of the centre was designed and constructed by the entrepreneur Gilbert van Schoonbeke. This commercial rather than residential district had rectangular blocks aligned to canals that were intended to lead to the port of Antwerp on the Scheldt. Van Schoonbeke also rebuilt the Friday Market and other public areas in the old city. He developed the St Laurentius neighbourhood as a residential suburb. He bought land from previous owners, built a neighbourhood centre, then divided the rest into plots that he sold. The entire agglomeration, including the suburbs, was quickly fortified in the 1560s by a bastioned trace. On the plan of 1568 van Schoonbeke's New City is shown under construction.[68]

'Renaissance' notions only began to have an impact on English urban design in the seventeenth century. New fortifications were not an issue with London or any English city; the medieval wall of London, which followed the trace of the Roman enclosure, separated the city proper from the suburbs. In the seventeenth century the West End was growing as a fashionable and expensive quarter. East London, and especially its suburbs, grew spectacularly as an industrial sector, with the population expanding from about 20,000 in 1600 to 100,000 in 1700. There was not much development northward. It is likely that the population of the city of London was declining in the late seventeenth century in favour of the

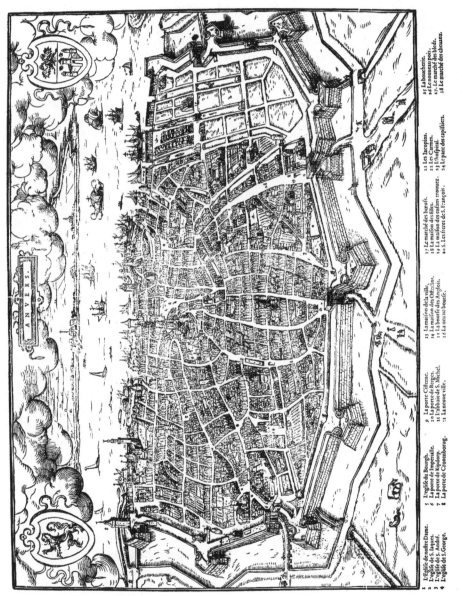

Figure 3.5 Guicciardini's plan of Antwerp in 1568

1. L'église de nostre Dame.
2. L'église de S. Iaques.
3. L'église de S. André.
4. L'église de S. George.
5. L'église du Bourgh.
6. La porte de Imperialle.
7. La porte de Kipdorp.
8. La porte de Cronenborgh.
9. La porte Citterne.
10. La porte de Berges.
11. L'abbaïe de S. Michel.
12. La neuve ville.
13. La maison de la ville.
14. La maison des Officiers.
15. La bourse des Anglois.
16. La neuve bourse.
17. Le marché des bœuf.
18. La maison des filles.
19. La maison des enfans trouvez.
20. S. Les freres de S. François.
21. Les Iacopins.
22. Les Carmes.
23. L'hôpital.
24. Le pain des capsifiers.
25. La boucherie.
26. Le comptoir pois.
27. Le marché des bleds.
28. Le marché des cheuaux.

88

suburbs.[69] Given that greater London doubled in size to half a million inhabitants during this single century, the suburbs illustrate even more graphically than the medieval suburbs had done the attraction of the city to immigrants and particularly to industrial workers.

Efforts to control suburban sprawl began with Elizabeth I's proclamation in 1580 forbidding all new building within three miles of any gate of the city, but they were fruitless. Suburban planning projects began with the Covent Garden suburb, between the city of London proper and Westminster, designed in 1630 as an aristocratic residential area by the court architect Inigo Jones, who had studied in Italy and was influenced by the style of Andrea Palladio. Covent Garden declined as fashion moved west, and by 1671 a vegetable market was in the square. Little remains of the original design today. Other squares were laid out in the West End, starting with Bloomsbury Square in 1661, St James's Square in 1665, and Piccadilly, designed by Sir Christopher Wren between 1682 and 1684. Soho Square was also laid out in the late seventeenth century, along with several new streets, including Downing, Buckingham and Essex Streets. Deliberate planning of this sort is not found in the other English cities until the eighteenth century.[70]

Indeed, London's urban fabric was curiously slow to react to opportunity enclosed within disaster. The plague of 1665 killed about 20 per cent of London's inhabitants, while the Great Fire of September 1666 left only 75 of 448 acres undamaged within the walls. The fire consumed over 13,000 houses and nearly all public buildings of the city, including the Royal Exchange, the Custom House, the halls of 44 of the city companies and the Guildhall, St Paul's and 87 of the 109 churches. The extent of the destruction made it theoretically possible to rebuild London more efficiently, straightening the old medieval street alignments and improving the movement of traffic. As it happened, the need to respect property boundaries limited what Charles II's government could do. Sir Christopher Wren planned a redesign, but it was not implemented. It would have imposed radial streets on a plan that was basically a grid, and it took no account of London's hilly topography. There was in fact some standardising of street widths and house types, and many new squares would be laid out in the eighteenth century, but London still honours its past.[71]

A Social Explanation of the Urban Plan?

Gideon Sjoberg, author of the first comprehensive study of pre-modern urbanisation since Max Weber, saw the cities controlled by a small 'feudal' elite. The inner city was thus dominated physically by public buildings and functionally by government and religion. While income from rents was socially respectable and provided the wealth of the occupants of the 'city' proper, marketing and crafts were considered demeaning, and those who supported themselves by them lived on the outskirts. Thus for Sjoberg the distinction between core and periphery was social in character. Status diminished as one proceeded outward toward the limits of the settlement. Sjoberg saw the breakthrough to the modern city occurring when the technology that made possible the Industrial Revolution of the eighteenth century drove out the household or domestic unit of production.

James Vance, by contrast, thought that the cities before the sixteenth century were pre-capitalist and attributed this to the great influence of the occupational guilds, which supposedly determined residential patterns through occupational quarters. While seeing residential patterns and space use much as Sjoberg did, Vance thus attributed them to a different cause. He explained the mixture of occupational groups in the city as the result of vertical rather than horizontal use of space: narrow street frontages, trade in the same building as the residence, and mixture of economic groups because journeymen, apprentices and servants all lived in the household of the master. Status was not based on wealth, or indeed on ownership of the land – Vance saw little evidence of land ownership apart from land use before the sixteenth century – but rather of ownership of the means of production and control of economic activity through the guilds. When the merchants lost touch with actual production and trading and in effect became rentiers, the guilds became anachronistic and declined. Zoning became by class rather than by guild, determined by rent-paying ability.[72]

Our discussion has shown the danger of generalising from ideal types. Sjoberg exaggerated the contrast between core and periphery and did not realize that it was breaking down in the late Middle Ages. There are examples of wealthy suburbs and poor centres, particularly in cities that grew when princes established their residences in the outskirts, such as Dresden and Turin.[73] On the basis of Coventry evidence, Keith Lilley has disputed the notion that the suburbs were poor while the wealthier persons lived in the central cities. Neighbourhoods were mixed, and crises affected mainly the poor throughout the city. Early modern London evidence has been used to argue both that the suburbs were poor and that the characteristic medieval mixture of economic levels in the neighbourhood was preserved into the seventeenth century.[74] On the whole, however, the facts are much more supportive of Sjoberg than of Vance, who attributed an influence to the craft organisations that they simply did not possess (see Chapter 5) and argued against all the evidence that the pre-modern urban economy was not capitalistic.

Tax records make it possible to trace and compare levels of wealth in different sectors of many cities. Some of the wealthiest as well as some of the poorest areas of Paris in 1571 were on the peripheries, and the richest was on the northeastern edge. The *Ile de la Cité* was no longer as wealthy as it had been in the late Middle Ages, but its eastern half was quite prosperous, whereas most areas of the left bank were poor. The poorest part of the city was between the walls of Philip Augustus and Charles V on the north, while the wealthy parts of the right bank were on the east. By the late sixteenth century people associated with the government and court lived mainly on the peripheries, a great change from the fifteenth century, for only there was there enough space for their *hôtels*. There was thus movement away from the crowded central city toward the peripheries and in some cases the suburbs in early modern Paris. As in the Middle Ages, the great merchants preferred to live in the largest streets, the quarter of St Jacques de l'Hôpital, the *Île de la Cité* and around the Cloth Hall. The poor often lived in the side streets that led away from these major arteries, and accordingly the quarters had a wide disparity of wealth.[75]

Other examples from earlier periods and smaller towns confirm this suggestion. The administrative sixths (later quarters) of late medieval Florence were roughly comparable in wealth, except for Oltrarno, the poorer suburb across the river from the central city. Within the quarters, however, there was a wide divergence in wealth and social composition among the enclaved parishes. These cases suggest that while the city–suburb dichotomy may be valid before 1348, the rapid changes thereafter may mean that street rather than entire quarter may be the more appropriate frame of reference for a wealth contrast.[76]

The plans of the earliest cities were extremely irregular, but their expansion into suburbs, and often the renovation of pre-existing sectors of the city, shows that an evolving and highly sophisticated level of rationality was being exercised in pre-modern urban design and planning, mainly by the city governments themselves. The municipal authorities were vitally concerned with the urban infrastructure. Medieval cities were generally in charge of their own buildings and of street and bridge maintenance. The all-important walls were maintained by the city authorities, initially to defend themselves against outsiders, including their own lords, but later, particularly in France and England, because they were required to do so by the national and regional/territorial governments to which they were losing their independence. Even to accomplish this much required sophistication. But the cities also took on other functions, including lawmaking, economic regulation, public health and justice. We cannot understand the complexity and evolution of the physical city, nor the power of the capital concentration that made it the centre of its region, without understanding the power mechanisms that resided in pre-modern urban government. We now turn to that topic.

Chapter 4 . . . .

Corporation and Community

All burghers of Zürich should be obedient in all matters and all things to the burgomaster, his councillors and the guild masters of Zürich, as God has ordained . . . and we ordain and will that all our ancient statutes and our charters, in all their other clauses and articles, and also our city court, have been and are eternal and will remain inviolate in all respects.[1]

(from the 'Konradbuch' of Zürich)

The Beginnings of Urban Government: Northern Europe

Max Weber noted that the city is not peculiar to the West, but the urban community is. His criteria for a 'full urban community' thus include not only the fortification and market, but also 'a court of its own and at least partially autonomous law; a related form of association; and at least partial autonomy and autocephaly, thus also an administration by authorities in the election of whom the burghers participated'.[2]

Most cities by 1100 were ruled by customs that had evolved from the laws of their local territories. They had initially been oral, but some were being committed to writing. Urban government is sometimes portrayed as originating in opposition to the town lords, but in fact the extent of municipal independence has been exaggerated by historians' concern with 'communes'. Guibert of Nogent, writing around 1115 of recent events in Laon, said that

'Commune' is a new and evil name for an arrangement for them all [the lords' subjects] to pay the customary head tax which they owe their lords as a servile due, in a lump sum once a year, and if anyone commits a crime, he shall pay a fine set by law, and all other financial exactions which are customarily imposed on serfs are completely abolished.[3]

Three sentences later he calls this a 'sworn association of mutual aid among the clergy, nobles, and people'. If we disregard the adjective 'evil', we see that Guibert correctly identified the features common to all communes: the recognition of the community as a corporation and the establishment of written guarantees that provided a basis in law for the respective rights of lord and town.

Not all the early communes were revolutionary. Some were peace associations, such as the Charter of Peace of Valenciennes of 1114 and the Institution of Peace of Laon of 1128, versions of which were given to other French towns. Members of the association pledged mutual assistance against danger. The charters provided penalties for fighting. The peace of the town, which initially extended only to members of the association, quickly came to include the city's territory. The territorialisation of personal law is a critical transition: newcomers to the sworn association of Laon had to build or buy real property within the town area within a year. But the communes cannot be equated with municipal independence: some places that were not communes were largely autonomous, while some communes achieved little power.

Not only were most communes not revolutionary, their long-term result was not democratic. Their councils were large as a percentage of the population of the towns in the early twelfth century, but they became more oligarchic as populations grew and as members of the councils either made their positions hereditary or co-opted their successors. The 'Establishments' of Rouen (granted shortly after 1200) provided that 100 'peers' would provide the pool from which city officials would be chosen. By 1291 natural attrition had reduced the number of peers to 25, a number insufficient to staff the two colleges of magistrates. Agitation led to a new system of 36 peers chosen for three-year terms. By this time the communes were unpopular, and the king abolished several in response to public demand.

In both Italy and the north, an oath association constituted the foundation of the urban community.[4] The members of the earliest town courts were generally called *scabini* (German *Schöffen*, French *échevins*); they were domain officials of the town lord. They generally served for life and represented the lord's interests. In the late twelfth and particularly thirteenth century, as town populations grew beyond the original *cité* and its nearest suburbs, a second body was often added, a council (German *Ratsherren*, French *jurés*) that represented the sworn association of the townsmen. They served for a briefer term, usually a year, after which they were rotated off for at least a year. In the founded towns of the German east and in some cities of northern Germany, there was a single council. In Flanders the *scabini* actually became the town council, and *jurés* had little importance.

Yet although the council of the community gradually assumed real power in most cities, the lord's *scabini* continued to function. Distinctions of competence between the two were often blurred. A major difference between them is that the *scabini* usually acted purely as a court that handled only those administrative matters that remained within the town lord's jurisdiction, while the community's representatives became a council with general administrative and legislative competence. In addition to the councils, some towns had one or more burgomasters or mayors, who chaired meetings and in some places controlled the militia.[5]

Most towns of Germany achieved some independence of their lords, generally bishops, beginning in the late eleventh century, and had developed specific municipal institutions by the mid- to late twelfth century. The movement for municipal independence atrophied in England after William the Conqueror.

Henry I gave a charter to London that did little beyond fixing the 'fee farm', the amount of money owed by town to crown. In other places, notably Canterbury, the guild merchant that early charters guaranteed to the urban communities was evolving into a town council by the mid-twelfth century. This transition is found in most towns after Richard I (1189–1199) and particularly John (1199–1216) granted charters that secured limited rights of self-government through a council.

Thus the earliest town charters were concerned mainly with relations between town and lord, with the community being given the right to choose officials without being specific about who was in the community or how the officials would be elected. The later charters are more concerned with the internal mechanics of elections.[6]

The charters differed in detail, but they shared fundamental characteristics. Procedural guarantees for townspeople were particularly important: they were to be judged only by the town court, with no obligation to leave the town to have their cases heard except for litigation involving their own rural properties. Members of the sworn association of the town were obligated to exact vengeance on anyone who injured another member without offering acceptable redress. Townspeople could sell their houses and move without hindrance, and were freed from many servile obligations. The amount that they could be fined for specified offences was fixed. They were normally freed from arbitrary taxation, the head tax (which was a mark of serfdom) and from military service except within a day's journey of the town. Burgesses were exempt from trial by ordeal and trial by battle, both of which favoured nobles – who often owed money to townspeople or were involved in litigation against them. Sworn testimony of witnesses was substituted, a clearly more rational mode of proof. Mature cities were normally given the right to a separate court and a 'guild', generally a merchant guild, although charters granted to newly founded towns lacked this feature.[7] While membership in the sworn association of the town was the frame of reference of the earliest charters on the continent, in England the concern was with membership in the merchant guild.

The 'freedom' (formal citizenship) in England bestowed the automatic right to practise a craft, while outsiders had to negotiate this with the civic authorities. Town judiciaries eventually preferred written evidence to oral testimony. Oral contracts were often subsequently copied (for a fee) in the book of the council. In southern France and Italy notaries kept written records that were considered legal records of first recourse. Townspeople were granted hereditary ground rents and the right to sell their property and leave it without obtaining the town lord's permission, called burgage tenure in England. Given the emphasis of the early charters on granting liberties to members of the sworn association, the territory of some early towns was called the 'liberty', thus emphasising that the magistrates had freedom of action in defined spheres, such as peacekeeping and protecting the persons and goods of members of the community.

But liberties are relative. Town lords always played an important role. Their rights usually included confirming newly elected members of the city council, even if they were chosen by the sworn association or by the previous council, or joining with the town government in choosing electors who would present a slate of nominees. Virtually all town lords could nullify the choice of an individual by refusing to install him. Lords held large amounts of land in all the cities, and rent was an important income for them as for townspeople. Their officials were the oldest urban elites, dominating the early councils and rarely yielding complete power to merchants.

Lords also collected tolls and fees, including in most places a substantial payment in return for giving the town such rights as issuing statutes and collecting taxes. Some charters gave control of the town walls to the city government, but many lords retained this right, and control of the gates gave them important leverage over the town. The lord had a representative in the town, variously called the bailiff, advocate or burgrave, who aided in law enforcement, handled criminal cases and supervised the mint. Some German towns were only able to buy out the right of the town lord to appoint these officials in the fourteenth century. Although the major French towns bought out the royal provost's rights in the early thirteenth century, this simply meant that they rather than he handled collection of the sums due to the king. In England the towns had this right and chose their own sheriffs.

Procedures for elections to city councils were cumbersome, for the brothers in the peace associations of the towns were quite suspicious of one another. Although city councils rotated their membership, this does not mean discontinuity of policy; the intent was to make certain that the emoluments of rule were spread among large numbers of amateurs. Especially from the late thirteenth century, the councils hired professional bureaucrats to implement the policies that the council fixed. There was broad agreement about what those policies should be, for the municipal elites consisted of merchants and landholders, and their policies reflected those interests. Once the lord's officials were reduced to a nominal role in the day-to-day administration of the town – and even this did not occur in England or France – conflicts over membership on the city councils almost always pitted hostile factions of merchants against one another, or newer commercial wealth against landed wealth, but rarely until the fourteenth century merchant against artisan. The issue was not what city governments should be able theoretically to do, but rather who should doing it to whom.

Medieval urban government was a family affair. In the early stages surviving members of city councils often chose the successors of their deceased colleagues, and sons were preferred. This is sometimes called rule by 'patricians', who dominated the city governments through merchant guilds. Later, as this gave way to guaranteed representation for occupational guilds, some urban constitutions prohibited close relatives from serving together on a the same council; but although the family element was reduced, it was never eliminated. Furthermore, not all members of the old city lineages were interested in government. Service in city administration was a political cul-de-sac, and as more opportunities in royal and other princely government opened after 1300, membership on city councils became less desirable.

To a greater extent than was once recognised, city government in northern Europe was linked to landownership in the town. Since land tends to pass in families while money does not, most cities had an old governing elite whose origins were in landholding and whose members only began moving into trade in the thirteenth century, and a newer commercial elite whose members were investing in land but whose lack of sufficiently ancient ancestors kept them out of offices.[8] Conflicts between these two elites erupted in the last quarter of the thirteenth century. Indeed, until town courts were functioning under a generally accepted legal framework, there is little evidence of merchants who were not also landowners serving on town councils.

Despite the frequent rotation of charges, public office cloaked an individual with authority and majesty. Members of city councils were given luxurious uniforms, sometimes in lieu of a salary: each alderman of Ghent received a uniform in 1366 that cost three times the annual wage of each town sergeant.[9] Foul language was actionable in the city courts, but it was *lèse majesté* when spoken in the presence of the magistrates or in criticism of them. In 1388 Robert Staffertone responded to a summons by his ward alderman

> 'that he had nothing whatever to say to him, and that he would not come to him ... [and] he made reply, that he wished the Alderman himself had come to him, and that he might then have kissed his rearward'. The board of aldermen noted 'that the said words were expressly uttered as well in disparagement ... [of] all the officers of the said city, and especially of such an officer as an Alderman, who represents the judicial status in the same' and imposed a 40-day jail term, which was commuted at the request of the offended alderman.[10]

Not all miscreants were this fortunate. In 1551 Richard Clidero of York was bound over to the ward court for having 'behaved himself disobediently and unfittingly to Master John Lewis, one of the aldermen of this city [York], for that he would not avail his bonnet to him going by him in the street, but said he would not cap to such churls' and under examination said 'openly he called him churl and if he called him poller [extortioner] he had said but truth'.[11]

Many towns developed by annexing parishes and suburbs that long maintained separate identities. The early cities' governments were thus pastiches of separate jurisdictions. The first reference to a collective magistracy for Cologne city only came in 1149, by which time it was probably the largest city in Germany.[12] Through the twelfth century the private 'sokes' of London, many of them church but also some lay, exercised some jurisdiction. A more unified city administration appears from 1200. York still had at least 14 private sokes in 1300. Parishes and wards had their own governing bodies. Even after they were incorporated into the larger city, they or their subdivisions – or in some cases groups of parishes (such as quarters or sixths) – were used for tax assessment and militia duty. Many town councils were composed of representatives of geographical sectors of the town rather than or in addition to occupational groupings.

The Normans encouraged French colonisation in England, and in several cases, notably Shrewsbury, Hereford, Norwich and Nottingham, two separate boroughs, English and French, resulted.[13] Lords maintained seigniories within and adjacent to the town walls. City and bourg at Narbonne were only brought under a single jurisdiction in 1338; the two Carcassonnes remained distinct until 1789, the two Coventries until 1345. While most bishops yielded temporal power within the walls to town governments, monastic town lords more often resisted secular encroachments. The conflicts of the burgesses of St Albans and Bury St Edmunds with the local abbots are notorious.

The Beginnings of Urban Government: Italy

The development of city government was more precocious in Mediterranean Europe than in the north. While the more independent city governments in the north grew out of sworn associations of all inhabitants, which were only later extended to territories, territorial communities are specified in the earliest concessions of rights to such places as Genoa and Lucca. The absence in Italy of strong local lay powers, together with the early lay encroachment on the bishops' jurisdiction, meant that much happened *de facto* and that formal charters of liberties were less significant than in the north. The German emperor was the legal lord of some north Italian towns, but he was rarely present. The development by the larger Italian cities of dependent *contadi* owes more to seizure of the bishop's powers than of those of the emperor (see Chapter 2).

By the late eleventh century, government by a varying number of noble 'consuls' was spreading in the Italian cities. By the 1160s some cities had multiple boards of consuls, and some also had senates. There was no Italian equivalent of the merchant guilds that chose the city councils in some cities of northern Europe in the twelfth and thirteenth centuries, particularly England and Flanders; the Italian cities had separate officials, such as 'consuls of the merchants', to handle commercial questions. Nobles who had property and clients in both the city and its rural environs dominated Italian political life in the early twelfth century, and the consuls, as their officials, were resented.

Thus from the 1150s some city governments appointed a *podestà* ('power'), who was usually an outsider who could be impartial between the feuding lineages. He assumed the executive, military and administrative functions of the consuls, who were implicated in the factional struggles. The procedures for choosing the *podestà* were as agonisingly complicated as the later scrutinies for membership on the city councils, usually involving narrow standards for qualification and several elections. The *podestà* was a transitional figure in a sense. The regime of consuls and *podestà* declined in the early thirteenth century in favour of multiple councils with different functions, although the *podestà*'s position was not abolished. In Tuscany, but rarely elsewhere, a separate *popolo*, made up of persons of the upper middle class who were not magnates, emerged as a separate organisation that assumed many of the commune's powers in the course of factional fighting that lasted from the 1240s into the early fourteenth century. The wealth of most *popolani* came from trade, and their lineages were less ancient and distinguished than those of the magnates.

There is no north European equivalent of the *popolo*, whose name unfortunately has given rise to myths of government by 'the people'. As the *popolo* seized the most essential functions of the commune in Florence and its satellites, political participation by persons who were not *popolani*, notably magnates, was restricted or precluded. Many persons were simply branded as 'magnates' to give justification for exiling them, regardless of their lineage. Although the *popoli* were being organised internally by guild affiliation by the late thirteenth century, they began as military organisations in quarters of the cities. Their ultimate victory over the magnates was essentially the triumph of wealth over lineage as the essential criterion of public participation. Yet even this broad distinction must be qualified, for *popolani* were often as wealthy as magnates, had rural property, fought on horseback – the leader of the *popolo* was generally called its 'captain' – and over time lineage became as important in the *popolo* as it had been for the magnates earlier.[14]

The situation continued in the late thirteenth century and afterwards, to be complicated by family feuds and by conflicts between factions, such as the famous wars between the Guelfs, who favoured the nominal lordship of the pope over the city, and the Ghibellines, who preferred the distant emperor. These 'parties' were based on extended families that founded their power on maintaining clienteles of retainers in particular quarters of the city and around family towers, just as the magnates had done. In Florence the Guelf party and its organs became a kind of secret police in the late thirteenth century; branding an opponent as Ghibelline was as sure to destroy him as calling him a magnate. The party had such financial strength that it was loaning money to the commune by 1277.[15]

Membership of the Italian city councils was theoretically broader than in the north, for geographical sectors of the city furnished representatives, rather than merchant guilds or lineages. But there are two major distinctions between city governments in Italy and the north: first, there is no northern equivalent of the Italian *popolo*, although vendettas are found everywhere. Second, and in part because component districts of the cities were stronger than in the north, and because the *popolo* became a sort of state within the state, paralleling and sometimes supplanting the formal government of the city, bureaucracy proliferated in Italy. Even as early as the thirteenth century the Italian cities were over-regulated and developed bureaucracies of a size and overlapping competences that few northern cities would attain even in the modern period. While the northern city governments were so understaffed that many could not fulfil the functions of regulation and peacekeeping that were expected of them, the Italians simply added council to council, resulting in paralysing inefficiency and venality.

The example of Perugia is typical: in the mid-thirteenth century there were three councils for the entire city, of 50, 100 and 500 members, each with an equal number of members from the five districts of the city; the council of 50 of the previous six months continued to serve; the *popolo* had a 200-member council, and the guild rectors and military companies had their own organisations. Membership had to be divided equally among *popolani* and magnates, and between city and suburbs, although most power was exercised by the officials of the *popolo*.[16] Particularly given the rapidity of rotation of magistracies – every six months at Perugia, every two months at Florence – this system gave the opportunity for public service to far more persons than were accommodated under the city regimes of the north. But it was also grossly inefficient, and rivalries between the different corporations that constituted the city, when added to the combustibility of family vendettas, caused endemic disorder.

The Changes of the Late Middle Ages

Europe began a period of major economic and political change in the last quarter of the thirteenth century. Before 1370 the essential institutions of urban government were in place that would remain nearly everywhere into the sixteenth century. Max Weber saw this as a transition from the 'patrician' city, dominated by magnates and merchant-landowners, to the 'plebeian' city, dominated by the *popolo* or similar organisations in Italy and by aristocratic and lineage-conscious guildsmen in the north, but never to the complete exclusion of the urban nobility. Recent work has generally seen this contrast as too stark but has substantially validated the family basis of urban government that it suggests.[17]

In the early thirteenth century the Great Council, with a membership of about 400, was the most powerful organ of Venice. It was a court and legislature, and chose the members of other councils. The most famous event in the city's constitutional development was the *Serrata* (closing) of this Council in 1297. It added enough new members to double its size. A few new members were added until 1323, when membership was made hereditary, and another 30 families in 1381. Venice was unusual in two respects: its oligarchy was a legally closed class until the mid-seventeenth century, but it included so many people that it was actually a larger group than the less formally defined elites of most other cities, particularly when the depopulations after 1348 made the Venetian oligarchy into a larger percentage of a reduced population.[18]

Broadly similar patterns emerge elsewhere. By 1293 the *popolo* ruled Florence. Thereafter a council of six priors ruled the city, one for each district, but they were now chosen also on the basis of guild affiliation: the seven 'greater', five 'middle' and nine 'lesser' guilds were represented; and since the priors were rotated every two months, power could be shared. Any election that did not produce the requisite representation on the priorate for any of these groups would be reheld.[19] The combination of professional and geographical requirements was common but not universal in Italy.

The choice of city councils continued to be cumbersome. At Florence 36 priors were chosen each year, and after their eligibility was verified in a 'scrutiny', their names were placed in a bag, and six were drawn every two months. Despite the rotation requirement, the wealthier guilds in fact continued to hold

99

most seats. Magnates were placed under severe civil disabilities, although the draconian measures taken against them at Florence were not replicated even elsewhere in Tuscany. But factional struggles continued, and from 1328 anyone approved for election by the scrutiny of that year became eligible in perpetuity. Later scrutinies could add names but not delete them except for cause. The scrutinies were enlarged after 1343, and by 1378 the Florentine elite consisted largely of persons whose families had not held office before 1348. The scrutiny was handled, with veto power over individuals' names, by the incumbent town government, who by now were called the *Signoria*, consisting of the priors and the captain of the *popolo*, the captains of the Guelf party, and officials of the local merchants' organisation, the *Mercanzia*.

Italian city government in the fourteenth century became an exercise in paranoid ineffectuality. Oligarchical though it was, the machinery of government prevented anyone from doing anything controversial short of an armed revolution. Siena is a good example. Between 1287 and 1355 the city was ruled by The Nine (the priors). The General Council of the Commune, called the Council of the Bell, consisted of 100 members from each of the city's three districts, but only half had to be members of the *popolo*. The Nine served for two-month terms, three per district. They were chosen by a complex electoral procedure, but half of the identifiable members of the Council of the Bell served on The Nine at some point. They had to be 30 years old or more, have been citizens for ten years, and out of office for a year between terms, and they could not be on the same Nine with business partners or close kin. During their terms they lived in the town hall, away from their families, and they could make no ordinances without the consent of two-thirds of the Council of the Bell. Finances were under a separate office, the Biccherna, which was outside the control of the Nine. Rotation guaranteed that the oligarchy was less tight than it appeared at first glance, and procedures were so cumbersome that only measures that attracted a broad consensus could be adopted.[20]

The municipal oligarchies in the Low Countries and northern France were opened up somewhat in the late thirteenth and fourteenth centuries. The Flemish struggles were played out against a backdrop of national conflict with the French that resulted in party formations (Claws, whose symbol was the Flemish lion, and pro-French Lilies) that are reminiscent of the Guelf–Ghibelline rivalry in Tuscany. Insurrections had led by 1302 to changes of regime in the major Flemish cities: two or more councils of *scabini* (*schepenen*) with distinct functions emerged, rotating annually, and membership was opened to craftsmen. But only in 1360 did the artisan guilds of the Flemish cities obtain a guaranteed right to certain seats on the councils. At Ghent, for example, the councils had 13 members each, but the weavers were guaranteed five seats per bench and the *poorters* (landowners) three. The other five were reserved for members of the 53 'small guilds', which were divided into groups for purposes of election.

While the old merchant guilds were dissolved on the continent, they continued to dominate most city councils in England. Wealth in long-distance trade remained the avenue to political power. Even when people who were nominally craftsmen served on city councils, they were generally the merchants within the craft, for example leather purveyors rather than people who actually made shoes. With the conspicuous exception of York, it was unusual for craft guilds to have corporate representation guaranteed on English town councils in the late Middle Ages, although individual wealthy craftsmen might serve. Most larger English towns had a single mayor's council by the thirteenth century, but in the fourteenth many added a second or 'Common' Council, often twice the size of the earlier one, which now became known as the 'Council of Aldermen'. The 26 member Court of Aldermen, chosen by ward, led the government of London, but the Common Council eventually took over the financial administration. It had grown to 200 members by the sixteenth century, by which time it was joined by a 'Common Hall' of several thousand members representing the liveried companies.[21]

In Germany also the ruling oligarchies were dominated by merchants who were members of nominally craft guilds. Municipal oligarchies in Germany faced less serious challenges than those of the Low Countries and Italy, perhaps because even at an early period they were more inclined to admit to the councils such 'craftsmen' as goldsmiths, who dealt in luxuries. The number of politically empowered guilds was generally smaller than in the Low Countries, but internally the guilds were more complex. The trades were sometimes divided into greater crafts, where merchants dominated, and lesser or common guilds, which had a stronger artisan element. Particularly in the Rhineland, the older elites were dominated by the descendants of the bishop's officials, particularly those who controlled his mint, and those who rendered military service on horseback, called the 'constabulary' in some patrician regimes. The city councils thus divided membership among the lineages (the old patrician families whose basis of power was landholding and service to the town lord), and the guilds, which were dominated by merchants but included artisans.

There was no serious challenge to the urban patriciates in France until the mid-thirteenth century. The consular form of government is found in the cities of southern France from the late 1120s and is associated with the development of a tradition there of written Roman law. The urban councils of the Midi had a large proportion of nobles, but merchants were entering the city governments in the thirteenth century, as trade gradually replaced rent as the most significant generator of urban capital. There is a perceptible regional difference: southern French cities had a stronger noble element – at Toulouse nearly a quarter of the *capitouls* (consuls) who served between 1380 and 1420 were nobles – while the northern towns were ruled by merchant patricians of relatively recent lineage who tried to imitate the nobles by acquiring rural land.[22]

The guilds thus entered urban political life in the French Midi between the mid-thirteenth century and around 1330, as in the north and Germany. But the politically recognised guilds did not include large numbers of persons, and the franchise was narrowed still further in the late fourteenth century, encouraged by the royal government. The seven consuls of Montpellier were reduced to six in 1393. When the consuls were rotated out in 1410, they claimed that there were no longer enough qualified men for the office. They thus agreed to give four of the six consular 'hats' to moneychangers, drapers, long-distance merchants and other purveyors of luxury goods, while two were reserved for the lesser guilds. Similar groupings are found in other cities. In cities with a strong lord the occupational guilds were actually his agents in ruling the city, punishing industrial infractions and in some cases criminal activity by their members. Paris is a superb example: the *Livre des Métiers* compiled in the 1260s includes the statutes of 102 craft organisations, but the crafts were strictly regulated by the crown and were never guaranteed seats in the city government.[23]

In northern Europe obsolete organs of government were usually abolished as new ones were established, except for the councils based on lineage and/or service to the town lord. In Italy, by contrast, the older councils were deprived of power but were retained. Given the large number of councils for which rotation was required in Italy, far more persons served in city government there than in the north, where municipal officeholding was accompanied by real responsibilities. Even the impotent offices became sources of patronage for families such as the Medici, for officeholding conveyed social prestige. Furthermore, most major public charges were salaried in Italy, while service on city councils in northern Europe was generally unremunerated until the fifteenth century. In Venice, given the large size of the nobility and thus the disparities of wealth within that class, by the fifteenth century some poorer nobles actually were relying on appointment to city offices to support themselves. Venetian patricians were eligible for membership on the Council and for about 800 other government positions. They monopolised political power, but some noble families were relatively poor and could not compete in the necessary displays of opulence. Since both elections and officeholding required expenditure from one's own funds, as was common in pre-modern government, the top group within the nobility held most posts and distributed the rest to their clients.[24]

In the north the disorders of the Hundred Years War led to the weakening of some older merchant lineages. New families often came from the environs of the towns into which they migrated, for example the Najac family of Toulouse and the more famous German case of the Fuggers of Graben-in-Schwaben and Augsburg.[25] But biological failure did not happen everywhere. The Hanse cities of the German north and east generally had a single council, dominated by patrician lineages whose wealth came from long-distance trade. Guild regimes were short-lived there. Farther south, the patriciate of Nuremberg was the most successful of northern Europe in keeping unchallenged power after 1370. Guild regimes were more successful elsewhere, particularly in the southwest, although they were not able to exclude the lineages until the fifteenth century, and even then mainly in cities where so many families had died out in the male line that they were unable to fill the offices to which they were entitled. An *Ammeister*, representing the guilds, sometimes replaced the burgomasters or took real power from them. In towns where the lord remained strong, guild regimes did not come to power or lasted only briefly. Given the domination of most artisan guilds by merchants and the place reserved even under guild regimes for older lineages – as many as half the places on many city councils and even more often the burgomastership – these regimes were anything but 'democratic'.[26] Christoph Scheurl in 1516 commented approvingly on the control of the government of Nuremberg by 42 leading families whose ancestors had been in the government since the earliest days, a group endowed by God with 'special wisdom': 'we admit no one into our Council ... whose parents and grandparents did not also sit in the council'. Five years later Nuremberg issued a Dance Law (dances in the town hall were important social occasions where deals were struck and marriages arranged) that named 43 families who, with their male descendants, could be invited to the dances.[27]

Thus the oligarchies governing the northern cities ossified. Several English towns (Colchester in 1430, Leicester, Northampton and York in 1489) restricted the electorate in view of recent disorders.[28] As mastership in guilds became increasingly a matter of employing journeymen and less of actual craftsmanship, and as the guild masters, particularly in the mercantile and more skilled artisan trades, tried to preserve their positions by restricting the admission of persons not related to an incumbent master, officeholding tended to run as strongly in guild as in patrician families. Surveys in several cities show remarkable similarity: the further into the fifteenth century one goes, the larger the percentage of persons and families who (or whose members) served repeatedly in the magistracy, and the larger the number of offices that they held. The rotation requirement simply meant that political families had to consolidate their domination by holding different offices.

The urban rebellions of late medieval Europe are well known. Richard Bonney's typology works nicely: food riots, riots against outsiders, riots resulting from faction rivalry, tax riots and major political rebellions.[29] The fact that he developed it in reference to the cities of the sixteenth century adds weight to the thesis that the 'modern' period forms no caesura in urban development. The cities had serious internal problems, but the most dangerous rebellions – the endemic Flemish revolts of 1323–8, 1338–49, 1379–85, 1438 and 1451–3; the revolt of Étienne Marcel at Paris in 1358; the urban rebellions in France 1380–3; the disorders at London in the 1380s that included but were not limited to the Peasants' Rebellion of 1381 – were not primarily disputes over internal issues in the cities. Rather, they concerned a policy of the prince, most often high taxation but occasionally a commercial matter, when the city authorities felt that one of their cherished privileges had been violated. The major exception is the Ciompi rebellion of Florence of 1378, which pitted the wool carders and their supporters against their employers. Although the Ciompi initially broadened the Florentine magistracy from 21 to 24 guilds, their experiment was over by 1382. *Balie* (commissions with extraordinary powers) were superimposed over the older councils. After several decades of even tighter aristocratic rule, the Medici assumed power in 1434. In Italy, interestingly, high taxes were municipally rather than regionally imposed, but they never gave rise to serious rebellion. The Biga–Busca conflicts in Barcelona between 1433 and 1462 have been interpreted as socially based but were actually more in the tradition of old versus new patriciates.[30]

103

Except in Germany, most rebellions led to more onerous princely restrictions on city governments rather than to greater independence, and least of all to increased participation by the middle and lower classes. The kings made sure that the city government of London was staffed with docile merchants who were ready to lend money to the crown. When sworn guilds entered some urban magistracies in Languedoc, they did so as agents of the prince to increase control, in the Parisian tradition, not as representatives of occupational constituencies. After the tax revolts of 1380–3 most French cities were governed by even tighter oligarchies than before, with a stronger element of lawyers and officeholders and a correspondingly diminished role for merchants. Royal *élus*, who began as financial officials in the late 1350s, gradually became linchpins of local administration. Yet the old elites were so corrupt that most French townspeople seem to have welcomed increased royal control.

The Birth of Public Administration in the Cities

Perhaps because the fundamental principles behind urban government were not challenged seriously, city administration became considerably more sophisticated in the fourteenth and fifteenth centuries. Councils generally had the right to legislate for their own citizens and territory, including a 'ban mile' outside the walls except in England, although in Germany in particular the laws of one council would have to be confirmed by its successor. Roman law and the medieval commentators favoured giving *universitates*, places with a corporate existence, the right to legislate for themselves, subject to confirmation by the prince, to whom a comprehensive legislative power was reserved. Sometimes a specific right to legislate was granted, as when Peter II of Aragon in 1204 gave to the consuls of Montpellier 'full power to legislate customs', although liberty to this extent was highly unusual. Most cities had jurisdiction over streets, markets, the walls, bridges and police matters, including industrial and trade regulations. Laws were commonly promulgated orally ('cried') in an assembly or from a balcony of the town hall. This practice persisted into the seventeenth century.[31]

The rise of despots (*signori*) to power is a central fact of public life in the cities of late medieval Italy. The lords of such smaller places as Mantua had never yielded to the kind of communal institutions associated with Florence, although in some, notably Ferrara and Verona, the eventual town lord began his rise as captain of the *popolo*. Factional struggles were the most intense in Europe, perhaps because of the absence of meaningful overlordship for the larger cities. Enemies were one's neighbours. Just as *podestà* had been imported to mediate between magnates and *popolani* in the late twelfth and thirteenth centuries, so in the fourteenth and fifteenth 'captains' were used to try to restore order between competing factions of *popolani*.

Even in the late thirteenth century local nobles began to usurp the functions of city councils, or more often simply gained control of electoral machinery and staffed the councils with their own people. The Visconti family, whose name betrays their origin as viscounts of the archbishop, were lords of Milan between 1277 and 1450. The most powerful Visconti, Giangaleazzo, also ruled Pavia and was designated duke of Milan in 1395 by the emperor. Probably only his premature death in 1402 prevented extension of his power into Tuscany. Typically, he preserved most of the old institutions in his cities – he did take sole control of finances – while controlling who actually held office. The last Visconti, Filippo Maria, was succeeded by his son-in-law, Francesco Sforza, whose descendants held power until they were toppled by the French invasion of 1494.

The Medici takeover of Florence is the most celebrated. The great families of Florence vied for power after 1382, building clienteles. The Albizzi initially seemed the most likely to achieve control, but dissatisfaction over the conduct of Florence's war with Milan, combined with complaints of rigged tax assessments, gave the Medici their opportunity. By 1434 Cosimo dei Medici controlled the major offices of Florence and had banished the Albizzi. He manipulated the scrutinies, used *balie*, rewarded his clients great and small with offices and loans, and perfected the art of behind-the-scenes manipulation to subvert the institutions of the commune. Even kings probably had less *de facto* control over their cities than Cosimo dei Medici and Francesco Sforza had over Florence and Milan. Much less obtrusive in his rule than Sforza, Cosimo seems to have been genuinely popular. He was succeeded by his son, grandson (the famous Lorenzo the Magnificent) and great-grandson, who was ejected by the French in 1494. The Medici returned in 1512 and eventually became grand dukes of Tuscany.

The pre-modern cities developed permanent bureaucracies and police forces. Only for England can a case be made that the royal government was more effective than city administrations, and techniques developed by the cities in the Low Countries, particularly in finance, were adopted by the regional governments, not vice versa. Virtually all cities were transacting their most important business in writing by 1300. Permanent records such as accounts and the proceedings of the councils were being kept in registers that gave succeeding governments a basis for action: for example, the tax assessment did not have to be entirely redone for each collection. Thus from the fourteenth century we have more information about how the city governments under councils actually functioned.

Such an achievement was carried through despite formidable obstacles. Even in towns whose lords retained little direct political power, the city governments did not control all territory within the walls. The castle of the prince or the residence of his official remained outside the town's competence. This was particularly important in the French towns, whose royal-bureaucratic element was a more important component of the municipal elite than elsewhere. The incorporation of suburbs left substantial territories outside. The territory of Ghent was complete after annexations around 1300, but two abbey villages remained independent, across bridges from the city. That of St Peter was a special problem, for it housed the largest concentration of the turbulent weavers. The city authorities could not pursue a suspected malefactor into the abbey village, nor could they enforce in St Peter debts that had been contracted in Ghent.

The churches held enormous amounts of urban real estate. In Canterbury this accounted for nearly two-fifths of the rent income in the city in the late fourteenth century, three-fifths in Gloucester in 1455, and 62 per cent in Oxford in 1312, although Oxford's figure was inflated by the university. Church properties, including both buildings and their environs such as cemeteries, were immunities where the city officials had no control. Churchyards were used as refuges by persons fleeing the law. The properties of the provost of St Donatian housed the largest concentration of prostitutes in late medieval Bruges. The church was adamant about its rights to give sanctuary. In 1386 the church excommunicated the bailiff of Ypres for seizing three murderers in a church. Although London limited felons to 40 days' grace in the churches, authorities in England always resented the immunity exercised in the bishop's close, which was often locked at night and thus barred access between parts of the city. The older organic towns had numerous small parishes – London, Lincoln, Norwich, York and Winchester had 110, 46, 61, 45 and 54 respectively – and this multiplied the number of places where malefactors could seek sanctuary.[32]

Although even in the quasi-independent Flemish towns the prince's bailiff handled much criminal prosecution and all capital cases, and the royal role in the English and French towns was even stronger. Once in place the councils could generally count on being able to fulfil their functions. In violation of modern notions of separation of powers, however, the governing organs of the premodern cities had overlapping spheres of competence, and this situation does not seem to have bothered anyone. In places with more than one council and where the electoral basis of the two was different, the older body tended to become ceremonial, although great prestige was attached to it, since lineage was usually the essential criterion for membership. In nominally craft regimes, guilds that were more oriented toward merchandising normally held more seats than did the artisan trades. Some larger cities, particularly in Germany, experienced disturbances over the composition of the city council, but in most cases these simply pitted new money against old. Furthermore, these conflicts pale in number and intensity beside disorders that were occasioned by taxation.

Discerning the normal operations of city government is rendered more difficult by the absence of clear lines between public and private. The operation of parallel governments of commune and *popolo* in Italy is the most conspicuous case, but some of the apparent difference between Italy and the north in terms of size of bureaucracy and weight of control by the city government is due to the reliance of northern city councils on such regulatory agents as guilds, parish magistrates and other unpaid officials who do not appear in the municipal accounts since their services were unremunerated. Parallel royal and municipal administrations in France and England must also be factored in.

Members of the council rotated duties, and usually a delegation of two or more sat at all times in the town hall to handle business. Finances were often separated from the council and entrusted to professional bureaucrats who did not lose office when the council changed. Cities employed attorneys, recorders, procurators or syndics both to handle (or give advice to the council on) important legal actions, usually as arbitrators among different authorities who were competing for jurisdiction, and to transact the city's business with foreign powers, such as other cities, the king or the pope. The larger towns had these officials in the fourteenth century, and virtually all had them in the fifteenth.[33]

City Finances

As is true of governments generally, pre-modern city councils were more adept at spending money than at raising it. Kings were expected to 'live of their own' and finance ordinary administration from domain revenues and 'regalian' (belonging only to the king) rights such as tolls and judicial fines. During peacetime a national government could survive for years without asking for taxes.

City governments did not have this luxury, for on them fell the necessity of enforcing order locally. Citizens could petition councils on matters public and private. Some problems of modern cities were not major concerns of their ancestors, but they handled most civil litigation, maintained streets and bridges, promulgated industrial regulations (usually in consultation with the guild concerned) and controlled trade. They dispensed charity to churches and almshouses. Some city councils administered the property of orphans. In France and England they paid large sums annually to the crown. They thus had continuing expenses, receiving and disbursing money on a more systematic basis than did royal governments, and they needed to have some idea in advance of their incomes. Yet only during the thirteenth century did many cities of northern Europe develop a tax base, and then in response to mounting debt.[34]

Some French and German towns used direct taxation, but most preferred indirect levies. In the early thirteenth century many began to levy excise duties on goods passing through the city gates, both imports and exports, and these rapidly became their major source of income. Excises were generally not collected directly by the city government but rather were 'farmed' to syndicates of persons, usually citizens of the town, who paid the government a lump sum for the right to collect the tax. Leasing the excises at the beginning of the fiscal year gave the city government a basic fund of money that it knew that it could spend, a primitive budget.

Taxation, however, required the prince's permission, and this came in return for a large fee. Furthermore, particularly after local rulers began auditing their cities' accounts in the thirteenth century, it became customary for the city governments to make 'presents' to the prince and various persons in his household, often of costly gold or silver items. As disorders mounted in the late Middle Ages, the city governments thus had to defend themselves with little aid from their rulers, and enforce the lords' often unpopular regulations with inadequate funds. The city governments incurred the expenses, but the ruler kept the incomes.

Thus the cities pioneered techniques of borrowing, some of which were later taken over by territorial governments. Government was a personal affair: city councillors were expected to spend their own funds on governmental projects, and when this did not suffice, to borrow. A major scandal erupted in Flanders in the late thirteenth century from the huge debts that city governments owed to the bankers of Arras. Arras itself collected a direct tax that in 1289 provided 84 per cent of the city's income.[35] After punishing the guilty parties for corruption, the Flemish counts granted the cities the right to levy excises at the gates. Some cities also began selling annuity rents, which amounted to primitive bond issues. The life annuity was an annual payment during the buyer's life, for which he or she gave the city government a lump sum, generally a multiple of the face value of the annuity. Perpetual annuities, which cost more and were inherited by the descendants of the purchaser, were somewhat less common.

Italian city finances were hurt by the constant turmoil and by the plurality of corporate groups that could legitimately claim to represent the city or a substantial part of its citizenry. Until the early thirteenth century some cities collected the direct tax that was theoretically owed to the emperor. Some north Italian towns also used the *estimo*, a proportional tax on property based on the sworn oral declaration of the taxpayer. City governments also exacted voluntary and forced loans from their wealthier citizens. The cities also taxed their *contadi*, often at punitive levels. But while Italian cities got most of their income from direct taxes, they also collected excises at the gates, as the northerners did. The Italian cities also borrowed heavily a century earlier than the northern towns had to. The *popoli*, other societies and the administrative districts of the city also had their own incomes and accounts, and the city government borrowed from them and at times required them to take responsibility for maintaining public works and buildings (see Chapter 6).[36]

The proliferation of magistracies in the Italian cities was accompanied by the use of more up-to-date techniques of accounting than were used in the north, but it is virtually impossible to derive an overall financial balance, since so much evidence either does not survive or was deliberately omitted. While the northern cities usually presented a single account for audit, Pisa had at least eight public treasuries. The amount of city expenditure grew enormously in the thirteenth century and continued to rise in the fourteenth, despite population decline. As the tax burden became insupportable, some cities tried to shift the tax load to the environs; but this simply depressed the *contado* and forced the cities to rely even more on agricultural imports from more distant places. Orvieto and later Florence even devised a version of the modern value-added tax, levying taxes at various stages on the transformations of grain as it was produced in the *contado* and made its way to the baker's oven.

Except in England, where most city income still came from market and industrial infractions, land rents and entry fees to the merchant guild or the freedom of the city, municipal finance and taxation became quite sophisticated in the late Middle Ages. Direct taxes tended to place the wealthier taxpayers at a relative disadvantage, and thus in the Low Countries and France most city governments continued to prefer indirect taxes, particularly excises. In France this was complicated by the increased reliance of the royal government after 1360 on indirect *aides*. The city governments often collected them, then kept the surplus over what they owed the crown. Direct taxes remained unusual in the north except in Germany, but even there many cities did not use them, preferring the excises that were the norm elsewhere. In virtually all cities where direct taxes were collected, assessment was done by written declaration rather than oral, but in Germany the assessors had to accept the oath of the taxpayer unless they had some reason to be suspicious. The Italian cities maintained tax assessors who compiled the registers themselves, although on the basis of information provided by the taxpayer. The city governments categorised their populations by wealth level. There was some variation about what kind of wealth was counted, but most cities used land, income, annuity rents and movable property, although taxing them at different rates. The upper income levels paid a higher percentage in tax than the middle classes, and the poorest were generally exempted altogether.

While in the thirteenth century much of the problem had been the lack of an adequate tax base, after 1300 city finances became much more conservative, and governments had enough revenue to cover their needs in ordinary years. Their expenses included ambitious programs of public works that helped make them attractive to immigrants; what village had walls or paved streets, permanent bridges or canals? City governments also engaged in conspicuous consumption that raised their costs.

The wars of princes, however, were the downfall of municipal solvency. Cities that were exposed to war had an enormous burden of maintaining the walls. The princes, enmired in feuds in which the cities were not directly involved, made inordinate demands on them for gifts and loans. The Italian cities were still maintaining their own armies into the sixteenth century, as well as elaborate fortifications.[37] Many cities of the Low Countries and northern France, caught in the rivalry of the French kings and the dukes of Burgundy, had debts by the mid-fifteenth century that were much larger than their normal annual income. As counts of Flanders, the dukes of Burgundy first took a large annual aid from the cities for permission to collect the excises, then from 1407 in Bruges and later elsewhere took instead one-seventh of the city's income from the excises. Other 'donations' were exacted from individual cities.[38] Thus excise rates were raised, including those on food. Some cities even established municipal lotteries. The cities were increasingly forced to sell annuity rents to their own citizens, and city governments sold one another's rents. At Lille the difference between solvency and debt was the prince. While the burden of taxes and loans combined multiplied nearly ninefold between 1510 and 1560, tax receipts only slightly more than doubled. Thus the city had to sell massive annuities, generally when the princes' demands were heaviest. Taxes and other sources of municipal income were normally sufficient to meet the local needs of government, but the imperatives of the central government threw the cities into crisis.[39]

Most Italian cities handled indirect taxes like the northerners, including the use of tax farmers, although in Italy the cities increasingly took over direct administration of the excises after 1350. When it came to direct taxation, however, the Italian cities were much more sophisticated. In contrast to the excises, direct taxes were not levied annually. Thus, as their expenses exceeded the revenues of the indirect taxes, city governments would try to meet their debt with a direct tax, which was considered a payment for emergencies rather than an ordinary source of revenue. But the assessment mechanism, based largely on what assets the taxpayer could not conceal, was primitive, and direct taxes were disliked by the wealthier citizens, whose hostility could hurt the city government most. The most famous direct tax levied by an Italian city in the Middle Ages is the *catasto* of Florence, first used in 1427 and established permanently in 1458. The system was similar to the modern income tax. The head of the household declared his assets. The family residence and personal furnishings were exempt, and the taxpayer received personal exemptions for himself, his wife and his minor children living at home. All forms of income were taxed, including rents and shares of the public debt. Thus

Assets of Conte di Giovanni Compagni. . . .

A house with furnishing which I inhabit, located in the parish of S. Trinita on the street of the Lungarno, 0 [not taxable].
A house in the parish of S. Trinita on the street of the Lungarno . . . which is rented to Niccolò and Tommaso Soderini for 24 florins per year, [capitalized] at 7 percent, 342–17–2 . . . .
One-half of two-thirds of some shops in the palace of the Aretti of Pisa . . . .
My share [of the rent] is 28 florins per year, more or less . . . . 400–0–0. . . .
He [Conte] has invested in a shop of the Lana [woollen cloth manufacturers] guild in the company of Michele di Benedetto di Ser Michele, the sum of 2000–0–0.[40]

Like their northern counterparts, the Italian cities had crushing debts. However, in contrast to the haphazard approach of the former, the Italians pioneered the funded public debt that was paid off through investments. At Genoa the various debts of the city were brought together in a municipal bank, the Casa di San Giorgio, in 1407. Florence established a public debt (*Monte*) in 1345, which combined the various obligations of the city into a single fund that paid 5 per cent interest. *Monte* shares were traded, and fathers of girls invested in them, for if they were bought when the child was born, they could yield a dowry at her maturity. They were an intelligent investment, for *monte* shares realised an annual average of 10–15 per cent, as opposed to 8–10 per cent for commercial enterprises and 5–7 per cent for land.[41]

Changes in the Sixteenth and Seventeenth Centuries

Changes in urban government in the two centuries after 1500 were matters of degree rather than the fundamental alteration of institutions. City councils became still more oligarchical, becoming virtually closed to all but the wealthiest by the seventeenth century. This usually happened by decoupling guild affiliation from eligibility requirements for the city council, although guildsmen could still serve as individuals. The emperor Charles V (ruled 1519–56) tried to deprive the guilds of their corporate political roles throughout his domains, although he had no objection to them as occupational associations. When possible his representative simply appointed the city councils, as he did at Utrecht in 1528 and at Ghent in 1540. In 1552 Charles ended the practice at Nördlingen of 12 guilds naming one city councillor each and the patricians the other 12 by abolishing the guilds outright. He substituted a council of 15 who chose their own successors. The councillors thus both were wealthy and had a family tie to the previous ruling body. Most Dutch city councils were chosen by the *vroedschap*, a group whose members served for life and co-opted their successors. Even Amsterdam, which had one of the most open elites in the early seventeenth century, saw an increasing number of rentiers on the council after 1650.[42]

The guilds thus reverted to something closer to their early functions of industrial regulation and charity. Guild membership had not always been connected to practising the trade even in the Middle Ages, and now that tenuous link was being lost. In places that still required guild membership for seats on the town council, some aristocrats joined poor guilds, such as fishermen and gardeners, assuming that mere artisans could never afford the time away from work to sit on the council.[43]

Apart from loyalty to the prince, the requirements for membership on city councils continued to be ancestry, wealth and landholding. The merchant element remained strong but, particularly in France, many city posts were staffed by royal officials and lawyers. Tax assessments show that the Parisian elite by 1571 was dominated by courtiers and bureaucrats, with financiers, medical doctors, barristers, notaries and (at the bottom of the elite tax list) merchant drapers. Lyon had more merchants, although even there the lawyers had high prestige and occupied numerous offices. Lille's patriciate was still dominated by merchants. Crafts there never had corporate representation on the council, and the informal policy of excluding Protestants in the sixteenth century contributed to narrowing participation. There was enough rotation, even in the inner circle, to ensure some new blood; two families that became very prominent in the late sixteenth and early seventeenth centuries first served in the government in the 1540s.[44]

However much modern democratic sensibilities are offended by restrictions of the franchise, that does not always translate into bad government. First, oligarchy cannot be equated with plutocracy. Most persons who held municipal offices in Ghent in the 1490s and lived in the St Michael's ward were in the second and third of five ascending levels of tax liability. Some of the wealthiest taxpayers were nobles who were simply not interested in city government. Prestige was not entirely a matter of wealth, but also adhered to 'solid, middle-class' persons.[45]

Second, although the urban oligarchies were undeniably narrow, they did not always rule coercively. Many English city leaders had a sense of community obligation and donated heavily to charity. Although the top levels of city administration were chosen from a small group, there was still considerable room for public participation in the wards and parishes and the liveried companies. While the aldermen of London chose their own successors, they did so from slates of candidates nominated by the freemen of the ward, and all taxpaying male householders could participate in other ward and parish business. As much as 10 per cent of London's male population held some public charge at this level in the early seventeenth century, and it was not purely a matter of giving them the appearance of importance without its substance. The aldermen of London did not have their own police force, and the militias of the companies defended the city during emergencies. They even sent members to oversee the food supply during periods of severe inflation when the city was trying to control prices.[46]

Most French cities were still governed in the seventeenth century by between three and six *échevins*, who rotated power, usually serving for one or two years. The boards of *échevins* had a rank order, and the first *échevin* was usually the mayor. A committee of *échevins* was usually on duty, as in the Middle Ages, but a formal meeting of the entire body was necessary for any important action to be taken. The council's main function was assessing and collecting taxes and negotiating with the royal government. The councils had a general competence in commercial and industrial regulations and enforcement, and they handled minor criminal infractions, but more potentially serious cases, and any that involved blood justice, went before the royal court in the city, which in turn was normally the chief town of its *bailliage* or *sénéchausée*.[47]

As in England, urban government in France was considerably less oligarchical at the parish level than at the top. At Paris the central government consisted of the *prévôt des marchands* (the *de facto* mayor) and four *échevins*, assisted by a council of 24 notables and 16 *quarteniers*, each of whom held office for life. Although the families of most *quarteniers* were still in commerce, they were quite well off; but those who reported to them, the *dizainiers* and *cinquanteniers*, were from an artisan milieu. After 1554 the *dizainiers* and *cinquanteniers* were forbidden to participate in city-wide elections; thus a split was developing between the upper levels, headquartered in the town hall, and the parish and quarter officials who were closer to the people whom they served. Similarly, the government of Rouen was a combination of city-wide and district representation: a Council of 24, actually of varying size, had six *conseillers-échevins*, all living ex-*conseillers-échevins*, one *quartenier* from each of the four quarters, six *pensionnaires*, the bailiff, and the royal officials attached to the *bailliage*. There was also a General Assembly for particularly important matters, which was actually attended by 100–200 persons. The Council of 24 served a three-year term, then was renewed by assemblies in the quarters nominating 12 men for the six general councillorships; the outgoing general councillors would then choose their successors from this slate. There was a regular 'course of offices', with younger members of the elite assuming less prestigious charges, then moving on to positions of greater responsibility. The only seriously contested election in the mid-sixteenth century was in 1566, at the height of the religious controversies. The city procurator, who managed negotiations with the crown, was chosen for life. There was a master of the public works. The parishes had their own officials as well, including treasurers and *centeniers* and *cinquanteniers* chosen by the council. These men were usually artisans who kept the authorities apprised of trouble and of the activities of transients.[48]

The *échevins* still had inadequate enforcement mechanisms and police power to enforce the unpopular measures that were decreed by the sovereign territorial state, and now had even more officials of the said state in the city watching over them. There were also competing sources of regulation, including governors of the *bailliage* of which the town was the centre, military commanders, courts, other royal officials and the church. In cities that had a *parlement*, the royal court became a new power broker in the sixteenth century. The *parlements* were issuing decrees by the second half of the century on most matters for which the city council had legislated earlier, including prices, wages, sanitation and poor relief. Meetings of the city council of Rouen thus diminished from an annual average attendance of 35 in the 1550s to 23 in the 1590s, and the agenda was often simply discussing how to accomplish what *Parlement* had ordered.[49]

The election and installation of major officers remained a highly ritualised affair. Decisions that had been made in private were formalised in lavish and usually symbolic public ceremonies. The electoral procedures used at Nantes were specified in a royal decree of 1598. The mayor and councillors submitted a slate of candidates to an assembly of eligible voters. The king personally chose the winner from the three who had the highest vote totals in the assembly. At Dijon the mayor chose the 20 members of the city council that would serve with him for his year in office. For other offices, nominations were made by members of the outgoing council and other notables. Voting – orally, not by secret ballot – was initially open to all householders, but in 1612 a property qualification was introduced that limited the franchise to several hundred.[50]

Given the extent of princely control, the question arises of what issues were contested in the elections. Public service was a sign of high status. It was generally not something that one did for personal advantage. Protestantism divided many cities, but municipal elections were not generally fought over political or economic programmes. In electorates that were always small and when councils were often co-opted to some degree, people whose virtue was recognised – which usually meant being from the right lineage – kept getting elected. Contests came from one group within the elite accusing another of graft, not over 'issues' in the modern sense of the term.

Yet the fact that local government was more open than appears on superficial examination shows that we are rarely dealing with closed elites. The patrician clubs of the late medieval German cities had an overriding preoccupation with heredity, and urban patriciates became even more concerned with defining their membership in the sixteenth century. But strict heredity made it impossible for the patrician lineages to fill all offices to which they were entitled. Thus some wealthy newcomers, mainly merchants and lawyers, were admitted, although the old lineages were much more prestigious and tried to keep themselves as exclusive as they could. The patriciates also increasingly included men from outside the town, often officials of the bishop or the territorial lord. Except in some port cities, the patricians increasingly became rentiers in both city and countryside, and in this way and through intermarriage moved toward the territorial nobility. The fact that Tuscany and Lombardy were basically extensions of Florence and Milan meant that the urban patriciate and territorial nobility were practically interchangeable. There was also a strong tendency for landed aristocracy and urban wealthy to merge in Spain, especially since the aristocrats controlled colonial trade. To some extent a vacuum was created by the withdrawal of members of the old patriciates to their rural estates; the offices were filled by officials, many of them lesser nobility, particularly those with legal training.[51]

Even at Venice, which had an unusually large but also closed elite from 1297, outsiders could buy nobility from 1646. Other north Italian cities compiled Golden Books on the Venetian model – Brescia in 1488, Genoa in 1528 and Padua in 1613 – but the practice of nobles staffing city office was so ingrained that most of them simply confirmed established practice. In some towns, such as Lübeck, older closed elite clubs co-existed with newer organisations that had less prestige but were still distinguished from commoners. Elites that were not defined by statute were technically open, but many unwritten rules and attitudes still kept them narrow. The most important differences were between elites whose economic basis of power remained relatively constant and those where it changed; and between those in which a mainly merchant elite kept control and those where merchants were replaced by lawyers, officeholders and rentiers.[52]

Thus an important change in the nature of the governing elites of the cities in the early modern period is linked to the quickening of the symbiosis of city and region that had begun in the Middle Ages. Urban elites virtually everywhere contained large numbers of nobles.[53] At Strasbourg in the sixteenth century, *Constofler*, all of them rentiers and most of them noble, held nearly one-third of the city offices and guildsmen the rest. But the guildsmen who participated in government at this level were also mainly rentiers, even including some noble guildsmen, wholesale merchants and goldsmiths. Genuine artisans held fewer than one-sixth of the major offices. The privileges of the *Constofler* were accepted by the guildsmen, who had ambitions to move into the top group. In practice, the share of the *Constofler* in the Great and Small Councils was usually filled by rotating 30–50 adult males. Their numbers increased somewhat after 1555, but until then there was no competition for offices among the patricians, because everyone who was eligible had to occupy one.[54]

The Urban Rebellions of Early Modern Europe

Violent conflicts in the cities seem to have become less serious in the early modern period than they were in the late Middle Ages. While most urban rebellions in the Middle Ages concerned princely taxation or violation of city privileges, religion was the main catalyst of disorder in the sixteenth century. The victory of Protestantism or Roman Catholicism was rarely accomplished peacefully.

Other conflicts involved outsiders, as at the famous carnival episode at Romans in 1579–80. The poor and vagrants were an element in petty crime but were rarely revolutionary.[55]

Religion, however, was an extremely volatile issue everywhere. In some German cities Lutheranism became a civic religion, as the municipal authorities simply took over the incomes – but in fairness also many of the duties – of the church: 'the church was added to the other elements of civic identity that characterized urban autonomy'. The new doctrine was often imposed from the top down, for the appeal of Lutheranism was much stronger to territorial princes and urban merchants and established guildsmen than to the peasants. Particularly in Switzerland and southern Germany, Lutheranism was a mainly urban movement. Most of the free imperial cities in Germany, which were concentrated in the south, recognised Protestantism at some point, although some later rejoined the Roman Catholics, and others that remained Roman Catholic granted toleration to Protestants.[56]

In France Calvinism became a major force in the 1550s, appealing mainly to merchants and lesser nobles. Most French cities saw ferocious internecine conflicts: in Troyes, Dijon and other cities, Protestants seized power at some point during the 1560s; but the zeal with which they obliterated religious images, combined with the fact that they were a small minority virtually everywhere, led inevitably to a quick resumption of Roman Catholic control, particularly after 1572.[57] The economic and social leaders of the cities generally followed the civic religion: thus they were Roman Catholic in France and Italy and Protestant in Germany and England. Except in places where a version of Protestantism became the state religion, the masses almost always remained Roman Catholic. Numerous exceptions exist to these generalisations, however. Religious conflict doubtless exacerbated social and economic tensions that were already present in many cities, but it appears rather endemic to the human psyche than a specifically urban phenomenon.

One reason for the relative quiet in the early modern cities may also be that while high levels of city taxation, and particularly allegations of rigged assessment, had occasioned problems in the late Middle Ages, taxation, although much higher now, was mainly national/regional. It is true that, particularly in France, local officials who were in charge of collecting taxes for the crown took the heat for what was not their responsibility. The tax revolt at Lyon in 1632 is an example. There was a large urban element in the *comuneros* agitation in Castile in 1520–1, particularly at Avila, where the elite initially supported the *comuneros*, then withdrew as they became more revolutionary. As was true of the great rebellions of the Middle Ages, both urban and rural elements were present. After 1521 the Iberian towns were generally peaceful. But in Germany and France the religious conflicts became endemic, in the first and second halves of the century respectively.

The English cities, with no tradition of independence, were the quietest of Europe. The French urban rebellions, like their rural counterparts, were directed against taxes or were bread riots, such as the 'Grand Rebeyne' of Lyon in 1529.

When bread prices rose after a bad harvest, and rumour spread that Italian spec-ulators had bought up the grain and exported it to Turin, mobs stormed the city granary and pillaged the houses of merchants. Order was quickly restored after the rebels made the mistake of leaving the city to check the grain reserves of a nearby monastery.[58]

Beginning with the La Rochelle revolt of 1627–8, the French rebellions assumed a more political context. Dijon saw rioting for a week in 1630 when the Estates of Burgundy were suppressed, but rumours of a new tax on wine were the immediate incitement. A vineyard worker called 'King Machas' led the rebellion in a virtual carnival atmosphere: it is called the 'Lanturelu' revolt after a popular song that the rebels sang to drumbeat. More serious rebellions occurred at Bordeaux in 1635 and again during the Fronde between 1648 and 1652. But national issues so dominated the Fronde that whether it was really an urban rebellion is problematical, for it was led by a group of notables who opposed the government of Cardinal Mazarin and the local *parlement*.[59] More specifically urban issues were involved in the rebellions of Palermo and Naples in 1647, following a harvest failure in 1646. The movement at Naples was led by a fishmonger, the charismatic 'Masaniello', who virtually ruled the city for ten days in the summer of 1647. But here too, high taxes and dynastic rivalries, in this case French intrigues to detach Naples from Spain, were incitements.[60]

The Prince and the *Populus*: City in State in Early Modern Europe[61]

The most obvious change in urban government during the sixteenth and seven-teenth centuries was the greater intrusion of territorial governments on urban autonomy. Yet this too was only a change of degree, for we have seen that town lords had always been quite powerful, even in Italy. The sovereignty doctrines of Roman law, situating ultimate authority with the prince, helped to erode muni-cipal liberties as Roman law spread as a coherent body of jurisprudence, first in the south, then in northern Europe in the fifteenth and sixteenth centuries. Most of the cities that were affected had written charters of liberties that went back to the eleventh or twelfth century. The newly codified law of the territorial state moved into the gaps not covered by these charters, which by now were very anti-quated. From a practical perspective this often did not mean much except for foreign relations; the old oligarchies continued to govern, and the regime of city councils was kept, but now they exercised a power expressly delegated from the town lord.[62] But the representatives of the territorial lords in the cities became much more intrusive everywhere in the sixteenth century.

Most English towns were royal by 1300. The rule of the Valois dukes of Bur-gundy in the Low Countries after 1384 meant a gradual termination of the long tradition of municipal independence there. After 1492 only Ghent attempted to defy the Spanish successors of the Burgundians. Royal control of the urban net-work in France was also of long-standing. Yet even there royal power over the cities expanded. Princes interfered with municipal elections; despite all the safe-guards, they sometimes announced the results in advance, quashed an election and appointed directly or ordered the election of specific candidates. Charles II of England revoked many borough charters after 1681, then reissued them with clauses giving the king the right to nominate town officials or veto nominations made locally. The French kings took advantage of the aftermath of the religious wars, when the number of *échevins* and eligibility requirements were changed in some places, and the Fronde of 1648–52, when the involvement of several towns compromised their bargaining positions. The government of Paris saw increasing intervention by the crown, decline of elections in favour of heredity and sale of offices, and growing social conflict.[63]

In the Middle Ages, when lords wanted something that under their charters the cities were not obligated to render, they had to bargain with the cities or face rebellions that, given the strength of the city walls, were hard to put down. But after 1500 most cities lacked the physical force to defy their princes. Their fortifi-cations gave them a certain defence, even against cannon, but city militias could not cope with the enormous mercenary armies of the kings. The cities probably suffered less from spectacular sacks than in the Middle Ages: the destruction of Rome in 1527 and of Antwerp in 1576 by the Spaniards and of Magdeburg by imperial troops in 1631 were unusual among the larger cities, but destruction was widespread in France during the religious wars, and the massacres perpe-trated in the Low Countries at Mechelen and Naarden were notorious.[64]

The changing role of the city in the early modern territorial state has given rise to simplistic typologies. Fernand Braudel has argued that the medieval city, which had concentrated commerce and later industry within its walls, was trans-formed into the rentier, consumer city of the early modern period, suggesting that the economic potential that some have ascribed to the earlier medieval city has been exaggerated. Yet neither princely control of urban institutions nor consu-mer cities in an economic sense were novelties of the period after 1500. Heinz Schilling has noted that schemes of ranking cities before 1650 have used mainly economic criteria, while thereafter the great cities were those with political privi-leges, which in turn fostered their economic growth.[65] But this overlooks the extent to which the economic importance of the greater medieval cities had been due to monopolies, rights and other privileges that had been conceded by princes, granted that in some cases they had been extracted by force.

Others hold that incorporation into the national state prevented the city from fulfilling its potential for political independence; thus the cities, through capitalism, had weakened the 'feudal' state, but were incorporated into its suc-cessor, the 'nation-state'. Charles Tilly and Wim Blockmans have argued that there was a conflict of interest between capitalists, whose pursuit of profit could not flourish under constraint, and centralising monarchies. But since the kings needed the money that was concentrated in cities, urban capitalism could only flourish in areas where central states were weak, which of course included many regions of medieval Europe. S. R. Epstein has rightly criticised this model, for in the Empire and to a lesser extent Italy and the southern Low Countries, cities that had been relatively independent in the Middle Ages became components of central states in the early modern period. In Sweden, Poland and Habsburg Castile, town development benefited from a centralised monarchy and its patronage. Much of the problem is probably how one defines town. The central states did promote new urban foundations, and they fostered rural industry; but they strictly limited the pretensions of the older large cities, specifically their claims to control their environs.[66]

The most politically independent cities in the Middle Ages were along the Mediterranean, Baltic and North Sea coasts. By 1700 the only relatively autonomous cities in these regions were Lübeck, Bremen, Hamburg, Genoa and Venice, and they were much less important economically than before. With the shift of economic power in the early modern period to the Atlantic, even the larger cities came under the increasing control of territorial states, not only of the national monarchies of the west, but of princes in Germany and city-based duchies such as Tuscany and Lombardy in Italy.[67]

We saw in Chapter 2 that urban regions did not correspond to political boundaries in the Middle Ages. But by 1700 they did. The development of the interregional economy under the aegis/domination of cities had created the economic base of modern states that now dominated the cities. But the fact that the cities lost political power was simply an adaptation to change of the environment. The economic functions of the urban sector as a whole were not adversely affected, although individual cities grew while others declined. Thus the development of the nation-state in the west, and of the territorial principality in Germany, was built on the regional foundation established earlier by the cities.

Chapter 5 . . . .

Social Structures and Infrastructures

The city-state (*polis*) originates so that man may live, but continues to exist that he may live well.[1]
(Aristotle)

The city was a large association or solidarity, consisting of numerous interlocking groups that were defined by neighbourhood of residence, occupation, educational level, status and lineage. In Chapters 1–2 we discussed how the economic nature of the city attracted immigrants and caused markets and hence jobs to diversify and expand. Chapter 3 discussed the physical layout of the urban environment and how space was utilised most effectively. Chapter 4 delineated the governing institutions that were developed in the cities to minimise interpersonal conflict. We shall now consider why towns were attractive as social centres: what non- or marginally-economic criteria caused people to move to a city and, once there, to remain?

Modern social class analysis is not useful for describing pre-modern urban populations. 'Classes' now are most often defined in economic or income-based terms, most broadly as upper, middle and lower classes. In pre-modern Europe 'status', which is more value-laden, is more satisfactory. Roland Mousnier has distinguished five bases for determining status: legal, social, economic, ideological and exercise of power. Prestige accrues to those who are closest to the centres of power or whose behaviour and functions most closely approximate to those of the powerful. Thus townspeople were disdained by writers in the twelfth century but not in the sixteenth, by which time wealthy urbanites were indistinguishable in many places from nobles, soldiering had lost its social prestige, and burgesses, at least in the west, were heavily involved in government through positions in administration and participation in representative assemblies. Max Weber distinguished social groups in terms of their relations to the market. Highest status was enjoyed by the property owner who had goods that could be sold or accumulated, as he wished. Less respect was given to persons who had goods or skills but who had to sell them in order to survive. Persons who had no property but could

119

perform manual labour formed the base of the social pyramid. Terms denoting status thus fit the pre-modern situation rather well, while classes, which are based on production of goods and accumulation of wealth without regard to ancestry, are more a feature of the modern period, not of capitalism per se as Mousnier thought, but rather of industrial as opposed to commercial capitalism.[2]

The Nature of Citizenship

Even by 1100 'citizens' were a distinct and privileged group within the urban community, and the status became progressively more restricted thereafter. From the late twelfth century most German town laws, building on Iberian prototypes, granted freedom to any serf who could live unchallenged in the town for a year and a day. But the maxim 'town air makes a person free' only spread later to France and the Low Countries, and it had little practical impact even in Germany, where most of the numerous serfs who lived in towns did so with their lords' consent. Town governments discouraged the immigration of serfs, and some required the newcomer to swear that he was free. Residence requirements were especially long in the south. Marseilles by the sixteenth century restricted citizenship to persons who had lived in the town ten years, owned property and married a local woman. The Tuscan cities characteristically demanded 30 years residence in the city.

Citizens could normally pass the status on to their wives and children, but newcomers had to pay an entry fee, take an oath to the town and meet conditions of residence, status and/or property. Citizens were expected to carry identification, since their home governments protected them when they travelled outside the walls. Since 'freedom of the borough', as citizenship was called in England, entailed tax exemption in one's home town and generally throughout the realm in places that had royal charters, some English towns began keeping lists of citizens who enjoyed the freedom.[3]

Most early charters also required citizens to own real estate within the town limits. This qualification remained important in the process of elevating citizenship to a preferred status. As the towns became larger, many newcomers could not afford houses, and accordingly rented accommodations. Persons holding houses, or particularly land, became a privileged group within the citizenry: in the cities of Flanders and some in Germany the word 'burgess' (*poorter, Bürger*) came to have a double meaning, of 'citizen' in the broad sense and of a group of citizens, usually those of ancient lineage, who owned land outright as opposed to paying ground rent on it. Frankfurt allowed newcomers a year and a day to acquire urban land worth 10 marks. Nuremberg based full citizenship on residence in two expensive central parishes, and wealthy newcomers could not buy property there without the consent of the city council.[4]

From the thirteenth century on 'freedom of the borough' in England could be acquired by inheritance from one's parents, enrolling as the apprentice of a burgess or paying an entry fine. Citizenship also came with membership in the merchant guild in places that had them, a group that did not include London. Most apprentices from the home counties, who made up a substantial part of the persons gaining the freedom of London in the late Middle Ages, came from landed county families who saw this as a good opportunity to expand their businesses in the capital. A royal charter of 1303 forbade anyone to practise a trade in London who did not enjoy the freedom of the city. After 1319 the freedom could only be gained by persons who were vouched for by six members of their crafts. By the sixteenth century freedom by apprenticeship could come only through one of the twelve 'liveried companies', although several hundred different crafts were practised in the city. The smaller towns were less rigid.[5]

Thus the citizens were a broad elite, rarely including as many as half the adult male residents of the community. From the ranks of the citizens the narrower elites who governed the city and controlled its social, economic and charitable institutions were formed. Restrictions on citizenship were more common in older cities that were trying to protect markets for their indigenous populations than in places that were expanding or lacked a rigid guild structure. The entry fees were usually charged in combination with some other standard that kept out those who could afford to pay but might be undesirable for other reasons. The result was that citizenship became limited to persons who were known and vouched for by a respected member of the community or who could bring letters attesting good conduct and good workmanship from their previous places of residence. Many immigrants seem to have lived in the city for some years before assuming citizenship. Ghent was most unusual in considering all persons citizens who registered with the aldermen within three days of entering the town.[6]

The fact that most cities had far more inhabitants than citizens raises the question of why a newcomer would want to become a citizen and in effect take the first step into the local elite. Citizens had the right to political participation and normally the right to sell goods on the town market without paying a fee, but they also had obligations that mere 'inhabitants' escaped, such as liability for direct taxation and service in the militia. The market fee that persons outside the freedom paid was so small that only the largest operators would find it advantageous to buy citizenship. Thus, especially after 1350, cities such as York were forcing artisans to buy the freedom as a condition of setting up business in the city; what had been a desired privilege was now being enforced for financial reasons by the city government. York and London were restrictive about citizenship – no more than one-quarter of London's adult males held the freedom in 1450 – but others, including Norwich and Exeter, were not. It depended on the range of economic and political activities for which the freedom was a prerequisite.[7]

Occupational Guilds and Working Conditions

Why was the city attractive to immigrants who had no hope or even intention of becoming citizens? First, the bitter internal conflicts over wages have obscured the fact that wages were always higher in the central place than in its environs. Even part-time work was thus desirable, particularly for workers who lived close enough to maintain residence in their native villages and work in the city for a few weeks when demand for labour was high. Since rural labourers could work more cheaply than urban artisans, whose wages were often fixed by guild statute, some masters, particularly in construction, which required a large but intermittently employed labour force, preferred to use them. In 1279 the bishop of Würzburg declared:

> that the carpenters cannot stop anyone from working on his own buildings in the city of Würzburg. Rather, anyone who wishes may have a foreign carpenter in his employ, and the other carpenters of the city are not to annoy or molest him.[8]

Second, the city had a much greater diversity of labour than the village. In simple terms, jobs were available. In places with weak or non-existent guilds, a newcomer could simply make and sell his products or services. Thus the occupational structure of the pre-modern cities provides important insight into their attraction for immigrants. At Nuremberg in 1363, a quarter of the master craftsmen in the city were purveyors of food and clothing that was consumed locally; another quarter were in metalworking, the chief export and the area in which specialisation was most advanced, and the rest worked in areas such as textiles and construction. At Ghent, which was strongly dependent on luxury textile exports, nearly 56 per cent of the city's workforce was supported by textiles in 1358; 11.1 per cent were in victualling, 9.6 per cent in transport and loading, 5.6 per cent in construction (this figure at Nuremberg was 5.8 per cent), 5.1 in clothing, and 5.0 per cent in leather and fur working.[9]

Thus even in cities whose economies were most driven by exports, at least a quarter of the workforce was occupied in trades that fed, housed and clothed the inhabitants of the city and those who lived close enough to the city to use its market regularly, the 'non-basic' producers (see Chapter 1). In the smaller towns, such as Winchester and even Tours, the figure is closer to half. Within this group, victualling is almost always the largest sector, although the percentage of food purveyors in the total population declines as the city becomes larger, followed (usually at some distance) by construction workers.[10]

This analysis continues to be valid for the sixteenth and seventeenth centuries. Between a quarter and a third of most town populations were still engaged in providing the necessities of food, clothing and shelter. At Norwich in 1525, textiles occupied nearly a third of the workforce. This had declined by 1569 to a fifth, but the change was accompanied by a growth in the percentage of persons who made clothing for local sale. The composite figure for distributive trades, purveyors of food and drink, leather trades and construction trades is 52 per cent in both years.[11] Comparisons of census data from 1516 and 1716–17 at Barcelona, a much larger city, show that in each period agriculture occupied 6–7 per cent of the workforce, fishing and other maritime occupations 3.5–4.5, construction 6–7, hides and leather 6–7, glass/ceramics 0.8–1.0, metal 3.5–4.5, food trades 3.6–5.6, commerce and transport 7.8–8.2, and the rest scattered. The biggest change was a drop in clothworkers from 15.2 per cent in 1516 to 12.3 per cent in 1716, and a similar decline in the number of widows from 17.4 per cent to 14.6 per cent.[12] The occupational profiles of six towns of widely diverse sizes over 251 years – Verona 1409, Como 1439, Frankfurt 1440, Monza 1541, Florence 1552 and Venice 1660 – confirm these patterns. When food distribution and agriculture are combined, Monza, by far the smallest and least commercial, was 39 per cent. Verona, Como and Frankfurt were 21–23 per cent, while Florence and Venice, by far the largest, were at 13 and 17 per cent. Textiles and clothing were 37 per cent at Verona, 41 and 43 per cent at Florence and Venice, and 25–30 per cent in the others; Florence and Venice had important textile exports, and each made fashionable clothing in addition to cloth. Metalwork was between 5 and 10 per cent in each, and leatherwork 2–8 per cent.[13]

We saw in Chapter 4 that many occupational guilds became politically powerful. However, their social and economic roles vary greatly between cities and always defy simple classification. First, there was no clear line between merchant and craftsman, either within or between guilds. Skilled craftsmen, such as weavers and goldsmiths, who produced exportable goods and sold them retail were obviously also merchants. The 'merchant' in the merchant guilds of the continent was a wholesaler. Membership in these guilds was not limited to wealthy or large-scale merchants, but it did confer the right to sell products that bore the town guild's seal of approval outside the town. Thus any craftsman who exported enough to make it worth his while to pay the entry fee would join the merchant guild. The English merchant guild, by contrast, gave its members the right to sell retail on the town market. Thus a prosperous shoemaker would pay the entry fee and sell his products directly. Lesser operators would sell their shoes wholesale to a member of the merchant guild, who would sell them retail. In both the continental and English cases, only members of the merchant guild could import goods into the town from outside, which gave them control over the food supply and strategic raw materials with industrial applications, such as dyes.

While municipal statutes gave the specifications for grades of cloth and fixed how much could be charged for a mug of beer, no city government tried to regulate how profits once made legally could then be spent or re-invested. Thus we have cases such as Mark Le Fayre of Winchester, who was active in business for about 50 years in cloth production and distribution, wine importing, and tavern- and innkeeping. He put out cloth to rural artisans, owned a house in Southampton and a country estate, and a dyeshop managed by a dyer to whom he paid a wage. He was a member of the merchant guild. John Stubbs of York called himself a barber in his will, but he also kept an inn whose accoutrements, not surprisingly, included a brewery.[14]

To complicate matters still further, some guilds permitted dual matriculation. The authorities frowned on it, and an English statute of 1363 required artisans to confine themselves to one craft, but in practice it was common. Although no one could practise two trades simultaneously, most cities permitted a person who had multiple professions, most often through inheritance or marriage (women could transmit claims to mastership to their children and sometimes to their husbands), to move between them as demand required. For example, a person might post bond as a moneychanger one year and as a broker the next: three hostellers at York in 1381 are called mercers in other sources. The dean of the brokers of Ghent in 1386 posted bond as a hosteller in 1373. The hostellers and the cloth wholesalers (*lakensniders*) posted bond separately, but it was common to change trades and thus appear in different years on different lists, then return to the original trade. This happened also at the opposite extreme, in professions that required little skill but could be learned on the job. Freemen of London and other English towns had the right to practise any single trade that they wished, regardless of their Company affiliation. There is little evidence of such crossovers before the 1570s, but thereafter they became more common.[15] Movement between occupations was also common in sixteenth-century Venice. Despite the overall growth of industry in the city, small-scale retailing attracted numerous persons – the number of mercers increased from 567 to 1747 between 1595 and 1690 – as woollen manufacturing declined, and most other guilds had loose structures and several branches of the trade that permitted considerable mobility.[16]

Even townspeople who were clearly either merchants or artisans were often in the same guild. Except in strictly service occupations, a hierarchy typically developed within the guild, with an elite importing the raw materials that went into the guild's product and selling it to their guild brothers who did the actual work. Thus a draper, who bought wool and dyes and put them out to various master artisans whose combined labour resulted in a finished piece of cloth that the draper would sell, would typically be a member of a weaver's guild, or occasionally the guild of the dyers or some other clothmaking trade. Although most grain was rarely obtained by bakers or millers but rather by persons who were not guild members at all or were grain measurers or shippers, master butchers controlled the meat supplies of the late medieval cities, often maintaining their own herds of beasts. The grocers of London are another good example. They were not greengrocers but rather persons who controlled the gross beam that was used for imported goods at the London weighing house. The prominent and most politically active grocers imported spices, while spice retailers constituted the majority of the guild membership. The apothecaries, a subordinate branch of the guild, also depended on the merchant grocers for their supplies.[17]

The London grocers illustrate another aspect of the politico-labour market in the late medieval and early modern cities. The wealthiest grocers paid for their spice imports by exporting wool, which they bought at the local markets where they sold the spices, through the Calais Staple. They were thus prominent in the both the import and export sides of clothmaking. The 'grocers' were accused unjustly in the 1380s of controlling the London food supply and driving prices up; in fact, the fishmongers, their great rivals, were far more involved in the food trade. Yet while the grocers handled the export of wool from London, the mercers did so from York.

Many guilds were umbrella organisations that included different and not always related occupations. Typically the separate occupations held their own meetings and devised their industrial regulations and standards, subject to approval by the guild deans and the city council. Which group furnished the guild's representative on the city council was frequently determined by rotation. After 1396 the council of Cologne was composed of representatives of 22 *Gaffeln*, five reserved for the merchants and 17 for groups of crafts of bewildering diversity; one included saddlers, artists, escutcheon makers and glassblowers.[18] Pistoia in 1330 had 40 professions but only eight guilds. While some guilds linked related crafts, others did not. At Strasbourg in the sixteenth century the guild *Zur Steltz* (At the Stilt) was dominated by metalworkers, particularly goldsmiths, but painters and printers were also in it.[19] Construction workers were often grouped into a single organisation, usually dominated by the carpenters and masons: the 'guilds of the Plaetse' at Ghent included six construction trades, each of which kept its own guild. The Plaetse had its own court to deal with infractions between members of different guilds within the group, and the six together were entitled to one of 26 seats on the two city councils.[20] Although after 1292 only 21 *arti* of Florence were eligible to choose priors (city councillors), 73 separate crafts were required to pay a tax in 1316. The list begins with the 21, then includes the rest, including painters, mattressmakers and mercers, who for purposes of council representation were considered part of the guild of doctors and druggists, one of the seven greater guilds.[21]

Thus, even in places that had guild-based political regimes, the formally recognised guilds do not even begin to take in the variety of occupations that were being practised. Saint-Omer had 52 trades with statutes approved by the *échevins* in the thirteenth century, but the number had grown to 93 by the fifteenth, and many other trades were unregulated. This does not show a zeal to over-regulate, but rather the decline of clothmaking for export and the growth of small guilds that produced for local consumers and exported through the regional markets of Bruges and Antwerp. At Ghent the troubles of the textile industry after 1275 were similarly reflected in the growth of the 'small guilds', which are first mentioned as a corporate group in 1317 and had an overdean by 1325. Their number was fixed at 59 by 1360. Perugia had 43 guilds in 1342.[22]

Trades that became large only after the list of officially approved guilds was drawn up often escaped guild regulation, although they might be regulated directly by the city council. Especially from the late fourteenth century, the prosperity of some towns was preserved by the development of new specialities as a dominant trade declined. Printing is the most obvious example. As broadcloth manufacture declined, coverlet makers took up some of the slack in Lynn and tapestry makers in York. Other towns kept up by marketing the cloth made in their rural environs.[23] The grain staple of Ghent cushioned the impact of the decline of the city's luxury textiles. Venice became noted for printing and the manufacture of musical instruments. While the cotton and linen of Venice succumbed to international competition, silk never did. Gold- and silversmithing, other jewellery including fine diamonds, and especially fine glasswork also became Venetian specialities.[24]

The size of the town and the complexity of its central functions are obviously tied to the level of occupational specialisation. Much of the reason for the relative unimportance of craft guilds in England was the small population base of the towns, which meant that the pool of masters was so small that separate administrations of guilds would have been wasteful.[25] Areas with strong export trades, where quality was an issue, tended to be those with the largest number of guild organisations. It is true that this could be carried to extremes: Ghent in 1358 had bread bakers, pastry bakers who were in the spicers' guild, and bakers who were not required to join either guild and were allowed to sell on specific markets in the city.[26] York had an unusual degree of specialisation, with separate crafts until the mid-fifteenth century for the smiths and marshals, who did virtually identical work, and for potters, pewterers and founders. Yet Lynn, which in 1389 had 43 social and religious confraternities, had no craft guilds, and most English cities had fewer than a dozen.[27]

Masters and Apprentices

Just as citizenship became more restrictive, so did mastership in the more prestigious occupational guilds after 1300. In contrast to modern labour unions, which are associations of employees, the guilds were organisations of employers, the masters. Thus the guilds tried to keep wages down and limit access to jobs. Most civic disturbances that involved the guilds and outsiders concerned representation on the city council, not economic issues, although there were struggles within the guilds, particularly between masters and journeymen, over technological questions, such as the introduction of the work clock and accordingly payment of wages by the hour and the length of the work day. Examples are the famous strike in 1539 of the 'Griffarians', the journeyman printers of Lyon, and the walkouts of the fullers against their weaver-employers in the Low Country cities.[28]

Some guilds, reacting to markets that were declining after 1348, made mastership hereditary in the male line. More often they simply restricted it in practice by charging much higher entry fees to newcomers than to sons of masters. Others limited automatic enfranchisement in the guild to eldest sons or to sons who were born after the father had become a master. Whether a masterwork was required or not, the fact that credentials were evaluated by a committee of masters from whom there was no appeal, the high entry fees, and the expensive banquet that new masters had to fund, all meant that access to mastership was difficult for outsiders. Yet there is immense variation between and within guilds with regard to heredity, and virtually everywhere it was stronger in theory than in practice. At York sons followed the father's profession 51 per cent of the time between 1397 and 1534. In the late fourteenth century about 50 per cent of the sons of barrelmakers of Bruges followed the father's trade, but by 1500 scarcely any did. Augsburg in the sixteenth century had a very high percentage of sons following fathers.[29]

The more prosperous and growing crafts were the least likely to be endogamous. Trades that required expensive equipment also tended to run in families. Yet high death rates meant that most families did not survive in the male line for more than a generation or two. Strict heredity could be catastrophic: the butchers of Ghent had 136 families of masters when the guild obtained heredity of mastership in 1302, 14 in 1469 and 2 in 1789.[30] Guild matriculation lists show that except when absolute heredity was practised, some newcomers could enter. Fathers commonly apprenticed their younger sons in guilds that were less prestigious and had lower entry fees than their own. But while individual guilds had a high turnover, few people took up occupations outside the artisan group; thus the son of a weaver might marry the daughter of a carpenter. Some artisan parents, mothers as well as fathers, passed their skills on to their daughters, thus giving them a means of livelihood as well as enhancing their marriageability. This explains why stem families throughout urban Europe had members both in related occupations and also in trades so diverse that no amount of in-house training or inheritance of industrial assets can explain them. Thus James Farr speaks of 'a correlation between guild exogamy and artisanal endogamy'.[31]

Even for the prestigious guilds the extent to which son succeeded father has been exaggerated. The London aldermen were very lineage-conscious; yet in the late Middle Ages only two-thirds of them were succeeded by their sons in the same profession. Only 51 per cent of the sons of artisans who were admitted to the freedom of the city between 1387 and 1534 followed the father's craft.[32] This pattern continues in early modern London, but Barcelona demonstrates more stability: a study of marriage contracts shows that 42 per cent of grooms had the same trade as their fathers, 12 per cent a different trade in the same general sector, and 46 per cent a completely different occupation Much of the explanation is group consciousness among merchants. High death rates prevented the formation of dynasties, as happened in many Italian cities. Intermarriage kept assets within the merchant group, which became a kind of extended kinship pool.[33]

Thus lineage was becoming as important a status question for guild masters as it was for the old patrician and merchant lines, but both groups had trouble excluding outsiders. Furthermore, restrictions on mastership did not make it impossible for newcomers to find jobs. Work was not reserved for masters. In the early stages a master was simply a craftsman who was recognised as competent by his peers. Industrial regulations and rules for accrediting masters become stricter after 1300, but the status divisions within the guild did not always correspond to a division of labour. Masters rarely completely lost touch with the technical aspects of their trades. Professional competence was easier for sons of masters, who were usually trained by their fathers if they lived long enough (the famous requirement of presenting a masterwork to the other masters of the guild is most commonly found only from the late fourteenth century on, and it was frequently used to disqualify outsiders), had the appropriate lineage and paid the entry fee. The master could own his own shop, hire journeymen and train apprentices.

Although the masters of the more respectable trades formed a middle class, not all masters were prosperous. The house was often the place of business, and rents were as out of reach as purchase prices for some, particularly in the large cities. Since not all masters could afford self-employment, with all the risks that this involved, some masters worked for others. One of the many reasons why guilds tried to limit the number of new masters is that guild pay scales normally required that masters be paid twice the rate of journeymen for the same job. Many cities had formal labour markets, used particularly for construction and textile jobs, where at the beginning of each work day persons desiring to be hired would present themselves.

Masters who had more work than they and their families could personally handle hired journeymen (workers by the day or *journée*, called *Gesellen* (fellows) in German). Journeymen were a diverse lot. Some were sons of local masters who could not afford to become masters themselves, but most were immigrants from the environs. They had to be qualified in their trades, but this could be learned through either apprenticeship or in-shop experience. Some masters relied on well-trained journeymen to manage their shops, and these people had long-term work opportunities. More often, contracts were short-term, for a day or week. Most labour was seasonal, dependent on the arrival of cargoes carrying the raw materials of the trade. In order to survive, a journeyman had to save a substantial part of his meagre income in order to tide him over, or have a working wife; most journeymen, however, seem to have remained single.

Thus many skilled artisans who were still actually making goods were not masters, as guild mastership increasingly became an aspect of elite status. Journeymen could vote in guild elections in a few places, although this was unusual, but wearing the livery, which conferred high standing, was restricted to a select group even among the masters. The officers of the company were chosen solely by the liverymen. Thus the term 'yeoman' in England, which initially indicated journeymen, was coming by the late fifteenth century to mean not only the journeymen, but also the lesser masters, who were close to their earning level. There were variations among the companies: the brewers' yeomanry, for example, consisted entirely of journeymen, and there were tensions between householders and yeomanry in most companies. A similar division occurred in Italy and elsewhere between the greater masters on one hand and the lesser masters and journeymen on the other.[34]

Not surprisingly, journeymen began to form their own organisations, which were rarely bound to a single locality and thus enhanced regional integration. They became potent forces in the fifteenth and sixteenth centuries, diminishing somewhat in the seventeenth. The shoemakers of the cities of the Upper Rhine formed an organisation in 1407, the ropemakers in 1389. They held periodic meetings to renew their rules. In the late fifteenth century, the journeymen bakers of Colmar, Strasbourg and Basel used what was nominally a social fraternity to coordinate a strike against their employers. Journeyman fraternities were most significant in Germany and France; they are also numerous in Spain, but less so in England and Italy, although the yeomen of the liveried companies of early modern London have been traced back to the journeymen fraternities of the late Middle Ages.[35]

Journeymen were considered a revolutionary element by city governments, which tried to prevent them from organising; for virtually all agitation for higher wages, which was a matter for the guild to decide but only with the approval of the city council, came from journeymen. The master beltmakers of Breslau in 1329 responded to a strike by the local journeymen with a lockout for a year, and the city council imposed a fine on any master who hired one of the rebels. The Rhenish city governments tried to develop a common policy toward the journeyman associations, notably through an ordinance that was first promulgated at Strasbourg in 1436. It subordinated the journeymen to their guilds and deprived them of drinking halls and even of the ability to act as a corporation, which precluded them from renting buildings. By the sixteenth century many brotherhoods had gone underground, using secret signs and handshakes and moving from town to town to contacts who would arrange work or lodging. The fact that disproportionate numbers of joiners became prominent in Huguenot activities in Troyes, Rouen and Dijon may have been due to a strong sense of corporate solidarity through their brotherhoods.[36]

The journeymen give us one window on an enduring characteristic of premodern urban populations: many of them were young, although as mastership became increasingly difficult for those who were not masters' sons to obtain, journeyman rank could sometimes be a lifetime career. Apprentices too were youthful. The father normally trained at least the son who would follow him into the guild. Formal apprenticeship outside the family was unusual except for a person whose father had died or who was not following his trade. But apprenticeship, whether formal or implied, is an important aspect of the urban labour market. Apprenticeship contracts were a costly investment for parents. Some required the master to handle the introduction of the young person to the guild, but completing apprenticeship was no guarantee of eventually becoming a master. The master always got the labour of his apprentice, beginning in unskilled jobs around the shop and ending with more professionally challenging tasks. Apprentices were usually paid low wages, and masters thus could cut costs by employing them. Terms of apprenticeship lengthened, often out of all proportion to the length of time needed to learn the trade, and ages at which it could begin rose in the fifteenth century, and was even in the early twenties with some guilds. Thus apprentices and journeymen, roughly age cohorts, with considerable free time to enjoy the licentious decadence associated with urban life, contributed to a 'youth culture'. They also competed for the same jobs. Masters who did not want the trouble of training apprentices could hire journeymen, or vice versa if the apprentices' generally lower wages were the issue. Since few documents refer to households having both apprentices and journeymen, scribal convention might determine which word was used for the same individual.[37]

The Guild and the Urban Family

Occupational guilds were closely associated with the household unit of production, which characterised most labour relations in the pre-modern cities. This leads us to a consideration of the urban family. While journeymen were frequently single, many guild statutes required masters to be married. Many guilds, assuming that all members of the master's family would contribute to its livelihood, limited the number of journeymen and apprentices whom a master might employ simultaneously, but some allowed bachelors and widowers to hire more outside help than married masters, to make up for the loss of family labour.[38]

Scholars have discerned a 'European' (really north European) marriage pattern in the pre-modern period, but it seems more valid for the cities than for rural Europe. It is characterised by a companionate marriage that comes from comparable ages of spouses and shared, albeit gendered, participation in making the family's income, in a unit of production centred on the household. The spouses also married later than in Italy, for they were expected to be able to support their households when they married and thus to live apart from the house and beyond the power of the husband's father. This also led to a high proportion of single persons in the cities. But the cities, unlike the rural areas, had a high rate of immigration, stimulated by high death rates as well as greater opportunities through liquidity of assets. City people married later than rural folk, on account of the absence of extended family support. Even among the elite, whose marriages were more often arranged by the parents than was true for artisans, marriage before the mid- to late twenties was unusual.[39]

Few urban families in the north contained more than two generations (parents and children) under the same roof, and more than three was almost unheard of. When the co-residential multigenerational family occurred in a city, the middle generation almost always dominated both its parents and its children, as the older couple became boarders. In the countryside the seniors' control of the family property could prevent their children, at least the younger ones, from marrying until the parents were gone; for the adult child had to have the parents' land in order to be independent and make a living. This was not true in the cities, where jobs were more plentiful; this indeed was a powerful inducement to migration to the cities. Italian urban families were more often multigenerational and there, in contrast to the north, the grandfather could maintain control over his descendants, much as he could in rural Europe in the north.

Women were given dowries everywhere if their parents had enough property to make one. Although the dowry was the wife's property, her husband could manage it during the marriage. The young couple often used it as a start-up fund to establish their independent household. Italian urban families were so anxious to attract proper husbands for their daughters that they gave such enormous dowries that they made it impossible for their sons to marry before the parents' demise.[40] North European dowries were more moderate, but two principles were valid virtually everywhere: a woman could take out of a marriage whatever she or her family had brought into it; and she got some share of common property, even if only for life. The 'Parisian' system allowed a daughter the option of returning her marriage portion and sharing with her siblings the parents' total estate when they died, or keeping the dowry and staying out of the inheritance. More importantly, the widow commonly received half the couple's common property and a one-third share of her husband's property for her lifetime. In Tuscany she could take her dowry into a second marriage; but if she did, her children remained with their father's family. Furthermore, while virtually all inheritance regimes in pre-modern Europe gave preference to males over females, partible inheritance, in which all heirs share the parents' estate, either without regard to age or gender or guaranteeing a lesser share to the daughters, was more common in the cities than in the rural areas. This brought property into the market and took it across family lines. Partible inheritance always benefited women, particularly those who remained single. Given the extent of financial liquidity in the towns, families did not have to alienate landed property to daughters and their husbands in order to provide for them.

The number of children per family was lower in the larger towns than in the rural areas, due both to high infant mortality rates in the cities and the fact that, particularly in Italy, urban children were likely to be sent away from home to nurses, and subsequently for education. In the north children remained at home longer and were expected to work in the family business. The number of young adults in the cities, by contrast, was high, as they migrated into the towns seeking training and/or better jobs. Women generally outnumbered men in the towns, and job opportunities were much better than in the countryside; for it was much easier for women to inherit money or rents than land.[41] The greater likelihood of finding a job that did not require landholding was undoubtedly a major cause of heavy immigration from the immediate environs of all cities.

Extended families, while not the norm anywhere, were more often found in Italy, and everywhere were more common among the merchants and urban nobles than among the artisans, for only the elite could afford large family complexes that provided separate quarters for the different generations. But even in the north, powerful extended families concentrated their holdings in particular parts of town. The family of the Ghent leader Jacob Van Artevelde lived in an extended complex around his house, each separate building owned by the male leader of the individual nuclear family.[42] Although most Italian families maintained separate residences and were nuclear in that sense, they nonetheless acted as an extended unit to a much greater extent than was true in the north. It was more common for Italian businesses to expect family members to join the firm than for businesses in the northern cities, although Nuremberg and other towns provide significant exceptions. Given the tendency of merchant lineages to intermarry, the northern business partnerships often involved in-laws.[43]

Pre-modern populations were much younger than now – usually half the population was under 25 – and urban populations were younger than rural ones. The age pyramid seems to have been most skewed toward the young in Italy. The high death rates in the cities led to a rapid turnover of assets, which in turn generated opportunities for acquisition and jobs for immigrants. Particularly after 1348, urban property descended into collateral branches of the family. Few people lived to maturity in a family with two living parents. When an adult died, his or her children were entitled to their share of the decedent's property. In the cities facilities for securing the property of children were vastly superior to the rural areas. Orphanages were established, although the sense of kin solidarity was so strong that few children were placed in them unless both parents and all other close kin were dead. In some cities the government took over management of the minor's assets, separating the share of the child(ren) from that of the surviving parent until the child's maturity, and this meant freezing capital for investment.[44]

Given the youth and transience of the urban populations, it is not surprising that the cities had a high level of crime.[45] Property crime seems to have been less serious in most towns than violence against persons. Most crime involved male against male, male against female mainly when a sexual offence was involved, but rarely women as aggressors except in verbal altercations. Most city police forces were too small to combat disorder effectively. Although the city governments regularly issued prohibitions against deadly weapons, requiring outsiders to leave them at the gates or their inns, in fact most people carried them. The cities had curfews, and they closed the city gates and taverns at sunset, and guild watches patrolled the streets, but most crime seems to have occurred at night. The large numbers of taverns and high consumption of alcohol also exacerbated the problem.

Punishments for violent acts were intended not only as retribution, but also to serve as a public example to deter such behaviour in the future. Most city statutes prescribed very severe penalties, financial and corporal, for persons who were actually convicted even of misdemeanours. Accordingly, most litigants preferred to use arbitration. Not until the fifteenth century in most cities, and in some considerably later, did city governments begin *ex officio* prosecution of crime in cases when the antagonists preferred to reach an accommodation.

The social dimension of urban crime does not entirely conform to modern expectations. Port cities and other places with large transient or youthful populations, such as university towns, were prone to violence. There was little middle-class crime except in connection with political rioting. The economic extremes, the very poor and the elite, were responsible for most violence. Many crimes by the poor doubtless went unreported and may contribute to the impression of a low incidence of property crime. Most violence was directed against persons of comparable social ranks: thus wealthy masters were not in great danger of assault from disgruntled occasional employees.

The elite accounted for most of the reported violence. This is connected to the persistence of vendettas among the urban aristocracy. As the city elites approached the territorial nobility socially, their lineage consciousness was translated into an adoption of this aspect of noble behaviour, even as the nobles became more inclined to live in the cities and profit from their markets. The Venetian nobles flouted the laws with impunity. There is a social dimension to the punishments at Venice. The wealthy were assessed higher fines than the poor for deeds involving honour, in which the entire ethos of the urban nobility was compromised by misbehaviour; yet for most misdeeds, particularly violent acts of which no gentleman need be ashamed, the poor were punished more severely than the wealthy, for violence by the poor threatened the social fabric, while that by the rich did not.[46]

No economic motive is present in such actions: elite violence against elite resulted from honour and status issues. Ghent became so factionalised that family-based groups wore distinctive clothing or badges to help distinguish friend from foe. A contract to commit premeditated murder was legally enforceable in the courts of Ghent. The Italian communes were born in the agitation against the feuds of magnates, but the *popolani* readily identified with this aspect of behaviour of their social superiors. The extended families of the Italian cities, and to a considerable extent the northern towns, based their power on land-ownership in specific neighbourhoods. The power of the family group was a magnet attracting lesser persons of the vicinity to the faction as clients. The feuds sometimes lasted for several generations, and until the fifteenth century the most that many city governments would do was declare and feebly enforce truces and try (with minimal success) to limit feuds to 'lawful' vendettas, meaning only to the offender if he was alive and to close relatives if he was not. Although Florence legislated against vendetta, the government was powerless to stop it. When peace was finally concluded, a reckoning was made, with homicides only cancelling each other if the decedents were of similar social ranks, injuries only cancelling each other if involving the same body part. The courts expected that relatives help one another in the feuding. A death unatoned could lead to a re-eruption of violence years after the original event, as happened in 1382 over the death in 1345 of the Ghent captain Jacob Van Artevelde.[47]

Urban Women

As a consequence of heavy immigration, all cities had a large number of single-person households, many of them, particularly from the late Middle Ages, women. The pre-modern cities were attractive to women. Their labour was more often rewarded by money than on the farm. There are significant differences in the legal position of women in Italy from those in the north, differences that are not peculiar to the cities. Unattached women had fewer protections in the south, and given the age gap between spouses were more likely than in the north to be widowed early and be unable to remarry.

In both Italy and the north there is more evidence of women in the middle echelons of the labour forces of the towns before 1300 than after. Thereafter they were gradually pushed out of the more responsible occupations and restricted to domestic service and 'traditional women's occupations' such as food preparation. Some have seen the change coming with the domination of the city governments by occupational guilds, which were strongly patriarchal and relegated women to a subordinate role, even restricting their ability to help their husbands in the family trade.[48]

Against the notion of a plotting patriarchy is the fact that possession of substantial property placed constraints on the economic and marital behaviour of everyone, men and women alike. Although fewer women pursued skilled crafts after 1300 than before, they are still found in great numbers in the middle and lower circles of the labour market. Since newcomers would not expect to move quickly into skilled work, the restrictions were more onerous on women who were already established in the town than on immigrants. While wives of masters would typically work in the household productive unit, single women and the wives of journeymen took other jobs.

A woman was the ward of her husband unless he emancipated her legally, making her an independent *femme sole*, able to handle her business without his intervention or liability. Although this degree of autonomy was unusual, women exercised considerable independence and discretion in practice. They were particularly numerous in household-based industries, and their second incomes were important for their families, especially in victualling and innkeeping and the other service trades. Their employment opportunities were not the equal of urban men, but they greatly exceeded those of rural women. First, although some guild regulations tried to limit wives helping husbands in their jobs, they did not end the practice. Guilds expected masters to be married, and in practice there was little official interference with what wives did in the shop.

Second, women disposed of considerable capital, most of it through inheritance, which they invested in business ventures. Women were more often their husbands' business partners in second marriages, using the capital recovered from the first marriage. Although artisans were largely site-bound, most merchants even after the 'commercial revolution' had to be away for part of the time, and their wives frequently managed the business in their absence. Some women were moneylenders. At Ghent they were usually about a quarter of the persons who paid the fee for this activity. They were also moneychangers, which took them into the area of banking. Margaret Ruweel of Bruges inherited a moneychanging business from her father, then married another changer. When he went bankrupt in 1370, her share was unaffected, and she thus preserved the family's business, because his creditors could not under Flemish law seize her property. A more colourful case is Celie Amelakens, daughter and wife of moneychangers of Ghent, who in different years was a moneychanger and a hosteller.[49]

Women were rarely independent wholesale traders, but they were ubiquitous as petty retailers. They were most numerous in low-status positions in the food trades, especially as vendors of ale, bread, fish, poultry and dairy goods. A sixteenth-century Munich list of those licensed to operate market stands shows only three men against 42 women, virtually all of whom were widows or wives of craftsmen who were indigent, incompetent or both.[50] In a fourteenth-century case over access to a square that was owned by a private family, the consuls of Montpellier used only one female witness, but the Bon Amic family called fifteen, most of them food retailers who rented space for their booths in the square directly from the Bon Amic or their tenants. The Nottingham poultry market was called the Womanmarket. The only area of victualling in which women are not found is butchering, which was exclusively a male preserve after 1300. In textiles they were most numerous in carding and spinning, although a few are found in other crafts. Women controlled the sale booths in the cloth hall at Ghent and many other cities.[51]

A list of the trades practised by urban women gives an exaggerated idea of their importance, for they were almost always outnumbered by men in the same trade. Some girls got professional training from their fathers that they took into marriage, given the extent of guild endogamy. Paris, and there only before 1300, and Cologne were the only large cities with separate women's guilds in the late Middle Ages; at Cologne they were especially active in the silk industry, where they organised their own guild in 1437, hired apprentices and held offices. But even here their husbands handled the long-distance trade side of the business. Cologne was exceptional, and in the sixteenth century the role of women in the crafts was narrowed still further.[52]

The presence of large numbers of domestic servants was a peculiarity of the cities, particularly the larger ones. This was the largest area of female employment. In the merchant streets of Hull and York in 1377, about 30 per cent of the unmarried population were in service.[53] Male servants are sometimes barely distinguishable from journeymen, but in the larger cities the two groups together sometimes constituted more than 15 per cent of the population and rarely less than 10 per cent.[54] Girls typically used the term of service as a way of saving for their dowries. The availability of servants in turn contributed to the comfort of those who had 'made it' in the city.

Given the size and vulnerability of the female population in the pre-modern cities, prostitution was rampant. Extramarital sexual activity was much more prevalent in pre-modern Europe than now and was more common in the cities than in rural communities. Under such circumstances prostitution was impossible to control effectively. Taverns and bathhouses frequently doubled as havens of prostitution.[55] The secular authorities did their best to restrict prostitutes to the disreputable quarters of the town, evidently as a matter of public order, as we see at London in 1393:

> Whereas many and divers affrays, broils, and dissensions, have arisen in times past, and many men have been slain and murdered, by reason of the frequent resort of, and consorting with, common harlots at taverns, brew-houses of huksters, and other places of ill-fame within the said city, and the suburbs thereof; ... [we forbid] that any such woman shall go about or lodge in the said city, or in the suburbs ... but they are to keep themselves to the places thereunto assigned, that is to say, the stews on the other side of the Thames [Southwark] and Cokkeslane.[56]

While poverty forced some women into prostitution, and female servants were prey to the desires of their masters and the masters' friends, this is not the whole explanation: for numerous married women turned to prostitution, and for others it was a second income in addition to a more respectable job. The attitude of city authorities was ambiguous: prostitutes were regularly fined and forced to wear badges of disgrace; yet many cities started maintaining public brothels in the later Middle Ages, a disreputable trade that suggests that their concern was less with the offence than with taking fines. The municipal whorehouses were only ended in the sixteenth century, first in Protestant cities, but soon in the Roman Catholics ones as well.

Prostitutes were commonly forced to live in a specific street or quarter, immortalised in such street names as the Alley of the Cows at Florence and Cock's Lane in several English cities. Curiously, many church immunity districts played host to prostitutes, probably because the lay authorities could not regulate them there. The stews of Southwark, in the liberty of no less a figure than the bishop of Winchester, were notorious. University towns had large numbers of prostitutes. Bruges, whose prostitutes catered to the foreign communities there, fined 131 prostitutes in 1351, but the number then quickly declined, as the fines were paid by the madams of consolidated establishments. Venice's prostitutes were even advertised as a major attraction of the city in a *Catalogue of the Principal and Most Honoured Courtesans of Venice*. Rome in 1650 had nine acknowledged prostitutes per 1000 inhabitants, or about 3.3 per cent of the female population between ages 15 and 65.[57]

Social and Charitable Fraternities

Most occupational guilds provided charity and fellowship for their members, sometimes – particularly in Italy and England – through an adjunct fraternity that was linked to the parent guild. The most famous are the *scuole* (confraternities) of the Venetian *arti* (guilds). Membership in the *scuola* was often compulsory for guild members.[58] Conversely, fraternities whose initial purpose was charity or devotion to a holy patron often catered primarily to one or two occupations. This happened especially when the fraternity was based on a parish church that was in a major concentration of members of the craft: the skinners of London received a charter in 1327 for a fraternity of Corpus Christi at the church of St John Walbrook, where many skinners resided. This fraternity became the liveried company of Skinners in 1393. The fraternity dedicated to St Antonin in 1345 became the Grocers' company in 1372.[59] Some occupational guilds in the cities of Languedoc also evolved out of confraternities. The importance of the parish is particularly clear in Italy and England, and in the Italian case led to the proliferation of fraternities, since the cities had more but smaller parishes than was usual in the north.

The large number of associations – parishes, fraternities, guilds, master-employee relations outside the guild – helped many immigrants adapt to life in the city.[60] In England the political weakness of the craft guilds probably contributed to the strength of the fraternities. So did the fact that the mysteries, which were the professional side of the organisations, regulating terms of employment and standards of production, had to submit their statutes to city authorities for ratification, while the fraternities did not. In 1389 the royal government ordered all guilds to report, but 'guild' in this context can mean occupational or charitable organisation. Thus the fraternities in England expanded into areas of craft regulation that usually were not in their purview on the continent. Even in cities that had craft guilds, such as London, they were far outnumbered by the fraternities.[61]

In France, too, many towns had numerous fraternities: Rouen and its suburbs had 130, Avignon 100 and Marseilles 40.[62] Particularly in southern France, the fraternities' social functions were paramount even when they linked persons practising the same trade. Members of the guild were expected to belong to its religious confraternity. Yet, although much has been made of the caritative aspect of the fraternities, most of them spent more money on their banquets than on charity, granted that these affairs helped to inculcate a sense of solidarity. As early as 1285 new matriculants in the guild of ironmongers at Trier were required to pay an entry fee of 20 shillings and fund a seven-course meal for the guild members and several city officials, and at its conclusion make additional payments to them. The members were to provide a decent burial for deceased brothers and sisters, and the organisation was to support impoverished members, but the amount of relief extended varied with the fortunes of the brotherhood's treasury. On balance, most fraternities seem to have been more social clubs than specifically charitable organisations.[63]

Journeymen were normally expected to join their guild's fraternity and, as we have seen, some journeymen had their own fraternity apart from that of the guild masters. As the guilds became increasingly oligarchical, and the artisans alienated from the merchants who dominated them, the rank and file turned increasingly to the fraternities, which in turn brought the fraternities under suspicion by the authorities. Florence abolished religious fraternities in 1419.[64] Confraternities multiplied in sixteenth-century Italy, but they generally became divorced from the occupational guilds after the Council of Trent in 1563 insisted that they be placed under clerical rather than lay control. Some of the larger cities of Counter-Reformation Italy had over 100 such brotherhoods, most of them based on the parish. Although this initially meant that they contained both rich and poor, the growing tendency after 1500 for rich and poor neighbourhoods to be distinguished inevitably led to wealthy and poor confraternities.[65]

In 1539 the fraternities were abolished in France by royal ordinance. In the following years some fraternities that had been attached to merchant organisations were restored, but the artisan brotherhoods were permanently banned in law, although in fact many continued to exist. In Germany most fraternities were disbanded in Protestant areas, but their functions were either absorbed by the guilds, which took on charitable duties toward poor members, or by private clubs, the latter especially in the Netherlands and England after 1700.[66]

Brotherhoods that were not linked to occupational groups were prayer societies, sponsoring devotions and maintaining the altars, relics and other assets of their home churches.[67] They sponsored processions that, given their parish affiliation, amounted to neighbourhood celebrations. A common treasury provided by membership dues and entry and burial fees ensured that brothers and sisters got a decent burial, often accompanied by vociferous mourners. Some fraternities had uniforms, a highly visible sign of identity. Most were small, although fraternities in some larger churches, such as the city cathedrals, had separate organisations in the various parishes, in effect becoming city-wide organisations. In such cases the financial outlays of membership effectively precluded membership by the poor.

Protection of the Consumer

'During the later middle ages urban economic activity was bound by more complex formal rules than had been the case in earlier centuries.'[68] Richard Britnell's delicate understatement refers to guild regulations that have become notorious for hampering the operation of the market and driving down production.

An absolutely free market has never existed. Everyone accepted the idea that some sort of public regulation was necessary. The vague feeling that there was a 'just price' for everything permeated market relations, especially in food and other essentials. The requirement that all goods entering the city be brought to a public market was to prevent large purchases before everyone had a chance to buy on equal terms. The justification used by guilds for their monopolies was that they controlled and regulated at a fair level the price of imports coming to the market.[69] In Max Weber's formulation:

> so-called 'urban economic policy' was basically characterized by its attempt to stabilize the conditions of the local urban economy by means of economic regulations in the interest of permanently and cheaply feeding the masses and standardizing the economic opportunities of tradesmen and merchants.[70]

Most regulation of goods for export was done through occupational guilds, with the approval of the city government. Guild statutes specified the number of threads per unit of length, the provenance of the wool, the mix of dyes and the cut of the cloth in excruciating detail. Guild inspectors relied on visitations and in some places anonymous denunciations to ensure quality. While these regulations raised costs, and some of them were probably a cloak to preserve entrenched markets by keeping outsiders from becoming masters, the city's export market depended on maintaining the reputation of its product.

Representative statutes from Ghent can show the concern of the city council for the quality of cloth:

> No one may dye long, broad and bordered cloth with madder. The fine for violation is £50 and the cloth confiscated.
> No one may exhibit or have cloth exhibited in his inn. The merchant who does it and the wholesaler who seeks it will each be fined £10, and the lords of the cloth hall may search or have searched as often as they wish. . . .
> No one may show or have cloth shown anywhere in Ghent except in the public hall.

No one may remake white cloth into green or sell it as blue, nor make dark green from light blue, nor dark blue nor dark black, because that would be evil and false. Wherever the certifiers of the public hall find such cloth, they may confiscate it.[71]

Yet however irksome such restrictions must have been, in all but the most luxury-driven urban industries, far more provisions of the guild statutes concern length of apprenticeship, entry fees to the guild, regulations of the fraternity, prohibitions against working outside the town, requirements that all persons practising the trade or selling on the local market be members of the guild, residence requirements, eligibility for guild offices, wages, and penalties for working on holidays and insults and physical attacks on other members of the guild. The guilds were at least as much social in character, attempting to regulate a broad range of conduct, as industrial and professional.[72]

Regulation of the export products of the city – in terms of the analysis that we developed in Chapter 1, regulation of basic producers – was significant, but most urban economies were dominated by the local market and central-place functions. Regulation of non-basic producers was intended to protect the local consumer, and consisted of quality and price controls. Consumers had to be kept satisfied to prevent rebellion. Thus the work of apothecaries, goldsmiths, chirurgien-barbers and particularly locksmiths was closely monitored.[73]

The most important and politically volatile internal markets were in food and drink. The authorities had to make certain that consumers got untainted meat and fish – no mean achievement before mechanical refrigeration – wine and beer that had the ingredients that their dispensers claimed, and bread of the legal weight from bakers and millers. The staple privileges of the cities, and the fact that expensive goods would naturally go to the market with the highest prices in relation to transport costs, meant that while food might be expensive in the cities in bad harvest years, it was rarely unavailable. Wine staples brought immense incomes to many cities and also assured a staggering level of alcohol consumption. In fifteenth-century Tours, the average consumption of wine was 148–178 litres annually per adult; 35 per cent of violent deeds are mentioned as connected with drunkenness. Bruges, with a population of about 40,000, had 54 taverns in 1441. Although drinking establishments were found throughout the cities, they were located disproportionately in the disreputable parts of town.[74]

The glories of a mythical tavern of Vienna are celebrated in a satirical poem from the 1260s:

One fine day, some Viennese burghers were carousing with their guests. The wine was the very best. Sorrow was metamorphosed into joy, and the food was fit for a prince, spiced with saffron and coloured with spice, so that to the gullet, twice stimulated, the wine tasted twice as good. So they sat in an arbour, eating and drinking the whole day long, until all their cares were gone. Whenever the waiter brought more food, the steward was right there, ready to fill any empty glass to the brim. .... And so they drank the wine. Some liked it warm and some liked it cold, so that the young got old and the old were young again.[75]

On the continent the cities had their own measures, with an official model usually kept at the town hall or some other public building, so that tavernkeepers could make their own measures from it. The councils fixed the price of wine and beer based on these quantities. In England the national assize of bread required bakers to charge a given price per loaf. When wholesale grain prices rose, the bakers sold smaller loaves, or loaves of mixed grain, for the fixed price. The problem of fixing the price of bread and ale continued to vex city authorities in the modern period. In England butchers and bakers sometimes went on strike to protest against the prohibition of passing their costs on to the consumer, but were nonetheless forced to work by the royal government.[76]

The monopolies of guilds were never complete. They concerned only goods made for sale on the market. People could, if they wished, build their own 'units of production' – their homes – bake their own bread there, weave cloth and slaughter meat for their own consumption. If they thereby got tainted goods, that was their problem. Selling them to someone else could be actionable, but not in every case. Despite the butchers' privileges, Antwerp allowed any citizen to slaughter as many as ten sheep and sell the carcasses in his or her house, but not to sell in a shop or to display them in front of the house.[77] The rural properties owned by townspeople complicate the picture, for the burgesses often received rents in kind or, in Italy, had sharecropping arrangements with their tenants. They could thus use meat and vegetables grown on their rural properties to feed their town establishments, although they could not sell them on the market.

Thus, particularly given the low level of technology and the small number of products available, even in the cities, many homeowners could largely bypass the market for everything but luxuries and food in large quantities. Most English cities required bakers to sell at their own homes, through a window or a shop in front of the domicile. They were not allowed to carry their bread from house to house for sale; the consumer had to come to them.[78] Elsewhere, bread could be sold by street vendors, and it could be baked in private homes everywhere.

The escapades of some weavers' guilds to the contrary, most urban guilds never fomented rebellions. Rather, they were agents of the local authorities. Night watches in many cities were the responsibilities of the guilds, and many city militias were recruited through guild quotas: neither function would have been entrusted to potential rebels. In England the number of craft guilds grew in the late Middle Ages at least in part because the city governments saw them as a convenient way of policing industry. Heather Swanson has argued that the presence of guilds may show more about the management styles of city governments than about the extent of occupational differentiation or corporate sensitivity among groups: thus Norwich preferred a centralised approach in which small crafts were affiliated with larger mysteries in a composite organisation, while York preferred to let even the smallest crafts have their own organisations.[79]

The French urban occupational guilds were substantially controlled by town lords even as early as the twelfth century. The crown kept strict control over the trades of Paris, and most occupational groups in Languedoc were regulated directly by the city administration, although usually by employing persons within the trade as overseers.[80]

The guilds' officers, usually chosen at the annual meeting, had wide discretion over their members. The chief officer of most guilds was the dean (other names include visitor, provost or master). He was assisted by a council chosen by the guild membership, and sometimes by a separate court that judged infractions of the guild's regulations and also disputes between guild members over private matters. Although a few prominent families tended to dominate the guilds, their oligarchies were less tight than the city councils, and some persons who were actually working craftsmen were active in guild affairs. The guild courts handled considerable litigation that now would go before a municipal court. The 'courts of assistants' of the London companies handled far more cases concerning their members than did the central courts of the city, including civil actions of diverse sorts and issues of petty violence. The jurisdictional issue was whether the defendant was a member of the company; the plaintiff need not be in the company or even a freeman, a fact that doubtless led to some in-house acquittals of dubious merit.[81]

Diversity of Goods, Central Place and the Birth of the Tertiary Sector

The diversity of goods available on its markets gave the city a powerful attraction as central place. Not all immigrants were poor. Some were quite well off, including not only merchants, particularly younger sons with money and talent, but also nobles. Most urban elites in Mediterranean Europe always contained rural nobles, and during the late Middle Ages and more strongly after 1500, this social pattern is found in the north, as nobles, attracted by the social attractions and purchasing opportunities on the urban market, spent increasing amounts of time in the chief cities of their regions.

A list of goods that were available on the urban markets but not on rural must focus on luxury and specialised items, even with food. In an area where mainly rye was grown, as in eastern Germany, the city market, with import facilities, might be the best place to obtain wheat. Hop beer is another example. Wine came through the cities. Bread in many more forms than the standard loaf was available in the cities, as were exotic meats and poultry, dried fruits and decorative metalwork. Some good cloth could be bought on small town if not on village markets, but the finest grades could only be obtained in the cities. Industrial regulations ensured that Flemish buyers of silks of Lucca would not be cheated, while there was a real danger of shoddy workmanship from unregulated village shops. Tapestries and embroideries, which came into high fashion in the late Middle

Ages, were urban industries. The cities had gold- and silversmiths who made the jewellery that was so prized by the elites everywhere, and also dabbled in money-lending and often brokerage, through their access to precious metals. Painters' guilds simply did not exist outside the cities. The quality of life was much enhanced by musicians, admittedly more of them employed by princes who lived in the town than by city people. Urban tailors made cloth into wearable clothing. Most large cities had a thriving market in used goods, evidently from people disposing of the clothes of deceased relatives, and they could be bought cheaply by immigrants and others. Numerous types of glassware and leather goods – white leather, purses, fashionable pointed shoes that no farmer would even want but which were prized by the elite – were available in the cities, as were specialists in aspects of construction whose greater sophistication is shown in the different styles of domestic architecture that characterize city and village. Mercers' guilds everywhere imported 'junk', mainly from other cities, that had a market in the central place but not in the lesser settlements, whose residents had to go to the city to obtain such goods. The manufacture of armaments was an important element of the gradual industrialising of many cities. This list deals only with consumer goods and does not take account of the brokerage, banking and shipping services that could be obtained only in the cities and were a powerful element of their attraction. The larger the city, the more of these goods was available, but few cities could boast that their artisans made all or even most of them. They were obtained through inter-city trade, as individual cities developed their own specialities that could only attract enough customers to be viable on a European-wide market that the city nexus, although not the individual city, provided.

The tertiary sector of the economy, which involved occupations that were not directly linked to the production of consumer goods, but rather provided services, was born in the commercial capitalism that gave rise to the cities and was one of their strongest attractions for outsiders. The service sector was vitally important in getting goods to the consumer, local and distant. Most service occupations, such as shippers, were not tightly regulated, although they did have guilds. They were also not highly paid. The most tightly regulated parts of the service sector were brokerage and innkeeping, moneychanging and moneylending. Moneychangers were found only in the larger cities but were essential underpinnings of the interregional trade that developed after 1300. Particularly in Italy they branched into banking; a money market developed, with investors speculating on the exchange rate through bills of exchange, which has similarities to the modern stock market. Moneylenders, often doubling as pawnbrokers, ranged from major operators to casual lenders of small amounts, but they and the moneychangers normally paid fines to the city and were closely watched. Virtually all towns required that goods that entered the city's territory be brought to market in the city and pay toll. They were then consigned to brokers, who delivered them to local merchants, who put them out for sale in the city. Most cities required the use of brokers and forbade merchants to deal directly with the producer:

No burgher from Ghent shall buy grain from another burgher of the city to re-export it, and no burgher from Bruges [may buy] from another burgher of Bruges ... and similarly for all other burghers of all other cities.[82]

Fees were charged by everyone in this process. Only the surplus remaining after the city's needs were met could be re-exported. But this also drove transaction costs up and gave an advantage to cities that were near their sources of raw materials, or at least whose merchants could buy at the source and import them directly. French grain was about 50 per cent more expensive in 1386-7 at Antwerp than at Ghent, through which it had passed.[83]

The nature of merchandising imposed travel. Even apart from the largely permanent merchant colonies in the major cities, whose occupants leased long term or even bought houses unless forbidden to do so by local statute, any place that would be visited by persons from farther away than half a day's journey had to have hotels. Toulouse, with a population of 25,000 in the late Middle Ages, had nearly 600 beds for perhaps 1000 transients. The hospices of St Julien and St Nicholas at Bruges had 73 beds between them, to accommodate over 200 persons at a time. Such figures show that numerous persons used one bed; eight was not uncommon. Florence had 235 innkeepers in 1353, and 622 in 1394, but the latter figure includes the enormous *contado*. London had 197 inns in 1397, in addition to the hospices for the poor and lodging extended by churches. Most cities of southern France had at least a score of inns, but some places with big transient populations such as Avignon and Lyon had many more.[84]

Social Values, the Tertiary Sector and the Urban Elites

Trade, if it is on a small scale, is to be considered vulgar; but if wholesale and on a large scale, importing large quantities from all parts of the world and distributing to many without misrepresentation ... seems to deserve the highest respect, if those who are engaged in it, ... satisfied with the fortunes they have made, make their way from the port to a country estate.[85]

The vogue for Cicero among the Italian humanists and their patrons in the civic aristocracies is well known. His attitude legitimised after the fact what was already their own dominant ethic. Although widespread reading of Cicero spread later in northern Europe, elite consciousness and sense of respectability and prestige were very much in accordance with his views. Hostellers, wholesalers, large-scale traders and rentiers were in all municipal elites. People who worked with their hands, practitioners of 'the vile mechanical arts', were not, although some of their descendants, who had expanded into the supply side of the industrial operation, were.[86]

Just as trade on a large scale was ennobling, while small-scale trading was demeaning, and just as trade per se was more respectable than industry, so within the craft sector differences in prestige and respectability developed between

143

trades with a commercial element and those that involved solely work with the hands. The Florentine distinction between greater and lesser guilds (*arti*) reflects this, as does the difference in some places between 'arts' and 'crafts'.

The urban nobility was at the apex of the elite. By the sixteenth century most writers were using 'patrician' to denote the dominant families of Germany and Italy, and French writers were applying it to their own towns. The Roman origin of the term contributed to its diffusion among the classically educated elites of post-Renaissance Europe. It is accurate for the early modern elites in suggesting inheritance through the father of political and economic privileges, and also some sense of group identity.[87]

Most cities had a two-tiered elite. An older group, called the 'lineages' in contemporary sources, based its power on landholding and rents but expanded into commerce during the thirteenth century. They were joined thereafter, and in many places largely supplanted, by a second group of 'honourable persons' whose wealth was gained through commerce but who then invested in land, in both the city and the rural environs, as a means of gaining 'respectability'. In the late Middle Ages in France, and in the sixteenth century elsewhere, professional persons, particularly lawyers, judges and other officials of the territorial prince began moving into the elites, primarily at the expense of the merchants.

Landholding was at the base of most city elites, as we saw in Chapters 1 and 2. The restrictions on political activity by 'magnate' families are largely a Tuscan phenomenon, and the term became more a personal designation for out-of-favour families than an indication of social milieu. In the cities of Bavaria and the Rhineland landed aristocrats, often descendants of the serfs of the early town lords, dominated most councils even as wealthy merchants muscled in alongside them. The landholding mystique continued to be very powerful and politically potent. Furthermore, while earlier rural magnates who moved into the town for part of the year branched into selling the products of their estates, first on the captive town market and then for exports, by the late Middle Ages merchants in both Italy and the north bought rural estates, intermarried with rural noble families, and for social reasons began working their way into the territorial nobility.

Rent from land was an important part of the patrician 'portfolio'. Given the high risks of commerce, this was only prudent. It does not show declining vigour or vitality, much less a 'treason of the bourgeoisie', as Marxist historians have proclaimed. Most merchants invested in land without giving up commerce: it was more secure, sometimes brought a good return, and helped with one's credit, and land speculation produced goods that could be used for town houses or sold. The activities of the Fuggers of Augsburg are an example of a combination of investment in land and commerce. Investment in rural land seems to have begun with the elite, but it quickly involved the middle classes as well.[88]

As landed nobles lived in towns and merchants bought land, merchant and noble families were intermarrying everywhere in the fourteenth and especially the fifteenth and sixteenth centuries. Many prominent urban families, particularly in France and Spain, bought titles of nobility. As a legally defined rank, nobility could be lost in a 'derogation of status' suit for inappropriate behaviour, such as working with the hands or engaging in petty commerce. The English urban elites thought themselves equal to the country gentry, styled themselves gentlemen or esquires and became clients of nobles. Some members of county ruling families became prominent at Norwich. Especially in London, the dissolution of the monasteries freed land in the city that was generally bought by gentry and lawyers; thus even as the gentry gained land and political power, they became partly urban, with the more prosperous gentlemen having dual residence in county and city. Prominent rural families were often in their town houses during the social 'season', which corresponded to terms at the great law courts. This sometimes meant a division of residence by function among family members, with the lawyer living in the city and the justice of the peace staying in the county.[89]

The landholding element had always been strongest in the Italian and German urban elites, but some power-sharing with the wealthier merchants was inevitable. Exclusive patriciates maintained themselves mainly in southern Germany and a few Italian cities, notably Venice, but lineage and officeholding became more important everywhere in determining standing within the elite. The number of patricians declined in many cities in the sixteenth century; the patriciate of Augsburg, then the largest city of southern Germany, was down to eight families by 1538, when 38 new families were added to it. Strasbourg's patriciate, by contrast, was becoming stronger and more politically active in the sixteenth century. Part of its vitality was due to the frequency with which nobles moved into the city, held office for a time, then returned to the land. A significant part of the nobility of Lower Swabia had links with the upper bourgeoisie of Strasbourg.[90]

An important aspect of elite self-consciousness was membership in social clubs or 'lineage halls', which were usually named, if somewhat inelegantly in the case of 'at the Donkey' (*zum Esel*) at Ravensburg, after the device on their coats of arms. Membership usually required the candidate to give up direct practice of his trade, and those entitled by inheritance to membership could lose it if they violated this rule.[91] By 1420:

> Things have reached the point in Constance that several people who are in the guilds have now figured out how to make associations, and also some people from the guilds have joined the Cat and other drinking halls, through which practice the guilds have been weakened. . . . Thus this is the ruling: Whoever it is, rich or poor, whose father has been in the guilds and who himself has been a guildsman, is forbidden in the future to join any pledged society, neither the Cat nor any other drinking hall, but must remain in his guild.[92]

The magistrates' vigilance came to naught: in 1430 the emperor allowed guildsmen to join the Cat.[93]

The patrician clubs became virtually synonymous with city government in some Hanse cities. Lübeck had two: the Circle Society was founded by the lineages in the fourteenth century, the Merchant Company in the fifteenth by the wealthier merchants to give themselves an association when they were denied membership in the Circle Society. Both were very exclusive. The Merchants' Company usually had 28–30 members, but the Circle Society, which 'restricted to the direct male descendants of the original five founding families', had only two members when it was dissolved at the beginning of the nineteenth century. Since seats were reserved for them on the city council, their very exclusivity created gaps that were filled by wealthy persons with less ancient lineage.[94]

Barcelona's patriciate was the 'honoured citizens', whose most distinctive mark for contemporaries were the fact that they were rentiers who did not work with their hands and controlled the city government. In 1510 a royal edict conferred nobility and the designation *ciutadans honrats* on about 100 named families. They and the gentry held a majority of seats in the committees that established the agenda for the governing body of Barcelona, the Council of the One Hundred. The edict also fixed a complex procedure for determining future admissions to the group. The honoured citizens were as endogamous as their need for dowries permitted, and the rate of biological failure was high. By the seventeenth century the group who gained the status by royal privilege, made possible by a separate accord of 1599, was considerably more numerous than the older group.[95]

Below the urban nobles were merchants of more recent lineage and craftsmen. Several criteria determined the status of trades. Nominally artisan guilds that were actually controlled by merchants enjoyed prestige. Prestigious trades were important to the well-being of the community, particularly procurement of food or raw materials that could be manufactured into goods that were either consumed locally or destined for export. If the market for the trade's product was large, and particularly if it was a monopoly, the prestige of the trade might exceed its lucrativity. Trades whose products were exportable generated income for the community and thus were highly regarded. The least respectable trades were those that were unhygienic or where manual labour could not be avoided. A hierarchy of prestige developed among guilds and was reflected in rank order in city-wide processions (Chapter 6), but individual citizens in undistinguished trades could gain wealth and respect if they were involved in the mercantile rather than industrial side of the business.

Naturally the prestige of individual crafts was not the same everywhere. In cities where the shippers controlled the grain supply or exported the city's products, they were among the most powerful and prestigious guilds, as happened in the Flemish and Hanse cities; but in the inland cities of France and Germany, whose supplies came overland, they were typically a poor group. The weavers were feared everywhere for disorderly tendencies. Yet weavers' guilds were much more powerful in Flanders and its neighbours than in southern France, for Flemish cloth was exported and the French product was not, and the Flemish weavers' guilds were dominated by merchant-drapers who procured the wool

146

and dyes. Direct access to the market was very important, for guilds whose members had to sell their products to wholesalers rather than selling them directly retail were less highly regarded. Similarly, the fact that the dyers did dirty work gave them low status in places that did not export much cloth; but the dye of the finer grades was part of its appeal, and thus in the larger cloth centres the dyers were prestigious. Fullers and other cloth workers were often employees of the weavers, who thus gained status as work-givers rather than workers.[96]

The victualling trades were vital to the survival of the community, but the status-laden question of raw materials and wholesale versus retail trade obtrudes. Bakers and millers were disliked, firmly regulated and uninfluential, in part because they depended on grain merchants for their supplies – granted that in some places the grain merchants were enrolled as bakers – in part because they worked with their hands. Nuremberg is unusual in having a powerful bakers' guild, probably because of the bakers' tie to the local financier Konrad Gross.[97] The butchers, by contrast, were powerful everywhere. They were renowned for being disorderly, for they were the only large group whose profession made necessary the possession of long knives, which the authorities tried to prohibit to others. The butchers' takeover of Paris in 1413 in support of Duke John the Fearless of Burgundy is notorious. They almost always had a prominent place in processions, gained heredity of mastership early and had at least one guaranteed seat on the city council. The more prominent butchers owned their own herds, and once the animals were slaughtered, the butchers sold the by-products to sausagemakers and leatherworkers, who thus depended on the butchers for their supplies. The butchers were linked to the fishmongers in some cities, with dual matriculation permitted in the guilds, but except in London and Winchester the fishmongers had little political influence.[98]

The brewers should be classified as a victualling trade, because the water was so contaminated that most persons drank something mildly fermented; without refrigeration, milk had to be consumed as cheese. Brewing in the rural areas was usually a by-occupation, particularly for women, who brewed ale rather than beer. In the cities, however, it became a highly professionalised trade due to the need to import hops, which were grown only in northern Germany before the fourteenth century. After hops were introduced into England in the fifteenth century, professional beer-brewers in the towns virtually drove out the alewives. Thus the brewers became importers, either of hops or of German or Netherlandish beer, and their status was accordingly enhanced.

Construction workers did not enjoy high standing. Building contractors used considerable amounts of unskilled labour, often from the suburbs of the town. The carpenters were almost always the largest construction trade in northern Europe, where wooden houses were the norm. The masons were less numerous than the carpenters but more highly skilled. They were still a partly itinerant group in the late Middle Ages, but in cities where they were organised they were almost as politically significant as the carpenters. The organisation of the construction industry generally benefited these two groups, for numerous specialities were required to complete a building. A contractor, usually a carpenter but sometimes a mason or other craftsman, directed projects, especially those under-taken by the city governments, and hired and paid workers in other trades.

Since the leatherworkers and metalworkers depended on others for their supplies, and their work was dirty and smelly, they rarely enjoyed high prestige, even though ironworking was expanding everywhere, and leather was coming back into clothing fashion in the late Middle Ages. The leatherworking trades were generally dominated by the tanners, who in some cities got control of the trade in hides by buying directly from the butchers, then restricting access for shoemakers and others.

Some of the richest and most prominent people of the towns – brokers, professional persons such as physicians and notaries, moneychangers, land-owners, innkeeper/hostellers, grain wholesalers, wool merchants – had separate guilds in some but not all cities. They often matriculated in a poorer guild that had the right to a seat on the city council, which they then dominated. The pro-fessionals in the town bureaucracy – attorneys, clerks, gendarmes – tended to have high status.

To conclude, occupational guilds were important, but they included such a diversity of economic and social levels that none was even remotely monolithic, and rarely did they gain total control of either the political or economic life of the cities in the late Middle Ages; and in cases where they did, this was usually ended in the sixteenth or seventeenth century. When fraternities are considered as guilds, however, their impact increases immeasurably on the social organisation of the pre-modern city.

Poverty and Poor Relief in the Cities

The city thus offered opportunities for persons of talent who also enjoyed a con-siderable degree of *fortuna*. In 1367 the weaver Jacob Fugger moved from the vil-lage of Graben-in-Schwaben (Ditch in Swabia) to Augsburg, where he expanded into the wool and cloth trades. He and his descendants invested in mines and eventually overseas exploration, and the family reached its high point in the early sixteenth century as bankers to the Holy Roman Emperors. Their success is very largely responsible for the great growth of late medieval Augsburg.

Unfortunately, most immigrants who streamed into the cities were farm workers who lacked the skill and connections to move immediately into good jobs, and *fortuna* is a fickle mistress. A characteristic of most central places is a greater gap between the resources of rich and poor than is present in small towns. Both food and rent required a much higher percentage of the labourer's income in the cities than in the rural areas, and many poor persons thus lived crowded into garrets, small outbuildings or tenements.[99]

It is a credit to the sense of civic obligation of the guildsmen and the mer-chant and landed elites with which they shared power that most cities developed institutions of poor relief that were far more sophisticated than those in rural Europe, however imperfect apologists for the modern welfare state may find them. In the early Middle Ages the only persons who received assistance, most of it distributed by churches, were those called 'poor' in the Bible: widows, orphans and those with severe physical disabilities. After 1300 the cities faced a growing incidence of economic poverty, large numbers of poor who were physically able to work but were unable to find steady jobs. Whether out of conscience or concern that poverty would lead to desperation and revolution, lay authorities thus became active in poor relief, subsidising and supervising church administration as well as establishing their own charities.[100]

Unfortunately, the extent of poverty is hard to measure. Determining income is difficult. Scarcely anyone except employees of the city governments received an annual salary. Guild masters lived on what was left over after they paid their workers and other business expenses. Most persons received wages, most often calculated by the work day or the week, but sometimes by the piece of work, particularly artisans to whom jobs were put out. In the summer, when the work day could be long, wages were high; they were much lower in the winter, when darkness falls early (virtually all guilds forbade nocturnal work). Efforts to calculate annual income by multiplying wages by the number of work days in the year (about 250 in most places, given rigid enforcement of holidays) are also unsuccessful, for few workers, even masters, were continuously employed. Second occupations provided relief to families. Even the poorest craftsman thus had to do some rational calculation, laying aside money during the good months to tide him over during the winter.

Persons below a given income were exempt from direct taxation virtually everywhere, but the tax floors varied between localities. They were usually so high that what we would call the lower middle class, including some self-supporting persons who owned a flat or even a house, were exempt as 'poor'. The fact that most urban tax records call between one-tenth and one-fifth of the population 'poor', and in some the misery index was nearly half, has led to unwarranted conclusions about the extent of indigence in the pre-modern city.[101] Far more persons received tax exemptions than received regular assistance from a poor table, parish or guild. The latter figure was usually between 3 and 10 per cent of the inhabitants. When the sources distinguish between genders and ages, they show that four to five times as many women and children as men were receiving assistance. This suggests that most men who had wives and children were able to support them. Thus we must distinguish when possible between the hard-core or structural poor and a larger number (another 10–15 per cent) who took charity occasionally but were able to work some of the time. This is still high by the standards of the modern developed world, but not by those of underdeveloped economies.

The availability of institutionalised poor relief was a major attraction of the cities. Most cities had 'hospitals', a term that includes foundations to aid transients for a night or two, orphanages and other long-term foundations for poor relief, and medical facilities. Many were for particular categories of the poor, such as lepers or the blind, rather than general almshouses to alleviate poverty. They ranged in capacity from several hundred unfortunates to fewer than ten.

Guild statutes required that local masters who were unemployed be given work in preference to outsiders.[102] To pass the work around, they also tried to limit the number of apprentices and journeymen that a single master could have. The fraternity attached to the guild dispensed charity to poor masters and sometimes journeymen, and in the fourteenth and early fifteenth centuries many city governments aided the guild almshouses with regular distributions of food, shoes and fuel. Unfortunately, few guild foundations were large enough to alleviate poverty significantly, and by 1450 it was mainly the larger and wealthier guilds, which had a substantial number of poor as well as the rich, that still maintained them.

Most parish organisations also dispensed poor relief, sometimes handled by the clergy but more often by lay churchwardens and sometimes confraternities who considered such donation of time and skill an important part of their Christian obligation. Sometimes the parish tables made direct distributions of food, clothing or money to the poor of the parish. Particularly in France and northern Spain, parishes kept registers of eligible recipients to whom tokens were given, which could be redeemed for food. Some pious donors who hoped to speed their passage into paradise established chantries or funded anniversary masses for their souls, but sometimes (much less often) left endowments that provided food distributions to the poor on the anniversary dates of their deaths. Some of these could give bread to hundreds of persons. A London riot in 1322 led to 52 deaths as the poor fought to get to the distribution site for food that had been provided in the testament of a local fishmonger.[103]

The older charities, which had endowments before 1350, were distributing charity to fewer persons after the depopulations caused by the plagues, but many thereby were able to increase the amount given per capita. But as immigration into the cities increased in the fifteenth century, local resources for almsgiving were being strained. The authorities were fearful of vagabonds, those without local roots. The visual was an important aspect of their fear. The council of Cologne threatened to expel from the city:

> all who sit before the churches with sickness or go on the street with open wounds and fractures. [They] must cover their wounds and fractures and not let them be seen, so that good people will suffer no stink or unpleasantness.

A statute also intoned:

> that many persons, both women and men, who circulate begging in the city are strong and healthy enough to work for their bread. ... Thus our lords decree that these healthy people must work and serve for their bread, and whoever refuses to do so will be expelled from the city. Any who refuse to leave and remain in the city anyway will be seized by the police and put in the city jail for a year on bread and water and then will be expelled physically from town.[104]

Thus in the late fifteenth and particularly sixteenth centuries many cities began expelling vagabonds or forcing them to work, supporting only the poor who were domiciled in the city. They kept better lists of eligible poor persons, so that the home market could be served. They also cut back on their assistance to private charitable foundations in the parishes and guild almshouses. By 1500 people who a century earlier would have been receiving charity in the cities – from city governments, guilds, churches, parishes or private foundations – were being sent on as vagrants, as the cities limited relief to the native-born and/or the 'deserving' poor. In the sixteenth century 9 per cent of the total criminal prosecutions at Brussels and 26 per cent at Antwerp were for vagabondage. The number of vagrancy prosecutions in London increased eightfold between 1560 and 1625, while population roughly doubled.[105]

The most optimistic estimate concedes that the purchasing power of London craftsmen declined by nearly a third in the sixteenth century.[106] The incidence of poverty and vagrancy accordingly rose, although probably not to the extent that some have maintained. Between 1534 and 1561 slightly over 5 per cent of the inhabitants of Lyon received some assistance from the municipal Almonry at some point, but in most cases only in emergencies.[107] Surveys show that 6.4 per cent of the population of Troyes was eligible for public assistance in the 1530s, but the number had grown to 16 per cent by 1551. Paris was giving assistance to 18,000 persons in 1627.[108] If Paris had a population of 250,000 inhabitants at that time, 7.2 per cent were receiving relief. Since standards of eligibility for assistance were much tighter than earlier, those receiving relief were the hard-core poor. Still, these figures confirm other suggestions that when genuine indigence is distinguished from tax poverty, social life in the cities appears far less bleak.

Major changes occurred in the administration of urban poor relief in the sixteenth century. Although city governments were careful to monitor eligibility, they became more generous in assisting the 'deserving' poor and those who could not help themselves, notably orphans. The record is considerably more dismal where national governments were able to dictate local policy, as in England, than in Germany and France, where the cities still made their own rules. The cities often issued tokens or scrip that could be redeemed for food at a local almshouse. Most cities also centralised the major private charities into a 'common chest'. The German cities that did this earliest were Protestant, starting with Nuremberg in 1522 and Strasbourg and Augsburg in 1523. They funded the 'common chest' with incomes seized from Roman Catholic charities and monasteries, as well as current church collections and private endowments. Roman Catholic cities quickly followed suit. In the Low Countries Ypres in 1525 established a common chest, administered by parish overseers. Bruges, Mons and others made similar reforms. The *quid pro quo* was that begging, which disturbed citizens' peace, was forbidden. With the wars and the Counter-Reformation, however, secular poor relief in the southern Low Countries ended in the second half of the sixteenth century, replaced by Roman Catholic relief as outlined in the decrees of the Council of Trent.[109]

In France too poor relief was being taken over by the city governments in the sixteenth century. At Troyes the parishes continued to be centres of poor relief, administered by elected lay churchwardens. In the 1520s and 1530s the city government took over most poor relief from the local hospitals, appropriating their revenues in the process. In 1545, following the examples of Lyon and Rouen in the 1530s, the hospital (Hôtel-Dieu) was reorganised under joint ecclesiastical and lay auspices. Begging was forbidden; poor children were to be trained in a craft (usually weaving) or put into domestic service, while able-bodied adults were given unskilled public works jobs.[110]

In Paris, which predictably had a serious poverty problem, public begging was outlawed in 1536. In 1544 the General Almonry (*Aumone générale*), more often called the Great Office of the Poor (*Grand Bureau des Pauvres*), was established with a board of governors drawn from among the city's notables to supervise the distribution of alms. The parishes were responsible for raising the money. Indigents had to make application to the authorities, who would determine whether the person qualified for assistance. Yet as early as 1551 a commission estimated that the number of persons receiving assistance had tripled. They insisted that only persons who had lived in Paris for at least five years and had worked in some respectable trade and had then fallen on evil days qualified for poor relief. Others were to be put to work on public projects.[111]

Lyon is the best-documented example of municipal response to the growing problem of poverty. The endowments of church almonries were simply appropriated in 1534 to fund a General Almonry, which kept lists of eligible poor, and inspectors visited the recipients regularly. The indigent received free medical treatment at the hospitals, and alms on a temporary or continuing basis as needed. Two hospitals for orphans and foundlings were opened, and primary education was provided for the boys and some of the girls. The Almonry paid the cost of apprenticing boys and funded dowries for the girls, although some of them were put into domestic service before marriage. Begging was strictly forbidden; the poor might be removed from the rolls if caught begging.[112]

In England, in contrast to the continent, most institutional almsgiving before the Reformation was still in the hands of the churches. Thus the dissolution of the monasteries and chantries forced local governments to act quickly. While private charity was still regarded as a Christian virtue, the national Poor Law of 1536 obliged the parishes to maintain funds for alms, but only for those who were physically incapable of working. Beginning with Bridewell in 1547, London established workhouses for the unskilled poor, mainly in areas that did not compete with domestic craftsmen. The term 'bridewell' quickly spread to workhouses in other towns. People were confined in them as punishment after repeatedly disregarding orders to work. The idea of semi-penal workhouses quickly spread to the continent. Rouen, Paris and Lyon began confining some poor in workhouses in the early seventeenth century, and a royal ordinance required this in all cities in 1656.[113]

Listing the problems of the cities makes them appear starkly unattractive places. Clearly, many of the immigrants who were attracted to them were people who felt that they had nothing to lose. Yet the inter-city networks of journeymen, the neighbourhood concentrations in many cities of immigrants from specific villages, the availability of part-time work in unskilled trades, the employment opportunities for masters with letters from their home guilds attesting their professional credentials, and the availability of charity during emergencies were important enticements for persons of at least minimal standing elsewhere.

The cultural life associated with the city is part of its attraction. While today immigrants can be misled into a disastrous move by media-driven fables of riches, no peasant was enticed to move to Florence by reading humanist tracts about the glories of the civic life. Residents of the environs heard tales of the central place, but the larger cities were also attracting newcomers from more distant regions after 1350, and these people had to have some hope, if not knowledge, of what awaited them. The information networks that contributed to a given city's reputation constitute a fascinating topic that unfortunately transcends the present study.

All cities fulfilled cultural functions. As material goods and services became concentrated in central places, so did cultural capital, and for many of the same reasons. Urban culture, to which we now turn, should be seen in terms of the analytical framework for the development of city life that we delineated in Chapters 1 and 2.

Chapter 6 . . . .

Material Culture and Cultural Environment

We arrived at Bruges, the finest city of the world. . . . The sea and the merchants from all nations who congregate there have made it the richest in goods, after Ghent the second city and capital of Flanders. For its site and its beauty one could scarcely find a city comparable to this: Bruges, my home town.[1]
(Anselme Adorno)

The City as Ideal

Anselm Adorno's praise of his native Bruges sounds unpolished in comparison to Leonardo Bruni's famous *Panegyric to the City of Florence*, which was conceived as a classically-inspired oration laden with references to ancient Rome.[2] The city as portrayed in panegyrics is often an ideal at odds with contemporary reality. Descriptions become more realistic in the late Middle Ages but many, particularly those done by humanists, are formulaic. The humanists inspired, but did not in each case cause, a renewed interest in the city's past that developed in the late Middle Ages. The proximity of ancient ruins fostered historical consciousness in Italy. The early humanists urged that the past be understood in its own terms. Unfortunately, they also considered history a branch of literature: Bruni simply lifted passages from Tacitus and applied them to Florence. But by the late fifteenth century urban historiography in Italy had moved beyond this: the city's past was to be reconstructed by using documents. Niccolò Machiavelli is best known for his political thought, but his *History of Florence* is notable for his use of the Florentine archives, as well as for drawing practical rather than moral lessons from the past.

Antiquity gave prestige to cities, as it did to families. Since documents were lacking, a myth explained the city's birth. The story of the Trojans moving west was incorporated into many stories of urban origins, including those of Venice and London. Any kind of orthographic coincidence would give rise to a legend:

Tours claimed to have the tomb of Aeneas' companion Turnus, and King Cole, father of St Helena, supposedly founded Colchester. York citizens knew that their city had been Roman Eboracum, but they also believed Geoffrey of Monmouth's tale that a 'King Ebrauk' had founded the city much earlier. When Henry VII entered York in 1486, he was met by a cortege that included King Ebrauk.[3]

More seriously, a tradition of municipal historiography was being developed, and not only in Italy. At Barcelona local antiquarians wrote more than 20 histories of the city between the fifteenth and eighteenth centuries.[4] German town clerks kept their cities' official chronicles, of which 18 survive from the Hanse cities alone. John Hooker's work on Exeter (*c.* 1575) and especially John Stow's *Survey of London* (1598) are the first English examples. There are several others in the seventeenth century, including Henry Manship's history of Great Yarmouth, which is important in showing that urban pride and 'civic memory' were not confined to the large cities.[5]

Rulers everywhere had control of public symbolism. Murals and sculpture in the town halls typically showed the city personified as a Roman goddess, and the magistrates wearing full regalia. Just as town seals often contained representations of the gates along with images of the patron saint and/or power images, such as a symbol of the king, so the niches in the gates of the larger cities were decorated with sculptures. At York, the mid-fourteenth century Mickelgate bar had the coats of arms of both the city and the king.[6] The Charles IV Bridge at Prague, finished around 1380, leading from the lower city, had coats of arms and sculptures of Kings Charles IV and Wenzel IV and the figure of Vitus, the patron saint of the city.

The City as Reality: Scenes, Smells and Sounds

Such luminaries as Adorno and Bruni to the contrary, the attractions of the pre-modern city did not include its physical environment. Perhaps because the towns grew so rapidly after 1100, there is little evidence of concern over waste disposal until after 1200 in Italy and still later in the north. No one thought of treating sewage to decontaminate it. The task was to take mostly organic mess outside the city, but scarcely any towns had subterranean conduits before the sixteenth century. What pipes existed were used to obtain fresh water, not dispose of sewage. The problem was exacerbated by the nature of some industrial processes. Urine was used in tanning and clothmaking. Dyers usually lived near streams into which they dumped their chemicals. The only source of fresh water at Cologne was the river Hürth, since the Rhine was contaminated, but it was turned into a 'blue river' by the dyeries built above it.[7] Most paper mills were in rural areas, but tanneries, although generally on the periphery of the town, were usually in populated areas, close enough to contribute to the pervasive miasma. The Tanners' Corner at Ghent was just outside the city proper, in St Peter's abbey village, a suburb favoured by weavers, in a sharp bend where the Scheldt joins a canal, trapping the fumes. Flax for linen, which was increasingly made in the cities from the late Middle Ages, was more environmentally noxious than wool, although since linen bleaching required open space, it was usually done near the walls.

Chickens and goats were everywhere. The presence of large animals in the streets, especially horses for transportation and pigs for food, created a manure problem. Municipal statutes constantly ordered owners to keep their pigs in sties rather than letting them wander the streets, but nobody tried to stop them from owning pigs. Reims in 1389 allowed no more than four pigs per household and confinement in a sty, which had to be cleaned at least twice per week.[8] In 1304 the parson and parishioners of St Benet Fink in London:

> complain that Roger de Euere has overthrown the fence . . . of the church-yard, so that pigs and other animals . . . enter it by night and day, and carry off the plants growing there, and commit other enormities in contempt of God and to the great damage of the church.[9]

Hence city governments and private citizens dug drainage ditches. Since they usually ran between the houses that shared them, complaints between neighbours were frequent. In 1310:

> John le Luter complains that the cess-pit of Robert de Chiggewelle's privy adjoins too closely his earthen wall . . . so that his house is inundated and his wall is rotted by the sewage. . . . Judgment after view that they clean the cess-pit at their common charges; and, at their discretion, either combine to build a stone wall in place of the earthen one, or each build a stone wall on his own pourparty.[10]

The idea of flushing waste presupposes indoor plumbing several centuries before it existed even in royal establishments. Whatever was produced in the house left it by the most commodious route, which was usually out the window. The cities tried to prevent citizens from dumping refuse into the streets, but the statutes were repeated so often that the magistrates' strictures were obviously having little impact.

> We [the magistrates of Bologna] order that no one throw or cause to be thrown into the piazza of the commune of Bologna or in the crossroads at the Porta Ravennate, any stinking or dead animals or rotten fish or shellfish or any filthy or stinking thing or foodscraps, sweepings, dung or prison filth.[11]

Chamber pots were emptied into the street from the upper storeys of houses, which were often jetties that projected into the street beyond the frontage of the lower floors. A famous tale has Louis IX of France being hit on his sacred head while en route to church by the contents of a chamber pot emptied from such a 'penthouse' into the street by a university student.[12] In 1305 Robert le Barber of London complained that his neighbour:

has constructed a gutter ... from which the water falls at his door ... and has built a jetty ... which obstructs his view, and that his chimney ... is too near the plaintiff's party-wall ..., causing danger of fire to his house.[13]

All cities had drainage canals, but they contaminated the drinking water supply. Streets commonly sloped toward the centre, where a channel would carry off the waste, but only if the pitch of the land was right. Defensive needs during the late Middle Ages also exacerbated the pollution problem: the cities had to build large and self-contained moats, which kept water in the city.

Human waste was the worst problem, and not all of it was produced in the residence. Most cities had Easement Alleys, Ordure Streets or some equally elegant designation near the main market. Public latrines were also common on bridges. Street names reflect functionality. Thus, just as Butchers' and Weavers' Streets were common, so in France were compounds of *rue* (street) and *merde* or *merdeux* (shit, shitty), which are found at Chartres, Amiens, Beauvais, Le Mans, Provins, Sens and Troyes, among others. Angoulême had a *rue Sale* (Dirty Street), Châlons-sur-Marne a Pee Alley (ruelle du Pipi), while Paris had its Stinking Hole.[14]

Recessed spaces built into the walls that served as property boundaries were used as privies and cesspits. Few houses had outdoor latrines, even in the back yards. In the fourteenth century the larger houses, especially those built in stone, had indoor privies that emptied the waste through a chute that led to a pit. Private citizens could not channel their waste into public drainage. Garbage collectors doubled as cesspit cleaners, such as the '*fify* masters' of Paris and the 'ordure count' of Buda. They seem to have been more concerned with removing debris than sewage. Nuremberg was unusual in requiring homeowners to maintain privies, but emptying them was always a problem: the privies of the prominent Tucher and Behaim families were only cleaned every 30 years. York in the early sixteenth century required that a cart be kept in every city ward to collect residents' waste. It was then conveyed outside the city, where farmers could use it as fertilizer.[15]

Matters became marginally better in the sixteenth and seventeenth centuries. In 1533, to stop the practice of emptying slops out of upper storey windows, the council of Amsterdam began requiring sinks drained by lead pipes in the upper storey rooms. From 1565 the city required privies on all plots of land.[16] Lead piping became much more common, and city sewers served the main streets, to which homeowners could have connections built at their own expense. But sanitation, particularly in the larger cities, remained elemental. The street was still the most convenient sewer.

The miasmas that such an environment emitted transcend the modern imagination. Odours leave no trace in the documentary sources unless someone complains about them. The food supply also caused problems. The cities generally required sale of meat and fish at the guildhalls, where they could be regulated carefully and the waste products disposed of. Since the fishmongers and butchers' halls were usually in proximity, the stench in their parts of the central city was overpowering. They were also on streams, so that the post-slaughter remains were thrown into the water. From 1409 Winchester required butchers to cut their residues into pieces smaller than four inches before dumping them into the Itchen, which unfortunately then meandered through the cathedral precinct.[17]

Speed was particularly critical with fish. 'All sea fish that comes fresh into Ghent shall immediately be displayed for sale, and it is not to be removed from the Fish Market before it is sold.'[18] In 1390 a mercer of London hired a carter to carry away rotten fish and dump them in a well in the suburbs. The fishmongers, whose reputation was at stake, asked for an inquest by the mayor and aldermen, who found that the mercer had also 'caused 24 barrels of salted eels to be carted, which were lying in a certain cellar ... the same being rotten and unwholesome for the human body, but which he purposed selling to the commonalty'. But the mercer's only punishment was loss of the fish, which were carried outside the city and buried.[19]

Yet much of London's legislation about sanitation came from royal concern about the stink. The king, not the city government, ordered the Shambles (slaughterhouses) moved from Cheapside to Westminster in the late fourteenth century.[20] In 1332 Edward III wrote to the mayor and bailiffs of York:

> The King, detesting the abominable smell abounding in the said city, more than any other in the realm from dung and manure and other filth and dirt wherein the streets and lanes are filled and obstructed, and wishing to provide for the protection of the health of the inhabitants and of those coming to the present parliament, orders them to cause all the streets and lanes of the city to be cleansed of such filth.[21]

Since the source of contamination was not removed, the stench got no better in the modern period: in 1600 the Provost of Paris ordered that:

> all carters carrying and conveying manure, materials emptied from privies, mud, and other filth, are forbidden to unload elsewhere than in ditches and gutters designated for this purpose ... and also all persons are forbidden to throw any water, filth or garbage from the windows onto the aforesaid streets and thoroughfares, either in the day or at night.[22]

The more things change, the more they stay the same.

Since the river on which most major cities were located was also the municipal sewer, fresh water was a critical issue. For most homeowners, themselves a minority of the population, a well in the backyard provided fresh water, but it was easily contaminated by seepage from privies. The monasteries and palaces were the first to pipe water from exterior streams and ponds, and the practice quickly spread to the cities. The royal palace at Westminster had water piped from the western suburb that is now called Hyde Park by 1169–70. London was the first city connected to an external fresh water source by pipes. In 1237 the city acquired a reservoir, then linked it to the 'Great Conduit' that was being built in

Cheapside. During the fourteenth and fifteenth centuries more pipes were built from the Great Conduit into different parts of the city. The flow was adequate to serve private homes, but not the needs of brewers in the streets near the Conduit, who in 1337 and again in 1345 were forbidden to fill their kegs at night, so that others would have enough. This basic system was still in place in 1666, after which a new aqueduct was built.[23]

The practice quickly spread to other cities. Hollowed tree trunks were used as pipes, since the joints between tiles leaked. Lead, its health hazards still unknown, was also used, particularly from the sixteenth century. The pipes were usually along the sides of the streets, not subterranean. Most cities also maintained public wells, supplied by rainwater as well as being piped in. Bamberg had 40 public wells, to which water was brought by a system of canals lined with wood and lead from mountain streams nearby. Bremen also pumped water by a large mill from the Weser to about 400 homes. Siena began a fountain in 1352, but the inhabitants of the neighbourhood paid most of the cost. Paris had about 20 fountains in the mid-seventeenth century, and the number was doubled under Louis XIV. Pumps were built at the Pont-Neuf, Pont des Tuileries, and Pont-Notre-Dame.[24] The cities also linked their reservoirs to fountains, generally on a main square. Unfortunately, there was no way to control the flow, and at high tides along the Seine much water was wasted. Most fountains were initially made of wood, but stone was being used for some even in the fourteenth century. The fountains were often works of art, and the availability of water enhanced the social aspect of the squares where they were situated.[25]

The city governments also maintained canals, initially for defence, then for trade. Milan's elaborate network of canals directed water away from the city into the moat, whence it was used to irrigate the suburbs. By 1346 Milan had a Street and Water office, with its 'judge' named by the duke.[26] The canals often became part of the street system of the cities; Venice, Bruges and Amsterdam are the most famous cases of barge traffic along canals serving the inner city as well as providing access with the outside, but they are not the only ones.

Numerous bridges crossed the rivers and canals. Dresden in 1295 instituted a tax on stalls in the cloth hall, where all local cloth had to be sold, to pay for repairs to the bridge.[27] The bridges were commercial and, less often, residential centres: London Bridge had 138 shops in 1358, and the Ponte Vecchio (Old Bridge), Florence's only crossing of the Arno until others were added in the fourteenth century, is famous. At least 15 bridges crossed the Gera river at Erfurt. Shops on the most centrally located one, the Mercers' Bridge (*Krämerbrücke*), were the main market for luxury items in the city.[28] In 1265 the city council bought from the cathedral chapter its ground rent on the stores on this bridge with the intention:

> in place of that bridge, which is now made of wood, to construct a stone bridge at the earlier opportunity, in order to prevent such damage from happening in the future as the city of Erfurt suffered recently, when fire destroyed this wooden bridge and a great part of the city on both sides of it.[29]

Access to the bridges was critical and difficult to maintain:

> No one may put kiosks or shops on the Count's Bridge except for French grapes and cheese and sweets. . . . Further, no one may stand or sit outside the gutter with vegetables nor any other goods between the foot of the Count's Bridge and the Hoogpoort [street], so that we can keep the street clear on both sides, except that people may stand with herrings inside the boundaries of the Fish Market, but not outside.[30]

The City as Habitation: Streets and Houses

The streets and squares of the pre-modern city were thus noxious and dangerous. They were also noisy. Public processions only made disorder official policy, albeit for a limited time. The town crier wandered the streets spreading information. Proclamations were read from balustrades of the town hall. In addition to what the city government sponsored, itinerant musicians, particularly fiddlers and pipers, perambulated the streets, playing for handouts but annoying many inhabitants. Since the guilds insisted that work be done in the open, noise from industrial operations, including the death throes of animals being slaughtered and their cries while being driven alive through the cities to the meat hall, were ever-present. Bells tolled the hours. Peddlers hawked their wares, and shopkeepers announced their goods.

Coarse entertainments were found everywhere. Girls whose virtue was compromised were immortalised by obscene processions. Some French cities chose a Plain Jane each year. Executions and mutilations became mass entertainment. Capital punishment was less common in the Middle Ages than in the modern period, but when it occurred, it was done publicly, gruesomely and in ceremonies intended to deter others from similar behaviour. The heads of political criminals were impaled on the city gates as a lesson to all.

Bull-baiting was common: from 1300 the butchers of Winchester were required to let their bulls be baited for entertainment before slaughtering them.[31] In Paris in 1425

> Four blind men wearing armour and each carrying a club were put into an enclosure in which there was also a strong pig. They were to have it if they could kill it. They fought this strange battle, giving each other tremendous blows with the clubs. . . . The blind men were led through Paris wearing their armour, with a great banner in front of them with a picture of a pig on it. In front of this went a man bearing a drum.[32]

The occupations of many urbanites were conducted from the home, but most other activities that are now done there, ranging from obtaining water to extended conversations to bodily functions, had to be conducted outside. The pervasive darkness limited what could be done at home. Penthouses kept light away from the lower storeys as well as from the street. Most houses had their narrow frontage on the street side, often sharing a wall extending into the back yard with adjacent houses, and this cut down on interior illumination. Candles and torches were fire hazards and did not help much. Street lights were rare. Paris's first lighting ordinance came in 1504, when residents were obliged to put lanterns in their windows. From 1558 one or more lanterns were supposed to be installed in each street and kept burning from 10 p.m. to 4 a.m., but enforcement was lax.[33]

Most cities had a statutory minimum width for streets, but these restrictions were often ignored, especially in the side, residential streets. In composite streets, where the sections of a long thoroughfare that succeeded each other without break served different functions, the separate sections often had different widths. Even within the same street, adjacent houses often projected different distances into the thoroughfare, hindering circulation. The widest streets usually provided access to the gates and/or the market. Residential streets were often narrower, and those that designate an occupation were usually the smallest.[34]

Since many towns were situated on hilltops for defensive reasons, many streets were extremely steep, with danger of floods and rapid descent of sewage. Stairs were provided for some, including platforms to allow pedestrians to catch their breath. At Metz access to the cathedral city was by the 'Stairs of the Chamber'. Chartres had steep streets, including stairs to link the upper town on the hilltop with the lower town. Other colourful names include 'The Steps of the Hanged', 'Steps of the Little Stag', 'Steps of the Rats' and 'Steps of the Slippery Harlot'.[35]

Most streets were narrow, irregular, and winding, particularly in the older, organic cities. Anything called 'rue Neuve' (New Street) is likely to be straighter and broader than other streets in the same town: for example the regular streets of the Villeneuve of the Temple at Paris and those of planned foundations or suburbs, such as at Reims.[36] In the old cities the larger streets, usually with a name such as *Grande Rue* or High Street, were sometimes as wide as 12 metres.

Paris was a notorious bottleneck. Perhaps because it has three discrete segments, one of which is an island, access was difficult. Even its main streets were unusually narrow, and many were still unpaved in 1500. The main roads, which ran north–south, had to cross the *Ile de la Cité* and were barely 6 metres across. Most streets, including those around bridges, ports and public squares, were considerably narrower. The bridges across the island were narrow and not aligned with the streets. Street frontages provided different passable widths (as buildings jutted out into the passageway) and were often hindered with scaffolding and crates of merchandise. Some streets were 1–2 metres across or even less; the ruelle du Paon-Blanc permitted one person to pass, but only a thin one. A rue Esquiche-coude (the name means 'scrunch the elbow') in Aix-en-Provence was so narrow that the two elbows of a passer-by could touch the facades of buildings on the two sides.[37]

Circulation was a manageable problem as long as most goods were transported on foot or pack animal. However, the incidence of transport wagons within the walls increased after 1300, and in the modern period personal carriages put a severe strain on circulation, for they could pass through only the main streets and sometimes, particularly in the older large cities, not even them.[38] The smaller streets were alleys sometimes no more than a metre across. The main streets of most major cities were paved, first in Italy and then in the north. Florence was completely paved by the time Villani wrote in 1338. Vienna's paved streets made a favourable impression on a distinguished Italian visitor in 1438.[39] At London paving began on a ward basis and quickly became city-wide, but homeowners had to pay for paving the portion of street that passed their property. The material was initially gravel, but cobblestones were common by the fourteenth century. The side streets were another matter, as were the main streets of the smaller towns. They were simply packed earth, and rain turned them into mudslides. The farther one moved from the city centre, the smaller, more serpentine and muddier the streets were likely to be.

Some streets were initially the private property of a landowner, but in the thirteenth century in Italy and the fourteenth in the north, they came to be considered public space and subject to municipal regulation. Street maintenance was a major expenditure in all city budgets, along with bridges and fortifications. Depending on whether the city was at war, Ghent spent between 5 and 25 per cent of its budget on public works (including bridges) in the fourteenth century; streets alone took 9 per cent of the income of Nantes in 1467, 18 per cent of that of Rennes in 1483. Most cities had officials in charge of streets and paving. They were usually part-time and most often were carpenters or masons.

Some cities required citizens to demolish structures that obstructed the streets or violated building codes, which were often a matter of local custom. A statute of Bologna ordered 'that no one is to keep outside the columns or walls of houses around the commune's courtyard any wood or barrel-hoops which might obstruct passage through the courtyard'.[40]

Wide streets served as markets in many cities, and the amount of buying and selling outside homes made the streets congested under the best of circumstances. Hucksters were everywhere. In 1475 the guild of cooks of London complained that the respectable members of their craft were being tainted because 'divers persons of the said craft with their hands dirtied and fouled are accustomed to draw and pluck other folk ... by their sleeves and clothes to buy their victuals'.[41] Access to the street was also hindered by external staircases and galleries. Four butchers of London were fined in 1345 'because that they obstructed the street of the Poultry with their benches, placed there for selling their meat'.[42]

Other impediments to circulation were private towers, in the north as well as in the French Midi and Italy, galleries or private or common balconies, external staircases and sometimes bridges that linked the upper storeys of family compounds. Towers were a common feature of Italian cityscapes in the twelfth and thirteenth centuries, but less so thereafter. Some collapsed and were not repaired, or the city government ordered their destruction because of the antisocial behaviour of their occupants. Some towers were divided into rental apartments, and stairs were put onto some for access from the street to apartments in the upper storeys.[43] The confiscation of aristocrats' towers permitted street widening and new public buildings in Florence and Bologna in the 1260s and 1270s.

Urban properties were identified by street name in northern Europe from the beginning of our period. Some names are obvious, such as High, Great or Middle Streets. Religious names, such as a chapel or church, were also common. Patronymic names, for prominent persons who dominated them, are found generally only for side streets. Others were named for a public work or an occupation, or had an economic-descriptive name. In Mediterranean France and Italy landmarks and city blocks were more often used to identify property locations until the fourteenth century, but thereafter street names became more common. Street corners were not marked with signs until later, a fact that doubtless confused transients and, given the dangers of wandering into unfamiliar neighbourhoods, kept them close to their inns.

Most places of business and many residences, however, were identified by signs by the early fourteenth century. They were commonly wooden or sometimes stone images on building corners, where they could serve a structural as well as decorative function. Sculpted images were also found above doors or in niches in the façade. Shops were usually adorned with painted signs, either on a flat board or suspended on a pole that projected into the street. The signs' topics range from the religious to the profane, with much from mythology, romance and scenes of daily life. The colourful names of some houses often described the kind of business conducted there. Houses of prostitution and taverns boasted signs that indicated the nature of the business and often the name of the building, which was generally taken from a previous owner, or a saint's name, or an animal or human associated with the trade practised in the house, or an astrological or cosmological symbol. The pictorial signs yielded to house numbers in the modern period. The house names that the signs contained, even if only pictorially, are often found in the tax registers, indicating that they were becoming part of a legal identification.[44]

The projecting signs, obviously intended to attract trade and distinguish one's own business from competitors, could also hinder access through the narrow streets. On 21 September 1375:

> At the prayer of the Commonalty, making plaint that the alestakes projecting in front of the taverns in Chepe, and elsewhere in the City, extended too far over the King's highway, so as to impede those riding there, and other persons, and, by reason of their excessive weight, did tend to the great deterioration of the houses in which they were placed; – it was ordained and granted by the Mayor and Aldermen, as a befitting remedy for the same, and all the taverners of the City being summoned, orders were given unto them ... that in future no one should have an alestake bearing his sign, or leaves, projecting or extending over the King's highway more than seven feet in length at the utmost.[45]

Although there was some amelioration of this situation through wider streets and squares in the sixteenth and seventeenth centuries, the practical impact of 'Renaissance' ideas of town planning has been overestimated. Urban renewal was difficult in older centres unless the authorities were willing to undertake deliberate demolition of existing streets, which was rarely feasible. There was some alteration of street plan in the quarters near the walls. Suburbs were more likely to have a master plan than the central areas, and in some rapidly growing cities the suburbs were overtaking the city centre in terms of demographic and sometimes economic importance. There are exceptions, such as Rome, but Renaissance theories, as discussed in Chapter 3, affected mainly new foundations, particularly those of a primarily military character. The problem of narrow, crooked streets remained serious in all but a few cities.[46]

In the early stages of urbanisation plots of land in the cities were large, usually in a trapezoidal shape of 14–15 metres on the street frontage, declining to 4–6 metres behind. This ratio between depth and width was often reversed in the Italian cities. While stone building was the norm in Italy, most town houses in northern Europe before 1100 were simple huts, but thereafter their plans became more complex. The house, generally gabled to facilitate drainage and provide an attic for storage, was usually on one side of the plot, and its neighbour on the other, leaving an open space between the buildings. They thus used in common a vacant space that led into a rear courtyard, which was often shared in the twelfth century but was subdivided thereafter.

But population increased more rapidly than land area, and subdivision of plots, and even of houses, produced overcrowding. Rows of houses had always been the norm in Italy, and this became true of the north during the late Middle Ages. The houses were now built directly adjacent to each other, sharing a common wall. Through the thirteenth century the hearth was usually on the street side of the house, with the kitchen directly behind it, and the smoke escaped through a hole in the roof. This was incompatible with multistorey structures, and in the thirteenth century the introduction of the chimney entailed repositioning the hearth to a side of the house, often along the wall that was shared with the neighbour.[47]

The shape of the houses also changed, with the narrow side with the gable on the street frontage, the longer side extending into the courtyard, particularly in the larger cities, where space was scarce. The gable was sometimes decorated with signs or statuary. Some street frontages in the old quarters of the cities were as tiny as 15 feet. The back yard might extend all the way to the roughly parallel street behind the house; thus one side of a secondary street might have only outbuildings of the houses on the main street, but the opposite side would have house fronts.[48]

Most people cooked on the interior hearth, keeping a fire going most of the time. Baking was hard except in an outdoor oven (most meat and vegetables were boiled). The back yards contained kitchens, though only in the case of the more elegant homes, privies and latrines, sometimes stand-alone ovens, a kitchen, a well or fountain, stalls, a garden, and in the case of the larger establishments, rooms and apartments that were rented.

As wood became scarcer, half-timbering became the norm for most urban houses in the north, with mud or plaster filling in the framework provided by the crossed beams. Half-timbering made possible multistoreyed buildings, and this style quickly spread.[49] Brick was introduced in the thirteenth century and became more common in the fourteenth. The street frontage might be of brick or stone, and the sides wattle and daub. The organic material in the walls, and particularly the straw in roofs, was a breeding ground for plague-bearing rats.[50]

Houses built entirely of stone were the norm in Italy, but in the north they were unusual except for aristocrats, although most towns had some. As early as 1179 the archbishop of Reims complained that the 'wealth and fortified houses' of the elite of Ghent had made them arrogant.[51] Stone houses yielded to brick after 1400. Wooden buildings were a fire hazard. Paris had long had a custom forbidding new building in wood, but from 1607 Henry IV started enforcing it and requiring that old structures be rebuilt. This cannot be generalised; the towns of the Midi had traditionally used stone, but the usage only spread significantly to the northern French towns from the second half of the seventeenth century.[52]

Half-timber buildings, and even more so stone and brick, were much heavier than the purely wooden shacks of the early cities. Thus the development of multistoreyed houses forced owners to build a stone or brick foundation and ground floor surmounted by one or more storeys of half-timbering. The growing use of stone cellars in the twelfth and especially thirteenth century gave houses stronger foundations and permitted higher structures, providing storage for goods, impossible in the essentially 'slab' or posthole cellars earlier.[53]

Since space was scarce in the cities, virtually all houses were multistoreyed; but while in the late thirteenth and early fourteenth centuries some even reached seven storeys, diminished need for living space after 1348 meant a reduction, and even the grandest patrician palaces rarely contained more than three storeys. Windows were rare, both because they weakened the house structurally and because medical opinion held that disease was in the air. Linen, hides and oiled parchment were used for windows as late as the fifteenth century, although glass was gradually coming into use from the thirteenth century.[54]

The fact that many crafts involved open fires, combined with the combustibility of the houses, meant that fire was a constant threat. The cities had fire brigades, but they were ineffective. A fire that began in a baker's house damaged or destroyed two-thirds of the buildings in Vienna in 1326.[55] Most roofs were initially of straw or thatch, but from 1212 London required new houses to have tile roofs, whose weight required a solid understructure. Since London had no city-wide fire between 1212 and 1666, it must have worked.[56] Elsewhere the requirement for tile or slate roofing came in the fourteenth century, but most cities phased it in by requiring only new construction to have the sturdier substance.[57]

The interior design of houses reflected the fact that most people worked out of their homes. A common house type in England, the Low Countries and northern Germany had a ground floor, a cellar for merchandise, a great hall on the first upper storey, where business associates and other important guests were received, and smaller rooms for domestic space on the second and third storeys. The upper storeys and cellars generally had lower ceilings than the ground-floor rooms. The hall might be parallel to the street, but this was feasible only with an undivided tenement of sufficient width. The solar, undercroft, hall and service areas were laid out in a row. A variant on this was to have two ranges of buildings, with shops on the street frontage and the hall and solar in the rear. In more elaborate structures, the hall was free-standing in the rear courtyard, while the gateway and shops were on the street frontage. The scarcity of land made this form unfeasible in the late Middle Ages except for public buildings: the famous Guildhall of York is of this type.[58]

During the thirteenth and fourteenth centuries cellars and vaulted undercrofts commonly had street access by stairs and could be used to display goods as well as for storage. In the fifteenth century the steps were usually removed, and they were used for storage only. Perhaps as a result of the growing importance of cloth (which rotted in damp, cool cellars, which wine needed), fifteenth- and sixteenth-century houses more often had larger shops and warehouses on the ground floor, while the family lived in the first upper storey. Taverns too were shifting from the cellars to the ground level in the fifteenth century.[59] For understandable reasons, many taverns were rented by their keepers from landowners who did not reside on the property.

With population growth in the thirteenth century, the houses were more often subdivided into individual rooms, often for renting. Italian magnates had always invested in rental properties, and in the thirteenth century this practice spread to the north. Tenements were often sublet, and rents became high in the thirteenth century. Still, apart from the great hall, there was little 'living space', usually just a room or two for sleeping (the entire family usually slept in the same room, until some concern for privacy developed after the fourteenth century) and eating. Some houses had only one room on the ground floor, particularly merchant frontages, but then went up several storeys. The more rooms there were on the ground floor – rarely more than three – the fewer above-ground storeys there were likely to be.[60] Ownership of houses was often divided. Sometimes this was simply a division of shares among heirs to apportion rental income, but some houses were physically partitioned. Particularly among the great merchants, after 1250 the warehouse was often separated from the family residence, or the ground floor became the warehouse while the family lived in the rear or the first upper storey. Garrets were also used for storage. Families would buy in bulk when possible to tide them across the winter and store food upstairs, although there were municipal statutes against hoarding.[61]

Except for the replacement of some half-timbered buildings with stone, and particularly brick, the exterior of most houses – half-timbering, with wattle and daub or rubble infilling, and the upper stories jettying over the lower – remained largely unchanged in the modern period, but some modifications were made to interior space. Partitions, ceilings and stairs replaced the large open halls, as privacy now became more desired.[62] More on the continent than in England, the number of storeys in urban houses increased in the modern period. This was not simply a question of congestion, but also of expansion of the physical facilities of the house, as individual family members had their own rooms, and some rooms were dedicated to specific purposes, even if this meant that they were not used continuously.[63] The movement to multi-room interiors was accompanied by the increased use of fireplaces as room dividers, with chimneys making it possible to heat more than one storey. Kitchens were moved from out-buildings to the main structure and took on additional functions, sometimes doubling as a child's or servant's bedroom.[64]

The City as Theatre

One of the most vibrant and original aspects of pre-modern urban culture was the number and variety of festivals and processions, replete with symbolic overtones, at least before the Reformation ended many of them. Fairs were often opened with a procession through the town, accompanied by minstrels. Some town lords and city governments provided a cow or bull that would be driven in the procession, sometimes with bright coloured fabrics and the horns adorned, then slaughtered to provide a banquet for the visiting merchants. A herald would read aloud the bans of the fair.[65] Weddings, christenings, funerals and processions of patron saints of parish churches were important neighbourhood festivities. When city-wide festivals are added to these celebrations, 'somebody was celebrating something in public most of the time. Most of these festivities required considerable expenditure on fine clothing and wine, giving business to local merchants and craftsmen'.[66] Mimes and jugglers could perform on streets more or less at will. Many cities had bellringers and bands or Waits, usually of three or four members, who, attired in the city's livery, played a glorious cacophony of wind instruments to accompany the processions. Some had guilds of minstrels, although usually the town piper was someone with a real job in some other line of work. Nuremberg maintained a city band of six or seven pipers in the fifteenth century, but most musical effort in the city processions came from the other participants, playing whatever could make noise, and eating the ceremonial meal that concluded the festival.[67]

The festivals included both celebrations that involved the entire citizenry, admittedly more in the sixteenth than in the seventeenth century, and others for specific social groups and neighbourhoods.[68] The urban festivals usually followed the folkloric calendar, which might (the Épinette at Lille was held during Lent) or might not (the Festival of the Forester at Bruges) correspond to the liturgical calendar. They allowed the inhabitants to let off steam, gave them a holiday from work, and inculcated religious devotion and a sense of majesty of the city. Only the larger towns had the population base, with the necessary skills, for the processions, which required considerable outlay of funds and were often organised on the basis of occupational guilds. Thus the festivals and processions were a function of the central place, attracting tourists from the environs, not always willingly. The residents of the *contado* of Florence were required to attend and contribute financially to the city's ceremonies, and there are signs in the fifteenth century that they resented it. In England, however, the processions seem to have enticed villagers to the town. The residents of the villages around

Leicester participated in the procession on Whit Monday at Leicester, whose Robin Hood plays were a major attraction.[69]

The most important church rite for civic identity was the cult of the patron saint, propitiating the holy person who had made the city great and whose continued posthumous intercession was desired. The saint's relics, a tactile reminder of his presence on earth in the form of an article of clothing, another item of close personal association, or most desirably a body part, were carried through the streets by priests and civic leaders in a usually annual procession that would culminate at the cathedral or other shrine dedicated to him or occasionally her. An important part of the civic myth was the explanation of how the relics got to the city and blessed it: either through translation, or the claim that they had been there all the time and had been discovered miraculously. The translation of the relics of St Mark to Venice, for example, was celebrated every 25 June. The patron saint was also the subject of much artwork, commissioned by the dedicatory church or the city.

The city elites consciously developed traditions, building on older myths that inculcated acceptable behaviour. Except for processions that had overtones of heresy or sedition, such as the flagellants, it was unusual for laypeople to participate in urban processions alongside the clergy before 1300, but thereafter it became the norm. 'The procession brought the sacrament into the city streets.'[70] Although many of the festivals occurred on church feast days, the civic authorities came to control them. The annual procession of the doge at Venice is a famous example:

> A dozen times a year or more, the leading office holders participated in lengthy processions, which could last as long as five hours, through the streets of the city, always winding their way back to the great basilica of St Mark where these hard-headed politicians humbled themselves before their protector saint.

The most famous civic ceremony was the marriage of Venice with the sea, celebrated on Ascension Day. The doge and other high civic officials presided and paraded. The marriage culminated when the doge threw a gold ring into the sea and intoned 'We espouse thee, O sea, as a sign of true and perpetual dominion'.[71]

Gregorio Dati has described the atmosphere in Florence on the feast day of St John the Baptist (24 June):

> The whole city is engaged in preparing for the feast. . . . Everyone is filled with gaiety; there are dances and concerts and songfests and tournaments and other joyous activities. Up to the eve of the holiday, no one thinks about anything else. Early on the morning of the day before the holiday, each guild has a display outside of its shops of its fine wares, its ornaments and jewels. There are cloths of gold and silk sufficient to adorn ten kingdoms. . . . Then at the third hour, there is a solemn procession of clerics, priests, monks, and friars . . . . There are many confraternities of men who assemble

at the place where their meetings are held, dressed as angels, and with musical instruments of every kind and marvellous singing. They stage the most beautiful representations of the saints. . . . Then . . . all of the citizens assemble under [the banner of] their district, of which there are sixteen. Each goes in the procession in turn .[72]

Many civic festivals involved the guilds. City-wide 'guilds of the whole' became prestigious, particularly the St George, Holy Trinity and Corpus Christi guilds of the English cities. They were charitable and social, linking the town wealthy and often regional landholders in a club. Trinity Guild Coventry, for example, had members who lived in the smaller towns of its region and regularly traded through the city, which was the central place of the Midlands and second only to London in the commercial hierarchy.[73] The entire fraternity was expected to attend the funeral of any brother, his child, wife or apprentice. Corpus Christi Day processions are first attested in the thirteenth century but quickly spread. The body in form of the Host was carried though the city, with guildsmen attired in uniforms that bore the livery of their trades.[74]

The order in which the city officials and guildsmen marched in the processions was fixed by local custom. Fights sometimes broke out over imputations of violated privilege. The highest almost everywhere were members of the great companies. The rank order of the crafts of Norwich was fixed around 1449, with the sheriff and his retinue at the head, followed by mercers, grocers, drapers, goldsmiths, and other more prestigious crafts and ending with shoemakers, barbers, curriers, smiths and reeders (thatchers).[75] Elsewhere the social and political structures of the town determined the character of the processions. At Erfurt, whose city council had a majority of guildsmen in the late Middle Ages, most processions included the entire citizenry, although a procession in which the relics of the local saints Adolar and Eoban were carried to the Frauenkirche involved only the city council and the cathedral canons. All citizens paraded at Strasbourg's Corpus Christi celebration. Although the early processions had included craft participation, by the late fifteenth century the patrician regime of Nuremberg was restricting direct participation in the civic festivals, including Corpus Christi, to the cathedral clergy and members of the leading families of the city. There was nothing of the elaborate rank order of trades found elsewhere. The celebration was not completely closed to non-patricians, for although council members carried the body of Christ, other leading citizens carried the canopy. Although the Corpus Christi processions were hierarchically structured, the members of the incumbent city council never marched as a unit.[76]

Virtually anything could provide the excuse for a city celebration, but gratitude and fear were the most common motivations. Many local ceremonies are first attested in the years following the Great Death. The rotation of the magistracy was usually accompanied by festivities. Deliverance from a major threat was also formalised: Ypres celebrated the raising of an English siege in 1383 with 'Garden Day', so designated because the English had withdrawn after the inhabitants raised a barricade of garden trellises on the city wall.

Particularly as territorial princes were ending the liberties of the larger cities, some of the most important urban festivals were the entries of the princes. These could involve the prince symbolically subjugating the city, as in the entry of Philip the Bold, duke of Burgundy, into Bruges on 26 April 1384 as its new count, following a recent rebellion. The procession included church and community, as the new prince took his oath to the strains of bells and music in the church of St Donatian.[77] When Louis XII of France made his entry into Genoa in 1507, he was met by a delegation of citizens, kneeling and begging for mercy. He forgave them in return for a huge indemnity, imposed penalties for rebellion, and burned the city's book of privileges.[78] Given that the French cities were docile, the royal entries there were symbolic but gentle. In a less constrained context, the cities also welcomed their princes in formal 'Joyous Entries', but in terms that suggested his beneficence.[79]

A major part of the pageantry in the cities of the continent involved jousting. The social ambitions of many great merchants could only be realised by a patent of nobility. Most personal libraries that have survived from the time before printing – in the case of townspeople these are quite small – include the major vernacular classics, such as the works of Chaucer in England and Boccaccio and Dante Alighieri in Italy, but have a preponderance of devotional material and chivalric legend. The jousts were grand entertainments that everyone who could fit onto the square could attend, but membership in the jousting societies was limited to the city elites and, as was true of the even more exclusive clubs, fostered group consciousness. Zaragoza was so known for tourneys and jousts that it was mentioned in *Don Quixote* for that reason.[80] In some German cities the jousting societies were forbidden initially but were later revived, and they may be more important even than intermarriage and landholding in the developing rapprochement of the rural nobility with the urban elites.

The largest marketplace of the city was commonly used for the jousts. They were organised in cooperation by the nobles and by the city elite, who wanted to give training to their own archers and crossbowmen as well as provide entertainment. In the fourteenth century the jousts had involved real fighting, but in the fifteenth the combats became highly ritualised, and the goals were less physical and more social/moral. This corresponds to an important change: while in the fourteenth century access to the nobility for the urban elites was through military prowess, landholding and intermarriage, in the fifteenth it was more often through officeholding in the prince's bureaucracy. Rulers such as the dukes of Burgundy grafted aspects of symbolism of the benevolent ruler onto the festivals. The towns cooperated by providing the money and locale for the spectacles that the princes wanted, but the jousts were no unmixed blessing for the towns, for they were expensive and sometimes destructive. The number of towns that organised tourneys declined in the fifteenth century; only the pressure of the dukes of Burgundy kept the Épinette of Lille going until 1486.[81]

Many urban processions thus featured the town militia companies or the shooters' guild, amounting to a muster. The London Midsummer Watch commemorated with an annual festival the guild watches that regularly patrolled the streets. Although disorder was generally petty, serious disturbances occurred in 1515. The Watch of 1521 was described by the Venetian ambassador: the guilds provided the marchers, but the aldermen maintained a watch in the wards to keep order. The procession included armed guards, Morris dancers, and seven 'gorgeous pageants: Pluto, the Tree of Life, a besieged castle, the Assumption, Saint George, Saint John the Evangelist, and John the Baptist'. A second account of the 1521 Watch, by the recorder of the Drapers' Company, confirms the factual accuracy of the Venetian's account; but for him, the celebration was the 'Mayor's Watch', in honour of the city government and the merchant guilds that furnished the ruling elite. The festivals were carefully orchestrated celebrations of the elite, but there was plenty for everybody, including bonfires and drink.[82]

Some jousting societies sponsored poetry or vocal competitions as part of the festivities, but this tradition precedes the tourneys. Arras, the major banking centre of the northwest before the fourteenth century, was the home of the poet–dramatist Adam de la Halle. Even in the thirteenth century the town already had two literary societies, the Confraternity of the Ardents and the Pui. Most of Adam's output is courtly, but the *Jeu de la Feuillée* (Play of the Bower), which is attributed to him but may not be his, includes a critique of crookedness in the Arras government.

Such literary societies became more numerous after 1300. 'The Company of the Jolly Sabre' at Toulouse held yearly competitions from 1324 and had officers and ceremonies that resembled those of the local university. A symbolic prize was given to the winner, in the Toulouse case a golden violet. The Toulouse society became the model for the statutes of later literary societies in the northern cities. During the fifteenth century the cities in the Low Countries also developed Chambers of Rhetoric, really guilds of rhetoricians. They and their individual members commissioned and wrote plays and poems, held public readings and sponsored competitions. They also debated theological and public policy issues.[83] Antwerp had three chambers of rhetoric in the early sixteenth century, which collaborated with the city government in sponsoring festivals. The Gilliflowers chamber organised a gathering of 14 chambers in 1561 'in a magnificent spectacle, called the Land's Jewel festival. There were 1328 men on horseback as well as many actors on 23 antique chariots and 196 illuminated ones'. The chambers also joined the city authorities in sponsoring entries for princes. They were suspended during the religious hostilities of the sixteenth century, then were revived in the seventeenth.[84]

Thus public theatrical productions became a commonplace of city life. Travelling troupes of actors provided entertainment, as did the miracle and morality plays staged by the guilds, performed as the wagons moved through the city during the Corpus Christi processions. The plays were important attractions for tourists and pilgrims. By the sixteenth century the 'Everyman' plays, which had been borrowed from the earlier Dutch *Elckerlijk*, were staples of the English processions.[85] Yet drama was still considered subversive, and only in the sixteenth century, with royal patronage, was much secular drama written, and that on classical models. Before 1600 London and Paris became centres of a professional and stationary theatre that provided entertainment to the urban masses, but always under the watchful eye of the crown: in the English case the supervision of the 'Master of the Queen's Revels'. The first professional theatre in Barcelona for which admission was charged was built the 1590s.[86] The Globe Theatre in London followed soon after.

The festival repertoire of the cities included feasts of fools, student plays and music productions and carnivals. Most cities had at least one youth confraternity, consisting of single and young married men of all social situations. They organised festivals, operated charivaris with 'rough music' against disapproved remarriages, and provided outlet for the exuberant spirits of the young. But in the sixteenth century their recruitment became limited to the wealthy, and their celebrations became part of the propaganda panoply of the city elite. The coarser entertainments were left from that point to Societies of Fools or Joyous Abbeys, which usually had a professional (especially artisan) or territorial (often neighbourhood) base of recruitment; the rich would have no part of them.[87]

The line between secular and profane was blurred, as the city elites and religious authorities carefully orchestrated the festivities to keep the fun under control. The annual carnival at Shrovetide figures prominently in the rituals of many cities and sometimes blended with other festivities. The Épinette of Lille was held on Shrove Tuesday, with a king chosen from among the city elite. After his investiture, a tournament was held to which contestants from throughout Flanders were invited. Most carnivals do not support the idea of the city as a focus of civility. 'The centrepiece of the official rituals of Carnival in Venice consisted of the ritualised chase and slaughter of twelve pigs and a bull in the small square next to the Palace of the Doges.' They made it into a judicial procedure, with the pigs sentenced to death. Although many high officials were embarrassed by it, it was such a popular tourist attraction that efforts to abolish it were unsuccessful. During the pig slaughter, there were other entertainments: acrobats, fireworks, bull chases in the individual neighbourhoods, boat races, mimed shows and tableaux.[88] Disorder at Shrovetide became such a threat to public order that the authorities in some towns tried to forbid the carnivals. In 1276 John le Hancrete was returning from celebrating the feast of St Michael to the house of William le Cuver,

> where he hired his bed by the day; [and] being very drunk . . . intending to lie down upon it, he took a lighted candle for the purpose of making his bed; which done, he left the candle burning, and fell asleep thereon.[89]

He perished in the fire.

City, Central Place and Culture

Since Greek antiquity, the Mediterranean city has been associated in literature with culture, refinement and order, with *urbanitas* framed in dichotomy to the less civilised *rusticas*. The northern cities did not have such talented publicists. Except in Italy rural culture dominated over urban until late in our period, and even then the urban elites were imitating the manners of the rural nobles, not vice versa. The ancient notion of the city nevertheless experienced a strong revival in the Renaissance, one of whose fundamental features was the resurrection of the idea of civic life as the basis for human association.[90]

Thomas A. Brady has vigorously criticised views that project the city as a force of civility:

> The unique historical character of the medieval European town as a forward-looking enclave in a sea of primitive feudal society is one of the finest creations of Liberal historiography, developed and nourished in various forms by Sismondi, Villari, Gierke, and Pirenne. ... [The] assumption of the political, social, and cultural uniqueness of the cities ... [is] the most damaging weakness of the whole literature [of Protestantism].[91]

In contrast to Brady, Lauro Martines has argued that there was a specifically urban life and culture in the late Middle Ages, as citizens worked in a network of family, quarter, parish, trade organisations and religious associations.[92]

Certainly the violent, dirty and ill-designed cities of the early twelfth century were something less than cultural capitals. Yet most of the cultural achievement of Europe after 1350 occurred in cities, although not necessarily because of the activity of citizens. Just as the economic and social characteristics of the city lured immigrants, so urban settlements once in place attracted cultural life; just as the industrial work force of the city was more diversified than that of the village, so the cities, particularly in Italy, had a high number of 'professional' persons such as notaries, lawyers, physicians and teachers.[93] Persons of talent went where there was money to support them, and this tended to be a city, whether because there was a court there or because of demand for the product. Tilman Riemenschneider, perhaps the greatest German sculptor from this period, is an artistic parallel to the merchant Jacob Fugger (Chapter 5). Riemenschneider was from rural Thuringia, migrated to Würzburg, apprenticed, then enrolled in the St Lucas guild as a journeyman. He became a master in 1505, working for bishops, his own city and small towns around, and eventually became mayor of Würzburg.[94]

Although most definitions of the urban region have focused on the economic and political roles of the city, religion and cult functions were much more important in the pre-modern period than now. Unfortunately, this important aspect of urbanisation is also the least quantifiable. The best known attempt to give statistical verity to cultural standing is Jacques Le Goff's misguided effort to determine the degree of urbanisation in the thirteenth century by the number of mendicant establishments in a given place, a classification that founders on the fact that some tiny places had as many friaries as some of the largest cities.[95] Most major cities had bishoprics that generally extended outside the town. As the town governments took over many of the secular functions of the bishops, the regional importance of the town was enhanced.[96]

Étienne François has used cultural indicators, specifically the presence of universities, book publications and publishing firms, and the residences of writers to show that a cultural hierarchy existed among the German cities by the seventeenth century that did not reflect their size or economic roles. While Augsburg, Cologne and Nuremberg occupy similar ranks in both the demographic and cultural hierarchies, Wittenberg, Jena, Heidelberg and Ingolstadt were more regionally important as intellectual centres than the much larger Gdánsk, Prague, Hamburg and Magdeburg. By 1700 Frankfurt served as the cultural capital of a large concentration of towns in western Germany, while Leipzig fulfilled this function in central Germany.[97] Germany appears unusual, however, in this decoupling of culture from other indices of urban function.

Thus, many aspects of the intellectual achievement of Europe between 1100 and 1700 bear the imprint of the city. Others, however, do not, and we must avoid the fallacy of assuming that simply because something was written or painted in a city, it was therefore a product of urban culture.

Education in the Cities

Religion and education were crucial and intertwined aspects of the city's central-place function. Although the clergy themselves rarely comprised more than 2–3 per cent of the population of the cities except for university towns, the churches employed, if intermittently, large numbers of laypeople, attracting skilled construction workers, painters and sculptors, gold- and silversmiths, jewellers, book illuminators and a host of others for work on their buildings and libraries. The wealth of the central-place church thus explains the presence of many artisans who probably could not have supported themselves by working solely for laypeople. The argument that concentration of wealth led to artistic patronage works as well for the church as for the bankers of Renaissance Italy. The Italian church as a whole was much wealthier than the northern churches, and much of the demand for religious art came from the churches. Bullion was being drained from northern Europe to Italy, not only to pay for luxuries imported from the east, but also in papal tithes and other payments. The popes used their money for conspicuous consumption and local wars. They did not spend much in northern Europe, but a great deal in Italy.

Levels of literacy in the vernacular languages were much higher in the cities than in the rural areas. Merchants had to keep written documents, and they corresponded frequently with business partners outside their home cities. On 22 December 1415 Tideman Brekelvelde wrote from Lübeck to Hildebrand and Sivert Veckinchusen in Cologne:

> Hildebrand, I have received your letter from Cologne in good order, in which you wrote me that our copper is still unsold. I am uneasy that it has

taken so long to make money, and it seems to me that it will soon be high time for it to make money, for the cloth has already been sold for some time, and you well know that that I am already in arrears to our partnership by a considerable sum. Moreover, Tideman Swarte has rendered accounts to us for everything ... and he wrote me that I should forward them to you. I have done so, and I hope that you receive the account at Bruges before you come to Cologne. ... On another matter, the house at Lüneburg has still not been sold. Herr Klaus has written me that he may not get more than 700 marks for it. I wrote him back that he should sell it for whatever he can get. Otherwise I know of nothing to write except stay healthy.[98]

The first urban schools were usually in the chief church of the city. While some elementary education for laypeople was available in rural areas, more specialised training, in the learned fields as in artisanship, could only be obtained in the cities, which had a wider demand radius. Once schools were established in the central city, which had a population base of merchants and bureaucrats who had to be literate, cultural opportunities expanded on the basic/non-basic principle (Chapter 1), for schools were basic producers that attracted outsiders, although their students were often transients.

The churches initially tried to control the education of the laity, but their monopoly was gone by 1250. The first lay urban schools were in the parishes, usually with a priest but sometimes with a layman as master. The larger the city and the more complex its parish organisation, the more church schools there were likely to be. This meant that schooling was under lay control from the beginning in the founded towns, but the clergy were stronger in the older, nuclear cities. The cities were not equally well provided with schools. Stralsund acquired a foundation charter in 1234, and had a parish school by 1278; there were two others by 1285, each likewise attached to a church. In 1319 the town acquired the right of patronage over all parish churches of the city area, which made the schools municipal. A similar chronology is true of Wismar and Rostock. Lübeck, the great merchant city, had fewer parish schools per capita than the others; Brunswick had twice the number of schools of Hamburg, although the two cities were of comparable size.[99]

Primary education was in Latin in most places outside Italy until the fourteenth century. Thereafter the city schools moved increasingly to the vernacular for instruction. The early town schools usually handled the elementary subjects, while the cathedral school was necessary for advanced subjects in the liberal arts, which had a specifically theological content. Before 1300 the church had effectively conceded the point that merchant children should be taught reading, writing and calculating, but church and city council continued sparring over which had the right to appoint the schoolmaster. The curriculum was really not at issue. By the early thirteenth century most city governments were hiring schoolmasters, really headmasters, who then appointed the other teachers. Particularly in the smaller towns, the town clerk might double as schoolmaster, since there was not enough work for the city to keep him busy. By the fifteenth century it was expected that children of the upper bourgeoisie, both boys and girls, would attend a parish school. Formal schooling was followed by a term in the family shop or learning the merchant's trade from the father. Given the nature of their clienteles, children of craftsmen were less likely to receive education than those of merchants, but it did occur. London statutes by the fifteenth century required new apprentices to be literate in English.[100]

The thirteenth and early fourteenth centuries witness a critical transition from Latin to the vernacular in lay education everywhere. The vernacular schools that were established in most cities in the west in the fourteenth century and in the fifteenth in Germany taught writing based on commercial correspondence. Not surprisingly, Italy was more precocious than the north in vernacular education. Giovanni Villani claimed that by 1338 some 8–10,000 children in Florence were being educated, both boys and girls. His figures may be inflated, but it is clear that in the late Middle Ages levels of literacy were quite high there.[101] Primary education usually started between ages 5 and 7 for both sexes, but girls were often returned home after gaining basic literacy. The boys continued, learning to read notarial acts and do elementary arithmetic. Secondary education continued this practical emphasis. It began with stories that could be understood by children, such as Aesop's Fables, then continued to emphasise literature, mainly Latin works in translation but also Italian vernacular works such as Dante Alighieri's *Divine Comedy* and Giovanni Boccaccio's *Decameron*. The pupils also studied chivalric literature for its moral content. Particularly from the turn of the fifteenth century Cicero was studied intensively, and the curriculum then was completed by Aristotle's *Politics* and *Nichomachean Ethics*.[102]

The picture is mixed outside Italy. Virtually all English grammar or secondary schools were in towns. Their numbers increased rapidly in the fifteenth and especially the sixteenth century, when most were founded and run by laypeople. In Flanders and Germany too the cities dominated secondary education. Bruges had a 'school of administration' and a school for rhetoricians in the fifteenth century, but the other Flemish cities had fewer schools than one might expect in view of their commercial preeminence. In Flanders it was common practice for merchant families by the second half of the fourteenth century, and for artisan families by the late fifteenth, to send their children to the French areas to learn the language, because it was necessary to conduct business. Antwerp was unusual in having perhaps 200 schools, including private schools for the children of merchants.[103]

As urban populations expanded, so did their governments. The Italian cities began keeping large numbers of documents in the late eleventh and twelfth centuries, and most of the larger towns of the north did so by the late thirteenth. There is evidence of registration of acts at Cologne by 1135. The first surviving act mentioning the 'intervention' of the aldermen of Ghent dates from 1147, with Tournai and Ypres following in 1160 and 1206. The judicial records and political and administrative decisions of the magistrates survive in register form, in the vernacular language, at Ghent from 1339, Mechelen from 1345, Leuven from 1362 and Antwerp from 1394. The Low Country cities were more precocious with financial records. Tournai has accounts from 1240, Ypres from 1267, Ghent and Bruges by the end of the thirteenth century. The aldermen of Ypres generated at least 8000 'fair letters' and debt recognitions between 1249 and 1300.[104]

While in the northern cities oral transactions were preserved by the parties coming voluntarily before the town council and its clerk, notaries recorded more agreements in the cities of Mediterranean France and Italy. The notaries' registers were considered public documents, and the notaries themselves enjoyed great prestige. Their acts were in Latin. Yet, although knowledge of Latin was much more widespread among the laity in Italy than in the north and contributed substantially to the cultural climate that produced the Renaissance, by the fourteenth century even some Italian city governments had clerks who not only handled their writing but also could translate Latin documents coming from the churches and notaries, as more councillors admitted that they could not understand Latin, and litigants rarely could.[105]

The city lived as much by numbers as by letters. Merchants had to calculate profits, debits and exchange rates, and know when to come to fairs. Workers were paid by the day and eventually by the hour. The earliest cities had bells in the church towers that were rung to signal the liturgical day, but the bells by 1300 were tolling time by secular hours. Most cities had mechanical clocks in a public place, usually the town hall.

Arithmetic and geometry were taught in the universities, but from a theoretical perspective. Oxford was unusual in offering a business course as a kind of 'university extension' from the early thirteenth century, but its content was more in the area of commercial writing and estate management than in calculation, and it was phased out in the fifteenth century.[106] Thus for commercial arithmetic, schools of reckoning grew up outside the universities, first in Italy and then in the north, but always in the cities. In 1338 Florence had six schools of reckoning; Nuremberg by 1613 had 48.[107] The curriculum was based on Fibonacci's *Abbaco*, a practical system that did not use an abacus but included arithmetic, algebra and geometry. Francesco Pegolotti's *Practice of Commerce* amounted to commercial arithmetic, illustrating the science with specific problems peculiar to merchants, such as double-entry bookkeeping. The *Treviso Arithmetic*, the first dated and printed arithmetic book of Europe, also illustrates calculation with practical examples from the business world:

> Three merchants have invested their money in a partnership, whom to make the problem clearer I will mention by name. ... Piero put in 112 ducats, Polo 200 ducats, and Zuanne 142 ducats. At the end of a certain period they found that they had gained 563 ducats. Required is to know how much falls to each man so that no one shall be cheated.[108]

The University and Urban Culture

Most universities were in cities. There were about 20 universities by 1300 and another 50 by 1500, usually founded by princes in their chief towns. In founding the University of Prague, the emperor Charles IV in 1348 noted the glories of the city, which he had raised to an archbishopric, how the university and his various other acts of patronage would cause the population of the town to grow, and unspecified attractions that a university town would have to immigrants. In founding the University of Erfurt in 1389, the pope noted the urban environment, in a fertile area with plenty of food, many inns, access by water and land, and other benefits to *scientia*. The charter of the University at Krakau in 1364 justified it because Krakau was the 'most important town' of Poland, but far away from other major schools.[109] Some city governments also took an active role in founding a university, usually by petitioning the town lord to make a formal request of the pope. This occurred at Cologne in 1388, Erfurt in 1389, Rostock in 1418–19, Leuven in 1425 and Basel in 1459–60. The municipal government of Rostock provided the land for the university buildings and financial support.[110]

The foundation of a university was no guarantee that a place would develop into a large city. The university could attract only persons who could not get comparable instruction nearer home. In Italy the universities flourished in medium-sized cities – Siena, Perugia, Ferrara – rather than in the largest places. Some territorial princes seem to have preferred to have the university in their second largest city rather than the capital. Thus the Lombard university was at Pavia. No second university was founded at Venice to complement that at Padua, whose university was founded before Venice conquered the city. Florence's university did reasonably well in the early stages but was transferred by the Medici to Pisa. In the north, London did not have a university until the modern period. Paris was the major exception in being both a major metropolis and the home of a university.[111] While some later German urban universities were successful, most, such as Tübingen and Ingolstadt, did not attract more than a few hundred students. Most universities were established in places that already had strong local schools that were simply gaining a higher faculty – we would now call it a graduate school – that qualified it for university standing: Trier, Erfurt and Cologne are the best examples.

The larger universities had a considerable impact on the urban fabric. Paris may have had 4000 masters and scholars around 1200, at least twice that by 1300. The overall rate of expansion of the city's population was much higher, but for much of our period the university accounted for between 5 and 10 per cent of the city's population.[112] At Oxford, Cambridge and probably Bologna, the percentages were even larger. As basic producers, the universities made a major contribution to the local economy. The first universities rented buildings, but they quickly acquired their own properties, which were usually concentrated in one part of town.

But there is a darker side to the relation of university and city. Oxford was a much more prosperous town before the university than later, due largely to bitter town–gown conflicts over rent, food, housing and especially student violence. Some streets in the university quarters were so dangerous that the city authorities simply left them unpoliced. Late medieval Oxford had a homicide rate that was more than double that of most other English cities, which in turn were more than double that of most modern cities.[113] Conditions were so bad at the university of Angers that 'good people' hesitated to send their sons there in the fifteenth century. The violence at Toulouse was notorious enough to be immortalised by a comment by Rabelais. Armed conflict occurred at Oxford between the Welsh and the English, at Orléans between the rival 'nations' of Picards and Champenois.

Further, the universities as agents of culture were curiously anomalous in the urban context. They were centres of scholarship, particularly in law and theology. The arts course, where most students began and ended their academic careers, spread Latin literacy enormously. But most original creative work was done outside the universities. The university curriculum was impractical for most urbanites; it became a way to move into the territorial bureaucracies through the humanist education that princes were fostering. While the universities were in cities, they did not offer a curriculum that was vital to most townsmen: private study was necessary for that.

Thus in both Italy and the north there is not much evidence of university education among city councillors until the fifteenth century. Their political careers resulted from their family and occupational bonds, not their educational level. The technical personnel, such as clerks, attorneys and accountants who were employed by the city governments more often had attended a university, for professional competence was their route to advancement. University education became increasingly common among the upper bourgeoisie, and accordingly the city councillors, from about 1450. More than half the aldermen of Antwerp in the seventeenth century had a university education. The number of university graduates in the city governments of Flanders was lower than at Leuven or Antwerp but higher than in the smaller communities, and the professional employees of the cities, such as attorneys and clerks, were much better educated than in the rural areas.[114] In Germany the picture is mixed. Most great families at Augsburg sent at least some sons to university, although those who were carrying on the family business more often got practical training, such as apprenticeship overseas. Of 1019 Augsburgers who enrolled at universities through 1500, Vienna had the highest number of matriculations, followed at a considerable distance by Leipzig, Ingolstadt and Heidelberg. Bologna and Padua were the only non-German universities that many Germans attended. The Bavarian and Austrian rulers relied on university-educated Augsburgers for bureaucracy, court and council, lawyers, tutors and physicians.[115]

The City and Religious Heterodoxy

The church and the lay establishment generally cooperated for most of the period covered by this book. Even as lay governments took over many duties once reserved to the ecclesiastical arm, landownership, cultural activity, and the fact that they employed so many people still gave the churches considerable power.

The lower orders in the cities appear to have been somewhat more inclined to religious heresy than the peasantry. When problems arose, they were magnified by the fact that city privileges and the difficulty of seizing a hostile town made suppression much more difficult than in the countryside. Some 'religious' disturbances in the cities were actually semi-political in nature. Such movements as the Humiliati in northern Italy, the Waldensians in southeastern France, the Cathars in southwestern France and the Lollards in England found a warm response in the towns. The Beguines were found in the cities but were not a specifically urban group, particularly the uncloistered Beguines, whose leanings toward heresy caused problems for the entire movement. Wandering preachers in Italy and Germany found enthusiastic listeners among the poor in town and countryside. The career of Girolamo Savonarola at Florence (1494–8) after the fall of the Medici can be used to support two propositions: that the urban masses were prone to religious enthusiasm, and that the authorities did not let matters get out of control for long. But rarely were city authorities outside Italy actively involved in the suppression of heresy. If the local bishop could not handle it, the territorial prince did.[116]

This changes somewhat in the sixteenth century. There is certainly no tie between capitalism and Protestantism, as R. H. Tawney following Max Weber thought. The birth, expansion and perpetuation of commercial capitalism in that heartland of Roman Catholicism, Italy, in itself belies the notion. While some Catholic businessmen made large charitable donations in expiation of their sins, the church was actively involved in commercial activities, including moneylending: 'the church became more infused with capitalism than the merchants became imbued with theology'. Usury, which had been forbidden by the popes, was not legitimised until long after 1500 in most areas that eventually became Protestant. Attempts to translate Luther's emphasis on lay reading of the Scriptures into a higher level of literacy among Protestants have failed. Some correlations are possible between craft groups and religion in northern Europe: trades that used a new technology or high skills, or developed outside the established guilds tended to have disproportionate numbers of Protestants.[117]

In southwestern Germany and Switzerland, Protestantism was a largely urban movement, as individual cities took the lead and princes followed. The proletarians turned Protestant only when their city governments did. Secular grievances against the city regime and its leaders tended to be turned against their religion. As the territorial states were consolidated, the princes' religious convictions determined what religion was officially followed in their cities. Similarly, Protestantism in France was associated very largely with the cities, which were unable to gain sufficient rural adherents to prevail. Troyes was probably typical. Scarcely any Roman Catholic clergy converted to Protestantism, but a disproportionate number of city councillors did. Family connections seem to have determined the religious stance of most merchants. As elsewhere, doctors, goldsmiths, apothecaries, printers, booksellers and paper merchants and in general those whose work required a high level of technical skill and/or were outside the guild structure joined the Protestants in disproportionate numbers. There was a tendency for older, politically powerful trades, and for artisans in construction and foodmongering to remain Roman Catholic. While textile workers were often Huguenot in other cities, few at Troyes were. Religious violence on both sides was associated mainly with artisans (see also Chapter 4).[118]

The Renaissance and Urban Humanism

At least in northern Europe, 'most literary activity was connected to the princely courts that happened to be in the cities, rather than being specifically urban'.[119] Important works of history, too numerous to catalogue here, were being produced in the Italian cities. Even in the thirteenth century, the Florentine notary Brunetto Latini (1220–1294) wrote works in Italian and French that extol public life and the governance of his city. His *Li Livres dou Tresor* was moulded by his study of Aristotle and Cicero, and he interpreted the experience of Florence in the light of their lessons.[120]

Dante Alighieri (1265–1321) evidently received his vast learning in the schools of Florence and by personal reading. The outward events of his career in the city, notably his vendetta-imposed exile from Florence, gave him a distaste for the political pretensions of the popes that he vented in *On Monarchy*. His *On the Eloquence of the Vulgar Tongue*, a justification of the use of the vernacular for serious expression, was written in Latin to reach the intended audience of scholars. His greatest work, the *Comedy*, was written in the Tuscan dialect during his exile and can hardly be considered a specific product of an urban environment, except for the posthumous locales assigned to the poet's personal enemies. The work of Giovanni Boccaccio, notably the stories in his *Decameron*, is much more bound than Dante's to human situations in Florence. Boccaccio's early work is original, but later in his career he became convinced by Petrarch that the vernacular was an unworthy vessel, and accordingly he spent the rest of his life on classical literary criticism.

We come thus to the problem of humanism and the Renaissance as urban movements. A working definition of humanism is the study of what now are called the 'humanities': art including painting and sculpture, philosophy including ethics, history for its moral lessons and above all literature. In the context of the Renaissance, 'literature' meant the classics of ancient Rome and to a lesser extent Greece. In the beginning this involved a slavishly uncritical use of classical rather than 'medieval' Latin and quotation of passages from the Latin classics instead of using one's own words. Although by the mid-fifteenth century the rigidity of the humanists' classicism was waning, and some of their works were appearing in translation, law and the natural sciences were denigrated. All ruling elites of Europe were receiving a classical education after the humanist curriculum spread to the northern universities in the late fifteenth century. Humanism does not refer to a secular as opposed to a religious attitude. In both Italy and the north, demand for religious art was extremely high, both from the churches and pious laypeople.

Such an antiquarian orientation was an anomaly in urban cultural life as it existed around 1350. What the schools taught and what educated adults read were not the same, but the great cultural achievements of the cities continued to be in more practical areas: history as a record of recent events of which the writer had some personal or documentary knowledge, expressed in the vernacular; entertaining stories; personal memoirs; and business records. Although the Renaissance is associated with the cities, it is most doubtful whether it would have had much impact if its leaders had not been patronised by the city rulers. Florence may be the partial exception, where reverence for the classics preceded the Medici, but it was fostered by them. Elsewhere, it flourished only with princes' patronage, then was imitated by those who sought the princes' favour. Humanism came late to Venice, which lacked a single ruler of the sort of the Medici, Visconti or the pope. And by that time, it was already a fashion to be imitated.

The Italian humanists exalted the city, seeing aspects of ancient Rome replicated in their own experience. Naturally there are differences: humanists at Florence, which preserved the form of republican institutions, at least in the early Medici period, praised the benevolence of their elites as heirs of the rulers of the Roman Republic. The Visconti of Milan preferred that their court humanists laud princes and emperors.

By the fifteenth century most humanists agreed that scholars should not immure themselves in the study but rather should be active in the affairs of their cities. The latter view took its inspiration from Cicero, a man of letters who also had a political career and died in defence of the liberty of his city. Cicero also had the good taste to invest his fortune in land. He was thus the perfect role model for the urban elites of pre-modern Europe. Ciceronian 'civic humanism' was important in the transfer of the humanist curriculum to the north, where university education was increasingly necessary for a public career.

Some humanists, particularly the early ones such as Coluccio Salutati, were officials or merchants of a city. Others, such as the Medici and Visconti, came from families that were not responsible for much cultural patronage until they had become rulers of their cities. The independent scholar or person of letters was rare. Urban princes commissioned the great buildings and works of art and literature; and their example was imitated by other wealthy citizens, more out of hubris than from intrinsic appreciation of classical culture.[121]

Thus humanism was a court culture, a 'program for the ruling classes' in Lauro Martines' famous formulation.[122] Italy was the richest place in the west, and the accumulation of capital was strongest in the cities. The urban elites had enough money to buy what they wanted. Paintings, sculpture, fine jewellery, even books were becoming items of conspicuous consumption and display: some early collectors of Greek manuscripts could not read them in their original language, but they were wonderful conversation pieces.[123]

The extent and breadth of private patronage of the arts was exceptional at Florence even among Italian cities, and no northern city comes even close. Pre-Medicean Florence had been unique in allocating to the guilds the responsibility of maintaining and adorning the main public buildings. Thus in the fourteenth century the wool merchants were responsible for the Duomo and the Piazza della Signoria and its loggia, while the cloth merchants handled the Baptistery and commissioned Ghiberti's famous doors, while the silk merchants were in charge of Orsanmichele, the grain market. The city government itself kept control of the Palazzo della Signoria. Smaller churches got state subsidies for building, and they too were often assigned to guilds. Since the *arti* were very aristocratic, a certain amount of guild hubris was involved in outspending the others. Individual merchants and guildsmen were the main patrons of the parish churches and the monasteries favoured by their families.

Such fourteenth-century Florentine banking families as the Bardi and Peruzzi were wealthy, but they did not patronize art.[124] The advent of the Medici to power in the fifteenth century is thus critical: three-fifths of the works of art now housed in Florence were donated by this family. To give public honour to their family, and because they genuinely appreciated architecture, painting, sculpture and literature, the Medici spent vast sums on the arts. Their example ended whatever moral constraints about ostentation were still at work elsewhere among the Florentine elite: individual patronage became more important than the corporate support of guilds.[125]

Patronage at Venice was very different. There the city patricians handled some major art patronage directly, and the rest was done by the Council and other organs of the government. The confraternities of Venice were also important patrons of the arts, but they were even more closely supervised by the state than they were elsewhere. The art works cultivated an image of the beneficence of the state: 'it is difficult to overemphasize the importance of art as state propaganda'. Thus at Venice it was the state, at Florence the individual guild and family that drove cultural achievements of the Renaissance.[126]

Outside Florence and Venice, the association of princes with humanism is almost unbreachable even in Italy: for example with the popes at Rome and Federigo da Montefeltro at Urbino. Cultural patronage at Milan was almost entirely in the hands of the Visconti and Sforza dukes, who cultivated an image of the ruler as patron of the major churches, particularly the cathedral, to which they diverted vast revenues. They also used their power over landholding to control private building, to the point where the elite of Milan did little building or artistic patronage until the fall of the Sforza in the sixteenth century.[127]

The status of the architect was considerably higher than that of painters and particularly sculptors. Much new building, sponsored both by city governments and other public institutions and by individuals, was done after 1400, but pre-existing street layouts and property boundaries hindered a comprehensive rebuilding (see Chapter 3). About 100 new *palazzi* were built at Florence in the fifteenth century; the city had only 10,000 taxpaying households in 1427, so the ratio was very high. The same general point can be made about other Italian cities.[128] Most of the new palaces were geometric blocks enclosing an interior courtyard, with private porticos on all sides; the Medici palace is an example. By end of the fifteenth century the porticos had also been shifted to the courtyard.[129] Yet new building was not limited to the cities, and princes also spent lavishly on their rural properties.

Painting and sculpture saw an evolution of more realistic styles, but neither was exactly a novelty of Renaissance urban culture. The great cathedrals and other churches of Europe had long been adorned externally and internally with sculpture. So were other public buildings such as town halls and guild houses, market squares and some private homes.[130] Sculpture had the advantage of imperishability: it could be kept outside, where, the bigger the better, it could enhance the reputation of the patron for magnificent monumentality. More than with architecture, painting and sculpture varied considerably in quality. For every genius there were hundreds of stonecarvers who could make gargoyles.

The City as Cultural Marketplace

The cultural importance of the German and Low Country cities appears much more clearly if we do not compare them with Florence, which was almost as untypical of Italy as of Europe as a whole. They were responsible for important artistic patronage, both of masterworks and of more mass-produced work. There were important art markets at both Ghent and Bruges. In 1357 Ghent had about 50 painters in a population of 50,000. About 100 painters were active in Bruges in the last quarter of the fifteenth century, of whom 40 were of foreign origin, most from northern France and Germany.[131] The painters not only did works for private homes, which were increasingly in demand, but also painted banners and buildings for the city governments, and they got a lot of business painting decorations for the city festivals. Manuscript illumination was also important at Bruges, but mainly for the counts of Flanders rather than urban patrons. Throughout the Low Countries, local painters sold their works at the city fairs.

The dukes of Burgundy were probably second only to the Medici in their cultivation of the arts. Both the city of Bruges and individuals in its elite were patronising the arts before the Burgundians became the city's princes, but the dukes and the Italian merchants living at Bruges commissioned far more than did the native Flemings. Ghent, where the dukes rarely resided, employed Hugo Van der Goes, and several important artists were born there. Hubert and Jan Van Eyck, who were not natives of the city, painted the *Adoration of the Lamb* at St Bavo's Cathedral on commission from the wealthy burgess Joos Vijt and his wife, Elisabeth Borluut. The arts at Ghent were never as strong as at Bruges and declined severely in the sixteenth century, while Bruges remained important for art.

The urban network that was already in place before the Renaissance provided the framework for an exchange of artistic technique. Flemish artists pioneered the use of oil-based paints, which Italian businessmen in Bruges saw before the Italian artists did. When Tommaso Portinari, branch manager of the Medici bank at Bruges, sent to Italy the 'Adoration Altarpiece' that Hugo Van der Goes had painted for him on commission, it caused a sensation and led to Italian adoption of the new medium.[132]

What appears new in the cities after 1400 is the development of a mass market for painting and sculpture. This made painters less dependent on advance commissions and in particular on wealthy patrons. Before the fifteenth century most houses had only utilitarian furniture: enough beds for the occupants, one or more storage chests, chairs and stools, a desk if home doubled as office, the tools of the trade, dishes, cutlery and candlesticks. As standards of living rose in the late Middle Ages and the middle classes began to buy luxury goods for the first time, houses became less spartanly furnished, as homeowners bought more furniture and pleasant decorations. In 1438 Aeneas Silvius Piccolomini, in a famous description clearly laden with politically-inspired hyperbole, portrayed the houses of Vienna as spacious, sturdy, with tasteful decorations (including pictures), well heated and with iron gates. The horses had roomy stalls, and many burghers even kept pet birds. The façades were splendid and adorned with pictures. He claimed that even a modest house in Vienna was comparable to the dwelling of a prince.[133]

The elites themselves were mobile; the same families rarely stayed in power for long, and as others got access to wealth and power, they got a taste for art. At Florence there is little evidence before the Medici period of paintings hanging in private homes. Thereafter those who could afford them filled their houses with high quality art. Mass production of paintings, however, comes at the end of the fifteenth century and particularly the sixteenth. By the seventeenth century some wealthy Florentines literally had hundreds of paintings in their homes.[134] Much of Titian's fame came from the high demand for his erotic nudes for bedrooms.

Cologne developed an independent market for art at the close of the Middle Ages. Literary evidence suggests that private home interiors were being decorated in the early sixteenth century. From the fourteenth century some painters were producing small works without an advance commission, suggesting that they expected to sell them on the market. As in Italy, religious art was commissioned by lay patricians as well as the churches. Yet as elsewhere, it is unwise to generalise about artistic tastes among the entire city elite: of 25 major lay patrons of art at Cologne, five families account for 15 names.[135]

Before the 1430s demand for art at Bruges came mainly from the church and court, but thereafter a mass market developed. Painters began making multiple copies of their own works in response to demand. The city built the *Pandt*, a gallery with 187 stalls for luxury craftsmen. Most of the painters who rented stalls there have left no mark on art history; they were simply craftsmen producing for a home decoration market.[136] Antwerp, the successor to Bruges' commercial functions in the sixteenth century, was also important both for commissioned art, which influenced the evolution of new styles as the elites' fashions 'trickled down', and also for the increasing demand for more mass-produced art, which found a mainly city market. Antwerp probably had 300 artists, including sculptors and engravers as well as painters, in a population of 100,000 in 1566; this is more than twice the number of bakers. The city still had 216 painters and

19 sculptors in 1616, which would represent a higher proportion of its diminished population than in 1566. An open art market was held every Friday. The Antwerp Bourse contained an area for the permanent display of paintings. Paintings were also sold at auction, and in the late sixteenth century some art retailers who were not themselves painters entered the business. Antwerp paintings were shipped to markets as distant as Spain and Scandinavia. Commissions were important, but there is a tendency from this period for favourite scenes to be painted in numerous copies for a wider market. Goldsmiths and makers of musical instruments were also numerous, and more stable than the painters and sculptors, who moved frequently to satisfy demand for their works.[137]

Printing

Crafts, education and commerce are linked by the development of printing with movable type, which was associated mainly with the cities. The early printers served a diverse clientele, including state authorities and bishops. Southern Germany and Italy dominated printing until about 1475. Thereafter it expanded to England and particularly the Low Countries. As a percentage of population, the Low Countries, Germany and Italy had the highest number of printers, with France and England far behind, a professional geography that mirrors levels of urbanisation. In the sixteenth century the establishment of a university in a city often came just after printing is first attested there, as happened at Frankfurt-an-der-Oder and Wittenberg. Marburg University was founded in 1527, and in the same year Johann Loersfeld from Erfurt (also a university town with a printing establishment) was named university printer. Basel and Cologne are good examples of the link between the university and printing: not necessarily institutional, but simply providing a demand for books. The first printers in Paris were Germans; and although they did not print for the university, they published classical texts and grammars that had a market among the students and masters.[138]

The link between printing and university was not absolute. Antwerp became a major printing centre, although it had no university. The number of titles produced there before 1501 was half-again as large as that of Leuven, a university town. Antwerp had over 400 printers by the 1570s, while Leuven had 42, and Ghent and Brussels about ten. The Antwerp printers were entrepreneurs who handled both typesetting and distribution of their works. Thus Antwerp had a large printing establishment even before the advent of Christopher Plantin (1514–1589), a crypto-Protestant immigrant from France who managed through judiciously flattering publications to gain royal favour and become the official state printer in the Low Countries. Government business gave him a monopoly over proclamations and statutes, and he published the Antwerp *Polyglot Bible* in various languages. The diversity and size of the population of Antwerp, including religious dissidents in exile from their homes – many English religious works of the 1520s and 1530s were printed in Antwerp and smuggled into England – contributed largely to making printing such a success there.

Printing in connection with cartography was also important: Abraham Ortelius printed the first atlas of several maps collected in the same printed volume in 1570 at Antwerp.[139]

The Italian cities were also important for printing, particularly Venice, where the firm of Aldus Manutius printed in Italic or humanistic font, the ancestor of the modern printed page. Religious works dominated the inventories of most early printers everywhere, but humanist books made the reputations if not the fortunes of the Italian publishers. Yet even Manutius had to be a businessman. He printed such exotica as the first complete edition of Aristotle's works in Greek published in the west, but his firm, the Aldine Press, also printed works that gained wide circulation. Desiderius Erasmus, one of the earliest authors whose reputation generated large demand for his original works, published through Manutius.[140] All successful printers published contemporary works, both literary and scientific. William Caxton, the first known English printer, published works that appealed to his own elevated cultural sense but also chivalric works that would sell well.

The cities were thus centres of an information revolution. Before 1450 most authors became known only to a limited readership by manuscript publication. Printing spread so rapidly, however, that virtually all contemporary authors by 1500 could find someone who would print their works, as long as a reasonable return could be expected. Thus not only were more writers becoming known, but their works were available in multiple copies. By 1600 even small towns usually had at least one printer. The resulting diffusion of literacy transcends our topic. Books were sold in shops throughout the cities, usually works of entertainment and didactic material: not only devotional books, but also health manuals, books on farming techniques, schoolbooks and the like. Printing thus became the important avenue by which 'civility' reached the citizen.

Printing made it possible for cities to develop municipal libraries. Although the cities had archives in the Middle Ages, most lacked libraries. In cities that had a university, its collection was the most substantial library. The Sorbonne in 1289 had over 1000 titles, but the English colleges only reached this size in the fifteenth century. The Medici collection became the nucleus of the Laurentian Library at Florence, while the 800-volume collection of Niccolò Niccoli was given to the city by his executors, the Medici, and became the origin of the first public library of Florence. Venice's library grew from the collection of the Greek Cardinal Bessarion, which was donated to the city in 1468. From 1535 the Venetian city library, the Libreria Marciana, was given a new building on St Mark's square opposite the doge's palace. These were not lending libraries in the modern sense, but rather collections of books that scholars could consult for reference.

Throughout our period in all but a few cities, private collections – and not just those of the aristocrats – dwarfed the municipal libraries. The beginnings might be modest. Hamburg's council in 1481 used a gift of 30 books owned by the burgomaster Hinrich Murmeister as the nucleus of a 'new library' in the town hall. They were not widely used: although Murmeister's express wish was that people read the books, his donation was forgotten. Several professors on the law faculty of the university at Leipzig willed their books to the town, which set up a library in the town hall. Nuremberg had the oldest and best municipal library in Germany, first mentioned in 1370 and supplemented by a donation in 1429–30 of books from a private citizen. The printers of Nuremberg were patronised by the town fathers, and by 1500 the library had 371 books. A tradition developed of private persons leaving their books to the city library.[141] Lyon had a Municipal Library from 1530, Aix-la-Chapelle from 1556, but in England Norwich in 1608 and Bristol in 1615 are the first examples.[142] Only in the industrial age did the possession of a large library that was intended to serve as a repository of knowledge become a characteristic of the city, as it had been in antiquity.

The large cities were the only places with enough internal market and distribution facilities for export to be able to publish major scholarly works. Printers also needed a skilled labour force, a high level of literacy, and start-up capital because the presses and paper were expensive. Printers in the small towns published mainly broadsides. To the extent that they printed books, these reached a wider market through the central place. Printers published what would sell and where they could sell it. Printing produced an information revolution, for religion and the classical curriculum, but also for the practical knowledge that was so important to urbanites. The development and distribution of the printing trade is thus a classic illustration of central-place theory that intellectually brings our story full circle.

Chapter 7 . . . .

Achievement, Rationality, Measure and Assessment: Concluding Reflections on Pre-Modern Urbanisation in Europe

The establishment of urban Europe in the six centuries after 1100 constituted the most profound man-made alteration of the landscape in the history of Europe. As with all human activity, this development came in response to a complex network of forces that were inherent in the human and physical environment. While many towns of 'old Europe' developed on re-populated Roman sites, others did not. Europe was dotted with villages, and some Roman ruins, that were either abandoned or whose development into cities atrophied. Once in place, however, the older cities did provide functional but rarely topographic models for the foundation of newer settlements, some of which evolved into genuine cities.

    The city developed at the intersection of the supply of and demand for goods, labour, and/or services. The precise nature of what each city needed and what it could provide in exchange determined its individuality and character. The town and the city are distinguished from the village, and from each other, by the extent, permanence and complexity of those exchanges. Simple definitions of the 'city' are always misguided, for the city by its very nature is multifunctional. The old cliché 'Whoever claims to understand this simply does not understand the complexity of the situation' has considerable relevance here. Of the older generation of theoreticians of urban origins, only Max Weber realised this. Accordingly, his characterisations of the nature of the city have provided the analytical framework for this book, particularly the first five chapters. Yet for all their differences, the cities of 'old Europe' developed a set of broadly delineated characteristics that in greater or lesser degrees are true of virtually all of them, and which distinguish the pre-modern cities as a group from those that have developed since the Industrial Revolution of the eighteenth century.

The first cities were political, religious and domanial centres that came to serve two functions: as markets for the agricultural surpluses of their environs, and for luxuries demanded by the secular and ecclesiastical lords of the settlements. As agricultural surpluses became larger in the late eleventh century, precisely at the time when the development of the large mechanical loom for weaving required a larger labour force, the markets became larger and increasingly complex, dealing with a greater variety and quantity of goods, and the city became a producer as well as a consumer.

Fundamental to this change also is the development of the 'tertiary' or service sector of the economy, which was always located principally in the towns. Although many 'service' personnel were involved in provisioning the city populations with food, industrial raw materials and luxuries, others developed techniques that brought the cities into increasingly close contact with one another and fostered the establishment of a European economic region that was centred on interlocking urban networks. A great increase in the money supply from the late twelfth century conditioned the expansion of the tertiary sector. Although money had always been used, until the twelfth century its inherent value was too great for all but the largest commercial transactions. The greater use of money lowered its value and made monetary exchange feasible for smaller quantities and for less exotic consumer goods than before. The use of arithmetical values for goods fostered exchange, cash payments as wages, the use of credit and fiduciary money, and economic interdependence. Commercial capitalism was born in the economic and monetary expansion of the central Middle Ages, as regional networks of small markets fed into larger central places that in their turn injected value into the economy through services, in providing mechanisms for credit, investment and exchange of an ever-greater variety and quantity of consumer goods.

Other fundamental changes came in the late thirteenth century, with the nearly simultaneous development of regular voyages between Italy and the North Sea ports and a contraction in the money supply. But the urban and commercial infrastructure that was in place by then did not change fundamentally. The exchange networks continued to be focused on the cities, which were able to market the surplus products of the regions that they served as central places, continued to provide a demand market for food and luxuries, and also provided the population base that was necessary for occupational diversity and specialisation. The cities had been created by the population expansion of the central Middle Ages, but the urban network was not destroyed by the later demographic setbacks. Rather, as distress mounted in the rural areas, the cities grew relatively through even higher levels of immigration, although most of them lost absolute numbers of residents. The great cities of 1500 were with rare exceptions the great cities of 1300, but with the difference that by the later date their domination of their economic regions was even stronger.

A new period of expansion began in the late fifteenth century. The supply of coin increased, then was fuelled by the infusion of new supplies of bullion into the economy from the Americas. A world market under European domination was developed. Commercial capitalism reached its fullest development. Yet the new development brought problems for many cities. Prices rose faster than wages, and vagrancy and poverty in the cities, which were already becoming serious during the late medieval contraction, became even worse. Although the proportion of Europe's population that lived in cities rose during the sixteenth and seventeenth centuries, most of the increase occurred in national capitals and ports whose fortunes were made in the colonial trade. Many of the greatest cities of the late Middle Ages stagnated, and the populations of some actually declined.

Much of the strength of the European urban system after 1100 had been the development of legal structures that guaranteed for corporations such as cities, as well as for individual persons, rights that could not be overturned by the territorial state without due process. But the cities lost most of their independence to the territorial states that contained them during the sixteenth and seventeenth centuries. National and regional capitals – some of them new creations such as Madrid, others such as London and Paris simply growing because of the increase in the state apparatus – became extremely large. The more balanced demographic structure of the European urban network before 1500 yielded to a few enormous cities. Yet although the changes altered the urban map in detail, they did not transform its fundamental structure. The earlier great cities continued to exist, although in many cases their importance became regional rather than inter-regional.

Change is inevitable over any period of history, and certainly one of six centuries, but the revolutionary period of pre-modern urbanisation was 1100–1300. The next four centuries saw consolidation and modifications of detail in the urban system, but no fundamental changes. The urban revolution created a system by which regions of Europe could accommodate local shortages and surpluses through a market mechanism that was centred on major population concentrations, which in effect justified their legal privileges and paid for their food by providing marketing and other services to the rural environs that had given them birth. Shortage and surplus existed not only in the production of goods and services, but also in the supply of labour. The cities provided outlets for population that could not be supported in the rural economy, as the large concentration of persons permitted the development of trades and industries that required large amounts of labour, and also specialised labour. The specialisation of the urban labour force made possible both the production of goods of high quality, particularly fine textiles and other luxury items where numerous talents were required, and also the manufacture of items with a limited market but which nonetheless enhanced the quality of life. Once on the urban market, these goods spread to the countryside. Urbanisation, and specifically the cities' functions of central place and capital concentration, had an impact on economic, social, cultural and political relations that was far out of proportion to the number of persons who actually lived in cities.

In an overwhelmingly rural environment, the very existence of the cities depended on the rational solutions that their leaders found for issues that confronted them. Modern scholars looking at the cities are often overwhelmed by what appear to be their appalling problems: high levels of violence, elementary sanitation, primitive technology, poverty, relative illiteracy – and the list goes on. Yet the city could not have maintained its population without heavy immigration, in view of the higher death rates there than in the rural areas, and immigration can only be explained as the result of large numbers of persons feeling, correctly or incorrectly, that their situations would be improved by moving into a city, most often one near their previous place of residence. The pre-modern cities should be seen not in the light of recent standards, which assume a much more sophisticated technology than was available earlier, but rather in terms of the functions that they fulfilled at the time and which on balance made them seem attractive to contemporaries. The cities provided employment and other opportunities for their residents and had a relatively open labour market for low and intermediate-level jobs that attracted newcomers. Their economic infrastructures and the cultural sophistication that supported them enhanced the quality of life not only for the cities' own residents, but for the entire regions that they served. City councils were not democratically elected, but countless opportunities existed for public participation through guild, confraternity and parish organisations, and public charges were rotated so frequently that most persons who so desired were able to serve their cities in some capacity. The city councils were not unresponsive to the needs of those whom they governed, and many of their members took on public service from a sense of obligation rather than desire for power. That their priorities were more on the side of maintaining order than on securing economic or social 'equality' centuries before such notions were coherently formulated even in theory is irrelevant in the light of their magnificent achievement.

Despite the immense variety of local circumstances, the cities of Europe developed institutions for regulating interpersonal conflict, social and cultural as well as economic linkages with their rural environs, market mechanisms, and land use patterns that were remarkably constant in all parts of Europe. These developments were rational responses to the circumstances that city-dwellers faced. The pre-modern period gave rise to cogent if broadly based urban types and an urban system that was based on the symbiosis of regional diversities. The development of mass industrialisation in the later eighteenth century and the attendant growth of industrial capitalism created a new set of challenges that transformed the cities more fundamentally than anything that had occurred since the late eleventh century. Surely no one, however, would be so misguided as to argue that these changes were so thorough that contemporary urbanisation can be comprehended without understanding its pre-modern foundation.

Notes

Preface

1. Braudel, *The Structures of Everyday Life*, pp. 517–18, 514.
2. The exception to the periodisation tendency is Marino Berengo, *L'Europa delle città: Il volto della società urbana europea tra Medioevo ed Età moderna* (Turin, 1999), a work of which I only became aware as I was completing work on this book. Berengo (p. xii) adopts a time frame from the early twelfth century to the peace of Westphalia (1648), for essentially the same reasons that cause me to de-emphasise 'medieval' and 'early modern'.
3. Nicholas, *The Growth of the Medieval City*, and *The Later Medieval City*, 1300–1500.

Chapter 1: Urban Europe Between the Industrial Revolutions

1. Hyde, 'Universities and Cities in Medieval Italy', p. 15.
2. 'Scholars who go on repeating Max Weber's anachronistic equation of the spirit of capitalism with Protestantism should find a way to conceal the abundant medieval data that contradict it' (Mumford, *Technics and Civilization*, p. 275). The problem is that Tawney, not Weber, made that equation.
3. Weber, *The Protestant Ethic and the Spirit of Capitalism*; Tawney, *Religion and the Rise of Capitalism*; Weber, *The City*; Weber, *General Economic History*, p. 153. For recent analyses, see Hohenberg and Lees, *The Making of Urban Europe, 1000–1950*, p. 23; Lachmann, *Capitalists in Spite of Themselves*, p. 45; Sjoberg, 'Cities in Developing and Industrial Societies', p. 227.
4. Weber, *The City*, pp. 66–8; Cipolla, *Before the Industrial Revolution*, pp. 102–4.
5. Weber, *General Economic History*, pp. 130–1.
6. Wallerstein, *The Modern World System*, Vol. I, pp. 119–20.
7. Weber, *General Economic History*, pp. 132–3; Swanson, *Medieval British Towns*, p. 121; Carter, *The Study of Urban Geography*, p. 86; Hohenberg and Lees, 'Urban Systems and Economic Growth'.
8. Wallerstein, *The Modern World System*, Vol. I, pp. 15–16; Van der Wee, 'Industrial Dynamics and the Process of Urbanization and De-urbanization in the Low Countries', pp. 309–11. Braudel, *Civilization and Capitalism*, pp. 89, 92, takes a similar view

in associating the city with capitalism, while insisting relentlessly on fundamental changes beginning in the late fifteenth century.

9. Numerous examples from other regions corroborate this observation. Milan, on the frontier between the Alpine Foreland, and the fertile flood plain of the Po River, affords a striking parallel (Haverkamp, 'Das Zentralitätsgefüge Mailands im hohen Mittelalter'). The most successful English towns were at the junction of 'contrasting agricultural regions' (Kermode, 'The Greater Towns 1300–1450', p. 446). For Low Country examples, see Van Uytven, 'Brabantse en Antwerpse centrale plaatsen (14de–19de eeuw)', p. 35.

10. Van der Woude, Nayami and de Vries (eds.), *Urbanization in History*, p. 13; Nicholas, 'Of Poverty and Primacy'.

11. Brennan, 'Town and Country in France, 1550–1750'.

12. Carter, *The Study of Urban Geography*, p. 26.

13. See discussion of the historiography of the terms 'basic' and 'non-basic' in Carter, *The Study of Urban Geography*, p. 104.

14. Marshall, *The Structure of Urban Systems*, p. 135.

15. Dickinson, *The West European City*, p. 326.

16. Boucheron, 'Water and Power in Milan, *c.* 1200–1500', p. 181.

17. De Vries, 'Problems in the Measurement, Description, and Analysis of Historical Urbanization', pp. 55–7; Perrenoud, 'Aspects of Fertility Decline in an Urban Settling: Rouen and Geneva'.

18. Sjoberg, 'Theory and Research in Urban Sociology', p. 162. Curiously, although recent research has de-emphasised the separation of town and countryside, the older view, of the town as an 'island', is much closer to how contemporaries in the pre-modern world conceived their towns and themselves as members of the urban community (Kugler, *Die Vorstellung der Stadt in der Literatur des deutschen Mittelalters*, p. 170).

19. Nicholas, *The Growth of the Medieval City*, p. 87.

20. The best documented example is Cologne. See Strait, *Cologne in the Twelfth Century*.

21. Britnell, *The Commercialisation of English Society, 1000–1500*, pp. 102–3.

22. The best survey of the monetary changes of the central Middle Ages is Spufford, *Money and Its Use in Medieval Europe*, pp. 109–86.

23. Carter, *Introduction to Urban Historical Geography*, pp. 46–7; Morris, *A History of Urban Form*, p. 107.

24. Swanson, *Medieval British Towns*, p. 19; Britnell, 'The Economy of British Towns 600–1300', p. 115; Morris, *History of Urban Form*, pp. 94–8. On the general question of town foundation as a means of establishing control, see Bartlett, *The Making of Europe*, esp. pp. 179–82.

25. Carter, *Introduction to Urban Historical Geography*, pp. 48–9.

26. Kermode, 'The Greater Towns 1300–1450', pp. 442–7; Laughton, Jones and Dyer, 'The Urban Hierarchy in the Later Middle Ages', p. 335.

27. Carter, *Introduction to Urban Historical Geography*, p. 1; Dickinson, *West European City*, p. 282; Morris, *History of Urban Form*, p. 110.

28. Braudel, *Civilization and Capitalism*, Vol. I. p. 501; Friedman, *Florentine New Towns*, pp. 5–171; Nicholas, *Later Medieval City*, p. 92.

29. Goose, 'In Search of the Urban Variable'.

30. de Vries, *European Urbanization, 1500–1800*, p. 42.

31. Clark and Lepetit, *Capital Cities and their Hinterlands*, pp. 1–2.

32. Britnell, 'The Economy of British Towns 1300–1540', p. 316. In 'The Black Death in English Towns', p. 197, Britnell discusses problems of the English towns before 1348

but argues that 'probably the most general determinant of the level of trade in towns
... was the level of spending by their rural neighbours, and many towns were affected
before 1348 by falling local demand'.

33. Goose, 'In Search of the Urban Variable', p. 181.
34. Schilling, *Die Stadt in der frühen Neuzeit*, pp. 22–3; Aston and Bond, *The Landscape of Towns*, p. 110; Van Uytven, 'Stages of Economic Decline'.
35. de Vries, *European Urbanization*, pp. 28–9.
36. de Vries, 'Problems in the Measurement, Description, and Analysis of Historical Urbanization', particularly Table 3.1, p. 45.
37. Marshall, *The Structure of Urban Systems*, Table 2.1, pp. 38–9.
38. Cowan, *The Urban Patriciate*, p. 39.
39. Discussion based on John U. Marshall, *The Structure of Urban Systems*, pp. 36–41.
40. François, 'Des républiques marchandes aux capitals politiques: remarques sur la hiérarchie urbain du Saint-Empire à l'Époque Moderne'; François, 'The German Urban Network between the Sixteenth and Eighteenth Centuries', pp. 84–9.
41. Hohenberg and Lees, *Making of Urban Europe*, p. 108.
42. Weber, *General Economic History*, pp. 169–73, 205–8.
43. Davis, *The Rise of the Atlantic Economies*, pp. 201.

Chapter 2: City and Region

1. Braudel, *Structures of Everyday Life*, p. 481.
2. Epstein, 'Cities, Regions and the Late Medieval Crisis: Sicily and Tuscany Compared', p. 10.
3. Marshall, *The Structure of Urban Systems*, p. 18.
4. Jack, *Towns in Tudor and Stuart Britain*, p. 140; Kermode, 'Northern Towns', pp. 662–4.
5. Swanson, *Medieval British Towns*, pp. 37–8.
6. Marshall, *The Structure of Urban Systems*, pp. 20–2.
7. Weber, *General Economic History*, pp. 207–8; for the Bruges figures, see Nicholas, 'The English Trade at Bruges in the Last Years of Edward III', pp. 37–9, for London, see Cobb (ed.). *The Overseas Trade of London*, p. xxxviii.
8. Kowaleski, 'Port Towns: England and Wales 1300–1540', p. 473.
9. James Vance developed this 'mercantile' theory of urban origins as a variant on Pirenne's classic 'wandering merchant' hypothesis. Although Vance's model was North America, the sequence applies just as well to the German east. See James Vance, *The Merchant's World*, pp. 277–97.
10. Smith, 'Types of City-size Distributions', pp. 35–7; Maria Bogucka, 'Between Capital, Residential Town, and Metropolis'.
11. Zipf, *National Unity and Disunity*. See discussion by Carter, *The Study of Urban Geography*, p. 36; Herbert and Thomas, *Cities in Space, City as Place*, pp. 62–3; Hohenberg and Lees, *Making of Urban Europe*, p. 56; de Vries, 'Problems', p. 50.
12. Smith, 'Types of City-size Distributions', pp. 20–1, 24, 26–7.
13. Russell, *Medieval Regions and Their Cities*, pp. 24–33, with formula p. 24.
14. See critique of Hohenberg and Lees, *Making of Urban Europe*, pp. 56–7.
15. de Vries, *European Urbanization*, pp. 95, 107; van der Woude, Nayami and de Vries, *Urbanization in History*, p. 2.

16. Discussion based on Peter Stabel, *Dwarfs Among Giants*, pp. 24–6, 39–43, 48–50, 66, table pp. 245–6; see also Prevenier, Sosson and Boone, 'Le réseau urbain en Flandre (XIIIe–XIXe siècle)', pp. 157–200, especially 176–7.

17. Stabel, *Dwarfs Among Giants*, pp. 28–30, 262–3. Stabel uses a population of 800 as the threshold of urbanisation, which in my opinion is far too low.

18. Stabel, *Dwarfs Among Giants*, pp. 55–6; see also Klep, 'Long-Term Developments in the Urban Sector of the Netherlands (1350–1870)', p. 212.

19. Klep, 'Urban Sector of the Netherlands', pp. 205–9; Hoppenbrouwers, 'Town and Country in Holland, 1300–1550', pp. 62–3.

20. Discussion based on Klep, 'Urban Sector of the Netherlands', p. 221; 't Hart, 'Cities and Statemaking in the Dutch Republic, 1580–1680', p. 665; de Vries and van der Woude, *The First Modern Economy*, pp. 59–62 and quotation p. 59.

21. Stabel, *Dwarfs Among Giants*, pp. 72–80.

22. Schilling, *Die Stadt in der frühen Neuzeit*, pp. 4–6.

23. Stabel, *Dwarfs Among Giants*, pp. 74–5; see also Moraw, 'Cities and Citizenry as Factors of State Formation in the Roman-German Empire of the Late Middle Ages', p. 637.

24. Von Thünen, *Isolated State*; Hohenberg and Lees, 'Urban Systems and Economic Growth', pp. 38–41; Vilfan, 'L'Approvisionnement des villes dans les confines germano-italo-slaves du XIVe au XVIIe siècle', pp. 53–7; Jack, *Towns in Tudor and Stuart Britain*, p. 150.

25. Christaller, *Central Places in Southern Germany*, pp. 19–21; Smith, 'Types of City-size Distributions', pp. 21–2; Carter, *Introduction to Urban Historical Geography*, pp. 86–8.

26. Marshall, *The Structure of Urban Systems*, pp. 139–79, 213.

27. Marktort, Amtsort, Kreisstadt, Bezirkstadt, Gaustadt, Provinzstadt, Landstadt; cf. Gilbert Rozman, 'Urban Networks and Historical Stages'; see also discussion by Carter, *Study of Urban Geography*, pp. 29–30.

28. Higounet, 'Centralité, petites villes et bastides dans l'Aquitaine médiévale', p. 46, applying Cristaller's theory of centrality to Périgueux, found two approximate circles (with corners to include small villages), of 21 km (half a day to the central market) and 36 km (one day) Most immigrants into the city came from the narrower circle, but goods consumed at Périgueux came from the larger one. Cited by Carpentier and Le Mené, *La France du XIe au XVe siècle: population, société, économie*, pp. 274–5.

29. Christaller, *Central Places*, esp. pp. 19–21, 27–36. See also discussion of central place theory by Carter, *Study of Urban Geography*, pp. 27–30.

30. Quoted from Mayer, 'A Survey of Urban Geography', pp. 89–90. For Germany, see discussion by Tom Scott and Bob Scribner, 'Urban Networks', pp. 119–29.

31. Dyer, ' "Urban Decline" in England, 1377–1525', pp. 266–8; Britnell, 'The Economy of British Towns 1300–1540', pp. 317–21.

32. Kelley, 'Dendritic Central-place Systems', pp. 221–34. See also discussion by Brennan, 'Town and Country in France, 1550–1750', pp. 268–9.

33. Duplessis, *Transitions to Capitalism in Early Modern Europe*, p. 92.

34. Kowaleski, *Local Markets and Regional Trade in Medieval Exeter*, pp.179–81, 268.

35. Mitford's account is analysed by Christopher Dyer, 'The Consumer and the Market in the Later Middle Ages', pp. 260–4, 279–80; see also Swanson, *Medieval British Towns*, p. 33.

36. Munro, 'The Symbiosis of Towns and Textiles'; Derek Keene, 'Small Towns and the Metropolis', pp. 231–7.

37. Chartier and Neveux, 'La ville dominante et soumise', pp. 57–62.

37. Campbell, Galloway, Keene and Murphy, *A Medieval Capital and Its Grain Supply*.
39. Campbell *et al.*, *Medieval Capital*, pp. 173–5; Chartier and Neveux, 'La ville domi-nante et soumise', p. 57; see also Jacquart, 'Paris: First Metropolis of the Early Modern Period', pp. 110–11. The area required to feed the city was somewhat smal-ler in the Low Countries, where yields on grain were high; Van Uytven, 'L'Approvi-sionnement des villes des anciennes Pays-Bas au Moyen Age', pp. 78–9.
40. For Ghent, see Nicholas, 'The Scheldt Trade and the 'Ghent War' of 1379–1385', pp. 256–8, and Nicholas, *The Metamorphosis of a Medieval City*, pp. 241–54. For Pader-born, see Schoppmeyer, 'Probleme der zentralörtlichen Bedeutung Paderborns im Spätmittelalter', pp. 106–9; see more generally Kießling, 'Herrschaft–Markt–Landbesitz. Aspekte der Zentralität und der Stadt-Land-Beziehungen spätmittelal-terlicher Städte an ostschwäbischen Beispielen', pp. 194–7. For Dordrecht, see Nicholas, *The Later Medieval City*, p. 42, and Hoppenbrouwers, 'Town and Country in Holland, 1300–1550', pp. 61–2. For Bruges, see Nicholas, *Medieval Flanders*, pp. 295–305 and literature cited.
41. De la Roncière, 'L'Approvisionnement des villes italiennes au Moyen Age (XIVe–XVe siècles)' pp. 43–4.
42. Irsigler, 'L'Approvisionnement des villes de l'Allemagne occidentale jusqu'au XVIe siècle', pp. 120–3; Jean-Pierre Kintz, 'L'Approvisionnement en vivres des villes des pays du Main et du Rhin Supérieur (XVIe–XVIIe siècles)', p. 259; Cipolla, *Before the Industrial Revolution*, p. 52.
43. Translated from Möncke (ed.), *Quellen zur Wirtschafts- und Sozialgeschichte mittel- und oberdeutscher Städte im Spätmittelalter*, p. 313.
44. Van Uytven, 'L'Approvisionnement des villes des anciennes Pays-Bas', pp. 88–90.
45. De la Roncière, 'L'Approvisionnement des villes italiennes au Moyen Age (XIVe–XVe siècles)' pp. 33–51; Aymard, 'L'Approvisionnement des villes de la Méditerra-née occidentale (XVIe–XVIIIe siècles)', pp. 167–70, 174–8.
46. Kowaleski, *Exeter*, pp. 83–9; Rappaport, *Worlds within Worlds*, pp. 67, 80; Chartier and Neveux, 'La ville dominante et soumise', pp. 53–5.
47. Hohenberg and Lees, *Making of Urban Europe*, p. 41.
48. Weber, *City*, p. 92.
49. Opll, 'Cities and the Transmission of Cultural Values in the Late Middle Ages and Early Modern Period: the Vienna Example', p. 124, including quotation.
50. Barron, 'London 1300–1540', p. 399.
51. Schilling, *Die Stadt in der frühen Neuzeit*, p. 8.
52. Rappaport, *Worlds within Worlds*, pp. 55–6.
53. Rosser, 'Crafts, Guilds and the Negotiation of Work in the Medieval Town', p. 11. For the Strycker case, see Cowan, 'Foreigners and the City', pp. 48–52.
54. de Olivera-Marques, 'Les villes portugaises au Moyen Âge (XIVe–XVe siècles)', p. 107. See in general Nicholas, *Later Medieval City*, pp. 280–7.
55. Carter, *Study of Urban Geography*, p. 263.
56. Calabi, 'The Jews and the City in the Mediterranean Area'.
57. Carter, *Introduction to Urban Historical Geography*, p. 92; Keene, 'The South-East of England', p. 579.
58. Cipolla, *Before the Industrial Revolution*, p. 194.
59. Smail, *Imaginary Cartographies*, pp. 111–12.
60. Brady, *Ruling Class, Regime and Reformation at Strasbourg 1520–1555*, pp. 140–2, 147–51.
61. Farr, *Artisans in Europe, 1300–1914*, pp. 58–9; Rosser, 'Crafts, Guilds and the Negotia-tion of Work in the Medieval Town', p. 9.

62. Malanima, 'An Example of Industrial Reconversion', pp. 63–6; Kowaleski, *Exeter*, pp. 1–41; Scott, 'Town and Country in Germany, 1350–1600', p. 222.

63. Chartier and Neveux, 'La ville dominante et soumise', p. 80.

64. Piergiovanni, 'Social and Economic Consequences of Structural Changes in the Ligurian Silk-weaving Industry from the Sixteenth to the Nineteenth Century'.

65. Gerd Wunder, 'Reichsstädte als Landesherrn' (*sic*); Schilling, *Die Stadt in der frühen Neuzeit*, p. 23.

66. Similarly, Bruges, which exported the cloth of the small centres of western Flanders, was reluctant to follow the lead of Ghent in suppressing rural industry. Nicholas, *Town and Countryside*, pp. 103–8.

67. Irsigler, 'Stadt und Umland im Spätmittelalter: zur zentralitätsfördernden Kraft von Fernhandel und Exportgewerbe', pp. 7–10. See more generally Irsigler, *Die wirtschaftliche Stellung der Stadt Köln im 14. und 15. Jahrhundert. Strukturanalyse einer spätmittelalterlichen Exportgewerbe und Fernhandelsstadt.*

68. Nicholas, *The Transformation of Europe, 1300–1600*, p. 302, after Wright, 'The Nature of Early Capitalism'.

69. Haverkamp, 'Das Zentralitätsgefüge Mailands im hohen Mittelalter', pp. 54–8; De la Roncière, 'L'Approvisionnement des villes italiennes au Moyen Age', p. 40.

70. Chittolini, 'Cities, "City-states", and Regional States in North-Central Italy', pp. 694–6.

71. Davidson, 'As Much for Its Culture as for its Arms'. Davidson explicitly rejects the term 'parasite'.

72. Scott, 'Town and Country in Germany, 1350–1600', p. 206.

73. See in general Moraw, 'Cities and Citizenry as Factors of State Formation in the Roman-German Empire of the Late Middle Ages'.

74. Wunder, 'Reichsstädte als Landesherrn', pp. 79–91. Wunder's arguments are paralleled by the case of Basel; see Juliane Kümmell, *Bäuerliche Gesellschaft und städtische Herrschaft im Spätmittelalter*. See also Kießling, 'Herrschaft–Markt–Landbesitz', pp. 189–92.

75. Dean, *The Towns of Italy in the Later Middle Ages*, pp. 138–9.

76. Belfanti, 'Town and Country in Central and Northern Italy, 1400–1800', pp. 295–6; Nicholas, *Later Medieval City*, pp. 87–92.

77. Epstein, 'Cities, Regions and the Late Medieval Crisis', esp. pp. 34–5, 40–1.

78. Nicholas, *Town and Countryside*, pp. 316–21.

79. Brennan, 'Town and Country in France, 1550–1750', pp. 253–5.

80. Nicholas, *Growth of the Medieval City*, pp. 154–5 and literature cited; Lilley, *Urban Life in the Middle Ages, 1000–1400*, pp. 53–5, 76–7, 83–92.

81. Nicholas, *Medieval Flanders*, p. 212; Prevenier *et al.*, 'Le réseau urbain en Flandre', p. 178; Stabel, *Dwarfs Among Giants*, pp. 87–8; Scott, 'Town and Country in Germany, 1350–1600', pp. 207–8.

82. Graus, 'Prag als Mitte Böhmens, 1346–1421'; Patze, 'Die Bildung der landesherrlichen Residenzen im Reich während des 14. Jahrhunderts'.

83. Marshall, *The Structure of Urban Systems*, p. 18.

84. Sánchez-León, 'Town and Country in Castile, 1400–1650', pp. 274–5, 277, 281–5.

85. David Ringrose, *Madrid and the Spanish Economy, 1560–1850*, pp. 180, 194, 255–7; López García and Madrazo, 'A Capital City in the Feudal Order'.

86. Gillespie, 'Dublin 1600–1700'.

87. Bogucka, 'Between Capital, Residential Town, and Metropolis', pp. 198–216; Andrzej Wyrobisz, 'Power and Towns in the Polish Gentry Commonwealth'.

88. Heller, *Labour, Science and Technology in the Age of Valois and Bourbon, 1500–1620*, p. 8.
89. Jacquart, 'Paris: First Metropolis of the Early Modern Period', pp. 105–8.
90. Nightingale, 'The Growth of London in the Medieval English Economy'; Glass-cock, 'England *circa* 1334', pp. 183–5; Baker, 'Changes in the Later Middle Ages', pp. 245–6; Derek Keene, 'Medieval London and Its Region'.
91. Rappaport, *Worlds within Worlds*, pp. 91–3.

Chapter 3: The Morphology of the Urban Plan

1. Vance, *The Continuing City*, p. 24.
2. Van Emden, 'Medieval French Representations of City and Other Walls', p. 543.
3. Dickinson, *West European City*, p. 29; Palliser, Slater and Dennison, 'The Topography of Towns 600–1300', p. 178.
4. Dickinson, *West European City*, pp. 5, 29, 326–8.
5. Leguay, *La rue au Moyen Age*, pp. 20–1.
6. Hohenberg and Lees, *Making of Urban Europe*, p. 31; Smail, *Imaginary Cartographies*, pp. 44–5; Nicholas, *Growth of the Medieval City*, p. 88; Dickinson, *West European City*, pp. 144–5.
7. Dickinson, *West European City*, pp. 272–5; Desportes, *Reims et les Rémois aux XIIIe et XIVe sièlces*, pp. 53–80.
8. Amelang, *Honored Citizens of Barcelona*, p. 4.
9. Dickinson, *West European City*, pp. 384–92.
10. Slater, 'Planning Britain's Largest Medieval New Town'. Cited with the author's permission. On the general subject of medieval town planning, see the still classic work of Maurice Beresford, *New Towns of the Middle Ages*; Lilley, *Urban Life*, pp. 159–63.
11. Nicholas, *Growth of the Medieval City*, p. 97 and literature cited; Carter, *Introduction to Urban Historical Geography*, pp. 48–9.
12. Reyerson, 'Medieval Walled Space', p. 99.
13. Grenville, *Medieval Housing*, p. 158; Schofield and Stell, 'The Built Environment 1300–1540', pp. 373–4.
14. Benjamin Arbel, 'The Port Towns of the Levant in Sixteenth-Century Travel Literature', pp. 151–64.
15. Nicholas, *Growth of the Medieval City*, pp. 92–6, 184–6.
16. Carter, *Introduction to Urban Historical Geography*, pp. 130–2.
17. For the suburban population, see Dickinson, *West European City*, pp. 318–19.
18. Tracy, 'To Wall or Not to Wall', pp. 84–5 and tables.
19. Reyerson, 'Medieval Walled Space', p. 92; Nicholas, *Later Medieval City*, pp. 72–3; Nicholas, *Growth of the Medieval City*, pp. 243–4; Tracy, *City Walls*, p. 6.
20. Reyerson, 'Medieval Walled Space', p. 101.
21. Zucker, *Town and Square*, pp. 64–5.
22. Dickinson, *West European City*, pp. 30–6; Faber and Lochard, *Montpellier: La Ville médiévale*, pp. 212–15.
23. Heers, *Espaces publics, espaces privés dans la ville*.
24. Steane, *The Archaeology of Power*, pp. 206–8.
25. From *ceap*, AS 'market'. At Winchester the eventual High Street was being called *ceapstraet* by the early tenth century. Martin Biddle, *Winchester in the Early Middle Ages*, p. 285.

26. Zucker, *Town and Square*, pp. 75–89.
27. Weber, *City*, pp. 66–8; Laughton, Jones and Dyer. 'The Urban Hierarchy in the later Middle Ages', p. 346.
28. Braudel, *Wheels of Commerce*, pp. 35, 38.
29. Carter, *Introduction to Urban Historical Geography*, pp. 154–6.
30. Dean, *Towns of Italy*, pp. 122–3.
31. Nicholas, *The Metamorphosis of a Medieval City*, pp. 77–8, after Napoléon De Pauw, *De Voorgeboden der stad Gent in de XIVe eeuw*, p. 89; for English examples of demarcation of sections of markets, see George Sheeran, *Medieval Yorkshire Towns*, p. 113.
32. Dickinson, *West European City*, pp. 63–78.
33. Dickinson, *West European City*, pp. 137–9.
34. Bechtold, *Zunftbürgerschaft und Patriziat*, pp. 101–2.
35. Heers, *Génes au XVe siècle*, pp. 55–9.
36. Keene, 'London from the Post-Roman Period to 1300', p. 201.
37. Gray (ed.), *The Oxford Book of Late Medieval Verse and Prose*, p. 18; spelling modernised.
38. Nicholas, *Growth of the Medieval City*, pp. 102–4, 187–9, and literature cited.
39. Carter, *Introduction to Urban Historical Geography*, pp. 151–3.
40. Leguay, *La rue au Moyen Age*, p. 131.
41. Nicholas, *Later Medieval City*, p. 82, after Raymond Cazelles, *Paris de la fin du règne de Philippe Auguste à la mort de Charles V, 1223–1380*, pp. 91–2.
42. Smail, *Imaginary Cartographies*, pp. 179–80.
43. Wheeler, 'Neighbourhoods and Local Loyalties in Renaissance Venice', p. 38.
44. Nicholas, *Metamorphosis*, pp. 19–20.
45. Leguay, *La rue au Moyen Age*, pp. 111–24; John Patten, *English Towns 1500–1700*, p. 36; Michael Camille, 'Signs of the City', p. 18.
46. Amelang, *Honored Citizens of Barcelona*, pp. 5–7; Keene, 'London from the Post-Roman Period to 1300', p. 192.
47. Carpentier and Le Mené, *La France du XIe au XVe siècle*, p. 489.
48. Nicholas, *Later Medieval City*, pp. 80–1.
49. Nicholas, *Later Medieval City*, pp. 50–6.
50. Nicholas, *Later Medieval City*, p. 75 after Keene, *Survey of Medieval Winchester*, pp. 130–1, 139–54, 417–18.
51. Leguay, *La rue au Moyen Age*, pp. 44–9.
52. Decavele, *Panoramisch Gezicht op Gent in 1534*.
53. Reyerson, 'Medieval Walled Space', pp. 105–6; Cowan, *Urban Patriciate*, p. 50.
54. Nicholas, *Metamorphosis*, pp. 84–9.
55. Goldthwaite, *The Building of Renaissance Florence*, pp. 2–22.
56. Tracy, *City Walls*, p. 8, with quotation p. 14; Michael Wolfe, 'Walled Towns During the French Wars of Religion (1560–1630)', p. 322.
57. Pollak, *Turin 1564–1680*, pp. 1–6, 41–9, 74–5 and plate 98.
58. Wolfe, 'Walled Towns During the French Wars of Religion', pp. 325–31; Chartier and Neveux, 'La ville dominante et soumisc', p. 121.
59. Carter, *Introduction to Urban Historical Geography*, p. 136.
60. Morris, *History of Urban Form*, p. 123.
61. Burke, *Towns in the Making*, pp. 69–71.
62. Burke, *Towns in the Making*, pp. 80–2.
63. Piet Lombaerde, 'Antwerp in its Golden Age', pp. 107–8, 120–2.
64. Burke, *Towns in the Making*, pp. 82–3; Dickinson, *West European City*, p. 426; Morris, *History of Urban Form*, p. 156.

65. Morris, *History of Urban Form*, pp. 158, 169; Friedrichs, *Early Modern City*, p. 27; Konvitz, *Cities and the Sea*, pp. 32–4.
66. Dickinson, *West European City*, pp. 426–9, 437.
67. Morris, *History of Urban Form*, pp. 185–8; Burke, *The Making of Dutch Towns*, pp. 141–53; Konvitz, *Cities and the Sea*, pp. 34–7.
68. Konvitz, *Cities and the Sea*, pp. 20–4; Lombaerde, 'Antwerp in its Golden Age', pp. 100–5.
69. Patten, *English Towns 1500–1700*, pp. 142, 188.
70. Aston and Bond, *Landscape of Towns*, pp. 113–14.
71. Morris, *History of Urban Form*, pp. 211–22.
72. Vance, *Continuing City*, especially pp. 131–5; Gideon Sjoberg, *The Pre-Industrial City*, pp, 108–45; see discussion by John Langton, 'Residential Patterns in Pre-industrial Cities'.
73. Dietrich, 'Merkantilismus und Städtewesen in Kursachsen', pp. 232–9.
74. Lilley, 'Decline or Decay?' pp. 235–65; Rappaport, *Worlds within Worlds*, p. 171, compared to Pearl, 'Change and Stability in Seventeenth-century London', p. 146.
75. Robert Descimon, 'Paris on the Eve of Saint Bartholomew', pp. 85–6, 92.
76. Nicholas, *Later Medieval City*, p. 77.

Chapter 4: Corporation and Community

1. Translated from the 'Konradbuch' of Zürich (1383), in Susanna Burghartz, *Leib, Ehre und Gut*, p. 213.
2. Weber, *City*, pp. 80–1.
3. Guibert of Nogent, *Self and Society in Medieval France: The Memoirs of Abbot Guibert of Nogent (1064?–c. 1125)*, p. 167.
4. Weber, *City*, pp. 108–14.
5. Nicholas, *Growth of the Medieval City*, pp. 141–55.
6. Swanson, *Medieval British Towns*, p. 95.
7. Weber, *City*, pp. 111–12, 183; Lilley, *Urban Life*, pp. 48–52.
8. On the thirteenth-century move of landowners into trade, see Strait, *Cologne in the Twelfth Century*, p. 76.
9. Nicholas and Prevenier (eds.), *Gentse Stads-en Baljuwsrekeningen (1365–1376)*, pp. 40–1.
10. Riley, *Memorials of London and London Life in the XIIIth, XIVth, and XVth Centuries*, p. 501.
11. Williams, *English Historical Documents, 1485–1558*, p. 993.
12. Strait, *Cologne*, pp. 35–56, 143–6.
13. Keene, 'London from the Post-Roman Period to 1300', p. 209; Rigby and Ewan, 'Government, Power and Authority 1300–1540', p. 292; Lilley, *Urban Life*, pp. 93–9.
14. Max Weber made an extremely suggestive analogy to the plebeians of ancient Rome, who like the *popolani* had their own organisation within the state and were dominated by wealthy merchants with social aspirations; *General Economic History*, pp. 325–6.
15. See Heers, *Parties and Political Life in the Medieval West*, for a convenient summary.
16. Blanshei, *Perugia 1260–1340*, pp. 53–6.
17. Weber, *City*, pp. 121–95.
18. Cowan, *The Urban Patriciate*, pp. 51–56; Chojnacki, 'Social Identity in Renaissance Venice', pp. 341–58.

19. A chronicler refers to 72 craft guilds with their own officials in Florence in the 1290s; Compagni, *Chronicle of Florence*, pp. xix, 37.

20. Bowsky, *A Medieval Italian Commune*, pp. 24–36, 54–92; Waley, *Siena and the Sienese in the Thirteenth Century*, pp. xv, 48; Nicholas, *Growth of the Medieval City*, pp. 314–15.

21. Rigby and Ewan, 'Government, Power and Authority 1300–1540', pp. 312, 292; Barron, 'London 1300–1540', pp. 403–4; Friedrichs, *Urban Politics in Early Modern Europe*, p. 12.

22. Rigaudière, *Gouverner la ville au Moyen Age*, p. 17; Carpentier and Le Mené, *La France du XIe au XVe siècle*, pp. 479–80.

23. Rigaudière, *Gouverner la ville*, pp. 172–89; Nicholas, *Growth of the Medieval City*, pp. 227–8.

24. Queller, *The Venetian Patriciate*; Cowan, *Urban Europe*, pp. 55–6.

25. Carpentier and Le Mené, *La France du XIe au XVe siècle*, pp. 482–3.

26. Pirenne's famous title *Belgian Democracy: Its Early History* leaps immediately to mind.

27. Strauss, *Nuremberg in the 16th Century*, p. 61; Cowan, *Urban Patriciates*, pp. 55–6.

28. Rigby, *English Society in the Later Middle Ages*, p. 175.

29. Bonney, *The European Dynastic States, 1494–1660*, pp. 407–16.

30. Carrère, *Barcelone*, pp. 687–96, 748–52, 771; Heers, *Parties and Political Life in the Medieval West*, pp. 235–43.

31. Rigaudière, *Gouverner la ville*, pp. 125–37; Beik, *Urban Protest in Seventeenth-Century France*, p. 75.

32. Kermode, 'The Greater Towns 1300–1450', pp. 458, 461; Swanson, *Medieval British Towns*, pp. 128–9; Nicholas, *Medieval Flanders*, pp. 355–6.

33. Rigaudière, *Gouverner la ville*, pp. 219–41.

34. Nicholas, *Growth of the Medieval City*, pp. 239–45.

35. Lestocquoy, *Patriciens du Moyen-Âge*, pp. 51–7.

36. Nicholas, *Growth of the Medieval City*, p. 257.

37. Cipolla, *Before the Industrial Revolution*, p. 53.

38. Nicholas, *Medieval Flanders*, p. 324.

39. DuPlessis, *Lille and the Dutch Revolt*, pp. 41–2.

40. Brucker, *The Society of Renaissance Florence*, pp. 6–7. Figures are in florins–soldi–denari.

41. Nicholas, *Later Medieval City*, p. 179; Lachmann, *Capitalists in Spite of Themselves*, pp. 84–5.

42. 't Hart, 'Cities and statemaking in the Dutch Republic, 1580–1680', p. 665; Cowan, *Urban Europe*, pp. 60–1.

43. Friedrichs, *Early Modern City*, pp. 43–60; Bonney, *European Dynastic States*, p. 404; Cowan, *Urban Europe*, pp. 60–1.

44. Descimon, 'Paris on the Eve of Saint Bartholomew', p. 92; Duplessis, *Lille and the Dutch Revolt*, pp. 30–1.

45. Derycke, *De Sint-Michielswijk in Gent (1480–1520)*, p. 84.

46. Barry, *The Tudor and Stuart Town*, p. 25; Friedrichs, *Urban Politics in Early Modern Europe*, p. 17; Rappaport, *Worlds within Worlds*, pp. 182–94; Pearl, 'Change and Stability in Seventeenth-century London', pp. 154–5.

47. Beik, *Urban Protest*, pp. 73–4.

48. Diefendorf, *Beneath the Cross*; Benedict, *Rouen during the Wars of Religion*, p. 36. The oligarchy at Troyes was somewhat narrower; see Roberts, *A City in Conflict*, pp. 13–17.

49. Beik, *Urban Protest*, pp. 94, 114; Benedict, *Rouen*, p. 34.

50. Friedrichs, *Urban Politics*, p. 14.

51. Cowan, *Urban Patriciate*, pp. 6–10.

52. Cowan, *Urban Europe*, pp. 55–6.
53. Sánchez-León, 'Town and Country in Castile, 1400–1650', pp. 280–1; Amelang, *Honored Citizens of Barcelona*, pp. 54–8.
54. Brady, *Strasbourg*, pp. 51, including table, 57–75.
55. Le Roy Ladurie, *Carnival: A People's Rising in Romans, 1579–1580*.
56. Of an immense literature, see particularly Brady, *Turning Swiss*; Moeller, *Imperial Cities and the Reformation*; Ozment, *The Reformation in the Cities*. The quotation is from Nicholas, *Transformation of Europe*, p. 390. Black, *Guilds and Civil Society in European Political Thought*, pp. 110–28 disputes the aristocratic character of German urban Protestantism.
57. Duplessis, *Lille and the Dutch Revolt*; Benedict, *Rouen during the Wars of Religion*; Benedict, *Cities and Social Change in Early Modern France*; Diefendorf, *Beneath the Cross*; Roberts, *A City in Conflict*; Farr, *Hands of Honor*. See in general the judicious discussion of Friedrichs, *Early Modern City*, pp. 317–23.
58. Chartier and Neveux, 'La ville dominante et soumise', pp. 214–15.
59. Beik, *Urban Protest*, pp. 126–33, 219–46.
60. Zagorin, *Rebels and Rulers, 1500–1660*, Vol. I: 247–52.
61. See in general Berengo, *L'Europa delle città*, pp. 39–110.
62. Van Caenegem, 'Bookish Law and Customary Law', pp. 119–33; Schilling, *Die Stadt in der frühen Neuzeit*, pp. 40–8.
63. Chartier and Neveux, 'La ville dominante et soumise', pp. 164, 176–7.
64. Friedrichs, *Early Modern City*, pp. 67, 71, 293.
65. Schilling, *Die Stadt in der frühen Neuzeit*, p. 59.
66. Tilly and Blockmans, *Cities and the Rise of States in Europe, 1000–1800*, pp. 8–9; Epstein, *Town and Country*, pp. 16–17.
67. Tilly, 'Cities and states in Europe, 1000–1800', pp. 573–4; Walter Hubatsch, 'Ziele und Massnahmen landesherrlicher Politik im Absolutismus gegenüber den Städten aus der Sicht des Verwaltungshistorikers', p. 34.

Chapter 5: Social Structures and Infrastructures

1. Aristotle, *The Politics*.
2. Mousnier, *Social Hierarchies 1450 to the Present*, pp. 945, esp. pp. 15, 34, 35–8.
3. Nicholas, *Growth of the Medieval City*, p. 202; Kowaleski, *Exeter*, pp. 192–7.
4. Nicholas, *Growth of the Medieval City*, p. 204; Nicholas, *Later Medieval City*, p. 58.
5. Barron, 'London 1300–1450', pp. 399–401; Rigby, *English Society in the Late Middle Ages*, p. 157.
6. Nicholas, *Town and Countryside*, p. 224; Nicholas, *Later Medieval City*, p. 56.
7. Kowaleski, *Exeter*, pp. 192–7; Patten, *English Towns 1500–1700*, p. 158.
8. Translated from Möncke, *Quellen*, pp. 106–7.
9. Nicholas, *Later Medieval City*, pp. 203–4; Nicholas, *Metamorphosis*, pp. 19–21.
10. Keene, *Medieval Winchester*, pp. 250–1; Chevalier, *Tours, ville royale (1356–1520)*, pp. 142–3; Goldberg, *Women, Work and Life Cycle in a Medieval Economy*, pp. 45–7, 60–3.
11. Calculated from the tables of Pound, 'The Social and Trade Structure of Norwich 1525–1575', pp. 129–47, 135, 137.
12. Amelang, *Honored Citizens of Barcelona*, pp. 16–17.
13. Cipolla, *Before the Industrial Revolution*, Table 2.7, p. 77.
14. Keene, 'Continuity and Development in Urban Trades, p. 6; Keene, *Survey of Medieval Winchester*, p. 1225; Swanson, 'Artisans in the Urban Economy', pp. 50–1.

15. Nicholas, *Metamorphosis*, pp. 145–46; Nicholas, *Later Medieval City*, p. 237; Hilton, *English and French Towns in Feudal Society*, p. 102; Swanson, 'Artisans in the Urban Economy', p. 50; Rappaport, *Worlds within Worlds*, p. 91.

16. Mackenney, *Tradesmen and Traders*, pp. 91–113.

17. Nightingale, *A Medieval Mercantile Community*. After years of disputing the grocers' control over the drug trade, the Apothecaries Company got a separate charter in 1615; Ward, *Metropolitan Communities*, pp. 117–19.

18. Nicholas, *Later Medieval City*, pp. 135, 205; Irsigler, *Die wirtschaftliche Stellung der Stadt Köln*, p. 230.

19. Brady, *Strasbourg*, p. 113.

20. Nicholas, *Metamorphosis*, p. 280; Boone, *Gent en de Bourgondische hergogen, ca. 1384–ca. 1453*, pp. 38, 73.

21. Nicholas, *Later Medieval City*, pp. 205–6; Cave and Coulson, *A Source Book for Medieval Economic History*, pp. 258–9.

22. Derville, 'Les métiers de Saint-Omer', p. 100; Nicholas, *Metamorphosis*, pp. 4–5; Dean, *Towns of Italy*, p. 127.

23. Kermode, 'The Greater Towns 1300–1450', p. 453.

24. Ciriacono, 'Les manufactures de luxe à Venise'.

25. Rigby, *English Society in the Later Middle Ages*, pp. 157–8.

26. Nicholas, *Metamorphosis*, pp. 252–3.

27. Swanson, 'Artisans in the Urban Economy', pp. 43–7; Hilton, *English and French Towns*, p. 69.

28. Farr, *Artisans in Europe, 1300–1914*, pp. 195–202.

29. Kermode, 'Sentiment and Survival', pp. 5–18; Farr, *Artisans in Europe*, pp. 248–56; Sosson, 'La Structure sociale de la corporation médiévale'.

30. Van Werveke, 'De Gentse Vleeschouwers onder het Oud Regime', pp. 3–32.

31. Farr, *Artisans*, p. 247.

32. Nicholas, *Later Medieval City*, p. 237 and literature cited; Swanson, *Medieval Artisans*, pp. 165–87.

33. Rappaport, *Worlds within Worlds*, pp. 309–14; Amelang, *Honored Citizens of Barcelona*, pp. 16–17; Kermode, 'Sentiment and Survival', p. 7.

34. Rappaport, *Worlds within Worlds*, pp. 217–25; Farr, *Artisans*, pp. 161–5.

35. Rosser, 'Crafts, Guilds and the Negotiation of Work in the Medieval Town', pp. 25–6; Nicholas, *Later Medieval City*, pp. 242–8; Rappaport, *Worlds within Worlds*, pp. 217–25; and in general Schulz, *Handwerksgesellen und Lohnarbeiter*.

36. Möncke, *Quellen*, pp. 166–7; Nicholas, *Later Medieval City*, p. 247, after Schulz, *Handwerksgesellen*, pp. 81–7, 89–97; Roberts, *City in Conflict*, pp. 77–9.

37. Swanson, 'Artisans in the Urban Economy', p. 43; Rigby, *English Society in the Later Middle Ages*, pp. 157–58; Nicholas, 'Child and Adolescent Labour in the Late Medieval City', pp. 1106–10; Nicholas, *Later Medieval City*, pp. 237–40.

38. Farr, *Artisans*, pp. 245–7.

39. For a recent survey of the immense literature, see Lynch, 'The European Marriage Pattern in the Cities'.

40. An immense historiography has grown up around enormous dowries given by aristocratic urban fathers in late medieval Italy. For an introduction, see Herlihy, *Medieval Households*; David Herlihy and Christiane Klapisch-Zuber, *Tuscans and Their Families*; Klapisch-Zuber, *Family and Ritual in Renaissance Italy*; and Chojnacki, *Women and Men in Renaissance Venice*.

41. Jack, *Towns in Tudor and Stuart Britain*, p. 21.

42. Nicholas, *The Van Arteveldes of Ghent*, pp. 12–16.
43. Cowan, *Urban Patriciate*, pp. 96–101.
44. Nicholas, *Later Medieval City*, pp. 277–80; Kermode, 'Sentiment and Survival', pp. 8–9; Cowan, *Urban Patriciate*, pp. 109–13.
45. See in general Nicholas, *Later Medieval City*, pp. 302–15.
46. Ruggiero, *Violence in Early Renaissance Venice*, pp. 66–75, 96.
47. Nicholas, 'Crime and Punishment in Fourteenth-Century Ghent', pp. 1168–73; and in general Nicholas, *Van Arteveldes*. For a Florentine statute against vendetta, see Dean, *Towns of Italy*, p. 188; for its persistence in practice, see Brucker, *Society of Renaissance Florence*, pp. 106–20.
48. Howell, *Women, Production, and Patriarchy in Late Medieval Cities*.
49. Murray, 'Family, Marriage and Moneychanging in Medieval Bruges', p. 117; Nicholas, *The Domestic Life of a Medieval City*, pp. 85–94.
50. On market women and for the Munich example, see Wiesner, *Working Women in Renaissance Germany*, pp. 134–42.
51. Reyerson, 'Public and Private Space in Medieval Montpellier', pp. 12–13; Nicholas, *Later Medieval City*, p. 269.
52. Herlihy, *Opera Muliebria*.
53. Kermode, 'Sentiment and Survival', pp. 10–11.
54. Cipolla, *Before the Industrial Revolution*, Table 2.10, p. 80.
55. Nicholas, *Later Medieval City*, pp. 274–7; Rossiaud, *Medieval Prostitution*; Burghartz, *Leib, Ehre und Gut*; Karras, *Common Women*, pp. 35–43.
56. Riley, *Memorials of London*, p. 535.
57. On the general situation of urban women in the sixteenth and seventeenth centuries, see Wiesner, *Women and Gender in Early Modern Europe*, pp. 149–85; King, 'The Woman of the Renaissance', pp. 207–49. The figure for Rome is calculated from Cipolla, *Before the Industrial Revolution*, p. 87.
58. Mackenney, *Tradesmen and Traders*, pp. 5–7, 46–65 for the Venetian brotherhoods; Black, *Early Modern Italy*, p. 159.
59. Robertson, *Chaucer's London*, pp. 84–5; Nightingale, *Medieval Mercantile Community*, pp. 178–81, 215–22; Barron, 'London 1300–1540', p. 432.
60. Kermode, 'Sentiment and Survival', pp. 5–6.
61. Swanson, 'Artisans in the Urban Economy', p. 50; Nightingale, *Medieval Mercantile Community*, pp. 177–8.
62. Hilton, *English and French Towns*, pp. 72–4.
63. Moncke, *Quellen*, pp. 122–3, and more generally Swanson, *Medieval British Towns*, pp. 128–9.
64. Brucker, *Society of Renaissance Florence*, p. 83.
65. Black, *Early Modern Italy*, pp. 159–65.
66. Huppert, *After the Black Death*, pp. 110–11; Louis Châtellier, *The Europe of the Devout*, pp. 204–12; Farr, *Artisans*, pp. 228–36.
67. This aspect is emphasized especially by Berengo, *L'Europa delle città*, p. 853.
68. Britnell, 'The Economy of British Towns 1300–1540', p. 331.
69. Jack, *Towns in Tudor and Stuart Britain*, pp. 50–1.
70. Weber, *City*, p. 73.
71. Translated from N. De Pauw, *De Voorgeboden der stad Gent in de XIVe eeuw (1337–1382)*, pp. 78–9.
72. See for example the statutes of the wool guild of Padua from 1384: Dean, *Towns of Italy*, pp. 128–32.

73. É. Husson. 'Les métiers du bâtiment à Dijon sous le "mécénat" de Philippe le Hardi, duc de Bourgogne', p. 131.
74. Leguay, *La rue au Moyen Age*, pp. 155–6.
75. Translated from Opll, *Nachrichten aus dem mittelalterlichen Wien* pp. 39–40.
76. Cipolla, *Before the Industrial Revolution*, p. 29; Hilton, 'Pain et cervoise dans les villes anglaises au Moyen Age', pp. 224–5; Jack, *Towns in Tudor and Stuart Britain*, p. 81.
77. Van Uytven, 'L'approvisionnement des villes . . . Pays Bas', p. 85.
78. Hilton, 'Pain et cervoise', p. 226–7.
79. Swanson, 'Artisans in the Urban Economy', pp. 46–7.
80. Nicholas, *Later Medieval City*, pp. 305–6; Barron, 'London 1300–1540', p. 404.
81. Rappaport, *Worlds within Worlds*, pp. 201–14.
82. Statute of 1364, translated from De Pauw, *Voorgeboden*, p. 85.
83. Nicholas, 'The Scheldt Trade and the "Ghent War" of 1379–1385', pp. 52–3.
84. Wolff, L'Approvisionnement des villes françaises au Moyen Age', p. 28; Van Houtte, 'Herbergswesen und Gastlichkeit im mittelalterlichen Brügge', pp. 177–87.
85. Cicero, *De Officiis*, p. 155.
86. Again 'the vile mechanical arts' is Cicero's term: *De Officiis*, p. 153.
87. Cowan, *Urban Patriciate*, pp. 4–5.
88. Boone, 'La terre, les hommes et les villes', pp. 157–8, 163–4.
89. Sheeran, *Medieval Yorkshire Towns*, p. 13; Jack, *Towns in Tudor and Stuart Britain*, pp. 23, 105–6.
90. Brady, *Strasbourg*, pp. 76–94.
91. Nicholas, *Later Medieval City*, pp. 187–9.
92. Translated from Möncke, *Quellen*, p. 281.
93. Bechtold, *Zunftbürgerschaft und Patriziat*, pp. 134–5, 144–8.
94. Cowan, *Urban Patriciate*, p. 42. The parallel with the butchers of Ghent, noted above, suggests a common ethic that overarched social barriers.
95. Amelang, *Honored Citizens of Barcelona*, pp. 26–31, 34–40.
96. Nicholas, *Later Medieval City*, pp. 218–27.
97. Löther, *Prozessionen in spätmittelalterlichen Städten*, pp. 66–76.
98. Kowaleski, *Exeter*, p. 126–38.
99. Laughton, Jones and Dyer, 'The Urban Hierarchy in the Later Middle Ages', p. 342; Cipolla, *Before the Industrial Revolution*, pp. 10, 32–3.
100. See in general Mollat, *The Poor in the Middle Ages*, particularly chapters 7–12.
101. See for example the table compiled by Cipolla, *Before the Industrial Revolution*, p. 15.
102. The charter of the shearers of Arras (1236), clause 16: 'Those who are fed at the expense of the city shall be put to work first'; Cave and Coulson, *Source Book*, p. 251.
103. Hanawalt, *Growing Up in Medieval London*, p. 18.
104. Nicholas, *Later Medieval City*, pp. 255–6, both translated from Friedrich Keutgen (ed.), *Urkunden zur städtischen Verfassungsgeschichte*, p. 302.
105. Muchambled, 'Les minorités: mythes et réalités', pp. 212–13; Beier, 'Social Problems in Elizabethan London', pp. 123–6.
106. Rappaport, *Worlds within Worlds*, pp. 130–50.
107. Davis, 'Poor Relief, Humanism, and Heresy', pp. 48–9.
108. Roberts, *City in Conflict*, pp. 20–1; Chaunu and Gascon, *L'Etat et la Ville*, p. 421.
109. Jütte, *Poverty and Deviance in Early Modern Europe*, pp. 105–7.
110. Roberts, *City in Conflict*, p. 20–1.
111. Diefendorf, *Beneath the Cross*, p. 20.

112. Discussion from Davis, 'Poor Relief, Humanism, and Heresy', pp. 17–64.
113. Chaunu and Gascon, *L'État et la Ville*, p. 421.

Chapter 6: Material Culture and Cultural Environment

1. Adorno, *Itinéraire d'Anselme Adorno en Terre Sainte (1470–1471)*, p. 489.
2. Bruni, *Panegyric to the City of Florence*.
3. Palliser, 'Civic Mentality and the Environment in Tudor York', p. 208. For a discussion of the myths of urban origins, see Rosser and Dennison, 'Urban Culture and the Church 1300–1540', pp. 339–40, and Rosser, 'Myth, Image and Social Process in the English Medieval Town', pp. 5–25.
4. Amelang, 'The Myth of the Mediterranean City', pp. 18 19.
5. Tittler, *Townspeople and Nation*, p. 121.
6. Steane, *Archaeology of Power*, p. 201.
7. Irsigler, 'L'Approvisionnement des villes de l'Allemagne' p. 131.
8. Leguay, *La rue au Moyen Age*, pp. 56–61.
9. Chew, *London Assize of Nuisance, 1301–1431*, p. 13.
10. Chew, *London Assize of Nuisance*, p. 35.
11. Dean, *Towns of Italy*, p. 50.
12. Leguay, *La rue au Moyen Age*, p. 42.
13. Chew, *London Assize of Nuisance*, p. 16.
14. Leguay, *La rue au Moyen Age*, p. 56.
15. Sheeran, *Medieval Yorkshire Towns*, p. 161. See in general Nicholas, *Later Medieval City*, pp. 332–4 and literature cited.
16. Morris, *History of Urban Form*, pp. 185–8; Konvitz, *Cities and the Sea*, pp. 34–7.
17. Keene, *Medieval Winchester*, p. 64.
18. Statute of 1369, translated from De Pauw, *Voorgeboden*, p. 105.
19. Riley, *Memorials of London*, pp. 517–18.
20. Robertson, *Chaucer's London*, pp. 23–4.
21. Sheeran, *Medieval Yorkshire Towns*, p. 160.
22. Quoted in Ranum, *Paris in the Age of Absolutism*, p. 63.
23. Keene, 'Issues of Water in Medieval London to *c.* 1300', pp. 167, 174–8; Riley, *Memorials of London*, pp. 200–1, 225.
24. Irsigler, 'L'Approvisionnement des villes de l'Allemagne', esp. pp. 120–3, 131; Dean, *Towns of Italy*, p. 28; Chartier and Neveux, 'La ville dominante et soumise', pp. 147–8.
25. Nicholas, *Later Medieval City*, pp. 338–9 and literature cited; Pounds, *Hearth and Home*, pp. 274–5.
26. Boucheron, 'Water and Power in Milan, *c.* 1200–1500', pp. 184–7.
27. Möncke, *Quellen*, pp. 130–1.
28. Nicholas, *Growth of the Medieval City*, pp. 99–100 and plan 10; Nicholas, *Later Medieval City*, p. 340.
29. Translated from Möncke, *Quellen*, pp. 72–5.
30. Translated from De Pauw, *Voorgeboden*, pp. 107–8.
31. Nicholas, *Later Medieval City*, p. 302 for discussion of these entertainments.
32. Shirley (ed. and trans.), *A Parisian Journal, 1405–1449*, pp. 205–6.
33. Lecuppre-Desjardin, 'Les lumières de la ville', pp. 29–30; Chartier and Neveux, 'La ville dominante et soumise', p. 154.

34. Dickinson, *West European City*, p. 24; Carter, *Study of Urban Geography*, p. 366.
35. Leguay, *La rue au Moyen Age*, pp. 39–42, 92–124.
36. Leguay, *La rue au Moyen Age*, pp. 44–9.
37. Favier, *Paris au XVe siècle, 1380–1500*, pp. 15, 22–6; Leguay, *La rue au Moyen Age*, pp. 12–15, 35.
38. Morris, *History of Urban Form*, p. 73.
39. Opll, *Nachrichten*, p. 134.
40. Dean, *Towns of Italy*, p. 50.
41. Myres, *English Historical Documents, 1327–1485*, p. 1102.
42. Riley, *Memorials of London*, p. 226.
43. Dean, *Towns of Italy*, pp. 39–41.
44. Camille, 'Signs of the City,' pp.1–36. See also Sheeran, *Medieval Yorkshire Towns*, p. 145.
45. Riley, *Memorials of London*, pp. 386–7, cited in slightly changed translation by Camille, 'Signs of the City', p. 22.
46. See above, Chapter 3, pp. 84–9.
47. Nicholas, *Later Medieval City*, p. 324.
48. Sheeran, *Medieval Yorkshire Towns*, p. 127.
49. Keene, 'London from the Post-Roman Period to 1300', pp. 193–4.
50. Patten, *English Towns 1500–1700*, p. 66.
51. Cited in Nicholas, *Medieval Flanders*, p. 121.
52. Chartier and Neveux, 'La ville dominante et soumise', pp. 141–2.
53. Keene, 'London from the Post-Roman Period to 1300', pp. 193–4.
54. Nicholas, *Later Medieval City*, pp. 322–3; Pounds, *Hearth and Home*, pp. 272–3.
55. Opll, *Nachrichten*, p. 70.
56. Palliser, Slater and Dennison, 'The Topography of Towns 600–1300', pp.182–3.
57. Nicholas, *Later Medieval City*, p. 330.
58. Grenville, *Medieval Housing*, p. 165; a convenient description of such a house, which was much more elaborate than what most city-dwellers occupied, is given in a lease of 1384, published in Myres, *English Historical Documents*, pp. 1140–1.
59. Schofield and Stell, 'The Built Environment 1300–1540', pp. 387–9.
60. Grenville, *Medieval Housing*, p. 169.
61. Nicholas, *Later Medieval City*, p. 323.
62. Burke, *Towns in the Making*, p. 96; Borsay, 'Early Modern Urban Landscapes, 1540–1800', pp. 101–2.
63. Dickinson, *West European City*, pp. 318–19.
64. Cowan, *Urban Europe*, pp. 127–9.
65. Leguay, *La rue au Moyen Age*, pp. 143–4.
66. Nicholas, *Later Medieval City*, p. 320, based on discussion of London by Hanawalt, *Growing Up in Medieval London*, pp. 16–17. See also in general Hanawalt and Reyerson, *City and Spectacle in Medieval Europe*.
67. Löther, *Prozessionen*, p. 113.
68. Chartier and Neveux, 'La ville dominante et soumise', p. 187.
69. Chittolini, 'Civic Religion and the Countryside in Late Medieval Italy', pp. 69–80; Laughton, Jones and Dyer. 'The Urban Hierarchy in the Later Middle Ages', p. 353.
70. Löther, *Prozessionen*, p. 135.
71. Muir, *Ritual in Early Modern Europe*, pp. 232–9, quotation p. 235; Muir, *Civic Ritual in Renaissance Venice*, p. 122 for the marriage with sea.

72. Quoted in Brucker, *Society of Renaissance Florence*, p. 77.
73. Laughton, Jones and Dyer, 'The Urban Hierarchy in the Later Middle Ages', p. 338.
74. Myres, *English Historical Documents, 1327–1485*, pp. 1064–5.
75. Myres, *English Historical Documents*, p. 1095.
76. Löther, *Prozessionen*, pp. 14, 85, 96–101, 140–71.
77. Murray, 'The Liturgy of the Count's Advent in Bruges', pp. 137–52.
78. Muir, *Civic Rituals*, p. 245.
79. Shirley, *Parisian Journal*, pp. 153–4.
80. Mateos Royo, 'All the Town is a Stage', pp. 165–89.
81. See in general Van den Neste, *Tournois, joutes, pas d'armes dans les villes de Flandre à la fin du moyen âge (1300–1486)*; Arnade, *Realms of Ritual*.
82. For special precautions taken by the city authorities, see precepts of 1385 and 1410 in Myres, *English Historical Documents*, p. 1067; Lindenbaum, 'Ceremony and Oligarchy', pp. 171–88 with quotation p. 171; Henry VIII ended the Midsummer Watch on grounds of disorder in 1539; Barron, 'London 1300–1540', p. 407.
83. Nicholas, *Later Medieval City*, pp. 299–300; Nicholas, *Medieval Flanders*, p. 348.
84. Waterschoot, 'Antwerp: Books, Publishing and Central Production before 1585', pp. 245–8, with quotation pp. 246–7.
85. Nicholas, *Later Medieval City*, pp. 316–18; James, 'Ritual, Drama and Social Body in the Late Medieval English Town', pp. 3–29.
86. Amelang, *Honored Citizens of Barcelona*, p. 198.
87. Chartier and Neveux, 'La ville dominante et soumise', pp. 180–1.
88. Muir, *Ritual in Early Modern Europe*, pp. 87–8, with quotation p. 87; Muir, *Venice*, pp. 160–6.
89. Riley, *Memorials*, p. 8.
90. Amelang, 'The Myth of the Mediterranean City', pp. 15–16.
91. Brady, *Strasbourg*, p. 13.
92. Martines, *Power and Imagination*, pp. 72–93.
93. Cipolla, *Before the Industrial Revolution*, pp. 83–5.
94. Kaufmann, *Court, Cloister, and City*, pp. 80–1.
95. Le Goff, 'Ordres mendiants et urbanisation dans la France médiévale'.
96. Marshall, *Structure of Urban Systems*, p. 14; Ennen, 'Stufen der Zentralität im kirchlich-organisatorischen und kultischen Bereich. Eine Fallskizze: Köln', p. 17.
97. François, 'German Urban Network', pp. 90–4.
98. Translated from Sprandel, *Quellen zur Hanse-Geschichte*, pp. 512–13.
99. Wriedt, 'Schulen und bürgerliches Bildungswesen in Norddeutschland im Spätmittelalter, pp. 152–72.
100. Swanson, *Medieval British Towns*, pp. 135–6.
101. Villani, quoted in Lopez and Raymond, *Medieval Trade*, p. 72.
102. Nicholas, *Later Medieval City*, pp. 292–3.
103. Limberger, 'No Town in the World Provides More Advantages', p. 59.
104. Prevenier, 'La conservation de la memoire par l'enregistrement dans les chancelleries princières et dans les villes des anciens Pays-Bas du moyen âge', pp. 559–62.
105. Waley, *Siena*, pp. 54, 156–9.
106. Cobban, *English University Life in the Middle Ages*, pp. 147–8.
107. Swetz, *Capitalism and Arithmetic*, pp. 13–18.
108. Swetz, *Capitalism and Arithmetic*, p. 138.
109. Kugler, *Vorstellung der Stadt*, pp. 144–6.

110. Wriedt, 'Stadtrat–Bürgertum–Universität am Beispiel norddeutscher Hanse-städte', pp. 499–523.

111. Hyde, 'Universities and Cities in Medieval Italy', pp. 14–15.

112. Ferruolo, *'Parisius-Paradisus'*, p. 32.

113. Hammer, 'Patterns of Homicide in Fourteenth-century Oxford', pp. 3–23.

114. Baetens, 'Le role d'Anvers dans la transmission de valeurs culturelles au temps de son apogee (1500–1650)', p. 43; Decavele, 'Het culturele en intellectuele network: middeleeuwen en 16de eeuw', pp. 371–84.

115. Kießling, 'Das gebildete Bürgertum und die kulturelle Zentralität Augsburgs im Spätmittelalter', pp. 571–84. Yet university-educated men were unusual in the government of Strasbourg and Ulm until after 1600. Brady, *Strasbourg*, pp. 189–90.

116. For a good summary, see Lambert, *Medieval Heresy*.

117. Discussion in Nicholas, *Transformation of Europe*, pp. 305–7, with quotation p. 306.

118. Roberts, *City in Conflict*, pp. 80–7.

119. For this important point, see Peters, *Literatur in der Stadt*, p. 138.

120. Discussed by Martines, *Power and Imagination*, pp. 115–23.

121. Martines, *Power and Imagination*, p. 241 speaks of 'Art: An Alliance with Power' and sees it under the aegis of patronage, reflecting the values of the patron, down to the background details of paintings.

122. Martines, *Power and Imagination*, p. 191.

123. Jardine, *Worldly Goods*, pp. 37–132.

124. Goldthwaite, *Wealth and the Demand for Art in Italy, 1300–1600*, pp. 2–3.

125. Hollingsworth, *Patronage in Renaissance Italy*, pp. 17–22, 33–7, 56–82; Martines, *Power and Imagination*, p. 242.

126. Hollingsworth, *Patronage*, pp. 97–154 and quotation p. 105.

127. Boucheron, *Le Pouvoir de bâtir*, especially pp. 130–97, 218–30.

128. Martines, *Power and Imagination*, p. 256. On the material and architectural aspects of building, see Goldthwaite, *The Building of Renaissance Florence*.

129. Burroughs, 'Spaces of Arbitration and the Organization of Space in Late Medieval Italian cities', pp. 64–100.

130. For a study of the use of symbolism in the structure and adornment of town halls to inculcate allegiance to the regime, see Tittler, *Architecture and Power*.

131. De Vos, 'Brügge und die Flämischen Primitiven in Europe', p. 318.

132. Hale, *The Civilization of Europe in the Renaissance*, p. 232.

133. Cited by Opll, *Nachrichten*, p. 134.

134. Goldthwaite, *Wealth and the Demand for Art*, pp. 47–8, 223–4.

135. Corley, *Painting and Patronage in Cologne, 1300–1500*, esp. pp. 24, 37, 306–12.

136. Wilson, *Painting in Bruges at the Close of the Middle Ages*, pp. 14, 87–131, 163–87.

137. Honig, *Painting and the Market in Early Modern Antwerp*, esp. pp. 13–17; Vlieghe, 'The Fine and Decorative Arts in Antwerp's Golden Age', pp. 173–85; Baetens, 'Le role d'Anvers dans la transmission de valeurs culturelles', p. 52.

138. On printing, see in general Eisenstein, *The Printing Press as an Agent of Change*.

139. Waterschoot, 'Antwerp: Books, Publishing and Central Production', pp. 233–7; Baetens, 'Le role d'Anvers dans la transmission de valeurs culturelles', p. 59.

140. Lowry, *The World of Aldus Manutius*.

141. Moeller, 'Die Anfänge kommunaler Bibliotheken in Deutschland', pp. 136–51.

142. Harris, *History of Libraries in the Western World*, pp. 110–14, 149–50.

Bibliography

Adorno, Anselm. 1978. *Itinéraire d'Anselme Adorno en Terre Sainte (1470–1471)*. Ed. Jacques Heers and Georgette de Groer. Paris: Éditions du Centre National de la Recherche Scientifique.

Amelang, James S. 1986. *Honored Citizens of Barcelona: Patrician Culture and Class Relations, 1490–1714*. Princeton: Princeton University Press.

Amelang, James S. 2000. 'The Myth of the Mediterranean City: Perceptions of Sociability', in A. Cowan, *Mediterranean Urban Culture 1400–1700*, pp. 15–30. Exeter: University of Exeter Press.

Approvisionnement (L') des villes de l'Europe occidentale au Moyen Age et aux Temps modernes. 1985. Centre Culturel de l'Abbaye de Flaran. Cinquièmes Journées internationals d'histoire, 16–18 septembre 1983. Auch: Abbaye de Flaran.

Arbel, Benjamin. 2000. 'The Port Towns of the Levant in Sixteenth-Century Travel Literature', in A. Cowan, *Mediterranean Urban Culture 1400–1700*, pp. 151–64. Exeter: University of Exeter Press.

Arnade, Peter. 1996. *Realms of Ritual: Burgundian Ceremony and Civic Life in Late Medieval Ghent*. Ithaca, N.Y., and London: Cornell University Press.

Astill, Grenville. 2000. 'General Survey 600–1300', in D. M. Palliser, *The Cambridge Urban History of Britain*, pp. 27–49. Cambridge: Cambridge University Press.

Aston, Mick and Bond, James. 2000. *The Landscape of Towns*. 2nd edn. Phoenix Mill, UK: Alan Sutton.

Aurell I Cardona, Jaume. 2000. 'Culture marchande et culture nobiliaire à Barcelone au XVe siècle', *Revue Historique* 613, pp. 33–53.

Aymard, Maurice. 1985. 'L'Approvisionnement des villes de la Méditerranée occidentale (XVIe–XVIIIe siècles)', in *L'Approvisionnement des villes*, pp. 165–85. Auch: Abbaye de Flaran.

Baetens, Roland. 1996. 'Le role d'Anvers dans la transmission de valeurs culturelles au temps de son apogée (1500–1650)', in *Cities and the Transmission of Cultural Values*, pp. 37–72. Brussels: Crédit Communal.

Bairoch, Paul. 1988. *Cities and Economic Development: From the Dawn of History to the Present*. Translated by Christopher Braider. Chicago: University of Chicago Press.

Baker, Alan R. H. 1973. 'Changes in the Later Middle Ages', in H. C. Darby (ed.), *A New Historical Geography of England Before 1600*, pp. 186–247. Cambridge: Cambridge University Press.

Barron, Caroline M. 2000. 'London 1300–1540', in D. M. Palliser, *The Cambridge Urban History of Britain*, pp. 395–440. Cambridge: Cambridge University Press.

211

Barry, Jonathan (ed.) 1990. *The Tudor and Stuart Town: A Reader in English Urban History, 1530–1688*. London: Longman.

Bartlett, Robert. 1993. *The Making of Europe: Conquest, Colonization and Cultural Change, 950–1350*. Princeton: Princeton University Press.

Bechtold, Klaus D. 1981. *Zunftbürgerschaft und Patriziat: Studien zur Socialgeschichte der Stadt Konstanz im 14. und 15. Jahrhundert*. Sigmaringen: Jan Thorbecke.

Beier, A. L. 1990. 'Social Problems in Elizabethan London', in J. Barry, *The Tudor and Stuart Town*, pp. 121–38. London: Longman.

Beik, William. 1997. *Urban Protest in Seventeenth-Century France: The Culture of Retribution*. Cambridge: Cambridge University Press.

Belfanti, Mario. 2001. 'Town and Country in Central and Northern Italy, 1400–1800', in S. R. Epstein, *Town and Country in Europe*, pp. 292–315. Cambridge: Cambridge University Press.

Bender, Thomas (ed.) 1988. *The University and the City: From Medieval Origins to the Present*. Oxford: Oxford University Press.

Benedict, Philip. 1981. *Rouen during the Wars of Religion*. Cambridge: Cambridge University Press.

Benedict, Philip (ed.) 1989. *Cities and Social Change in Early Modern France*. London: Unwin Hyman.

Bennett, Judith M. 1996. *Ale, Beer, and Brewsters in England: Women's Work in a Changing World, 1300–1600*. Oxford: Oxford University Press.

Berengo, Marino. 1999. *L'Europa delle città: Il volto della società urbana europea tra Medioevo ed Età moderna*. Turin: G. Einaudi.

Beresford, Maurice. 1967. *New Towns of the Middle Ages: Town Plantation in England, Wales, and Gascony*. New York and Washington: Frederick A. Praeger.

Biddick, Kathleen. 2000. 'Becoming Collection: The Spatial Afterlife of Medieval Universal Histories', in B. A. Hanawalt and M. Kobialka, *Medieval Practices of Space*, pp. 223–41. Minneapolis: University of Minnesota Press.

Biddle, Martin. 1976. *Winchester in the Early Middle Ages: An Edition and Discussion of the Winton Domesday*. Oxford: Clarendon.

Black, Antony. 1984. *Guilds and Civil Society in European Political Thought From the Twelfth Century to the Present*. Ithaca, N.Y.: Cornell University Press.

Black, Christopher F. 1999. *Italian Confraternities in the Sixteenth Century*. Cambridge: Cambridge University Press.

Black, Christopher F. 2001. *Early Modern Italy: A Social History*. London: Routledge.

Bland, Alfred E.; Brown, Philip A. and Tawney, Richard H. (eds.) 1914. *English Economic History: Select Documents*. London: G. Bell.

Blanshei, Sarah Rubin. 1976. *Perugia 1260–1340: Conflict and Change in a Medieval Italian Urban Society*. Transactions of the American Philosophical Society, n.s. 66, part 2. Philadelphia: American Philosophical Society.

Blockmans, Wim. 1989. 'Voracious States and Obstructing Cities: An Aspect of State Formation in Preindustrial Europe', *Theory and Society* 18, pp. 733–55.

Bogucka, Maria. 1996. 'Between Capital, Residential Town, and Metropolis: The Development of Warsaw in the Sixteenth to Eighteenth Centuries', in P. Clark and B. Lepetit, *Capital Cities and their Hinterlands*, pp. 198–216. Aldershot: Scolar.

Bok, Marten Jan. 2001. 'The Rise of Amsterdam as a Cultural Centre: The Market for Paintings, 1580–1680', in P. O'Brien, D. Keene, M. 'tHart and H. van der Wee, *Golden Ages in Antwerp, Amsterdam and London*, pp. 186–209. Cambridge: Cambridge University Press.

Bonney, Richard. 1991. *The European Dynastic States, 1494–1660*. Oxford: Oxford University Press.

Boone, Marc. 1990. *Gent en de Bourgondische hergogen, ca. 1384–ca. 1453: Een sociaal-politieke studie van een staatsvormingsproces*. Brussels: Paleis der Academiën.

Boone, Marc. 1996. 'La terre, les hommes et les villes: Quelques considérations autour du thème de l'urbanisation des propriétaires terriens', in *Cities and the Transmission of Cultural Values*, pp. 153–73. Brussels: Crédit Communal.

Borsay, Peter. 2000. 'Early Modern Urban Landscapes, 1540–1800', in P. Waller, *The English Urban Landscape*, pp. 99–114. Oxford: Oxford University Press.

Bottin, Jacques, and Conatella Calabi (eds.) 1999. *Les Étrangers dans la ville. Minorité et espace urbain du bas Moyen Âge à l'époque moderne*. Paris, Éditions de la Maison des sciences de l'homme.

Boucheron, Patrick. 1998. *Le Pouvoir de bâtir: Urbanisme et politique édilitaire à Milan (XIVe–XVe siècles)*. Rome: École française de Rome.

Boucheron, Patrick. 2001. 'Water and Power in Milan, *c.* 1200–1500'. *Urban History* 28, pp. 180–93.

Bowsky, William M. 1981. *A Medieval Italian Commune: Siena Under the Nine, 1287–1355*. Berkeley and Los Angeles: University of California Press.

Brady, Thomas A., Jr. 1978. *Ruling Class, Regime and Reformation at Strasbourg, 1520–1555*. Leiden: E. J. Brill.

Brady, Thomas A., Jr. 1992. *Turning Swiss: Cities and Empire, 1450–1550*. Cambridge: Cambridge University Press.

Braudel, Fernand. 1981–1984. *Civilization and Capitalism, 15th–18th Century*. Vol. I. *The Structures of Everyday Life. The Limits of the Possible*. Vol. II. *The Wheels of Commerce*. Vol. III. *The Perspective of the World*. New York: Harper & Row.

Braunfels, Wolfgang. 1988. *Urban Design in Western Europe: Regime and Architecture, 900–1900*. Chicago: University of Chicago Press.

Brennan, Thomas. 2001. 'Town and Country in France, 1550–1750', in S. R. Epstein (ed.), *Town and Country in Europe*, pp. 250–71. Cambridge: Cambridge University Press.

Britnell, Richard H. 1994. 'The Black Death in English Towns', *Urban History* 21, pp. 195–210.

Britnell, Richard H. 1996. *The Commercialisation of English Society, 1000–1500*. 2nd edn. Manchester: Manchester University Press.

Britnell, Richard H. 2000a. 'The Economy of British Towns 600–1300', in D. M. Palliser, *The Cambridge Urban History of Britain*, pp. 105–26. Cambridge: Cambridge University Press.

Britnell, Richard H. 2000b. 'The Economy of British Towns 1300–1540', in D. M. Palliser, *The Cambridge Urban History of Britain*, pp. 313–33. Cambridge: Cambridge University Press.

Brodt, Bärbel. 2000. 'East Anglia', in D. M. Palliser, *The Cambridge Urban History of Britain*, pp. 630–56. Cambridge: Cambridge University Press.

Brucker, Gene A. 1969. *Renaissance Florence*. New York: John Wiley.

Brucker, Gene A. (ed.) 1971. *The Society of Renaissance Florence: A Documentary Study*. New York: Harper and Row.

Brucker, Gene A. 1988. 'Renaissance Florence: Who Needs a University?' in T. Bender, *City and University*, pp. 47–58. Oxford: Oxford University Press.

Bruni, Leonardo. *Panegyric to the City of Florence*. Translated by Benjamin G. Kohl in Benjamin G. Kohl and Ronald G. Witt with Elizabeth B. Welles (eds.), *The Earthly Republic:*

Italian Humanists on Government and Society, 1978, pp. 135–75. Philadelphia: University of Pennsylvania Press.

Bruwier, Marinette. 1992. 'Etudes sur le réseau urbain en Hainaut de 1350 à 1850', in *Le Réseau Urbain en Belgique*, pp. 251–316. Brussels: Gemeentekrediet.

Buisseret, David (ed.) 1998. *Envisioning the City: Six Studies in Urban Cartography*. Chicago: University of Chicago Press.

Burghartz, Susanna. 1990. *Leib, Ehre und Gut: Delinquenz in Zürich Ende des 14. Jahrhunderts*. Zürich: Chronos Verlag.

Burke, Gerald L. 1956. *The Making of Dutch Towns: A Study in Urban Development from the Tenth to the Seventeenth Centuries*. London: Cleaver-Hume.

Burke, Gerald L. 1971. *Towns in the Making*. New York: St. Martin's.

Burke, Peter. 1974. *Venice and Amsterdam: A Study of Seventeenth-Century Elites*. London: Temple Smith.

Burroughs, Charles. 2000. 'Spaces of Arbitration and the Organization of Space in Late Medieval Italian Cities', in B. A. Hanawalt and M. Kobialka, *Medieval Practices of Space*, pp. 64–100. Minneapolis: University of Minnesota Press.

Calabi, Donatella. 2000. 'The Jews and the City in the Mediterranean Area', In A. Cowan, *Mediterranean Urban Culture 1400–1700*, pp. 56–68. Exeter: University of Exeter Press.

Camille, Michael. 2000. 'Signs of the City: Place, Power, and Public Fantasy in Medieval Paris', in B. A. Hanawalt and M. Kobialka, *Medieval Practices of Space*, pp. 1–36. Minneapolis: University of Minnesota Press.

Camille, Michael. 2001. 'Signs on Medieval Street Corners'. In *Die Strasse*, pp. 91–117.

Campbell, Bruce M. S.; Galloway, James A.; Keene, Derek and Murphy, Margaret. 1993. *A Medieval Capital and Its Grain Supply: Agrarian Production and Distribution in the London Region c. 1300*. Historical Geography Research Series No. 30. London: Institute of British Geographers.

Carpentier, Élisabeth and Le Mené, Michel. 1996. *La France du XIe au XVe siècle: population, société, économie*. Paris: Presses Universitaires de France.

Carrère, Claude. 1967. *Barcelone: Centre économique à l'époque des difficultés, 1380–1462*. 2 vols. Paris and The Hague: Mouton.

Carter, Harold. 1983. *An Introduction to Urban Historical Geography*. London: Edward Arnold.

Carter, Harold. 1995. *The Study of Urban Geography*. 4th edn. London: Edward Arnold.

Cave, Roy C. and Coulson, Herbert H. (eds.) 1936. *A Source Book for Medieval Economic History*. New York: Bruce.

Cazelles, Raymond. 1972. *Paris de la fin du règne de Philippe Auguste à la mort de Charles V, 1223–1380*. Paris: Hachette.

Cerman, Markus, and Knittler, Herbert. 2001. 'Town and Country in the Austrian and Czech Lands, 1450–1800', in S. R. Epstein, *Town and Country in Europe*, pp. 176–201. Cambridge: Cambridge University Press.

Chartier, Roger and Neveux, Hugues. 1981. 'La ville dominante et soumise', in E. Le Roy Ladurie, *La ville classique*, pp. 15–286. Paris: Éditions du Seuil. *Histoire de la France urbaine*, ed. Georges Duby, III.

Châtellier, Louis. 1989. *The Europe of the Devout: The Catholic Reformation and the Foundation of a New Society*. Cambridge: Cambridge University Press.

Chaunu, Pierre and Gascon, Richard. 1970. *L'Etat et la Ville*. Paris: Presses Universitaires de France.

Chevalier, Bernard. (n.d.) *Tours, ville royale (1356–1520)*. Paris: Nauwelaerts.

Chevalier, Bernard. 1982. *Les bonnes villes de France, du XIVe au XVIe siècle*. Paris: Aubier Montaigne.

Chevalier, Bernard. 1995. *Les bonnes villes, l'État et la société dans la France de la fin du XVe siècle*. Orléans: Paradigme.

Chew, Helena M. (ed. and trans.) 1973. *London Assize of Nuisance, 1301–1431*. London: London Record Society.

Chittolini, Giorgio. 1989. 'Cities, "City-states", and Regional States in North-Central Italy', *Theory and Society* 18, pp. 689–706.

Chittolini, Giorgio. 1990. 'Civic Religion and the Countryside in Late Medieval Italy', in T. Dean and C. Wickham (eds.), *City and Countryside in Late Medieval and Renaissance Italy: Essays Presented to Philip Jones*, pp. 69–80. London: Hambledon.

Chojnacki, Stanley. 1994. 'Social Identity in Renaissance Venice: the Second *Serrata*', *Renaissance Studies* 8, pp. 341–58.

Christaller, Walter. 1966. *Central Places in Southern Germany*. Translated by C. W. Baskin. Reprint from 1933 original, Englewood Cliffs, N.J.: Prentice-Hall.

Cicero. *De Officiis*. With an English translation by Walter Miller, 1928. London: William Heinemann.

Cipolla, Carlo M. 1994. *Before the Industrial Revolution: Urban Society and Economy, 1000–1700*. Third edn. New York: W. W. Norton.

Ciriacono, S. 1988. 'Mass Consumption Goods and Luxury Goods: The De-industrialization of the Republic of Venice from the Sixteenth to the Eighteenth Century', in H. Van der Wee, *The Rise and Decline of Urban Industries in Italy and in the Low Countries*, pp. 41–61. Leuven: Leuven University Press.

Ciriacono, Salvatore. 1996. 'Les manufactures de luxe à Venise: contraintes géographiques, gout méditerranéen et compétition internationale (XIVe–XVIe siècle)', in *Cities and the Transmission of Cultural Values in the Late Middle Ages and Early Modern Period*, pp. 235–51. Brussels: Crédit Communal.

Cities and the Transmission of Cultural Values in the Late Middle Ages and Early Modern Period: Records. 1996. Brussels: Crédit Communal, Collection Histoire in 8o, no. 96.

Clark, Peter (ed.) 1976 *The Early Modern Town: A Reader*. London: Longman.

Clark, Peter (ed.) 1995. *Small Towns in Early Modern Europe*. Cambridge: Cambridge University Press.

Clark, Peter and Lepetit, Bernard (eds.) 1996. *Capital Cities and their Hinterlands in Early Modern Europe*. Aldershot: Scolar.

Clark, Peter and Slack, Paul (eds.) 1972. *Crisis and Order in English Towns, 1500–1700: Essays in Urban History*. London: Routledge and Kegan Paul.

Clark, Peter and Slack, Paul. 1976. *English Towns in Transition, 1500–1700*. Oxford: Oxford University Press.

Cobb, Henry S. (ed.) 1990. *The Overseas Trade of London: Exchequer Customs Accounts 1480–1*. London: London Record Society.

Cobban, Alan B. 1999. *English University Life in the Middle Ages*. Columbus: Ohio State University Press.

Compagni, Dino. 1986. *Chronicle of Florence*. Translated, with an introduction and notes, by Daniel E. Bornstein. Philadelphia: University of Pennsylvania Press.

Corfield, Penelope J. 1990. 'Urban Development in England and Wales in the Sixteenth and Seventeenth Centuries', in J. Barry, *The Tudor and Stuart Town*, pp. 35–62. London: Longman.

Corfield, Penelope J. and Keene, Derek (eds.) 1990. *Work in Towns, 850–1850*. Leicester: Leicester University Press.

Corley, Brigitte. 2000. *Painting and Patronage in Cologne, 1300–1500*. Turnhout: Harvey Miller.

Corsten, Severin. 1978. 'Der frühe Buchdruck und die Stadt', in B. Moeller, H. Patze and K. Stackmann, *Studien zum städtischen Bildungswesen*, pp. 9–32.

Cowan, Alexander. 1986. *The Urban Patriciate: Lübeck and Venice, 1580–1700*. Cologne and Vienna: Böhlau, Quellen und Darstellungen zur hansischen Geschichte, neue Folge.

Cowan, Alexander. 1998. *Urban Europe, 1500–1700*. London: Edward Arnold.

Cowan, Alexander. 2000. 'Foreigners and the City: The Case of the Immigrant Merchant', in A. Cowan, *Mediterranean Urban Culture 1400–1700*, pp. 45–55. Exeter: University of Exeter Press.

Cowan, Alexander (ed.) 2000. *Mediterranean Urban Culture 1400–1700*. Exeter: University of Exeter Press.

Darby, H. C. (ed.) 1973. *A New Historical Geography of England Before 1600*. Cambridge: Cambridge University Press.

Davidson, Nicholas. 2000. ' "As Much for its Culture as for its Arms": The Cultural Relations of Venice and its Dependent Cities, 1400–1700', in A. Cowan, *Mediterranean Urban Culture 1400–1700*, pp. 197–214. Exeter: University of Exeter Press.

Davis, Natalie Zemon. 1975a. 'Poor Relief, Humanism, and Heresy', in N. Z. Davis, *Society and Culture in Early Modern France*, pp. 48–49. Stanford: Stanford University Press.

Davis, Natalie Zemon. 1975b. *Society and Culture in Early Modern France*. Stanford: Stanford University Press.

Davis, Ralph. 1973. *The Rise of the Atlantic Economies*. Ithaca, N.Y.: Cornell University Press.

De la Roncière, Charles. 1985. 'L'Approvisionnement des villes italiennes au Moyen Age (XIVe–XVe siècles)', in *L'Approvisionnement des villes*, pp. 33–51. Auch: Abbaye de Flaran.

de Olivera-Marques, H. 1994. 'Les villes portugaises au Moyen Âge (XIVe–XVe siècles), in *Villes et sociétés urbaines au Moyen Âge: Hommage à M. le Professur Jacques Heers*, pp. 105–12. Paris: Presses de l'Université de Paris-Sorbonne.

De Pauw, Napoléon. (ed.) 1885. *De Voorgeboden der stad Gent in de XIVe eeuw (1337–1382)*. Ghent: C. Annoot-Braeckman.

De Vos, Dirk. 1992 'Brügge und die flämischen Primitiven in Europe', in V. Vermeersch (ed.), *Brügge und Europa*, 318–57. Antwerp: Mercatorfonds.

de Vries, Jan. 1984. *European Urbanization, 1500–1800*. Cambridge, Mass.: Harvard University Press.

de Vries, Jan. 1990. 'Problems in the Measurement, Description, and Analysis of Historical Urbanization', in A. Van der Woude, A. Nayami and J. de Vries, *Urbanization*, pp. 43–60. Oxford: Clarendon.

de Vries, Jan, and Van der Woude, Ad. 1997. *The First Modern Economy: Success, Failure, and Perseverance of the Dutch Economy, 1500–1815*. Cambridge: Cambridge University Press.

Dean, Trevor (ed.) 2000. *The Towns of Italy in the Later Middle Ages*. Manchester: Manchester University Press.

Dean, Trevor and Wickham, Chris (eds.) 1990. *City and Countryside in Late Medieval and Renaissance Italy: Essays Presented to Philip Jones*, pp. 69–80. London: Hambledon.

Decavele, Johan. 1975. *Panoramisch Gezicht op Gent in 1534*. Brussels: Pro Civitate.

Decavele, Johan. 1992. 'Het culturele en intellectuele netwerk: middeleeuwen en 16de eeuw', in *Le Réseau Urbain en Belgique*, pp. 365–84. Brussels: Gemeentekrediet.

Derville, Alain. 1994 . 'Les métiers de Saint-Omer'. In P. Lambrechts and J.-P. Sosson (eds.), *Les Métiers au Moyen Âge*, pp. 99–108. Actes du Colloque international de Louvain-la-Neuve, 7–9 Octobre 1993. Louvain: Université Catholique de Louvain.

Derycke, Laurence. 1999. *De Sint-Michielswijk in Gent (1480–1520): een sociaal-topografische reconstructie.* Ghent: Verhandelingen der Maatschappij voor Geschiedenis en Oudheidkunde te Gent, XXIV.

Descimon, Robert. 1989. 'Paris on the Eve of Saint Bartholomew: Taxation, Privilege, and Social Geography', in P. Benedict, *Cities and Social Change,* pp. 69–104. London: Unwin Hyman.

Desportes, Pierre. 1979. *Reims et les Rémois aux XIIIe et XIVe siècles.* Paris: A. and J. Picard.

Dickinson, Robert E. 1951. *The West European City: A Geographical Interpretation.* London: Routledge & Kegan Paul.

Diefendorf, Barbara. 1991. *Beneath the Cross: Catholics and Huguenots in Sixteenth-Century Paris.* Oxford: Oxford University Press.

Dietrich, Richard. 1983. 'Merkantilismus und Städtewesen in Kursachsen', in V. Press, *Städtewesen und Merkantilismus in Mitteleuropa,* pp. 222–85. Cologne and Vienna: Böhlau.

Donkin, R. A. 1973. 'Changes in the Early Middle Ages'. In H. C. Darby, *A New Historical Geography of England Before 1600,* pp.75–135. Cambridge: Cambridge University Press.

Duplessis, Robert. 1991. *Lille and the Dutch Revolt: Urban Stability in an Era of Revolution.* Cambridge: Cambridge University Press.

Duplessis, Robert. 1997. *Transitions to Capitalism in Early Modern Europe.* Cambridge: Cambridge University Press.

Dyer, Alan. 2000. '"Urban decline" in England, 1377–1525', in T. R. Slater, *Towns in Decline, AD 100–1600,* pp. 266–88. Aldershot: Ashgate.

Dyer, Christopher. 1994. 'The Consumer and the Market in the Later Middle Ages', in C. Dyer *Everyday Life in Medieval England,* pp. 257–81. London: Hambledon.

Dyer, Christopher and Slater, Terry R. 2000. 'The Midlands', in D. M. Palliser, *The Cambridge Urban History of Britain,* pp. 609–38. Cambridge: Cambridge University Press.

Eisenstein, Elizabeth L. 1979. *The Printing Press as an Agent of Change: Communications and Cultural Transformations in Early-modern Europe.* 2 vols. Cambridge: Cambridge University Press.

Ennen, Edith. 1979. 'Stufen der Zentralität im kirchlich-organisatorischen und kultischen Bereich. Eine Fallskizze: Köln', in E. Meynen, *Zentralität,* pp. 15–21. Cologne and Vienna: Böhlau.

Epstein, Steven R. (ed.) 2001. *Town and Country in Europe, 1300–1800.* Cambridge: Cambridge University Press.

Epstein, Steven R. 1991. 'Cities, Regions and the Late Medieval Crisis: Sicily and Tuscany Compared', *Past and Present* 130, 3–50.

Faber, Ghislaine and Lochard, Thierry. 1992. *Montpellier: La Ville médiévale.* Paris: Imprimerie Nationale.

Farr, James R. 1988. *Hands of Honor: Artisans and their World in Dijon, 1550–1650* Ithaca, N.Y.: Cornell University Press.

Farr, James R. 2000. *Artisans in Europe, 1300–1914.* Cambridge: Cambridge University Press.

Favier, Jean. 1974. *Paris au XVe siècle, 1380–1500.* Paris: Hachette.

Ferruolo, Stephen C. 1988. '*Parisius-Paradisus:* The City, its Schools, and the Origins of the University of Paris', in T. Bender, *University and City,* pp. 22–43. Oxford: Oxford University Press.

François, Étienne. 1978. 'Des républiques marchandes aux capitals politiques: remarques sur la hiérarchie urbain du Saint-Empire à l'Époque Moderne', *Revue d'Histoire Moderne et Contemporaine* 25, pp. 587–603.

François, Étienne. 1990. 'The German Urban Network between the Sixteenth and Eighteenth Centuries: Cultural and Demographic Indicators', in A. Van der Woude, A. Nayami and J. de Vries, *Urbanization*, pp. 84–100. Oxford: Clarendon.

Friedman, David. 1988. *Florentine New Towns: Urban Design in the Late Middle Ages*. Cambridge Mass.: MIT Press.

Friedrichs, Christopher R. 1995. *The Early Modern City, 1450–1750*. London: Longman.

Friedrichs, Christopher R. 2000. *Urban Politics in Early Modern Europe*. London: Routledge.

Galloway, James A. 2001. 'Town and Country in England, 1300–1570', in S. R. Epstein, *Town and Country in Europe*, pp. 106–31. Cambridge: Cambridge University Press.

Ganshof, François L. 1943. *Étude sur le développement des villes entre Loire et Rhin au Moyen Âge*. Paris: Presses Universitaires de France.

Gerbet, Marie-Claude. 'Patriciat et noblesse à Barcelone à l'époque de Ferdinand le catholique: Modalités et limites d'une fusion', in *Villes et sociétés urbaines au Moyen Âge*, pp. 133–140. Paris: Université de Paris-Sorbonne.

Gerhard, Dietrich. 1981. *Old Europe: A Study of Continuity, 1000–1800*. New York: Academic Press.

Gillespie, Raymond. 1996. 'Dublin 1600–1700: A City and its Hinterlands', in P. Clark and B. Lepetit, *Capital Cities and their Hinterlands*, pp. 84–104. Aldershot: Scolar.

Glasscock, Robin E. 1973. 'England *circa* 1334', in H. C. Darby, *A New Historical Geography of England Before 1600*, pp. 136–85. Cambridge: Cambridge University Press.

Glennie, Paul. 2001. 'Town and Country in England, 1570–1750', in S. R. Epstein, *Town and Country in Europe*, pp. 132–55. Cambridge: Cambridge University Press.

Goldberg, P. J. P. 1992. *Women, Work, and Life Cycle in a Medieval Economy: Women in York and Yorkshire, c. 1300–1520*. Oxford: Clarendon.

Goldthwaite, Richard A. 1980. *The Building of Renaissance Florence: An Economic and Social History*. Baltimore: Johns Hopkins University Press.

Goldthwaite, Richard A. 1993. *Wealth and the Demand for Art in Italy, 1300–1600*. Baltimore: Johns Hopkins University Press.

Goose, N. R. 1986. 'In Search of the Urban Variable: Towns and the English Economy, 1500–1650', *Economic History Review*, ser. 2, 39, pp. 165–85.

Goose, Nigel. 1990. 'English Pre-Industrial Urban Economies', in J. Barry, *The Tudor and Stuart Town*, pp. 63–73. London: Longman.

Graus, Frantisek. 1979. 'Prag als Mitte Böhmens, 1346–1421', in E. Meynen, *Zentralität*, pp. 22–47. Cologne and Vienna: Böhlau.

Gray, Douglas (ed.) 1985. *The Oxford Book of Late Medieval Verse and Prose*. Oxford: Clarendon.

Grenville, Jane. 1997. *Medieval Housing*. London: Leicester University Press.

Guibert of Nogent. 1970. *Self and Society in Medieval France: The Memoirs of Abbot Guibert of Nogent (1064?–c. 1125)*. Edited with an introduction and notes by John F. Benton. The translation of C. C. Swinton Bland revised by the editor. New York: Harper and Row.

Hale, John. 1994. *The Civilization of Europe in the Renaissance*. New York: Atheneum.

Hammer, Carl I. 1978. 'Patterns of Homicide in Fourteenth-century Oxford'. *Past and Present* 78, pp. 3–23.

Hanawalt, Barbara A. 1993. *Growing Up in Medieval London: The Experience of Childhood in History*. Oxford: Oxford University Press.

Hanawalt, Barbara A. 2001. 'The Contested Streets of Medieval London'. In *Die Strasse*, pp. 140–157.

Hanawalt, Barbara A. and Kobialka, Michal (eds.) 2000. *Medieval Practices of Space*. Minneapolis: University of Minnesota Press.

Hanawalt, Barbara A. and Reyerson, Kathryn L. (eds.) 1994. *City and Spectacle in Medieval Europe*. Minneapolis and London: University of Minnesota Press.

Harris, Chauncy D. and Ullman, Edward L. 1945. 'The Nature of Cities', *Annals of the American Academy of Political and Social Science* 242, pp. 7–17.

Harris, Michael H. 1995. *History of Libraries in the Western World*. 4th edn. Metuchen, N.J.: Scarecrow.

Hauser, Philip M. and Schnore, Leo F. (eds.) 1965. *The Study of Urbanization*. New York: John Wiley.

Haverkamp, Alfred. 1979. 'Das Zentralitätsgefüge Mailands im hohen Mittelalter', in E. Meynen, *Zentralität*, pp. 48–78. Cologne and Vienna: Böhlau.

Heers, Jacques. 1971. *Gênes au XVe siècle: Civilisation méditerranéenne, grand capitalisme, et capitalisme populaire*. Paris: Flammarion.

Heers, Jacques. 1977. *Parties and Political Life in the Medieval West*. Amsterdam: North Holland.

Heers, Jacques. 1984. *Espaces publics, espaces privés dans la ville: Le Liber Terminorum de Bologne (1294)*. Paris: Éditions du Centre National de la Recherche Scientifique.

Heller, Henry. 1996. *Labour, Science, and Technology in the Age of Valois and Bourbon, 1500–1620*. Cambridge: Cambridge University Press.

Herbert, David T. and Thomas, Colin J. 1997. *Cities in Space: City as Place*. 3rd edn. London: David Fulton.

Herlihy, David and Klapisch-Zuber, Christiane. 1985. *Tuscans and Their Families: A Study of the Florentine Catasto of 1427*. New Haven. Yale University Press.

Herlihy, David. 1990. *Opera Muliebria: Women and Work in Medieval Europe*. Philadelphia: Temple University Press.

Higounet, Charles. 1985/1987. 'Centralité, Petites Villes et Bastides dans l'Aquitaine Médiévale', in J.-P. Poissou, P. Loupès and G. Dupeux, *Les petites villes du Moyen Age à nos jours*, p. 46. Paris. Colloque Bordeaux, Centre National de la Recherche Scientifique.

Hilton, R. H. 1992. *English and French Towns in Feudal Society: A Comparative Study*. Cambridge: Cambridge University Press.

Hilton, Rodney H. 1985. 'Pain et cervoise dans les villes anglaises au Moyen Age', in *L'Approvisionnement des villes*, pp. 221–29. Auch: Abbaye de Flaran.

Hirschfelder, Gunther. *Die Kölner Handelsbeziehungen im Spätmittelalter*. Cologne: Stadtmuseum, 1994.

Hoftijzer, Paul. 2001. 'Metropolis of Print: The Amsterdam Book Trade in the Seventeenth Century', in P. O'Brien, D. Keene, M. 'tHart and H. van der Wee, *Golden Ages in Antwerp, Amsterdam and London*, pp. 240–63. Cambridge: Cambridge University Press.

Hohenberg, Paul M. and Lees, Lynn Hollen. 1996. 'Urban Systems and Economic Growth: Town Populations in Metropolitan Hinterlands, 1600–1850', in P. Clark and B. Lepetit, *Capital Cities and their Hinterlands*, pp. 26–50. Aldershot: Scolar.

Hohenberg, Paul M., and Lees, Lynn Hollen. 1985. *The Making of Urban Europe, 1000–1950*. Cambridge, Mass.: Harvard University Press.

Hollingsworth, Mary. 1994. *Patronage in Renaissance Italy: From 1400 to the Early Sixteenth Century*. Baltimore: Johns Hopkins University Press.

Honig, Elizabeth A. 1998. *Painting and the Market in Early Modern Antwerp*. New Haven: Yale University Press.

Hoppenbrouwers, Peter C. M. 2001. 'Town and Country in Holland, 1300–1550', in S. R. Epstein, *Town and Country in Europe*, pp. 54–79. Cambridge: Cambridge University Press.

Howell, Martha C. 1986. *Women, Production, and Patriarchy in Late Medieval Cities*. Chicago: University of Chicago Press.

Hubatsch, Walter. 1983. 'Ziele und Massnahmen landesherrlicher Politik im Absolutismus gegenüber den Städten aus der Sicht des Verwaltungshistorikers', in V. Press, *Städtewesen und Merkantilismus in Mitteleuropa*, pp. 30–44. Cologne and Vienna: Böhlau.

Huppert, George. 1986. *After the Black Death: A Social and Economic History of Early Modern Europe*. Bloomington, Ind.: Indiana University Press.

Husson, É. 1994. 'Les métiers du bâtiment à Dijon sous le "mécénat" de Philippe le Hardi, duc de Bourgogne', in P. Lambrechts and J.-P. Sosson (eds.) , *Les Métiers au Moyen Âge*, pp. 129–42. Actes du Colloque international de Louvain-la-Neuve, 7–9 Octobre 1993. Louvain: Université Catholique de Louvain.

Hyde, J. K. 1988. 'Universities and Cities in Medieval Italy', in T. Bender (ed.), *University and the City*, pp. 13–21. Oxford: Oxford University Press.

Irsigler, Franz. 1979. 'Stadt und Umland im Spätmittelalter: zur zentralitätsfördernden Kraft von Fernhandel und Exportgewerbe', in E. Meynen, *Zentralität*, pp. 1–14. Cologne and Vienna: Böhlau.

Irsigler, Franz. 1979. *Die wirtschaftliche Stellung der Stadt Köln im 14. und 15. Jahrhundert: Strukturanalyse einer spätmittelalterlichen Exportgewerbe und Fernhandelsstadt*. Wiesbaden: Franz Steiner.

Irsigler, Franz. 1985. 'L'Approvisionnement des villes de l'Allemagne occidentale jusqu'au XVIe siècle', in *L'Approvisionnement des villes*, pp. 117–44. Auch: Abbaye de Flaran.

Irvine, Frederick M. 1989. 'From Renaissance City to Ancien Régime Capital: Montpellier, *c*. 1500–c. 1600', in P. Benedict, *Cities and Social Change*, pp. 105–33. London: Unwin Hyman.

Isenmann, Eberhard. 1988. *Die deutsche Stadt im Spätmittelalter*. Stuttgart: Eugen Ulmer.

Jack, Sybil M. 1996. *Towns in Tudor and Stuart Britain*. New York: St. Martin's.

Jacquart, Jean. 1996. 'Paris: First Metropolis of the Early Modern Period', in P. Clark and B. Lepetit, *Capital Cities and their Hinterlands*, pp. 105–18. Aldershot: Scolar.

James, Mervyn. 1983. 'Ritual, Drama and Social Body in the Late Medieval English Town', *Past and Present* 98, pp. 3–29.

Janeczek, Andrzej. 2001. 'Town and country in the Polish Commonwealth, 1350–1650', in S. R. Epstein, *Town and Country in Europe*, pp. 156–75. Cambridge: Cambridge University Press.

Jardine, Lisa. 1996. *Worldly Goods: A New History of the Renaissance*. New York: Doubleday.

Jütte, Robert. 1994. *Poverty and Deviance in Early Modern Europe*. Cambridge: Cambridge University Press.

Karras, Ruth Mazo. 1996. *Common Women: Prostitution and Sexuality in Medieval England*. New York: Oxford University Press.

Kaufmann, Thomas Da Costa. 1995. *Court, Cloister, and City: The Art and Culture of Central Europe, 1450–1800*. Chicago: University of Chicago Press.

Keene, Derek. 1985. *Survey of Medieval Winchester*. 2 vols. Oxford: Clarendon.

Keene, Derek. 1989. 'Medieval London and Its Region', *The London Journal* 14, pp. 99–111.

Keene, Derek. 1990. 'Continuity and Development in Urban Trades: Problems of Concepts and the Evidence', in P. J. Corfield and D. Keene (eds.), *Work in Towns*, pp. 1–16. Leicester: Leicester University Press.

Keene, Derek. 1995. 'Small Towns and the Metropolis: The Experience of Medieval England', in J.-M. Duvosquel and E. Thoen, *Peasants and Townsmen in Medieval Europe: Studia in Honorem Adriaan Verhulst*, pp. 223–38. Ghent: Snoeck-Ducaju & Zoon.

Keene, Derek. 2000a. 'London from the Post-Roman Period to 1300', in D. M. Palliser, *The Cambridge Urban History of Britain*, pp. 187–216. Cambridge: Cambridge University Press.

Keene, Derek. 2000b. 'The Medieval Urban Landscape, AD 900–1540', in P. Waller, *The English Urban Landscape*, pp. 74–98. Oxford: Oxford University Press.

Keene, Derek. 2000c. 'The South-East of England', in D. M. Palliser, *The Cambridge Urban History of Britain*, pp. 545–82. Cambridge: Cambridge University Press.

Keene, Derek. 2001. 'Issues of Water in Medieval London to *c.* 1300'. *Urban History*, 28, pp. 161–79.

Kelley, Klara Bonsack. 1976. 'Dendritic Central-place Systems', in C. A. Smith (ed.). *Regional Analysis*, 2 vols, Vol. I: pp. 221–34. London: Academic Press.

Kermode, Jennifer. 1999. 'Sentiment and Survival: Family and Friends in Late Medieval English Towns', *Journal of Family History* 24, pp. 5–18.

Kermode, Jennifer. 2000a. 'Northern Towns', in D. M. Palliser (ed.), *The Cambridge Urban History of Britain*, pp. 657–79.

Kermode, Jennifer. 2000b. 'The Greater Towns 1300–1450', in D. M. Palliser (ed.), *The Cambridge Urban History of Britain*, pp. 44–165. Cambridge.

Keutgen, Friedrich. (ed.) 1901. *Urkunden zur städtischen Verfassungsgeschichte*. Berlin: Emil Faber.

Kießling, Rolf. 1978. 'Das gebildete Bürgertum und die kulturelle Zentralität Augsburgs im Spätmittelalter', in B. Moeller, H. Patze and K. Stackmann, *Studien zum städtischen Bildungswesen*, pp. 553–85.

Kießling, Rolf. 1979. 'Herrschaft–Markt–Landbesitz. Aspekte der Zentralität und der Stadt–Land–Beziehungen spätmittelalterlicher Städte an ostschwäbischen Beispielen', in E. Meynen, *Zentralität*, pp. 180–218. Cologne and Vienna: Böhlau.

Kießling, Rolf. 1995. 'Markets and Marketing, Town and Country', in R. W. Scribner, *Germany*, pp. 145–79.

King, Margaret L. 1991. 'The Woman of the Renaissance', in E. Garin, *Renaissance Characters*, pp. 207–49. Chicago: University of Chicago Press.

Kintz, Jean-Pierre. 1985. 'L'Approvisionnement en vivres des villes des pays du Main et du Rhin Supérieur (XVIe–XVIIe siècles)', in *L'Approvisionnement des villes*, pp. 257–64. Auch: Abbaye de Flaran.

Kishy, Fiona (ed.) 2001. *Music and Musicians in Renaissance Cities and Towns*. Cambridge: Cambridge University Press.

Klapisch-Zuber, Christiane. 1985. *Family and Ritual in Renaissance Italy*. Chicago: University of Chicago Press.

Klep, Paul M. M. 1992. 'Long-Term Developments in the Urban Sector of the Netherlands (1350–1870)', in *Le Réseau Urbain en Belgique*, pp. 201–42. Brussels: Gemeentekrediet.

Konvitz, Josef W. 1978. *Cities and the Sea: Port City Planning in Early Modern Europe*. Baltimore: Johns Hopkins University Press.

Kowaleski, Maryanne. 1995. *Local Markets and Regional Trade in Medieval Exeter*. Cambridge: Cambridge University Press.

Kowaleski, Maryanne. 2000. 'Port Towns: England and Wales 1300–1540', in D. M. Palliser, *The Cambridge Urban History of Britain*, pp. 467–94. Cambridge: Cambridge University Press.

Kugler, Hartmut. 1986. *Die Vorstellung der Stadt in der Literatur des deutschen Mittelalters*. Munich: Artemis Verlag.

Kümmell, Juliane. 1983. *Bäuerliche Gesellschaft und städtische Herrschaft im Spätmittelalter*. Constance: Wolfgang Hartung-Gorre.

Lachmann, Richard. 2000. *Capitalists in Spite of Themselves: Elite conflict and Economic Transitions in Early Modern Europe*. Oxford: Oxford University Press.

Lambert, Malcolm. 1992. *Medieval Heresy: Popular Movements from the Gregorian Reform to the Reformation*. 2nd edn. Oxford: Blackwell.

Lambrechts, Pascale and Sosson, Jean-Pierre (eds.) 1994. *Les Métiers au Moyen Âge: Aspects économiques et sociaux*. Actes du Colloque international de Louvain-la-Neuve, 7–9 Octobre 1993. Louvain: Université Catholique de Louvain.

Langton, John. 1990. 'Residential Patterns in Pre-industrial Cities: Some Case Studies from Seventeenth-century Britain', in J. Barry, *The Tudor and Stuart Town*, pp. 166–205. London: Longman.

Laughton, Jane; Jones, Evan and Dyer, Christopher. 2001. 'The Urban Hierarchy in the Later Middle Ages: A Study of the East Midlands'. *Urban History* 28, pp. 331–57.

Le Goff, Jacques. 1970. 'Ordres mendiants et urbanisation dans la France médiévale', *Annales. Économies. Sociétés. Civilisations* 25, pp. 924–46.

Le Roy Ladurie, Emmanuel. (ed.) 1981. *La ville classique: De la Renaissance aux Révolutions*. Paris: Éditions du Seuil. *Histoire de la France urbaine*, ed. Georges Duby, III.

Le Roy Ladurie, Emmanuel. 1979. *Carnival: A People's Rising in Romans, 1579–1580*. New York: George Braziller.

Lebrun, François. 1985. 'L'Approvisionnement des villes françaises aux temps modernes', in *L'Approvisionnement des villes*, pp. 145–54. Auch: Abbaye de Flaran.

Lecuppre-Desjardin, Élodie. 1999. 'Les lumières de la ville: recherche sur l'utilisation de la lumière dans les cérémonies bourguignonnes (XIVe–XVe siècles)'. *Revue Historique* 609, pp. 23–43.

Leguay, Jean-Pierre. 1981. *Un réseau urbain au Moyen Age: les villes du duché de Bretagne aux XIVème et XVème siècles*. Paris: Librairie Maloine.

Leguay, Jean-Pierre. 1984. *La rue au Moyen Age*. Rennes: Ouest France.

Leguay, Jean-Pierre. 1994. 'Les métiers de l'artisanat dans les villes du duché de Bretagne aux XIVe et XVe siècles', in P. Lambrechts and J.-P. Sosson (eds.), *Les Métiers au Moyen Âge*, pp. 157–204. Actes du Colloque international de Louvain-la-Neuve, 7–9 Octobre 1993. Louvain: Université Catholique de Louvain.

Lestocquoy, Jean. 1945. *Patriciens du Moyen-Âge: Des Dynasties bourgeoises d'Arras du XIe au XVe siècle*. Arras: Mémoires de la Commission Départementale des Monuments Historiques du Pas-de-Calais, V.

Lilley, Keith D. 2000. 'Decline or Decay? Urban landscapes in late-medieval England', in T. R. Slater, *Towns in Decline, AD 100–1600*, pp. 235–65. Aldershot: Ashgate.

Lilley, Keith D. 2002. *Urban Life in the Middle Ages, 1000–1450*. London: Palgrave.

Limberger, Michael. 2001. ' "No Town in the World Provides More Advantages": Economies of Agglomeration and the Golden Age of Antwerp', in P. O'Brien, D. Keene, M. 'tHart and H. Van der Wee, *Golden Ages in Antwerp, Amsterdam and London*, pp. 39–62. Cambridge: Cambridge University Press.

Lindenbaum, Sheila. 1994. 'Ceremony and Oligarchy: The London Midsummer Watch', in B. A. Hanawalt and K. L. Reyerson, *City and Spectacle*, pp. 171–88. Minneapolis and London: University of Minnesota Press.

Lombaerde, Piet. 2001. 'Antwerp in its Golden Age: "One of the Largest Cities in the Low Countries" and "One of the Best Fortified in Europe" ', in P. O'Brien, D. Keene, M. 'tHart and H. Van der Wee, *Urban Achievement in Early Modern Europe*, pp. 99–127. Cambridge: Cambridge University Press.

López García, José Miguel and Madrazo, Santos M. 1996. 'A Capital City in the Feudal Order: Madrid from the Sixteenth to the Eighteenth Century', in P. Clark and B. Lepetit, *Capital Cities and their Hinterlands*, pp. 119–142. Aldershot: Scolar.

Lopez, Robert S. and Raymond, Irving W. (eds.) 1955. *Medieval Trade in the Mediterranean World: Illustrative Documents Translated with Introductions and Notes.* New York: Columbia University Press.

Lösch, A. 1954. *The Economics of Location.* New Haven: Yale University Press.

Löther, Andrea. 1999. *Prozessionen in spätmittelalterlichen Städten: Politische Partizipation, obrigkeitliche Inszenierung, städtische Einheit.* Cologne: Böhlau.

Lowry, Martin. 1979. *The World of Aldus Manutius: Business and Scholarship in Renaissance Venice.* Ithaca, N.Y.: Cornell University Press.

Lynch, Katherine A. 1991. 'The European Marriage Pattern in the Cities: Variations on a Theme by Hajnal', *Journal of Family History* 16, pp. 79–96.

Mackenney, Richard. 1987. *Tradesmen and Traders: The World of the Guilds in Venice and Europe, c. 1250–c. 1650.* Totowa, N.J.: Barnes and Noble.

Malanima, P. 1988. 'An Example of Industrial Reconversion: Tuscany in the Sixteenth and Seventeenth Centuries', in H. Van der Wee, *The Rise and Decline of Urban Industries in Italy and in the Low Countries,* pp. 63–74. Leuven: Leuven University Press.

Mänd, Anu. 2001. 'Avenues of Approach: The Street as Ceremonial Space in Late Medieval Livonian Festival'. In *Die Strasse,* pp. 167–181.

Marin, Brigitte. 2001. 'Town and Country in the Kingdom of Naples, 1500–1800', in S. R. Epstein, *Town and Country in Europe, 1300–1800,* pp. 316–31. Cambridge: Cambridge University Press.

Marnef, Guido. 1996. *Antwerp in the Age of Reformation: Underground Protestantism in a Commercial Metropolis.* Baltimore: Johns Hopkins University Press.

Marshall, John U. 1989. *The Structure of Urban Systems.* Toronto: University of Toronto Press.

Martines, Lauro. 1979. *Power and Imagination: City-States in Renaissance Italy.* New York: Random House.

Mateos Royo, José A. 1999. 'All the Town is a Stage: Civic Ceremonies and Religious Festivities in Spain during the Golden Age', *Urban History* 26, pp. 165–89.

Mayer, Harold M. 1965. 'A Survey of Urban Geography', in P. M. Hauser and L. F. Schnore (eds.), *The Study of Urbanization,* pp. 81–113. New York: John Wiley.

McRee, Benjamin R. 1994. 'Unity or Division? The Social Meaning of Guild Ceremony in Urban Communities', in B. A. Hanawalt and K. L. Reyerson, *City and Spectacle,* pp. 180–207. Minneapolis and London: University of Minnesota Press.

Meynen, Emil (ed.) 1979. *Zentralität als Problem der mittelalterlichen Stadtgeschichtsforschung.* Städteforschung, Reihe A: Darstellungen, Band 8. Cologne and Vienna: Böhlau.

Moeller, Bernd. 1972. *Imperial Cities and the Reformation: Three Studies.* Philadelphia: Fortress.

Moeller, Bernd. 1978. 'Die Anfänge kommunaler Bibliotheken in Deutschland', in B. Moeller, H. Patze and K. Stackmann, *Studien zum städtischen Bildungswesen,* pp. 136–151.

Moeller, Bernd; Patze, Hans and Stackmann, Karl (eds.) 1978. *Studien zum städtischen Bildungswesen des späten Mittelalters und der frühen Neuzeit.* Bericht über Kolloquien der Kommission zur Erforschung der Kultur des Spätmittelalters 1978 bis 1981. Göttingen: Vandenhoeck & Ruprecht, 1983. Abhandlungen der Akademic der Wissenschaften in Göttingen. Philologisch-historische Klasse, no. 137.

Mollat, Michel. 1986. *The Poor in the Middle Ages: An Essay in Social History.* Translated by Arthur Goldhammer. New Haven and London: Yale University Press.

Möncke, Gisela (ed.) 1982. *Quellen zur Wirtschafts-und Sozialgeschichte mittel-und oberdeutscher Städte im Spätmittelalter.* Darmstadt: Wissenschaftliche Buchgesellschaft.

Moraw, Peter. 1985. *Von offener Verfassung zu gestalteter Verdichtung. Das Reich im späten Mittelalter 1250 bis 1490*. Propyläen Geschichte Deutschlands 3. Berlin: Propyläen Verlag.

Moraw, Peter. 1989. 'Cities and Citizenry as Factors of State Formation in the Roman-German Empire of the Late Middle Ages', *Theory and Society* 18, pp. 631–62.

Morris, Anthony E. J. 1979. *History of Urban Form: Before the Industrial Revolutions*. 2nd edn. New York: John Wiley.

Mousnier, Roland. 1973. *Social Hierarchies 1450 to the Present*. New York: Schocken.

Muchambled, Robert. 1996. 'Les Minorités: Mythes et Réalités', in *Cities and the Transmission of Cultural Values in the Late Middle Ages and Early Modern Period*, pp. 207–23. Brussels: Crédit Communal.

Muir, Edward. 1981. *Civic Ritual in Renaissance Venice*. Princeton: Princeton University Press.

Muir, Edward. 1997. *Ritual in Early Modern Europe*. Cambridge: Cambridge University Press.

Mumford, Lewis. 1934. *Technics and Civilization*. New York: Harcourt, Brace.

Mumford, Lewis. 1938. *The Culture of Cities*. New York: Harcourt, Brace.

Munro, John H. 1999. 'The Symbiosis of Towns and Textiles: Urban Institutions and the Changing Fortunes of Cloth Manufacturing in the Low Countries and England, 1270–1570', *Journal of Early Modern History* 3, 1, pp. 1–74.

Murphy, Kenneth. 2000. 'The Rise and Fall of the Medieval Town of Wales', in T. R. Slater, *Towns in Decline, AD 100–1600*, pp. 193–213. Aldershot: Ashgate.

Murray, James M. 1988. 'Family, Marriage and Moneychanging in Medieval Bruges', *Journal of Medieval History* 14, pp. 114–25.

Murray, James M. 1994. 'The Liturgy of the Count's Advent in Bruges, from Galbert to Van Eyck', in B. A. Hanawalt and K. L. Reyerson, *City and Spectacle*, pp. 137–52. Minneapolis and London: University of Minnesota Press.

Myres, A. R. (ed.) 1969. *English Historical Documents, 1327–1485*. London: Eyre and Spottiswoode.

Nicholas, David. 1970. 'Crime and Punishment in Fourteenth-Century Ghent', *Revue Belge de Philologie et d'Histoire* 48, pp. 289–334, 1141–76.

Nicholas, David. 1971. *Town and Countryside: Social, Economic, and Political Tensions in Fourteenth-Century Flanders*. Bruges: De Tempel.

Nicholas, David. 1978. 'The Scheldt Trade and the "Ghent War" of 1379–1385', *Bulletin de la Commission Royale d'Histoire* 144, pp. 180–359. Revised edition published in 1996 in David Nicholas, *Trade, Urbanisation and the Family: Studies in the History of Medieval Flanders*. Aldershot: Variorum.

Nicholas, David. 1979. 'The English Trade at Bruges in the Last Years of Edward III'. *Journal of Medieval History* 5, pp. 23–61.

Nicholas, David. 1985. *The Domestic Life of a Medieval City: Women, Children, and the Family in Fourteenth-Century Ghent*. Lincoln, Nebr.: University of Nebraska Press.

Nicholas, David. 1987. *The Metamorphosis of a Medieval City: Ghent in the Age of the Arteveldes, 1302–1390*. Lincoln, Nebr.: University of Nebraska Press.

Nicholas, David. 1988. *The Van Arteveldes of Ghent: The Varieties of Vendetta and the Hero in History*. Ithaca, N.Y.: Cornell University Press.

Nicholas, David. 1990. 'The Governance of Fourteenth-Century Ghent: The Theory and Practice of Public Administration', in B. S. Bachrach and D. Nicholas (eds.), *Law, Custom, and the Social Fabric in Medieval Europe: Essays in Honor of Bryce Lyon*, pp. 235–60. Kalamazoo: Medieval Institute Publications.

Nicholas, David. 1991. 'Of Poverty and Primacy: Demand, Liquidity, and the Flemish Economic Miracle, 1050–1200', *American Historical Review* 96, pp. 17–41.

Nicholas, David. 1992. *Medieval Flanders*. London: Longman.

Nicholas, David. 1995. 'Child and Adolescent Labour in the Late Medieval City: A Flemish Model in Regional Perspective', *English Historical Review* 110, pp. 1103–31.

Nicholas, David. 1997a. *The Growth of the Medieval City: From Late Antiquity to the Early Fourteenth Century*. London: Longman.

Nicholas, David. 1997b. *The Later Medieval City, 1300–1500*. London: Longman.

Nicholas, David. 1999. *The Transformation of Europe, 1300–1600*. London: Edward Arnold.

Nicholas, David, and Prevenier, Walter (eds.) 1999. *Gentse Stads- en Baljuwsrekeningen (1365–1376)*. Brussels: Paleis der Academiën.

Nightingale, Pamela. 1995. *A Medieval Mercantile Community: The Grocers' Company and the Politics and Trade of London, 1000–1485*. New Haven: Yale University Press.

Nightingale, Pamela. 1996. 'The Growth of London in the Medieval English Economy', in R. Britnell and J. Hatcher, *Progress and Problems in Medieval England: Essays in Honour of Edward Miller*, pp. 89–106. Cambridge: Cambridge University Press.

O'Brien, Patrick; Keene, Derek; 'tHart, Marjolein and Van der Wee, Herman. 2001. *Urban Achievement in Early Modern Europe: Golden Ages in Antwerp, Amsterdam and London*. Cambridge: Cambridge University Press.

Opll, Ferdinand. 1995. *Nachrichten aus dem mittelalterlichen Wien. Zeitgenossen berichten*. Vienna: Böhlau.

Opll, Ferdinand. 1996. 'Cities and the Transmission of Cultural Values in the Late Middle Ages and Early Modern Period: The Vienna Example', in *Cities and the Transmission of Cultural Values*, pp. 121–35. Brussels: Crédit Communal.

Origo, Iris. 1963. *The Merchant of Prato: Francesco di Marco Datini*. Harmondsworth: Penguin.

Ozment, Steven. 1975. *The Reformation in the Cities: The Appeal of Protestantism to Sixteenth-Century Germany and Switzerland*. New Haven: Yale University Press.

Palliser, David M. 1990. 'Civic Mentality and the Environment in Tudor York', in J. Barry, *The Tudor and Stuart Town*, 206–43. London: Longman.

Palliser, David M. (ed.) 2000. *The Cambridge Urban History of Britain*. Vol. I: *600–1540*. Cambridge: Cambridge University Press.

Palliser, David M.; Slater, Terry R. and Dennison, E. Patricia. 2000. 'The Topography of Towns 600–1300', in D. M. Palliser, *The Cambridge Urban History of Britain*, pp. 153–86. Cambridge: Cambridge University Press.

Parker, Geoffrey. 2000. 'The Artillery Fortress as an Engine of European Overseas Expansion, 1480–1750', in J. D. Tracy, *City Walls*, pp. 386–416. Cambridge: Cambridge University Press.

Patten, John. 1978. *English Towns 1500–1700*. Hamden, Conn.: Archon.

Patze, Hans. 1972. 'Die Bildung der landesherrlichen Residenzen im Reich während des 14. Jahrhunderts', in W. Rausch (ed.), *Stadt und Stadtherr im 14. Jahrhundert. Entwicklungen und Funktionen*, pp. 1–54. Linz: Österreichischer Arbeitskreis für Stadtgeschichte.

Pearl, Valerie. 1979/1990. 'Change and Stability in Seventeenth-century London', in J. Barry, *The Tudor and Stuart Town*, pp. 139–65, reprinted from *London Journal*, 5.

Perrenoud, Alfred. 1990. 'Aspects of Fertility Decline in an Urban Settling: Rouen and Geneva', in A. Van der Woude, A. Nayami and J. de Vries, *Urbanization*, pp. 243–63. Oxford: Clarendon.

Peters, Ursula. 1983. *Literatur in der Stadt. Studien zu den sozialen Voraussetzungen und kulturellen Organisationsformen städtischer Literatur im 13. und 14. Jahrhundert*. Tübingen: Max Niermeyer.

Phythian-Adams, Charles. 'Ceremony and the Citizen: The Communal Year at Coventry, 1450–1550', in P. Clark and P. Slack, *Crisis and Order in English Towns, 1500–1700*, pp. 57–85.

Piergiovanni, P. Massa. 1988. 'Social and Economic Consequences of Structural Changes in the Ligurian silk-weaving Industry from the Sixteenth to the Nineteenth Century', in H. Van der Wee, *The Rise and Decline of Urban Industries in Italy and in the Low Countries*, pp. 17–40. Leuven: Leuven University Press.

Pirenne, Henri. 1956. *Medieval Cities: Their Origins and the Revival of Trade*. New York: Doubleday (reprint).

Pirenne, Henri. 1963. *Early Democracies in the Low Countries: Urban Society and Political Conflict in the Middle Ages and the Renaissance*. New York: Harper & Row.

Planitz, Hans. 1963. *Die deutsche Stadt im Mittelalter: Von der Römerzeit bis zu den Zunftkämpfen*. Cologne and Graz: Böhlau.

Pollak, Martha D. 1991. *Turin 1564–1680: Urban Design, Military Culture, and the Creation of an Absolutist Capital*. Chicago: University of Chicago Press.

Pound, J. F. 1976. 'The Social and Trade Structure of Norwich 1525–1575', in P. Clark, *The Early Modern Town*, pp. 129–47. London: Longman.

Pounds, Norman J. G. 1973. *An Historical Geography of Europe, 450 BC–AD 1330*. Cambridge: Cambridge University Press.

Pounds, Norman J. G. 1989. *Hearth and Home: A History of Material Culture*. Bloomington: Indiana University Press.

Pounds, Norman J. G. 1994. *An Economic History of Medieval Europe*. 2nd edn. London: Longman.

Press, Volker. 1983a. 'Der Merkantilismus und die Städte', in V. Press, *Städtewesen und Merkantilismus in Mitteleuropa*, 1–14. Cologne and Vienna: Böhlau.

Press, Volker (ed.) 1983b. *Städtewesen und Merkantilismus in Mitteleuropa*. Cologne and Vienna: Böhlau.

Prevenier, Walter. 1996. 'Culture et groupes sociaux dans les villes des anciens Pays-Bas au Moyen Age', in J.-M. Duvosquel, J. Nazet and A. Vanrie, *Les Pays-Bas Bourguignons: Histoire et Institutions. Mélanges André Uyttebrouck*, pp. 340–359. Brussels: Archives et Bibliothèque de Belgique.

Prevenier, Walter. 1998. 'La conservation de la memoire par l'enregistrement dans les chancelleries princières et dans les villes des anciens Pays-Bas du moyen âge', in K. Borchardt and E. Bünz, *Forschungen zur Reichs-, Papst- und Landesgeschichte. Peter Herde zum 65. Geburtstag von Freunden, Schülern und Kollegen dargebracht*, pp. 551–64. Stuttgart: Anton Hiersemann.

Prevenier, Walter; Sosson, Jean-Pierre and Boone, Marc. 1992. 'Le réseau urbain en Flandre (XIIIe–XIXe siècle): composantes et dynamique', in *Le Réseau Urbain en Belgique*, pp. 157–200. Brussels: Gemeentekrediet.

Queller, Donald E. 1986. *The Venetian Patriciate: Reality versus Myth*. Urbana, Ill.: University of Illinois Press.

Raiser, Elisabeth. 1969. *Städtische Territorialpolitik im Mittelalter: Eine vergleichende Untersuchung ihrer verschiedenen Formen am Beispiel Lübecks und Zürichs*. Historische Studien, Heft 406. Lübeck and Hamburg: Matthiesen Verlag.

Ranum, Orest. 1968. *Paris in the Age of Absolutism*. Bloomington, Ind.: Indiana University Press.

Rappaport, Steve. 1989. *Worlds Within Worlds: Structures of Life in Sixteenth-century London*. Cambridge: Cambridge University Press.

Réseau Urbain [Le] en Belgique dans une perspective historique (1350–1850). Une approche statistique et dynamique. Actes. Het stedelijk netwerk in België in historisch perspectief (1350–1850). Een statistische en dynamische Benadering. Handelingen. 1992. Brussels: Gemeentekrediet, Historische Uitgaven, reeks in-8o, nr. 86.

Reyerson, Kathryn L. 1997. 'Public and Private Space in Medieval Montpellier: The Bon Amic Square', *Journal of Urban History* 24, pp. 3–27.

Reyerson, Kathryn L. 2000. 'Medieval Walled Space: Urban Development vs. Defense', in J. D. Tracy, *City Walls*, pp. 88–116. Cambridge: Cambridge University Press.

Rigaudière, Albert. 1993. *Gouverner la ville au Moyen Age.* Paris: Anthropos.

Rigby, Stephen H. 1995. *English Society in the Later Middle Ages: Class Status, and Gender.* London: Macmillan.

Rigby, Stephen H. and Ewan, Elizabeth. 2000. 'Government, Power and Authority 1300–1540', in D. M. Palliser, *The Cambridge Urban History of Britain*, pp. 291–312. Cambridge: Cambridge University Press.

Riley, Henry T. (ed. and trans.) 1868. *Memorials of London and London Life in the XIIIth, XIVth, and XVth Centuries: Being a Series of Extracts, Local, Social, and Political from the Early Archives of the City of London, A. D. 1276–1419.* London: Longmans, Green, and Co.

Ringrose, David R. 1983. *Madrid and the Spanish Economy, 1560–1850.* Berkeley: University of California Press.

Roberts, Penny. 1996. *A City in Conflict: Troyes during the French Wars of Religion.* Manchester: Manchester University Press.

Robertson, Durant W., Jr. 1968. *Chaucer's London.* New York: John Wiley.

Rosser, Gervase. 1989. *Medieval Westminster, 1200–1540.* Oxford: Clarendon.

Rosser, Gervase. 1996. 'Myth, Image and Social Process in the Medieval English Town', *Urban History* 23, pp. 5–25.

Rosser, Gervase. 1997. 'Crafts, Guilds and the Negotiation of Work in the Medieval Town', *Past and Present* 154, pp. 3–31.

Rosser, Gervase and Dennison, E. Patricia. 2000. 'Urban Culture and the Church 1300–1540', in D. M. Palliser, *The Cambridge Urban History of Britain*, pp. 335–69. Cambridge: Cambridge University Press.

Rossiaud, Jacques. 1988. *Medieval Prostitution.* Oxford: Basil Blackwell.

Rozman, Gilbert. 1978. 'Urban Networks and Historical Stages', *Journal of Interdisciplinary History* 9, pp. 65–91.

Ruggiero, Guido. 1980. *Violence in Early Renaissance Venice.* New Brunswick, N.J.: Rutgers University Press.

Russell, Josiah C. 1972. *Medieval Regions and Their Cities.* Bloomington: Indiana University Press.

Rutledge, Elizabeth. 1995. 'Landlords and Tenants: Housing and the Rented Property Market in Early Fourteenth-century Norwich', *Urban History* 22, pp. 7–24.

Sakellariou, Eleni. 2000. 'The Cities of Puglia in the Fifteenth and Sixteenth Centuries: Their Economy and Society', in A. Cowan, *Mediterranean Urban Culture 1400–1700*, pp. 97–114. Exeter: University of Exeter Press.

Sánchez-León, Pablo. 2001. 'Town and Country in Castile, 1400–1650', in S. R. Epstein, *Town and Country in Europe*, pp. 272–91. Cambridge: Cambridge University Press.

Schilling, Heinz. 1993. *Die Stadt in der frühen Neuzeit.* Munich: R. Oldenbourg.

Schofield, John and Stell, Geoffrey. 2000. 'The Built Environment 1300–1540', in D. M. Palliser, *The Cambridge Urban History of Britain*, pp. 371–93. Cambridge: Cambridge University Press.

Schofield, John and Vince, Alan (eds.) 1994. *Medieval Towns*. Madison: Fairleigh Dickinson University Press.

Schofield, John. 1984. *The Building of London from the Conquest to the Great Fire*. London: British Museum Publications.

Schoppmeyer, Heinrich.1979. 'Probleme der zentralörtlichen Bedeutung Paderborns im Spätmittelalter', in E. Meynen (ed.). *Zentralität als Problem der mittelalterlichen Stadtgeschichtsforschung*, pp. 92–124. Cologne and Vienna: Böhlau.

Schulz, Knut. 1985. *Handwerksgesellen und Lohnarbeiter: Untersuchungen zur oberrheinischen und oberdeutschen Stadtgeschichte des 14. bis 17. Jahrhunderts*. Sigmaringen: Jan Thorbecke.

Scott, Tom. 2001. 'Town and Country in Germany, 1350–1600', in S. R. Epstein, *Town and Country in Europe*, pp. 202–28. Cambridge: Cambridge University Press.

Scott, Tom and Scribner, Bob. 1995. 'Urban Networks', in R. W. Scribner, *Germany*, pp. 113–43. London: Edward Arnold.

Scribner, Bob [Robert W.] (ed.) 1995. *Germany: A New Social and Economic History*. Vol. I: *1450–1630*. London: Edward Arnold.

Sheeran, George. 1998. *Medieval Yorkshire Towns: People, Buildings and Spaces*. Edinburgh: Edinburgh University Press.

Shirley, Janet (ed. and trans.) 1968. *A Parisian Journal, 1405–1449*. Oxford: Clarendon.

Sjoberg, Gideon. 1960. *The Preindustrial City: Past and Present*. New York: Free Press.

Sjoberg, Gideon. 1965a. 'Cities in Developing and Industrial Societies', in P. M. Hauser and L. F. Schnore, *The Study of Urbanization*, pp. 213–67. New York: John Wiley.

Sjoberg, Gideon. 1965b. 'Theory and Research in Urban Sociology', in P. M. Hauser and L. F. Schnore. *The Study of Urbanization*, pp. 157–89. New York: John Wiley.

Slater, Terry R. 1996. 'The European Historic Towns Atlas', *Journal of Urban History* 22, pp. 739–49.

Slater, Terry R. 2000. *Towns in Decline, AD 100–1600*. Aldershot: Ashgate.

Slater, Terry R. 2002. 'Planning Britain's Largest Medieval New Town: Ideology, Geometry, Metrology and Practicalities in Thirteenth-century Salisbury'. Paper delivered at International Medieval Congress, University of Leeds, 11 July.

Smail, Daniel Lord. 1999. *Imaginary Cartographies: Possession and Identity in Late Medieval Marseille*. Ithaca, N.Y.: Cornell University Press.

Smail, Daniel Lord. 2000. 'The Linguistic Cartography of Property and Power in Late Medieval Marseille', in B. A. Hanawalt and M. Kobialka, *Medieval Practices of Space*, pp. 37–63. Minneapolis: University of Minnesota Press.

Smith, C. T. 1967. *An Historical Geography of Western Europe Before 1800*. New York: Frederick A. Praeger.

Smith, Carol A. 1990. 'Types of City-size Distributions: A Comparative Analysis', in A. Van der Woude, A. Nayami and J. de Vries, *Urbanization*, pp. 20–42. Oxford: Clarendon.

Sombart, Werner. 1924. *Der moderne Capitalismus: historisch-systematische Darstellung des gesamt-europäischen Wirtschaftslebens von seinen Anfängen bis zur Gegenwart*. 6th edn. Munich: Duncker and Humblot.

Sosson, Jean-Pierre. 1966. 'La Structure sociale de la corporation médiévale: l'exemple des tonneliers de Bruges de 1350 à 1500', *Revue Belge de Philologie et d'Histoire* 44, pp. 457–78.

Sprandel, Rolf (ed.) 1982. *Quellen zur Hanse-Geschichte*. Darmstadt: Wissenschaftliche Buchgesellschaft.

Spufford, Peter. 1988. *Money and Its Use in Medieval Europe*. Cambridge: Cambridge University Press.

Stabel, Peter. 1992. 'Markt en hinterland: de centrale functies van de kleinere steden in Vlaanderen tijdens de late middeleeuwen en het begin van de moderne tijd', in *Le Réseau Urbain en Belgique*, pp. 341–63. Brussels: Gemeentekrediet.

Stabel, Peter. 1997. *Dwarfs among Giants: The Flemish Urban Network in the Late Middle Ages*. Leuven-Apeldoorn: Garant.

Steane, John M. 2001. *The Archaeology of Power: England and Northern Europe, AD 800 to 1600*. Stroud, UK: Tempus.

Strait, Paul. 1974. *Cologne in the Twelfth Century*. Gainesville, Fla.: University Presses of Florida.

Strasse, Die. Zur Funktion und Perzeption öffentlichen Raums im späten Mittelalter. 2001. Internationales Round Table Gespräch Krems an der Donau, 2. und 3. Oktober 2000. Vienna: Verlag der österreichischen Akademie der Wissenschaften.

Strauss, Gerald. 1966. *Nuremberg in the 16th Century*. New York: John Wiley.

Swanson, Heather. 1989. *Medieval Artisans: An Urban Class in Late Medieval England*. Oxford: Basil Blackwell.

Swanson, Heather. 1990. 'Artisans in the Urban Economy: The Documentary Evidence from York', in P. J. Corfield and D. Keene (eds.), *Work in Towns*, pp. 42–56. Leicester: Leicester University Press.

Swanson, Heather. 1999. *Medieval British Towns*. London: Macmillan.

Swetz, Frank J. 1987. *Capitalism and Arithmetic: The New Math of the 15th Century, including the full text of the* Treviso Arithmetic *of 1478*. Translated by David Eugene Smith. La Salle, Ill.: Open Court.

Tawney, Richard H. 1926. *Religion and the Rise of Capitalism: A Historical Study*. New York: Harcourt Brace.

't Hart, Marjolein. 1989. 'Cities and Statemaking in the Dutch Republic, 1580–1680', *Theory and Society* 18, pp. 663–87.

't Hart, Marjolein. 2001. 'Town and Country in the Dutch Republic, 1550–1800', in S. R. Epstein (ed.), *Town and Country in Europe, 1300–1800*, pp. 80–105. Cambridge: Cambridge University Press.

Thrupp, Sylvia L. 1948. *The Merchant Class of Medieval London*. Ann Arbor: University of Michigan Press.

Thünen, Johann Heinrich von. 1966. *Isolated State*. An English translation of *Der isolierte Staat*, translated by Carla M. Wartenburg. Edited with an introduction by Peter Hall. Oxford, N.Y.: Pergamon.

Tilly, Charles. 1989. 'Cities and States in Europe, 1000–1800', *Theory and Society* 18, pp. 1–18.

Tilly, Charles and Blockmans, Wim. 1994. *Cities and the Rise of States in Europe, 1000–1800*. Boulder, Colo.: Westview.

Tittler, Robert. 1991. *Architecture and Power: The Town Hall and the English Urban Community, c. 1500–1640*. Oxford: Clarendon.

Tittler, Robert. 2001. *Townspeople and Nation: English Urban Experiences, 1540–1640*. Stanford: Stanford University Press.

Tracy, James D. 2000a. 'To Wall or Not to Wall: Evidence from Medieval Germany', in J. D. Tracy, *City Walls*, pp. 71–87. Cambridge: Cambridge University Press.

Tracy, James D. (ed.) 2000b. *City Walls: The Urban Enceinte in Global Perspective*. Cambridge: Cambridge University Press.

Trigger, Brian. 1972. 'Determinants of Urban Growth in Pre-industrial Societies', in P. J. Ucko, R. Tringham and G. W. Dimbleby (eds.), *Man, Settlement and Urbanism*, pp. 575–99. Cambridge, Mass.: Schenkman.

Van Caenegem, R. C. 1994. 'Bookish Law and Customary Law: Roman Law in the Southern Netherlands in the Late Middle Ages', in R. C. Van Caenegem, *Law, History, the Low Countries and Europe*, pp. 119–33. London: Hambledon.

Van den Neste, Evelyne. 1996. *Tournois, joutes, pas d'armes dans les villes de Flandre à la fin du moyen âge (1300–1486)*. Paris: École des Chartes.

Van der Wee, Herman. 1988a. 'Industrial Dynamics and the Process of Urbanization and De-urbanization in the Low Countries from the Late Middle Ages to the Eighteenth Century: A Synthesis', in H. Van der Wee, *The Rise and Decline of Urban Industries in Italy and in the Low Countries*, pp. 307–81. Leuven: Leuven University Press.

Van der Wee, Herman (ed.) 1988b. *The Rise and Decline of Urban Industries in Italy and in the Low Countries (Late Middle Ages–Early Modern Times)*. Leuven: Leuven University Press.

Van der Wee, Herman. 1996. 'Urban Culture as a Factor of Demand in the Economic History of Late Medieval and Early Modern Europe', in *Cities and the Transmission of Cultural Values*, pp. 7–16. Brussels: Crédit Communal.

Van der Woude, Ad; Nayami, Akira and de Vries, Jan (eds.) 1990. *Urbanization in History: A Process of Dynamic Interactions*. Oxford: Clarendon.

Van Emden, Wolfgang G. 2000. 'Medieval French Representations of City and Other Walls', in J. D. Tracy, *City Walls*, pp. 530–72. Cambridge: Cambridge University Press.

Van Houtte, Jan A. 1983. 'Herbergswesen und Gastlichkeit im mittelalterlichen Brügge', in H. C. Peyer (ed.), *Gastfreundschaft, Taverne und Gasthaus im Mittelalter*, pp. 177–87. Munich and Vienna: Oldenbourg.

Van Uytven, Raymond. 1985. 'L'Approvisionnement des villes des anciennes Pays-Bas au Moyen Age', in *L'Approvisionnement des villes*, pp. 75–116. Auch: Abbaye de Flaran.

Van Uytven, Raymond. 1992. 'Brabantse en Antwerpse centrale plaatsen (14de–19de eeuw)', in *Le Réseau Urbain en Belgique*, pp. 20–79. Brussels: Gemeentekrediet.

Van Uytven, Raymond. 1995. 'Stages of Economic Decline: Late Medieval Bruges', in J.-M. Duvosquel and E. Thoen (eds.) *Peasants and Townsmen in Medieval Europe: Studia in honorem Adriaan Verhulst*, pp. 259–69. Ghent: Snoeck-Ducaju & Zoon.

Van Werveke, Hans. 1948. 'De Gentse Vleeschouwers onder het Oud Regime: Demografische studie over een gesloten en erfelijk ambachtsgild', *Handelingen der Maatschappij voor Geschiedenis en Oudheidkunde te Gent*, n.s. 3, pp. 3–32.

Vance, James E., Jr. 1970. *The Merchant's World: The Geography of Wholesaling*. Englewood Cliffs, N.J.: Prentice-Hall.

Vance, James E., Jr. 1990. *The Continuing City: Urban Morphology in Western Civilization*. Baltimore: Johns Hopkins University Press.

Verhulst, A. E. 1964. 'Bronnen en problemen betreffende de Vlaamse landbouw in de late Middeleeuwen', *Agronomisch-Historische Bijdragen* 6, pp. 205–35.

Vilfan, Sergij. 1985. 'L'Approvisionnement des villes dans les confines germano-italo-slaves du XIVe au XVIIe siècle', in *L'Approvisionnement des villes*, pp. 53–74. Auch: Abbaye de Flaran.

Villes et sociétés urbaines au Moyen Âge: Hommage à M. le Professur Jacques Heers. 1994. Paris: Université de Paris-Sorbonne.

Vlieghe, Hans. 2001. 'The Fine and Decorative Arts in Antwerp's Golden Age', in P. O'Brien, D. Keene, M. 'tHart and H. Van der Wee, *Golden Ages in Antwerp, Amsterdam and London*, pp. 173–85. Cambridge: Cambridge University Press.

Vogel, Thomas. 1994. *Fehderecht und Fehdepraxis im Spätmittelalter am Beispiel der Reichsstadt Nürnberg (1404–1438)*. Frankfurt am Main: Peter Lang.

Waley, Daniel. 1991. *Siena and the Sienese in the Thirteenth Century*. Cambridge: Cambridge University Press.

Waller, Philip (ed.) 2000. *The English Urban Landscape*. Oxford: Oxford University Press.

Wallerstein, Immanuel. 1976, 1980. *The Modern World System*. 2 vols. New York: Academic Press.

Ward, Joseph P. 1997. *Metropolitan Communities: Trade, Guilds, Identity, and Change in Early Modern London*. Stanford: Stanford University Press.

Waterschoot, Werner. 2001. 'Antwerp: Books, Publishing and Central Production before 1585', in P. O'Brien, D. Keene, M. 'tHart and H. Van der Wee, *Golden Ages in Antwerp, Amsterdam and London*, pp. 233–48. Cambridge: Cambridge University Press.

Weber, Max. 1958. *The City*. Translated and edited by Don Martindale and Gertrud Neuwirth. New York: Free Press.

Weber, Max. 1995. *General Economic History*. With a New Introduction by Ira J. Cohen. Translated by Frank H. Knight. New Brunswick, NJ: Transaction Publishers, reprinted from Greenberg Publisher, 1927.

Weber, Max. 1992. *The Protestant Ethic and the Spirit of Capitalism*. Translated by Talcott Parsons; introduction by Anthony Giddens. New York: Routledge, reprinted from 1930 edn.

Wheeler, Joseph. 2000. 'Neighbourhoods and Local Loyalties in Renaissance Venice', in A. Cowan, *Mediterranean Urban Culture 1400–1700*, pp. 31–42. Exeter: University of Exeter Press.

Wiesner, Merry E. 2000. *Women and Gender in Early Modern Europe*. 2nd edn. Cambridge: Cambridge University Press.

Wiesner, Merry E. 1986. *Working Women in Renaissance Germany*. New Brunswick, N.J.: Rutgers University Press.

Williams, C. H. (ed.) 1967. *English Historical Documents, 1485–1558*. London: Eyre and Spottiswoode.

Wilson, Jean C. 1998. *Painting in Bruges at the Close of the Middle Ages: Studies in Society and Visual Culture*. University Park, Pa.: Pennsylvania State University Press.

Wolfe, Michael. 2000. 'Walled Towns During the French Wars Of Religion (1560–1630)', in J. D. Tracy, *City Walls*, pp. 317–48. Cambridge: Cambridge University Press.

Wolff, Philippe. 1985. 'L'Approvisionnement des villes françaises au Moyen Age', in *L'Approvisionnement des villes*, pp. 11–31. Auch: Abbaye de Flaran.

Wriedt, Klaus 1978a. 'Stadtrat–Bürgertum–Universität am Beispiel norddeutscher Hansestädte', in B. Moeller, H. Patze and K. Stackmann, *Studien zum städtischen Bildungswesen*, pp. 490–523.

Wriedt, Klaus. 1978b. 'Schulen und bürgerliches Bildungswesen in Norddeutschland im Spätmittelalter', in B. Moeller, H. Patze and K. Stackmann, *Studien zum städtischen Bildungswesen*, pp. 152–72.

Wright, William J. 1995. 'The Nature of Early Capitalism', in R. W. Scribner, *Germany*, pp. 181–208.

Wrigley, E. A. 1990. 'Brake or Accelerator? Urban Growth and Population Growth Before the Industrial Revolution', in A. Van der Woude, A. Nayami and J. de Vries, *Urbanization*, pp. 101–12. Oxford: Clarendon.

Wrigley, E. Anthony. 1985. 'Urban Growth and Agricultural Change: England and the Continent in the Early Modern Period', *Journal of Interdisciplinary History* 15, pp. 683–728.

Wunder, Gerd. 1979. 'Reichsstädte als Landesherrn', in E. Meynen, *Zentralität*, pp. 79–91. Cologne and Vienna: Böhlau.

Wyrobisz, Andrzej. 1989. 'Power and Towns in the Polish Gentry Commonwealth: The Polish-Lithuanian State in the Sixteenth and Seventeenth Centuries', *Theory and Society* 18, pp. 611–30.

Zagorin, Perez. 1982. *Rebels and Rulers, 1500–1660.* Vol. I: *Society, States, and Early Modern Revolution: Agrarian and Urban Rebellions.* Cambridge: Cambridge University Press.

Zipf, George K. 1941. *National Unity and Disunity: The Nation as a Bio-Social Organism.* Bloomington, Ind.: Principia.

Zucker, Paul. 1959. *Town and Square: From the Agora to the Village Green.* New York: Columbia University Press.

Index

'*Urban Europe, 1100–1700* is a wide-ranging study of urban life and development in medieval and early modern Europe. It is well written coherent and comprehensive, and benefits from David Nicholas' vas bank of knowledge concerning the urban environment of the medie and early modern world.' **Penny Galloway**, *Bristol University*

This timely textbook by a leading scholar is a broadly interdisciplina work that breaks new ground by emphasising the links between the late medieval and early modern cities.

Urban Europe, 1100–1700:

- examines the common social, governmental, economic and intellectual roles played by most pre-modern cities
- views cities as originating in local market relations, then expandir with the growing complexity of their functions into regional centr of culture, government and exchange
- adopts an organic, evolutionary and environmental approach, particularly in its application of geographical systems to early urbanisation
- makes extensive use of maps and original source material to illustrate aspects of the urban experience.

David Nicholas' study will appeal to students and scholars of histor geography and urban studies. Sociologists and political economists v also value its demonstration of the continuing relevance of the thoug of Max Weber, while urban planners will find its analysis of the rationality of pre-modern cities highly useful.

David Nicholas is Kathryn and Calhoun Lemon Professor of History Clemson University. His previous publications include fourteen boo most recently a two-volume history of medieval urbanisation (199' and *The Transformation of Europe, 1300–1600* (1999).

palgrave macmillan

Illustration: Detail from *Plan de la Ville de Strasbourg, 1548*. Reproduced courtesy of the Germanisches National Museum. Research by Image Select International.

ISBN 0-333-94983-8

9 780333 949832

90101

www.palgrave.com